Business and Government in Canada

Business and Government in Canada: Selected Readings

edited by

K. J. Rea
J. T. McLeod

Methuen

Toronto   London   Sydney   Wellington

Library of Congress Catalog Card Number 72-94383

SBN 458 90110 5 Hc
     458 90370 1 Pb

Printed and bound in Canada
     2   3   4   5   73   72   71   70

Contents

SECTION THREE — POLICIES TO LIMIT AND TO COUNTERACT MARKET FORCES 201

Part 6 — Policies to Promote Manufacturing in Canada

Part 7 — Policies Affecting the Resource-Based Industries

Part 8 — Area Development Policies

Part 9 — Labour Policies

Part 10 — Consumer Protection Policies

SECTION FOUR — TOWARD A NEW POLITICAL ECONOMY

Part 11 — Re-Thinking Old Assumptions

PREFACE

This is a book about capitalism. In most Western nations in the twentieth century, government not only directs the "public" sector but also plays an important and growing role in the "private" sector of the economy. Under contemporary capitalism it is scarcely possible to understand the operation of the economic system if the role of the state as a regulator of industry is ignored.

There may have been a time when it was possible to study "capitalism" as an economic system that had a relatively limited relationship to the state and politics. It was once argued that if the state kept its hands off business activity, all would turn out for the best: productivity and the public welfare would be maximized. But the slogan "That government is best which governs least" has slipped very far from fashion, and it is now clear that completely laissez-faire arrangements do not exist and never have existed in Canada or in any other Western nation. Still, the economic institutions and political ideology that we call "capitalistic" have by no means passed from the contemporary scene.

The expanding role of the state in economic life has shifted our assumptions and altered our practices; but the debate continues as to what are the proper or "best" relationships between business and government. Probably no issue of political life during the past two centuries has sparked more controversy than the relationship of the state to economic affairs. That is the subject of this volume; capitalism is now closely inter-related with the state, and that is where the cut and thrust of public policy is sharpest in political economy today.

Our interest lies in the role of the state in economic life, but in a special and particular way. We might approach this study by focusing upon either the public or the private sectors of the economy, either "macro" considerations of monetary and fiscal policy or more "micro" considerations of government regulation of industry. We have made a deliberate choice of the latter alternative. Obviously there already exists a vast literature on matters of monetary and fiscal public policies to stablize the capitalist economy. This material is easily accessible and relatively familiar. Recent "post-Keynesian" generations of students have grown up with stabilization policies, the logic of which they now take for granted. So will we. We will assume, heroically perhaps, that fiscal and monetary policies can be used to maintain reasonably full employment and reasonably stable price levels in a "capitalistic" market economy.

What students and the general public may now be relatively less familiar with is the logic underlying the massive and comprehensive collection of policies by which our governments seek to influence the internal operations of our economic system. To what extent and for what reasons do governments deliberately influence the functioning of markets and the behavior of individual producers, consumers, and resource owners?

Strangely enough, these are questions that have been neglected by Canadian social scientists. Our economists have tended to concentrate on evaluating specific policies in the light of highly abstract theoretical models of doubtful relevance, while our political scientists are increasingly preoccupied with "value free" behavioral and quantitative studies. The two academic disciplines have drifted apart and left the central question of what kind of system we have evolved almost untended. That central question, we believe, is precisely the point at which the two disciplines intersect and should be most practically and socially useful. That central question is the focus of this book.

It is undeniably true that the economic system we call capitalism has been altered almost beyond recognition in recent decades. As state regulation of industry steadily advanced in the Western world, the free enterprise system has been transformed into a "welfare state" in which governments broadly assume that they know not only what is "best" for the economy but what is "best" for business. At present in Canada it is impossible to discover a single industry that has not come under deliberate government regulation, either directly or indirectly.

And yet most of us continue to discuss the system in terms of "theory of capitalism," a theory with both economic and political implications. Contemporary society still recognizes and pays lip service to this theory. It is a powerful and often persuasive set of inter-related principles by which advocates of capitalism explain and interpret the operation of a market society as it is or ought to be. Although the theory of capitalism for the most part may be neglected in practice, the capitalist ideology abides and is constantly invoked by politicians as well as businessmen. It remains an important part of the intellectual underpinning of the Western world. Emphatically there is a general philosophy of capitalism, as Part 1 makes clear.

But as Part 2 makes equally clear, that philosophy has undergone substantial modification in the twentieth century. It has been altered and adapted into the more nebulous and inadequately articulated concept of "collectivism". The capitalist beliefs remain; but the invisible hand of the market society has become the visible hand of state regulation.

The theory of capitalism becomes very much confused by the assumption introduced by some of its defenders that society is "naturally" organized on the basis of private property and competitive markets. They fail to see that, far from being "natural," capitalism may just as reasonably be regarded as an intellectual construct and an artificial order invented to explain the emerging industrial society of the nineteenth century. In other words, capitalism is more of a theory than it is a fact, more of a myth than a reality. It is extremely difficult, if not impossible, as we will demonstrate in Section Two, to make the realities of the market conform to the theory of the competitive model, even when the state with all its power strives deliberately to do so.

Moreover, when we look at the actual policies pursued by the state in Western nations, we find in many segments of the economy that the policies do not reflect much or any of the orthodox capitalist theory. As we will show in Section Three, public policy in Canada, as in most Western countries, is not even strongly committed to the maintenance of competition, the basic self-regulatory aspect of commercial enterprise under the capitalist theory.

How is it possible to reconcile the conflict between theory and practice, and the lofty generalizations of sections One and Four with the somewhat more pedestrian descriptive material in sections Two and Three? The actual practice of today's capitalism is difficult to explain in abstract theoretical terms, and still more difficult to relate to the body of theory that is supposed to explain how the system works. An orthodox "liberal" reconciliation of our practical policies with our traditional ideology is to say that we depart from the theoretical model of the system in discreet and more or less "knowable" ways, and that our public policies are means merely of offsetting these departures. This view is not so easy to accept after we have examined the vast array of often contradictory policies that the state actually implements. Therefore, we have included a wide selection of descriptive material in sections Two and Three to illustrate the real degrees of divergence between traditional capitalist theory and our present practices.

Although our selections cannot be comprehensive, they may suffice to show how most of these policies have a logic of their own, a logic that bears no relation whatever to the traditional theory of a capitalist market economy. How then are we to understand the nature of our system? Might it be possible to move toward a new political economy that could encompass these disparate elements? It is our impression that the existing system now departs so much from the capitalist norm that we can no longer hope to understand contemporary issues in terms of obsolete ideas, ideas that probably even at their inception were no more than marginally descriptive. Many of the

particular public policies now being pursued may be misguided and perverse because politicians, and the public they try to satisfy, do not compre-
hend the consequences of what they are doing.

We are in serious danger of ending up with political policies that make
no sense economically and economic policies that make no sense politically.
This is why we end the volume with a plea for rethinking old assumptions
and developing a new and more sophisticated political economy.

We hope this volume will not be read merely as one more eclectic antho-
logy, but as a book with a thesis. Facts without ideas are meaningless. Therefore, although we have tried to assemble a useful collection of information
on our topic, our main purpose has been to provoke the reader into asking
what it means.

We are indebted to the authors and their publishers who have permitted
us to use their work. Our own editorial efforts, including the introductions
to the parts, are our collective responsibility; the selections in sections One
and Four are principally the work of J. T. McLeod, and those in Two and
Three are that of K. J. Rea.

1

Ideology

PART ONE

The Capitalist

Ideology

INTRODUCTION

"Capitalism" is a very tricky word. Certainly it is one of the most controversial and elusive terms in political economy. A "capitalist," or "individual enterprise" system of economic relations emerged gradually in Western Europe as medieval forms of economic oragnization faded away. In 1776, Adam Smith coined the phrase the "invisible hand" to describe the system of individual initiative that he advocated and that we have come to know as free enterprise. The word "capitalism" did not come into widespread common usage until the end of the nineteenth century, and people have been arguing about its meaning and virtues ever since.

In large measure, the history of the last two or three centuries is the history of capitalism; there is, however, no single time or place in history to which we can point and say, "that was when pure capitalism flourished," or "that was when capitalism reached its peak". The phenomenon known as capitalism has undergone constant change, and it continues to evolve today in response to changing social circumstances. The nature and direction of its change in the future can only be guessed at. What we must concern ourselves with first is a definition of capitalism so that we may at least be clear on our terminology before we grapple with the content of the subject.

There are almost as many definitions of capitalism as there are writers on the subject. Usually, capitalism is defined in some broad way as an economic institution characterized by private ownership and private property, the profit motive, consumer sovereignty or consumer choice, competition, and a

3

market system in which prices allocate economic resources. The capitalist ideology maintains that these characteristics of the "free enterprise" system are good and desirable.

Not everyone would agree with so simple and general a definition of capitalism, and it is easy to raise objections to it. Many of these characteristics of capitalism may be found in other economic systems. For example, in the medieval economy and in the ancient slave economies of classical Greece and the Roman Empire, many merchants and traders sought profits, but we do not call those economic systems "capitalistic". Similarly, it can be argued that not all capitalist corporations seek to maximize profit, but seek instead to achieve relatively modest and stable returns on investment and aim at maximizing control of a market rather than maximizing profit. At least some degree of consumer sovereignty or consumer choice exists in both socialist and communist economies. Then too, contemporary writers such as J.K. Galbraith have suggested that the manipulation of the consumer by advertising techniques severely limits consumer sovereignty under capitalism. Moreover, many kinds of economic competition existed in various pre-capitalist economies, and certain forms of competition may be found between state-owned enterprises in communist countries. Furthermore, as Professor Lindblom's essay in Section Four indicates, both communist and socialist countries often use a system of market prices to measure efficiency and allocate resources; markets are not found exclusively in capitalist countries.

Because these characteristics of capitalism may also be found in other economic systems, we are driven back to the essence or basis of contemporary capitalism in the first characteristic that was mentioned in our definition: private ownership or private property. Thus it cannot be too strongly emphasized that the core of the system and the fundamental characteristic of twentieth-century capitalism is private economic decision-making, private ownership, and private property.

The capitalist insistence upon private ownership of the means of production is based upon two principal considerations. First, because ownership of productive property involves power over the lives of other individuals, it is preferable that such power be diffused among as many property owners as possible rather than held by any one owner or institution such as the state. Second, it is argued that economic innovation and technological progress will be facilitated when each individual minds his own business and strives to increase his own profit, and has a profound personal incentive to do so. Many people believe, or assume, that man's desire to acquire, protect, and expand his property is "natural" or "instinctive," and that men are both happier and more productive when they possess property of their own. Proponents of this view find support in the writings of contemporary zoologists and ecologists such as Konrad Lorenz (*On Aggression*) and Robert Ardrey (*The Territorial Imperative*).

But there exists an extremely wide variety of arguments in support of the capitalist ideology. Innumerable writers have extolled the virtues of capitalism and presented a wide range of arguments urging the superiority of capitalism to any alternative economic system. The best known advocacy of free enterprise, and a major landmark in economic literature, is Adam Smith's *The Wealth of Nations*. Since the publication of that classic work, the capitalist ideology has spread, flourished, and become one of the most astonishingly successful ideologies ever known to man. As many observers have remarked, however, it is surprising that, since 1776, there has been no book published in defence of capitalism that has been universally acknowledged as "great" or regarded as "basic" to an understanding of the system. In modern times the capitalist ideology has penetrated Western society as rapidly and pervasively as any other social doctrine, but there is no one particular apology or interpretation of capitalism that has captured the popular imagination. Fascism has its *Mein Kampf,* and communism has its *Manifesto* and *Das Kapital.* To what single volume can we point as providing the core of capitalist doctrine?

If no one such sovereign volume exists, advocates of capitalism can at least point to the whole body of normative theory in contemporary economics, plus the long tradition of "liberal" political philosophy from Hobbes and John Locke, to John Stuart Mill and beyond. This state of affairs makes the case for capitalism extensive and highly sophisticated, but it does not simplify our task of distilling the arguments in favor of the free enterprise system. Still, we must make the attempt, even at considerable risk of over-simplification.

Essentially the case for capitalism boils down to two main propositions: an economic argument and a political argument. If we take capitalism to be a system principally characterized by private decision making about privately owned property, the economic argument for it is mainly in terms of incentives. Individuals will act rationally in the market to maximize their own production and profit, and hence to maximize total productivity. Individuals will work harder because they are working for themselves. It is suggested that without private property and the search for profits, the major economic incentive would be removed. Individual initiative would be lessened, and the processes of invention and the application of inventions would be inhibited, thereby tending to decrease total productivity.

It is argued further that to leave individual entrepreneurs free to compete in a market will result automatically in an optimum allocation of resources, maximizing consumer satisfaction or total economic "welfare". This point is fundamental to the thesis advanced by most defenders of capitalism, but it need not be labored here because it is an implicit or explicit assumption that pervades many of the readings in Part I, and because we return to it in both sections Two and Four.

The political argument for capitalism is mainly that it provides a firmer basis for individual liberty and individual freedom than any other system. It is argued that democracy and individual liberty have flourished historically side by side with the rise of capitalism. Private property is regarded not only as the basis of capitalism but also as the basis of individual liberty; if an individual has private property, it is more difficult for the state or for society to deprive him of his liberty. Capitalism is said to emphasize both individualism and rationality, and both are extremely important to the maintenance of democracy and of political liberty. Thus the political dimension of capitalism is extremely important. Democracy and capitalism are held to be mutually reinforcing.

On the other hand, it is obvious that capitalism does not *guarantee* liberty. In many countries today, private property and capitalism go hand in hand with fascism, authoritarianism or dictatorship. Capitalism and private property are to be found, for example, in Portugal, in Spain, and in many countries of South America that live under systems of political dictatorship. Similarly, a high degree of both consumer choice and political freedom are to be found in socialist countries such as Britain and Sweden, which have moved a long way from the capitalist economic system. Capitalism and democracy may be inter-related, but they are by no means synonymous or identical. In the prevailing view, capitalism is an economic institution, whereas democracy is a political institution. The one does not necessarily depend upon the other. It is entirely possible to point to nations and periods of history in which we can find capitalism without political freedom, and political freedom without capitalism. We will return to this problem in Section Four.

Having indicated some of the breadth and complexity of the topic, let us turn to the individual readings. Part I opens with a selection from the late Karl Polanyi's *The Great Transformation,* a book that many scholars regard as one of the most seminal works published in recent decades. In that book Polanyi contends that the high-water mark of laissez-faire and the nineteenth century's one hundred years peace were based upon four pillars: the international balance-of-power system, the gold standard, a self-regulating market, and the liberal state. But by 1914, he insists, these four pillars had crumbled, and laissez-faire was dead except as an ideology of wishful thinkers and an abstract model for economic theorists. The twin theses of *The Great Transformation* are that "pure" nineteenth-century capitalism was an historical aberration, a short-lived "utopian" departure from the historical norm of social restrictions on commercial activity, and that completely free markets destroy "community". In the selection excerpted here, Polanyi examines the fundamental question of whether laissez-faire was "natural" or not, and plumps for the negative.

The subsequent selections in Part I are both easier reading and more orthodox. E. V. Rostow makes a strong case in *Reading 2* that capitalism and private property are indispensable bulwarks of liberty. Although Rostow is an advocate of limited economic planning, and the book from which this reading is taken bears the title *Planning for Freedom,* he insists that planning will diminish freedom if private property is eroded.

This theme is amplified in the selection that follows. *Reading 3* is from Friedrich von Hayek's *The Constitution of Liberty,* a work less well known than, but superior to, his *Road to Serfdom.* Hayek, an Austrian economist teaching in Chicago, presents a succinct case maintaining that the substitution of state allocation of resources for market allocation infringes not only upon individual freedom but also upon the rule of law. That these ideas have been widely adopted in Canada is demonstrated by *Reading 4.* In the following selection, Professor Milton Friedman of the University of Chicago offers a more sweeping and empirical indictment of public economic controls. Friedman is one of the most incisive thinkers and lively writers of the so-called Radical Right, a noted economic theorist best known to lay readers for his advocacy of the "negative income tax". His essay presents a sophisticated conservative view of the limited role of government in a free society.

These authors appear to be swimming against the present tide of rising public restrictions on private enterprise. The reader may sense that the proponents of capitalism are today somewhat on the defensive. For better or for worse, the social objectives and economic theories of the defenders of capitalism are under heavy pressure from those who urge an enlarged role for the state in economic life. The development of the "mixed" private and public economy of contemporary collectivism is examined in Part 2.

1   Birth of the Liberal Creed*

Karl Polanyi

Economic liberalism was the organizing principle of a society engaged in creating a market system. Born as a mere penchant for non-bureaucratic methods, it evolved into a veritable faith in man's secular salvation through a self-regulating market. Such fanaticism was the result of the sudden aggravation of the task it found itself committed to: the magnitude of the sufferings that were to be inflicted on innocent persons as well as the vast scope of the interlocking changes involved in the establishment of the new order. The liberal creed assumed its evangelical fervor only in response to the needs of a fully deployed market economy.

To antedate the policy of *laissez-faire,* as is often done, to the time when

*From: *The Great Transformation* by Karl Polanyi (1944) (reprinted by permission of the author's estate and publisher).

this catchword was first used in France in the middle of the eighteenth century would be entirely unhistorical; it can be safely said that not until two generations later was economic liberalism more than a spasmodic tendency. Only by the 1820's did it stand for the three classical tenets: that labor should find its price on the market; that the creation of money should be subject to an automatic mechanism; that goods should be free to flow from country to country without hindrance or preference; in short, for a labor market, the gold standard, and free trade.

To credit François Quesnay with having envisaged such a state of affairs would be little short of fantastic. All that the Physiocrats demanded in a mercantilistic world was the free export of grain in order to ensure a better income to farmers, tenants, and landlords. For the rest their *ordre naturel* was no more than a directive principle for the regulation of industry and agriculture by a supposedly all-powerful and omniscient government. Quesnay's *Maximes* were intended to provide such a government with the viewpoints needed to translate into practical policy the principles of the *Tableau* on the basis of statistical data which he offered to have furnished periodically. The idea of a self-regulating system of markets had never as much as entered his mind.

In England, too, *laissez-faire* was interpreted narrowly; it meant freedom from regulations in production; trade was not comprised. Cotton manufacturers, the marvel of the time, had grown from insignificance into the leading export industry of the country—yet the import of printed cottons remained forbidden by positive statute. Notwithstanding the traditional monopoly of the home market an export bounty for calico or muslin was granted. Protectionism was so ingrained that Manchester cotton manufacturers demanded, in 1800, the prohibition of the export of yarn, though they were conscious of the fact that this meant loss of business to them. An Act passed in 1791 extended the penalties for the export of tools used in manufacturing cotton goods to the export of models or specifications. The free trade origins of the cotton industry are a myth. Freedom from regulation in the sphere of production was all the industry wanted; freedom in the sphere of exchange was still deemed a danger.

One might suppose that freedom of production would naturally spread from the purely technological field to that of the employment of labor. However, only comparatively late did Manchester raise the demand for free labor. The cotton industry had never been subject to the Statute of Artificers and was consequently not hampered either by yearly wage assessments or by rules of apprenticeship. The Old Poor Law, on the other hand, to which latter-day liberals so fiercely objected, was a help to the manufacturers; it not only supplied them with parish apprentices, but also permitted them to divest themselves of responsibility towards their dismissed employees, thus throwing much of the burden of unemployment on public funds. Not even the Speenhamland system was at first unpopular with the cotton manufacturers; as long as the moral effect of allowances did not reduce the productive capacity of the laborer, the industry might have well regarded family endowment as a help in sustaining that reserve army of labor which was urgently required to meet the tremendous fluctuations of trade. At a time when employment in agriculture was still on a year's term, it was of great importance that such a fund of mobile labor should be available to industry in periods of expansion. Hence the attacks of the manufacturers on the Act of Settlement which hampered the physical mobility of labor. Yet not before 1795 was the repeal of that Act carried— only to be replaced by more, not less, paternalism in regard to the Poor Law. Pauperism still remained the concern of squire and countryside; and even harsh critics of Speenhamland like Burke, Bentham, and Malthus regarded themselves less as representatives of industrial progress than as propounders of sound principles of rural administration.

Not until the 1830's did economic liberalism burst forth as a crusading passion, and *laissez-faire* become a militant creed. The manufacturing class was pressing for the amendment of the Poor Law, since it prevented the rise of an industrial working class which depended for its income on achievement. The magnitude of the venture implied in the creation of a free labor market now became apparent, as well as the extent of the misery to be inflicted on the victims of improvement. Accordingly, by the early 1830's a sharp change of mood was manifest. An 1817 reprint of Town-send's *Dissertation* contained a preface in praise of the foresight with which the author had borne down on the Poor Laws and demanded their complete abandonment; but the editors warned of his "rash and precipitate" suggestion that outdoor relief to the poor should be abolished within so short a term as *ten* years. Ricardo's *Principles*, which appeared in the same year, insisted on the necessity of abolishing the allowance system, but urged strongly that this should be done only very gradually. Pitt, a disciple of Adam Smith, had rejected such a course on account of the innocent suffering it would entail. And as late as 1829, Peel "doubted whether the allowance system could be safely removed otherwise than gradually."[1] Yet after the political victory of the middle class, in 1832, the Poor Law Amendment Bill was carried in its most extreme form and rushed into effect without any period of grace. *Laissez-faire* had been catalyzed into a drive of uncompromising ferocity.

A similar keying up of economic liberalism from academic interest to boundless activism occurred in the two other fields of industrial organization: currency and trade. In respect to both of these *laissez-faire* waxed into a fervently held creed when the uselessness of any other but extreme solutions became apparent.

The currency issue was first brought home to the English community in the form of a general rise in the cost of living. Between 1790 and 1815 prices doubled. Real wages fell and business was hit by a slump in foreign

---

[1]Webb, S. and B., *op. cit.*

exchanges. Yet not until the 1825 panic did sound currency become a tenet of economic liberalism, *i.e.*, only when Ricardian principles were already so deeply impressed on the minds of politicians and businessmen alike that the "standard" was maintained in spite of the enormous number of financial casualties. This was the beginning of that unshakable belief in the automatic steering mechanism of the gold standard without which the market system could never have got under way.

International free trade involved no less an act of faith. Its implications were entirely extravagant. It meant that England would depend for her food supply upon overseas sources; would sacrifice her agriculture, if necessary, and enter on a new form of life under which she would be part and parcel of some vaguely conceived world unity of the future; that this planetary community would have to be a peaceful one, or, if not, would have to be made safe for Great Britain by the power of the Navy; and that the English nation would face the prospects of continuous industrial dislocations in the firm belief in its superior inventive and productive ability. However, it was believed that if only the grain of all the world could flow freely to Britain, then her factories would be able to undersell all the world. Again, the measure of the determination needed was set by the magnitude of the proposition and the vastness of the risks involved in complete acceptance. Yet less than complete acceptance would have spelt certain ruin.

The utopian springs of the dogma of *laissez-faire* are but incompletely understood as long as they are viewed separately. The three tenets—competitive labor market, automatic gold standard, and international free trade—formed one whole. The sacrifices involved in achieving any one of them were useless, if not worse, unless the other two were equally secured. It was everything or nothing.

Anybody could see that the gold standard, for instance, meant danger of deadly deflation and, maybe, of fatal monetary stringency in a panic. The manufacturer could, therefore, hope to hold his own only if he was assured of an increasing scale of production at remunerative prices (in other words, only if wages fell at least in proportion to the general fall in prices, so as to allow the exploitation of an ever-expanding world market). Thus the Anti-Corn Law Bill of 1846 was the corollary of Peel's Bank Act of 1844, and both assumed a laboring class which, since the Poor Law Amendment Act of 1834, was forced to give their best under the threat of hunger, so that wages were regulated by the price of grain. The three great measures formed a coherent whole.

The global sweep of economic liberalism can now be taken in at a glance. Nothing less than a self-regulating market on a world scale could ensure the functioning of this stupendous mechanism. Unless the price of labor was dependent upon the cheapest grain available, there was no guarantee that the unprotected industries would not succumb in the grip of the voluntarily accepted task-master, gold. The expansion of the market system in the nineteenth century was synonymous with the simultaneous spreading

THE CAPITALIST IDEOLOGY 11

of international free trade, competitive labor market, and gold standard; they belonged together. No wonder that economic liberalism turned into a secular religion once the great perils of this venture were evident.

There was nothing natural about *laissez-faire*; free markets could never have come into being merely by allowing things to take their course. Just as cotton manufacturers—the leading free trade industry—were created by the help of protective tariffs, export bounties, and indirect wage subsidies, *laissez-faire* itself was enforced by the state. The thirties and forties saw not only an outburst of legislation repealing restrictive regulations, but also an enormous increase in the administrative functions of the state, which was now being endowed with a central bureaucracy able to fulfill the tasks set by the adherents of liberalism. To the typical utilitarian, economic liberalism was a social project which should be put into effect for the greatest happiness of the greatest number; *laissez-faire* was not a method to achieve a thing, it was the thing to be achieved. True, legislation could do nothing directly, except by repealing harmful restrictions. But that did not mean that *government* could do nothing, especially indirectly. On the contrary, the utilitarian liberal saw in government the great agency for achieving happiness. In respect to material welfare, Bentham believed, the influence of legislation "is as nothing" in comparison with the unconscious contribution of the "minister of the police." Of the three things needed for economic success—inclination, knowledge, and power— the private person possessed only inclination. Knowledge and power, Bentham taught, can be administered much cheaper by government than by private persons. It was the task of the executive to collect statistics and information, to foster science and experiment, as well as to supply the innumerable instruments of final realization in the field of government. Benthamite liberalism meant the replacing of Parliamentary action by action through administrative organs.

For this there was ample scope. Reaction in England had not governed —as it did in France—through administrative methods but used exclusively Parliamentary legislation to put political repression into effect. "The revolutionary movements of 1785 and of 1815-1820 were combated, not by departmental action, but by Parliamentary legislation. The suspension of the Habeas Corpus Act, the passing of the Libel Act, and of the 'Six Acts' of 1819, were severely coercive measures; but they contain no evidence of any attempt to give a Continental character to administration. Insofar as individual liberty was destroyed, it was destroyed by and in pursuance of Acts of Parliament."[2] Economic liberals had hardly gained influence on government, in 1832, when the position changed completely in favor of administrative methods. "The net result of the legislative activity which has characterized, though with different degrees of intensity, the period

---

[2]Redlich and Hirst, J., *Local Government in England*, Vol. II, p. 240, quoted A. V. Dicey, *Law and Opinion in England*, p. 305.

since 1832, has been the building up piecemeal of an administrative machine of great complexity which stands in as constant need of repair, renewal, reconstruction, and adaptation to new requirements as the plant of a modern manufacture."[3] This growth of administration reflected the spirit of utilitarianism. Bentham's fabulous Panopticon, his most personal utopia, was a star-shaped building from the center of which prison wardens could keep the greatest number of jailbirds under the most effective supervision at the smallest cost to the public. Similarly, in the utilitarian state his favorite principle of "inspectability" ensured that the Minister at the top should keep effective control over all local administration.

The road to the free market was opened and kept open by an enormous increase in continuous, centrally organized and controlled interventionism. To make Adam Smith's "simple and natural liberty" compatible with the needs of a human society was a most complicated affair. Witness the complexity of the provisions in the innumerable enclosure laws; the amount of bureaucratic control involved in the administration of the New Poor Laws which for the first time since Queen Elizabeth's reign were effectively supervised by central authority; or the increase in governmental administration entailed in the meritorious task of municipal reform. And yet all these strongholds of governmental interference were erected with a view to the organizing of some simple freedom—such as that of land, labor, or municipal administration. Just as, contrary to expectation, the invention of labor-saving machinery had not diminished but actually increased the uses of human labor, the introduction of free markets, far from doing away with the need for control, regulation, and intervention, enormously increased their range. Administrators had to be constantly on the watch to ensure the free working of the system. Thus even those who wished most ardently to free the state from all unnecessary duties, and whose whole philosophy demanded the restriction of state activities, could not but entrust the self-same state with the new powers, organs, and instruments required for the establishment of laissez-faire.

This paradox was topped by another. While laissez-faire economy was the product of deliberate state action, subsequent restrictions on laissez-faire started in a spontaneous way. Laissez-faire was planned; planning was not. The first half of this assertion was shown above to be true. If ever there was conscious use of the executive in the service of a deliberate government-controlled policy, it was on the part of the Benthamites in the heroic period of laissez-faire. The other half was first mooted by that eminent liberal, Dicey, who made it his task to inquire into the origins of the "anti-laissez-faire" or, as he called it, the "collectivist" trend in English public opinion, the existence of which was manifest since the late 1860's. He was surprised to find that no evidence of the existence of such a trend could be traced

---

[3]Ilbert, *Legislative Methods*, pp. 212-13, quoted A. V. Dicey, *op. cit.*

save the acts of legislation themselves. More exactly, no evidence of a "collectivist trend" in public opinion *prior* to the laws which appeared to represent such a trend could be found. As to later "collectivist" opinion, Dicey inferred that the "collectivist" legislation itself might have been its prime source. The upshot of his penetrating inquiry was that there had been complete absence of any deliberate intention to extend the functions of the state, or to restrict the freedom of the individual, on the part of those who were directly responsible for the restrictive enactments of the 1870's and 1880's. The legislative spearhead of the countermovement against a self-regulating market as it developed in the half century following 1860 turned out to be spontaneous, undirected by opinion, and actuated by a purely pragmatic spirit.

Economic liberals must strongly take exception to this view. Their whole social philosophy hinges on the idea that *laissez-faire* was a natural development, while subsequent anti-*laissez-faire* legislation was the result of a purposeful action on the part of the opponents of liberal principles. In these two mutually exclusive interpretations of the double movement, it is not too much to say, the truth or untruth of the liberal position is involved today.

Liberal writers like Spencer and Sumner, Mises and Lippmann offer an account of the double movement substantially similar to our own, but they put an entirely different interpretation on it. While in our view the concept of a self-regulating market was utopian, and its progress was stopped by the realistic self-protection of society, in their view all protectionism was a mistake due to impatience, greed, and shortsightedness, but for which the market would have resolved its difficulties. The question as to which of these two views is correct is perhaps the most important problem of recent social history, involving as it does no less than a decision on the claim of economic liberalism to be the basic organizing principle in society. Before we turn to the testimony of the facts, a more precise formulation of the issue is needed.

In retrospect our age will be credited with having seen the end of the self-regulating market. The 1920's saw the prestige of economic liberalism at its height. Hundreds of millions of people had been afflicted by the scourge of inflation; whole social classes, whole nations had been expropriated. Stabilization of currencies became the focal point in the political thought of peoples and governments; the restoration of the gold standard became the supreme aim of all organized effort in the economic field. The repayment of foreign loans and the return to stable currencies were recognized as the touchstones of rationality in politics; and no private suffering, no infringement of sovereignty, was deemed too great a sacrifice for the recovery of monetary integrity. The privations of the unemployed made jobless by deflation; the destitution of public servants dismissed without a pittance; even the relinquishment of national rights and the loss of constitutional liberties were judged a fair price to pay for the fulfillment of the requirement of sound budgets and sound currencies, these *a priori* of economic liberalism.

The thirties lived to see the absolutes of the twenties called in question. After several years during which currencies were practically restored and budgets balanced, the two most powerful countries, Great Britain and the United States, found themselves in difficulties, dismissed the gold standard, and started out on the management of their currencies. International debts were repudiated wholesale and the tenets of economic liberalism were disregarded by the wealthiest and most respectable. By the middle of the thirties France and some other states still adhering to gold were actually forced off the standard by the Treasuries of Great Britain and the United States, formerly jealous guardians of the liberal creed.

In the forties economic liberalism suffered an even worse defeat. Although Great Britain and the United States departed from monetary orthodoxy, they retained the principles and methods of liberalism in industry and commerce, the general organization of their economic life. This was to prove a factor in precipitating the war and a handicap in fighting it, since economic liberalism had created and fostered the illusion that dictatorships were bound for economic catastrophe. By virtue of this creed democratic governments were the last to understand the implications of managed currencies and directed trade, even when they happened by force of circumstances to be practicing these methods themselves; also, the legacy of economic liberalism barred the way to timely rearmament in the name of balanced budgets and free enterprise, which were supposed to provide the only secure foundations of economic strength in war. In Great Britain budgetary and monetary orthodoxy induced adherence to the traditional strategic principle of limited commitments upon a country actually faced with total war; in the United States vested interests—such as oil and aluminum—entrenched themselves behind the taboos of liberal business and successfully resisted preparations for an industrial emergency. But for the stubborn and impassioned insistence of economic liberals on their fallacies, the leaders of the race as well as the masses of free men would have been better equipped for the ordeal of the age and might perhaps even have been able to avoid it altogether.

Secular tenets of social organization embracing the whole civilized world are not dislodged by the events of a decade. Both in Great Britain and in the United States millions of independent business units derived their existence from the principle of *laissez-faire*. Its spectacular failure in one field did not destroy its authority in all. Indeed, its partial eclipse may have even strengthened its hold since it enabled its defenders to argue that the incomplete application of its principles was the reason for every and any difficulty laid to its charge.

This, indeed, is the last remaining argument of economic liberalism today. Its apologists are repeating in endless variations that but for the policies advocated by its critics, liberalism would have delivered the goods; that not the competitive system and the self-regulating market, but interference with that system and interventions with that market are responsible for our ills. And this argument does not find support in innumerable recent infringements of economic freedom only, but also in the indubitable fact that the movement to spread the system of self-regulating markets was met in the second half of the nineteenth century by a persistent countermove obstructing the free working of such an economy.

The economic liberal is thus enabled to formulate a case which links the present with the past in one coherent whole. For who could deny that government intervention in business may undermine confidence? Who could deny that unemployment would sometimes be less if it were not for out-of-work benefit provided by law? That private business is injured by the competition of public works? That deficit finance may endanger private investments? That paternalism tends to damp business initiative? This being so in the present, surely it was no different in the past. When around the 1870's a general protectionist movement—social and national—started in Europe, who can doubt that it hampered and restricted trade? Who can doubt that factory laws, social insurance, municipal trading, health services, public utilities, tariffs, bounties and subsidies, cartels and trusts, embargoes on immigration, on capital movements, on imports—not to speak of less open restrictions on the movements of men, goods, and payments—must have acted as so many hindrances to the functioning of the competitive system, protracting business depressions, aggravating unemployment, deepening financial slumps, diminishing trade, and damaging severely the self-regulating mechanism of the market? The root of all evil, the liberal insists, was precisely this interference with the freedom of employment, trade and currencies practiced by the various schools of social, national, and monopolistic protectionism since the third quarter of the nineteenth century; but for the unholy alliance of trade unions and labor parties with monopolistic manufacturers and agrarian interests, which in their shortsighted greed joined forces to frustrate economic liberty, the world would be enjoying today the fruits of an almost automatic system of creating material welfare. Liberal leaders never weary of repeating that the tragedy of the nineteenth century sprang from the incapacity of man to remain faithful to the inspiration of the early liberals; that the generous initiative of our ancestors was frustrated by the passions of nationalism and class war, vested interests, and monopolists, and above all, by the blindness of the working people to the ultimate beneficence of unrestricted economic freedom to all human interests, including their own. A great intellectual and moral advance was thus, it is claimed, frustrated by the intellectual and moral weaknesses of the mass of the people; what the spirit of Enlightenment had achieved was put to nought by the forces of selfishness. In a nutshell, this is the economic liberal's defense. Unless it is refuted, he will continue to hold the floor in the contest of arguments.

Let us focus the issue. It is agreed that the liberal movement, intent on the spreading of the market system, was met by a protective countermovement tending towards its restriction; such an assumption, indeed, underlies our own thesis of the double movement. But while we assert that the inherent absurdity of the idea of a self-regulating market system would have eventually destroyed society, the liberal accuses the most various elements of having wrecked a great initiative. Unable to adduce evidence of any such concerted effort to thwart the liberal movement, he falls back on the practically irrefutable hypothesis of covert action. This is the myth of the antiliberal conspiracy which in one form or another is common to all liberal interpretations of the events of the 1870's and 1880's. Commonly the rise of nationalism and of socialism is credited with having been the chief agent in that shifting of the scene; manufacturers' associations and monopolists, agrarian interests and trade unions are the villains of the piece. Thus in its most spiritualized form the liberal doctrine hypostasizes the working of some dialectical law in modern society stultifying the endeavors of enlightened reason, while in its crudest version it reduces itself to an attack on political democracy, as the alleged mainspring of interventionism.

The testimony of the facts contradicts the liberal thesis decisively. The antiliberal conspiracy is a pure invention. The great variety of forms in which the "collectivist" countermovement appeared was not due to any preference for socialism or nationalism on the part of concerted interests, but exclusively to the broader range of the vital social interests affected by the expanding market mechanism. This accounts for the all but universal reactions of predominantly practical character called forth by the expansion of that mechanism. Intellectual fashions played no role whatever in this process; there was, accordingly, no room for the prejudice which the liberal regards as the ideological force behind the antiliberal development. Although it is true that the 1870's and 1880's saw the end of orthodox liberalism, and that all crucial problems of the present can be traced back to that period, it is incorrect to say that the change to social and national protectionism was due to any other cause than the manifestation of the weaknesses and perils inherent in a self-regulating market system. This can be shown in more than one way.

First, there is the amazing diversity of the matters on which action was taken. This alone would exclude the possibility of concerted action. Let us cite from a list of interventions which Herbert Spencer compiled in 1884, when charging liberals with having deserted their principles for the sake of "restrictive legislation."[4] The variety of the subjects could hardly be greater. In 1860, authority was given to provide "analysts of food and drink to be paid out of local rates"; there followed an Act providing "the inspection of gas works"; an extension of the Mines Act "making it penal to employ boys under twelve not attending schools and unable to read or

---

[4]H. Spencer, *The Man vs. the State,* 1884.

write." In 1861, power was given "to poor law guardians to enforce vaccination"; local boards were authorized "to fix rates of hire for means of conveyance"; and certain locally formed bodies "had given them powers of taxing the locality for rural drainage and irrigation works, and for supplying water to cattle." In 1862, an Act was passed making illegal "a coal-mine with a single shaft"; an Act giving the Council of Medical Education exclusive right "to furnish a Pharmacopoeia, the price of which is to be fixed by the Treasury." Spencer, horror-struck, filled several pages with an enumeration of these and similar measures. In 1863, came the "extension of compulsory vaccination to Scotland and Ireland." There was also an Act appointing inspectors for the "wholesomeness, or unwholesomeness of food"; a Chimney-Sweeper's Act, to prevent the torture and eventual death of children set to sweep too narrow slots; a Contagious Diseases Act; a Public Libraries Act, giving local powers "by which a majority can tax a minority for their books." Spencer adduced them as so much irrefutable evidence of an antiliberal conspiracy. And yet each of these Acts dealt with some problem arising out of modern industrial conditions and was aimed at the safeguarding of some public interest against dangers inherent either in such conditions or, at any rate, in the market method of dealing with them. To an unbiased mind they proved the purely practical and pragmatic nature of the "collectivist" countermove. Most of those who carried these measures were convinced supporters of *laissez-faire*, and certainly did not wish their consent to the establishment of a fire brigade in London to imply a protest against the principles of economic liberalism. On the contrary, the sponsors of these legislative acts were as a rule uncompromising opponents of socialism, or any other form of collectivism.

Second, the change from liberal to "collectivist" solutions happened sometimes over night and without any consciousness on the part of those engaged in the process of legislative rumination. Dicey adduced the classic instance of the Workmen's Compensation Act dealing with the employers' liability for damage done to his workmen in the course of their employment. The history of the various acts embodying this idea, since 1880, showed consistent adherence to the individualist principle that the responsibility of the employer to his employee must be regulated in a manner strictly identical with that governing his responsibility to others, *e.g.*, strangers. With hardly any change in opinion, in 1897, the employer was suddenly made the insurer of his workmen against any damage incurred in the course of their employment, a "thoroughly collectivistic legislation," as Dicey justly remarked. No better proof could be adduced that no change either in the type of interests involved, or in the tendency of the opinions brought to bear on the matter, caused the supplanting of a liberal principle by an antiliberal one, but exclusively the evolving conditions under which the problem arose and a solution was sought.

Third, there is the indirect, but most striking proof provided by a comparison of the development in various countries of a widely dissimilar political and ideological configuration. Victorian England and the Prussia of Bismarck were poles apart, and both were very much unlike the France of the Third Republic or the Empire of the Hapsburgs. Yet each of them passed through a period of free trade and *laissez-faire,* followed by a period of antiliberal legislation in regard to public health, factory conditions, municipal trading, social insurance, shipping subsidies, public utilities, trade associations, and so on. It would be easy to produce a regular calendar setting out the years in which analogous changes occurred in the various countries. Workmen's compensation was enacted in England in 1880 and 1897, in Germany in 1879, in Austria in 1887, in France in 1899; factory inspection was introduced in England in 1833, in Prussia in 1853, in Austria in 1883, in France in 1874 and 1883; municipal trading, including the running of public utilities, was introduced by Joseph Chamberlain, a Dissenter and a capitalist, in Birmingham in the 1870's; by the Catholic "Socialist" and Jew-baiter, Karl Lueger, in the Imperial Vienna of the 1890's; in German and French municipalities by a variety of local coalitions. The supporting forces were in some cases violently reactionary and antisocialist as in Vienna, at other times "radical imperialist" as in Birmingham, or of the purest liberal hue as with the Frenchman, Edouard Herriot, Mayor of Lyons. In Protestant England, Conservative and Liberal cabinets labored intermittently at the completion of factory legislation. In Germany, Roman Catholics and Social Democrats took part in its achievement; in Austria, the Church and its most militant supporters; in France, enemies of the Church and ardent anticlericals were responsible for the enactment of almost identical laws. Thus under the most varied slogans, with very different motivations a multitude of parties and social strata put into effect almost exactly the same measures in a series of countries in respect to a large number of complicated subjects. There is, on the face of it, nothing more absurd than to infer that they were secretly actuated by the same ideological preconceptions or narrow group interests as the legend of the antiliberal conspiracy would have it. On the contrary, everything tends to support the assumption that objective reasons of a stringent nature forced the hands of the legislators.

Fourth, there is the significant fact that at various times economic liberals themselves advocated restrictions on the freedom of contract and on *laissez-faire* in a number of well-defined cases of great theoretical and practical importance. Antiliberal prejudice could, naturally, not have been their motive. We have in mind the principle of the association of labor on the one hand, the law of business corporations on the other. The first refers to the right of workers to combine for the purpose of raising their wages; the latter, to the right of trusts, cartels, or other forms of capitalistic combines, to raise prices. It was justly charged in both cases that freedom of contract or *laissez-faire* was being used in restraint of trade. Whether workers' associations to raise wages, or trade associations to raise prices were in question, the principle of *laissez-faire* could be obviously employed by interested parties to narrow the market for labor or other commodities. It is highly significant that in either case consistent liberals from Lloyd George and Theodore Roosevelt to Thurman Arnold and Walter Lippmann subordinated *laissez-faire* to the demand for a free competitive market; they pressed for regulations and restrictions, for penal laws and compulsion, arguing as any "collectivist" would that the freedom of contract was being "abused" by trade unions, or corporations, whichever it was. Theoretically, *laissez-faire* or freedom of contract implied the freedom of workers to withhold their labor either individually or jointly, if they so decided; it implied also the freedom of businessmen to concert on selling prices irrespective of the wishes of the consumers. But in practice such freedom conflicted with the institution of a self-regulating market, and *in such a conflict the self-regulating market was invariably accorded precedence*. In other words, if the needs of a self-regulating market proved incompatible with the demands of *laissez-faire,* the economic liberal turned against *laissez-faire* and preferred—as any antiliberal would have done—the so-called collectivist methods of regulation and restriction. Trade union law as well as antitrust legislation sprang from this attitude. No more conclusive proof could be offered of the inevitability of antiliberal or "collectivist" methods under the conditions of modern industrial society than the fact that even economic liberals themselves regularly used such methods in decisively important fields of industrial organization.

Incidentally, this helps to clarify the true meaning of the term "interventionism" by which economic liberals like to denote the opposite of their own policy, but merely betray confusion of thought. The opposite interventionism is *laissez-faire* and we have just seen that economic liberalism cannot be identified with *laissez-faire* (although in common parlance there is no harm in using them interchangeably) . Strictly, economic liberalism is the organizing principle of a society in which industry is based on the institution of a self-regulating market. True, once such a system is approximately achieved, less intervention of one type is needed. However, this is far from saying that market system and intervention are mutually exclusive terms. For as long as that system is not established, economic liberals must and will unhesitatingly call for the intervention of the state in order to establish it, and once established, in order to maintain it. The economic liberal can, therefore, without any inconsistency call upon the state to use the force of law; he can even appeal to the violent forces of civil war to set up the preconditions of a self-regulating market. In America the South appealed to the arguments of *laissez-faire* to justify slavery; the North appealed to the intervention of arms to establish a free labor market. The accusation of interventionism on the part of liberal writers is thus an empty slogan, implying the denunciation of one and the same set of actions according to whether they happen to approve of them or not. The only principle economic liberals can maintain without inconsistency is that of the self-regulating market, whether it involves them in interventions or not.

To sum up. The countermove against economic liberalism and *laissez-faire* possessed all the unmistakable characteristics of a spontaneous reaction. At innumerable disconnected points it set in without any traceable links between the interests directly affected or any ideological conformity between them. Even in the settlement of one and the same problem as in the case of workmen's compensation, solutions switched over from individualistic to "collectivistic," from liberal to antiliberal, from *"laissez-faire"* to interventionist forms without any change in the economic interest, the ideological influences or political forces in play, merely as a result of the increasing realization of the nature of the problem in question. Also it could be shown that a closely similar change from *laissez-faire* to "collectivism" took place in various countries at a definite stage of their industrial development, pointing to the depth and independence of the underlying causes of the process so superficially credited by economic liberals to changing moods or sundry interests. Finally, analysis reveals that not even radical adherents of economic liberalism could escape the rule which makes *laissez-faire* inapplicable to advanced industrial conditions; for in the critical case of trade union law and antitrust regulations extreme liberals themselves had to call for manifold interventions of the state, in order to secure against monopolistic compacts the preconditions for the working of a self-regulating market. Even free trade and competition required intervention to be workable. The liberal myth of the "collectivist" conspiracy of the 1870's and 1880's is contrary to all the facts.

Our own interpretation of the double movement is, we find, borne out by the evidence. For if market economy was a threat to the human and natural components of the social fabric, as we insisted, what else would one expect than an urge on the part of a great variety of people to press for some sort of protection? This was what we found. Also, one would expect this to happen without any theoretical or intellectual preconceptions on their part, and irrespective of their attitudes towards the principles underlying a market economy. Again, this was the case. Moreover, we suggested that comparative history of governments might offer quasi-experimental support of our thesis if particular interests could be shown to be independent of the specific ideologies present in a number of different countries. For this also we could adduce striking evidence. Finally, the behavior of liberals themselves proved that the maintenance of freedom of trade—in our terms, of a self-regulating market—far from excluding intervention, in effect, demanded such action, and that liberals themselves regularly called for compulsory action on the part of the state as in the case of trade union law and antitrust laws. Thus nothing could be more decisive than the evidence of history as to which of the two contending interpretations of the double movement was correct: that of the economic liberal who maintained that his policy never had a chance, but was strangled by shortsighted trade unionists, Marxist intellectuals, greedy manufacturers, and reactionary landlords; or that of his critics, who can point to the universal "collectivist" reaction against the expansion of market economy in the second half of the nineteenth century as conclusive proof of the peril to society inherent in the utopian principle of a self-regulating market.

2 Capitalism as a Condition of Freedom*

Eugene V. Rostow

. . . It should be altogether possible for capitalist democracy in the United States to carry out enlightened economic programs, in pretty much its present posture of legal and social organization, and without giving up either capitalism or democracy.

The obverse of this proposition has equal force: neither political nor social freedom for the individual, as ultimate goals of American life, can be imagined without the working reality of American capitalism. In this perspective, capitalism is not merely one among many alternative methods for organizing commerce and industry: it is a system of power which accomplishes a reasonably wide dispersal of economic authority and of economic opportunity within the society. American capitalism divides influence into independent focal points which are relatively unprotected against the impact of competition and technological change, although some are linked by relations of reciprocity as well as of conflict. This quality of pluralism is an essential condition of American liberty.

Astute practitioners of the art of semantics urge that a new word be substituted for "capitalism" in this connection. Its connotations are unfavorable, they say, especially in Europe and Asia. It evokes disastrous memories of imperialism and unemployment, exploitation and brutality, of opulent bankers and starving hordes of barefoot workmen. Jacques Maritain proposes that the mild and protective economic environment of the present era in the West be called one of Economic Humanism, and others have suggested less felicitious and more defensive substitutes for "capitalism."

There are advantages, however, in confronting the fact that it is capitalism we are talking about, after all, capitalism and its rivalry with socialism as competing principles of economic order.

Capitalism is not a static concept of unalterable meaning. Its present legal

*From: *Planning for Freedom: The Public Law of American Capitalism* (New Haven, Yale University Press, 1959), Chapter 3 (reprinted and abridged by permission of publisher).

position is one of steady change, under evolving rules of law which define rights of property in terms of overriding public interests. The ballot has long since proved mightier than the safe deposit box. Taxes, welfare programs, and programs to mitigate the trade cycle have revolutionized the atmosphere of ordinary living in the Western world.

Capitalism today hardly resembles its ancestors, the capitalist regimes of the late middle ages or the early industrial period. We have come a long way from the slums and sweatshops which are the popular image of nineteenth-century capitalism. Some of the economic historians contend that Dickens, Engels, and Disraeli were lurid and inaccurate, and that the popular image is a myth. Whether or not the older pictures were overdrawn, there can be no doubt of the advance that has taken place in the conditions of life among the working people of Western communities during the last century.

But for all its development, capitalism is still recognizably a system that permits and protects the private ownership of property, and the making of private decisions about its use. There is still a difference between the rights of property in the Soviet Union and in the United States. And that difference, even if it is called a difference of degree, is crucial to the possibility of personal and political freedom.

It should by now be apparent, both in theory and in practice, that Democratic Socialism is a contradiction in terms. Neither personal nor political freedom could survive a monopolization of power by the state, nor indeed its monopolization by any other group of institutions under unified control within a society. Socialist societies can have good, bad, or indifferent economies, educational systems, armies or churches. There is no inherent reason why the state cannot conduct the steel industry or the railways as well or as badly as it conducts an atomic energy program, the traffic controls at air fields, or the weather service. Indeed, it would be hard to demonstrate that government administration of the railroads would necessarily be worse than the railroad administration now prevailing in the United States. The American preference for capitalism represents more than inertia, inherited loyalties, and a belief in its superior efficiency. It rests ultimately on a recognition of its role in the strategy of freedom. Unless the members of an opposition can make a living without the permission of the government; unless they can function as a political party, obtain newsprint and presses, hire meeting halls, publish freely; unless they can have access to television without complete dependence on the good will and sporting instincts of the government in power, their opposition is bound to be a feeble, meaningless force, existing only by sufferance. Capitalism is a vital part of the price of liberty.

The point has never been more sharply put than by Harold Laski. Laski was acutely conscious of the shortcomings of capitalism, and quite unaware of its economic processes. He considered himself a Socialist, though not a Communist. But he was also, perhaps even more emphatically, a democrat and a libertarian. In his writing on the conditions of freedom, he was one of the fervent modern spokesmen for pluralism—the dispersal and federalization of authority among the people and institutions of society—as the indispensable basis of liberty. He urged that great inequality in economic power was incompatible with freedom. It was his prediction, denied by what has happened since both in Britain and in the United States, that universal suffrage would never succeed in mitigating the political power of wealth. But he saw the other side of the coin with clarity. "If in any state," he wrote, "there is a body of men who possess unlimited political power, those over whom they rule can never be free. For the one assured result of historical investigation is the lesson that uncontrolled power is invariably poisonous to those who possess it. They are always tempted to impose their canon of good upon others, and, in the end, they assume that the good of the community depends upon the continuance of their power."[1] "There will never be liberty," he continued, "in any state where there is an excessive concentration of power at the centre."[2]

Many of the theorists of Socialism, including Laski himself, have experimented with the notion of decentralized Socialism. They have considered cooperatives, syndical groups, guilds and other forms of industrial organization which would have the advantages of dispersed power, without the supposed disadvantages of private property. In their systems of Socialism, the managers of state-owned enterprises would be given great discretion, although they would be ultimately answerable to the state.

The status of management in such decentralized socialist enterprises has sometimes been analogized to that of the men who direct great American corporations. By and large, the managers of these vast enterprises have achieved extraordinary freedom from the influence of stockholders, and an extraordinary capacity for self-perpetuation. The stockholders are the legal source of the managers' power, as the nominal owners of their companies' property. But in many publicly held companies the stockholders obey the managers, not the management the stockholders. The managers "own" their companies, for all practical purposes, although their investment is usually small. The stockholders accept the managers' advice, and re-elect them regularly, voting them also the generous option and pension plans which have become so popular.

Corporations of this kind present American law with difficult questions of responsibility. The stockholders of many publicly held companies discharge their duties in the most perfunctory manner, and allow the corporate management, for long periods of time, almost complete freedom, tempered only

---

[1]*Liberty in the Modern State* (New York, Harper, 1930), pp. 2-3.
[2]*Ibid.*, p. 64.

by the managers' own standards of behavior, and their concern for the possibility of an accounting.[3]

The question is occasionally put, whether the situation in the United States would be very different if all or a good deal of the stock of the United States Steel Corporation, and of other like corporations, were owned by the government, and voted at annual meetings by the Secretary of Commerce. Could not such a preservation of the forms of capitalism preserve also its desirable flexibility, and its relative freedom from governmental control? Would not such a solution establish active and intelligent procedures of review for the stewardship of the managers, who are at law trustees of other people's money? Experiments along this line have been proposed as a general policy by some leaders of the Labour party in England. "Decentralization" has become a popular slogan also in the Soviet Union, and in other countries which suffer from traffic jams in the machinery for making decisions.

Public ownership of the stock of great companies would provide adequate oversight for the internal affairs of American corporations. But the remedy would be far worse than the disease. For Socialism via stock ownership would involve as complete a monopolization of power as any other form of Socialism. If applied to any considerable segment of American commerce or industry, the effects of such an approach would be ruinous.

The government would of course be a most vigilant stockholder. In the nature of things, the government as stockholder would necessarily assert effective control over the policy of the corporations involved. Government officials are conscientious and diligent, by and large, and no civil servant charged with responsibility for the government's shares in a corporation would be as casual and as careless as many private investors are in voting their own shares. Such has been American experience with government-owned corporations, from the Panama Canal Company to the various banks, barge lines, and other incidental enterprises which belong to the United States Government. And experience with government-owned companies in Britain, France, and Italy is not notably different. Some are imaginative and active, others relatively routine. The head of the Italian government-owned oil company is a man of great influence and power, as is the Director of Electricité de France. But all these companies, the good and the bad alike, are in the end subject to sustained control by the state.

There is no possible objection to this fact so long as the state-owned sector is a relatively small share of the whole economy. Indeed it would be most objectionable if the pattern were otherwise, and the state passively allowed its funds to be spent without effective supervision.

The objection arises only if a program of genuine Socialism is put into effect, and the state becomes the sole employer of labor, or the sole signi-

---

[3]Discussed at some length in "To Whom and for What Ends Is Corporate Management Responsible?" a chapter of Edward S. Mason, ed., *The Corporation in Modern Society* (Cambridge, Harvard University Press, 1960) , p. 46.

ficant employer, save for a fragmentary private sector devoted to the manufacture and sale of handicrafts and the like. Consider the position of Mr.
Molotov, who was . . . removed as Foreign Minister of the Soviet Union,
after forty years of considerable experience, for the offense of having
caucused with some friends before a meeting of the Politburo. He could not
return to private law practice or run for the Senate. He was not made
president of a Moscow bank, or head of a great can or typewriter company,
or rector of a university, or chief of the Russian Red Cross. His future was
at the mercy of the government, the monopolist of respectable employment
at his level. No manager ultimately dependent on the smiles and frowns of
the government, however decentralized the system of Socialism might
become, would dare give a man in Molotov's position a reasonable job. For a
small man, discharged from the government service as "disloyal," or "a
security risk," or an opponent of the regime in any other guise, the problem
would be even more hopeless. Men of stature sometimes defy a tyrant and
survive, because they are too conspicuous to be punished. So it was with
Croce under Mussolini's rule. But a defenseless minor official in disfavor
with a socialist regime would be lucky to find work in the mines, as the
malcontents have done in Czechoslovakia.

The problem is not uniquely a political one. During the war a minor
official was fired from a government post on the day a Congressional committee revealed that he had once written an innocent and enthusiastic book
in praise of nudism, illustrated in part with topical photographs of himself.
His boss discharged him when the news arrived, without a hearing, and
indeed without pausing for breath. It is hard to be altogether unsympathetic
to the director of the agency. He had troubles enough in Congress without
taking on the defense of nudism. The implications of the episode, however,
are not such as to encourage making the government the ultimate employer
of labor in the United States. Starvation is hardly an appropriate penalty
for nonconformity—even when nonconformity includes a period of nudism.

The problem is not exclusively governmental, it exists wherever concentrated power exists. In the early thirties, it wasn't easy for a union organizer
to stay in many company towns of Pennsylvania or West Virginia. It isn't
easy for a union organizer, or for a representative of the NAACP, to remain
in many parts of the South today. And there have been times when life
was not a bed of roses for a member of the Progressive Mine Workers of
America who happened to live in United Mine Workers' territory.

Under such circumstances, there can be no reality in the idea of personal
or political freedom.

Even if the case for the possibility of Democratic Socialism were more
convincing, the risks of tyranny would surely be greater in a socialist state
than in one of dispersed authority. Why should such risks be accepted, if
Capitalist Democracy can reasonably meet the universal demand for employment stabilization and social security; the achievement of a widely shared,
rising standard of living; and the opening of educational and social oppor-

tunities to the whole population? As Morris R. Cohen once said:

A government of limited powers, which cannot indoctrinate all its citizens with its dogmas and does not make all of its citizens directly dependent on it for their daily bread, cannot possibly be so dangerous to free thought and to all the achievements of art and science which depend on free thought. In view of the inherent uncertainty of all human arrangements, can we afford the risk of putting all our eggs into one basket and depending on one central government to exercise unlimited power? History does not show any example of genuine intellectual progress under a regime of absolute power. We must allow for variation and research, so that the existing good may not prevent the better from coming into being.[4]

The force of this conclusion is strongly and often emotionally resisted in many quarters. The socialist tradition is of great political influence abroad, and has a more pervasive place in this country than is sometimes realized. Many men who function politically as Socialists are patently democrats in their working faith, and that fact, so evident in the politics of Western Europe and of Asia, has tended to obscure the inevitable consequences of genuinely socialist action—that is, the abolition of private property and the public ownership of all means of production. Both the historical role of Socialists in the process of reform and their identification with widely accepted ideals of progress have given to Socialism a quite general position of acceptance, indeed of authority, not often challenged in the intellectual world of the West.

For the democratic socialist movements of Western countries took the initiative, during the last hundred years, in giving leadership and impetus to many nonsocialist programs of humanitarian advance. They helped to establish new attitudes of respect toward manual work and manual workers within the factory system. Through the growth of trade unions, which were often led by Socialists, they helped achieve a status of dignity and security for the working man, and an opportunity for him to participate in the life of society on terms which everywhere begin to approach those of equality. The socialist movement and the development of unions were among the forces serving to mitigate the dominance of the middle classes in Western society, and, for better or for worse, to change its style. The efforts of Socialists and other reformers were important in promoting the acceptance by all modern societies, however bourgeois, of the principle that the state has fundamental responsibilities for the economic welfare of citizens.

Socialist influences were not alone in persuading Western democracies to accept this view. In one sense, its acceptance became inevitable once universal suffrage was achieved, through the long political battles of the nineteenth century, vindicating the ideals of the American and the French

---

[4]*Faith of a Liberal* (New York, Holt, 1946), p. 106.

revolutions. Agrarian protest made its contribution . . . and so did religious and humanitarian movements of many kinds. Two universal wars, which demanded the solidarity of the entire population, gave great impetus to the feeling that a community which sends men to the front should protect them in times of peace against unemployment, the accident of disease, and the unproductiveness of old age.

In recent years, of course, the manifest success of Western capitalist communities in raising standards of living, and in meeting the demand for other forms of social progress, has somewhat weakened the economic if not the political appeal of socialist programs, at least in the industrialized countries of the West. In a society visibly accomplishing rapid advances in its standard of living and social services, it is not so plausible as it used to be to contend that the nationalization of the means of production was the one sure road to social Utopia.

Despite the obsolescence of its economic platform, the socialist movement has immense political momentum in many Western countries. It is gaining rapidy throughout Asia and Africa. In part, the gain of the socialist idea in Asia and Africa reflects the prestige and political power of China and the Soviet Union; in part, it is a reaction to the mixed and often disastrous economic record of most of the countries recently liberated from imperial control. In 1957, for the first time, the world bought more copies of *Das Kapital* than of the Bible.

It is therefore of some importance to emphasize at the outset that if the analysis presented here should be correct, the economics of Socialism is not only erroneous, but irrelevant. The central rallying cry of Socialism—public ownership of the means of production—is one of the least pertinent of all the issues of modern economic policy. Public ownership of industry would not assure full employment under conditions of stability, nor much change the problem of achieving it. It would not guarantee the highest possible rate of economic progress, nor make it easier to secure the cost advantages of improved technique and more efficient management. Nor would Socialism as such necessarily lead to more equality in the distribution of incomes than prevails in many capitalist communities which use modern death and income taxes. Neither economic theory nor economic history suggests that the public ownership of productive property is a significant part of any plans realistically addressed to the elimination of unemployment and social insecurity, and the achievement of steady increases in the standards of living. Public ownership may sometimes be an easy escape from otherwise insoluble dilemmas of private monopoly, or of widespread bankruptcy in a declining industry, such as the British coal industry, or the railroads of many countries. But it has nothing to do with the general problem of keeping the resources of a modern economy fully and usefully employed, either in the United States or in the Soviet Union.

It is one of the gayer paradoxes of political controversy that "Keynesism" is a recognized heresy in the demonology of Communism, ranking with

Bukharinism and Bebelism, and just below Trotskyism and Titoism, as offenses against the faith. It was one of the damaging charges leading to Earl Browder's expulsion from the Communist party, even though the unfortunate Browder denied having read the British economist.

The Communists have good reason to treat the work of Keynes and other modern Western economists as a threat to their orthodoxy. For Keynes' writings, and the wide literature of which they are a part, rest on a core of generally agreed ideas about how to manage a capitalist economy. If the economists are right, the premises of Marxism are wrong. In their universe, as Galbraith sums it up, "instead of revolution there would be a budget deficit."[5] This challenges head on the familiar Marxist argument, widely accepted during the last few generations, that the capitalist system suffers from "inherent contradictions," galloping monopoly, and progressive impoverishment of the working classes; that it cannot be reformed in a socially acceptable way; that it has so far managed to survive only by promoting wars; and that unless it is replaced by a form of Socialism, it will end by destroying civilization in an orgy of unemployment, Fascism and war.

If this series of propositions is denied, the Marxist cause loses the appeal of its intellectual conviction. It abandons even the pretense of being what it claims so often to be—the only "scientifically" correct interpretation of history. It becomes a naked call to class warfare. Without its theory of economics and of history, Marxism breaks contact with the tradition of rational humanism, from which Western life has drawn so much of its moral force, and its impulse for self-improvement. The somber and dedicated fanatics who man the world-communist movement say, in all probability believe, that the existing order must be overturned because it can produce only suffering, exploitation, and tragedy. No attack on their position can hope for success without confronting this premise.

In dealing with modern problems of economic planning and control, Marxism is a sterile literature, offering nothing—a body of dogma, not a useful technique of analysis. Yet its influence is strongly felt among men of all classes. It has spread erroneous ideas, especially about the relation of government to industry and of wages to profits, which often militate against effective action in dealing with the problems of managing modern societies. And in Europe and Asia the incubus of socialist ideas has been one of the most important causes for the relative failure of socialist governments during the postwar period.

That failure is one of the melancholy events of the century. Socialists took office in many countries at the end of the war. Generally humane and well-intentioned men of the democratic tradition, they had long since ceased to be revolutionary ogres and had become symbols of progressive aspiration. Despite some remarkable achievements in advancing welfare, however, their

---

[5]*The Affluent Society*, p. 67.

administrations have not been notably successful, especially in stimulating growth. Quite often, they were prisoners of their own doctrine and therefore unable to rally working class support for more promising programs of liberal progress. The rank and file of the socialist parties are historically suspicious of their leaders, who more than once have followed the example of Pierre Laval and Ramsay MacDonald. For this reason, socialist leaders have had to devote time and attention to proving their loyalty to party principles, and especially to the cause of nationalization. Too often these doctrines have impaired their view both of domestic and of foreign policy, committing them to high wages and excessive inflation at home, and occasionally to pacificism or myopia abroad. The relative failure of socialist governments heightens the risks of even more extreme political divisions in many countries of Europe and Asia.

For the economic theories of Karl Marx are by no means the only, or even the most important, sources of strength of Socialism as a political movement. In many countries, . . . political parties committed to the program of Socialism have been successfully identified in peoples' minds with the yearning for equality. The protest against inequality is a smoldering political emotion. From time to time it becomes a call to arms, which may erupt as Jacobinism or worse. Americans have been spared, in large part, the divisive influence of a party system which splits the country into Disraeli's two nations of the rich and the poor. The illogical American party system, which requires most issues to be compromised within the parties, and not between them, is a strong force for unity within American society. But other countries have not been so fortunate.

It is a curious fact that capitalism is an idea which does not stir much passionate feeling among the mass of the people. The general opinion, as Tocqueville observed, seems rather soberly and passively acquiescent in capitalism, not affirmatively enthusiastic about it. "Wall Street" is not an expression of love and affection in the ordinary vocabulary of the American people. Even the official priests tend to be rather apologetic.

Yet the capitalist principle in economic organization has been and is a remarkable success. In the material realm it has accomplished a rate of economic growth and an enlargement of social and economic opportunity totally unmatched in any previous state of history. As a force affecting the conditions of human life, it has been an integral part of a great explosion, which has swept away old forms and permitted a release of creative energy, a degree of freedom for the human imagination, rarely equaled.

These improvements have been achieved at considerable costs. The great migrations of men and classes, both within societies and among the continents, have had their victims. Aristocracies of wealth have not proved obviously superior, save in energy, to those of family or caste. The supremacy of the market as a measure of values has threatened to weaken the power of the ideal in Western cultures. Prolonged depressions exacted their cruel toll. Old age is still too often a period of waste and decay. The incidence of illness falls at random on society, frequently bringing economic and social disaster in its wake.

But, on balance, the record of capitalism is one of extraordinary and general advance. And through its historical alliance with political democracy, capitalism has submitted to its own extensive and far-reaching reform. It took many years of struggle—often of violent, bitter struggle—before the battle was won. But it seems to be safely won today. That fact, so shocking to the logic of the early socialist prophets, is one of the most important features of Western political and economic life. For all their influence, the great chieftains of industry and finance are now docile and co-operative, by and large, in accepting the consequences of universal suffrage.

These comments on capitalism are not intended to suggest that the status quo is ideal, or that American society no longer requires the devoted zeal of its strong reforming conscience. For all the progress which has been made, our situation offers the Puritan spirit plenty of work for the indefinite future. Further advances in solving social and economic problems may well require further extensions of government authority, without establishing a threatening concentration of power in the state. The openness of Western society is a flexible quality. It could survive as many changes in the next thirty years as it did during the last thirty, without ceasing in any sense to be a guarantee of freedom. What freedom could not survive is a genuinely socialist program of massive nationalization, or the development of governmental regulations having an equivalent effect.

In this sense, competitive capitalism is a characteristic expression of the American culture. In all its arrangements, American society manifests a preoccupation with the problem of power. Persistently, almost instinctively, its policy is always to avoid concentrations of authority as a threat to the possibility of freedom. Capitalism stands with federalism, the separation of powers, the disestablishment of religion, the antitrust tradition, the autonomy of educational bodies, and the other major articles of the American creed, in expressing a deep suspicion of authority. Americans are committed pluralists, if not quite anarchists, in their social attitudes, willing to concede to Caesar only as much power as circumstance may require.

The law for the government of capitalism now in process of development has much to recommend it, however, beyond the important but rather negative advantage of not constituting a menace to the possibility of liberty. It should permit something far more exhilarating than a routine and stablized performance by the economy, grinding out full employment and ample leisure, without much effort, or pride of craft.

The American standard of living is not nearly so high as our national penchant for self-congratulation makes it out to be. If certain components of the standard of living not usually included in the indices are taken into account, it may not even be the highest in the world. Education is a matter of vital concern to every family. Neither the cost nor the quality of public education is reflected in statistics of per capita expenditure for consumption, or most other measures of the standard of living. The American people are beginning to realize that their public education is provided on a mass scale, but that its average quality is below that offered in many other countries. Similarly, if, in measuring standards of living, one counted the low quality of much American housing, the chaos of most American cities, the quality and organization of American health services, and the spotty character of our social insurance, the result might be a wholesome shock to American pride. We do not, of course, measure economic performance in such sensible ways. As Kenneth Galbraith has recently pointed out, fulfilling his duty as our most useful iconoclast since Thorstein Veblen, the statistics solemnly assume that consumer expenditures on tobacco, liquor, and patent medicines have the same social utility, dollar for dollar, as expenditures for essential housing, food, education, or health.[6] They make no distinction between money spent for good or bad housing, for shoddy merchandise, or for overpriced or even harmful commodities or services. Yet even these statistics show an increase of only 60 per cent, or less than 2 per cent a year, in per capita personal consumption expenditures between 1929 and 1957, in constant prices. And in 1957, the average amount spent for consumption by each person in the United States was $1,638, which hardly represents affluence by any standard.

With a reasonable measure of foresight, energy and luck, however, the next fifty years should permit a substantial real improvement in American and Western standards of living, and a start toward significant improvement in most of the countries of Asia, Africa, and South America. For the Western countries the improvement could well be so conspicuous, in terms even of Galbraith's dour criteria, as to justify calling it the end of poverty as our most important economic problem. For the world as a whole, that target is more remote and far less certain. The difficulty of mitigating the burden of poverty in many parts of Asia, Africa, and South America —indeed, the risk of further declines in standards of living there—is one of the crucial elements of American foreign policy, defining a major future claim against American output.

3   Economic Policy and the Rule of Law *

Friedrich A. von Hayek

The old formulae of laissez-faire or non-intervention do not provide us with an adequate criterion for distinguishing between what is and what is

---

[6] *The Affluent Society*, chap. 9.
*From: *The Constitution of Liberty* (Chicago, University of Chicago Press, 1960), pp. 231-32 (reprinted by permission of author and publisher).

not admissible in a free system. There is ample scope for experimentation and improvement within that permanent legal framework which makes it possible for a free society to operate most efficiently. We can probably at no point be certain that we have already found the best arrangements or institutions that will make the market economy work as beneficially as it could. It is true that after the essential conditions of a free system have been established, all further institutional improvements are bound to be slow and gradual. But the continuous growth of wealth and technological knowledge which such a system makes possible will constantly suggest new ways in which government might render services to its citizens and bring such possibilities within the range of the practicable.

Why, then, has there been such persistent pressure to do away with those limitations upon government that were erected for the protection of individual liberty? And if there is so much scope for improvement within the rule of law, why have the reformers striven so constantly to weaken and undermine it? The answer is that during the last few generations certain new aims of policy have emerged which cannot be achieved within the limits of the rule of law. A government which cannot use coercion except in the enforcement of general rules has no power to achieve particular aims that require means other than those explicitly entrusted to its care and, in particular, cannot determine the material position of particular people or enforce distributive or "social" justice. In order to achieve such aims, it would have to pursue a policy which is best described—since the word "planning" is so ambiguous—by the French word *dirigisme,* that is, a policy which determines for what specific purposes particular means are to be used.

This, however, is precisely what a government bound by the rule of law cannot do. If the government is to determine how particular people ought to be situated, it must be in a position to determine also the direction of individual efforts. We need not repeat here the reasons why, if government treats different people equally, the results will be unequal, or why, if it allows people to make what use they like of the capacities and means at their disposal, the consequences for the individuals will be unpredictable. The restrictions which the rule of law imposes upon government thus preclude all those measures which would be necessary to insure that individuals will be rewarded according to another's conception of merit or desert rather than according to the value of their services have for their fellows—or, what amounts to the same thing, it precludes the pursuit of distributive, as opposed to commutative, justice. Distributive justice requires an allocation of all resources by a central authority; it requires that people be told what to do and what ends to serve. Where distributive justice is the goal, the decisions as to what the different individuals must be made to do cannot be derived from general rules but must be made in the light of the particular aims and knowledge of the planning authority. As we have seen before, when the opinion of the community decides what different people shall receive, the same authority must also decide what they shall do.

This conflict between the ideal of freedom and the desire to "correct" the distribution of incomes so as to make it more "just" is usually not clearly recognized. But those who pursue distributive justice will in practice find themselves obstructed at every move by the rule of law. They must, from the very nature of their aim, favor discriminatory and discretionary action. But, as they are usually not aware that their aim and the rule of law are in principle incompatible, they begin by circumventing or disregarding in individual cases a principle which they often would wish to see preserved in general. But the ultimate result of their efforts will necessarily be, not a modification of the existing order, but its complete abandonment and its replacement by an altogether different system—the command economy.

While it is certainly not true that such a centrally planned system would be more efficient than one based on a free market, it is true that only a centrally directed system could attempt to insure that the different individuals would receive what someone thought they deserved on moral grounds. . . .

4   Freedom in Canada *

Canadian Chamber of Commerce

The Canadian Chamber of Commerce as a movement believes in and supports the economic system of private competitive enterprise based on individual freedom of choice and personal initative and responsiblity. We also believe that one of the basic aims of public policy should be the maintenance of personal freedom and an atmosphere in which individuals are free to make their own choice as to how or when they will spend their incomes. These individual choices, we believe, collectively provide the great stimulating and controlling force governing the provision of goods and services.

Canada can be great and properous only if all individuals have the incentive of adequate reward for risk, energy, initiative and enterprise, along with the right to enjoy the fruits thereof.

We recognize the responsibility of society to help those individuals incapable of providing for themselves, but do not believe that it is the business of the State to provide those services which the individual can supply for himself. Social security must not become an end in itself and Canadians must beware of looking to the State to provide security to such an extent that the individual loses incentive to provide for himself.

If ever business, or the people in general, come to believe that they can

*From: Canadian Chamber of Commerce, *Submission to the Royal Commission on Health Services* (March, 1962), pp. 27-28 (reprinted by permission).

turn to government in every difficulty, the springs of initiative and self-reliance will run dry. We put our faith in the responsibility and the resourcefulness of individuals operating under the private competitive enterprise system, believing that these factors will ensure the highest possible standard of living for the whole Canadian people. . . .

In conclusion our feelings on the subject of freedom were well expressed by a Standing Committee on Finance of the Senate:[1]

"Above all, it is important to keep alive in the minds of the people of the nation an understanding of what freedom means. People may clamour for security—many are doing that today—but it should never be forgotten that if personal freedom is sacrificed for personal security provided by Governments, the individual can have no guarantee that in the end he will have either freedom or security."

5   Competitive Enterprise: Canada's Economic System *

Canadian Chamber of Commerce

Canada's economic system is based upon competitive enterprise. This system, which permits maximum individual freedom, encourages the exercise of individual initiative, broad dispersal of decision making, and the most economic allocation of human and material resources. It promotes dynamic economic growth and a steady rise in living standards. One of the major roles of government in such a system is to maintain an equitable and favourable climate for private action.

The operation in Canada of the competitive market economy, motivated by opportunities of profit and the dangers of loss, is responsible in large measure of the improvements in social and living standards which have been achieved over the years. The competitive enterprise system develops maximum managerial capabilities, technical knowledge, operating skills and competitive attitudes required for sound growth. The profit motive exercises a determining influence upon the use of resources, the level of savings, the volume of investment, and it compels private enterprise to operate efficiently.

---

[1]*Report of the Proceedings of the Standing Committee on Finance of the Senate, No. 5, Thursday, June 16, 1955.*

*From: Canadian Chamber of Commerce, 1967-68 Statement of Policy (Montreal, 1968), pp. 12-14 (reprinted by permission).

The role of government is: (a) to establish, promote and enforce the rule of law in all relations between individuals and between groups in the economy including the government; (b) to foster an equitable and favourable climate for the private sector, enabling it to utilize its resources, both human and material, with the utmost efficiency; the greater the efficiency in this respect, the better able is this sector of the economy to contribute to the improvement of the nation's social environment; and (c) to give appropriate encouragement and financial support to the provision of social capital, consistent with the growth of the economy.

Sustainable social betterment depends on healthy competitive enterprise. The responsibility of business includes proposing and promoting sound solutions to social and public problems.

Competitive markets function best when the public is well informed and understands the principles of our economic system. To this end, the Chamber is committed to further the public understanding of our economic system and the essential role played by the profit motive.

The Annual Reviews of the Economic Council of Canada have depicted great potential for long term economic growth in Canada. If Canada is to realize this potential, however, and attain the goals outlined by the Council, rational and consistent policies must be developed and followed by business and by government at all levels. Sustained, well balanced economic growth cannot be based on a succession of opportunistic decisions as the needed policies, for the most part, can be effective only in the longer term, particularly where they are concerned with such basic questions as education and training, research and patterns of investment and trade.

As the Council points out, the attainment of maximum growth for the future rests on sound national economic and industrial policies, as well as on the efforts of individual businessmen. Thus, the goals, and the means of reaching them, are a matter of prime concern to all Canadians.

Recommendations:

1. *that each Canadian business carefully examine the Goals for 1970 suggested by the Economic Council of Canada, translate them into individual objectives and then enlist its resources, human and material, to attain these objectives.*

2. *that business promote a greater appreciation and understanding of our economic system, and take advantage of every opportunity to bring to Canadians, and particularly employees, the story of the role of business in the economy, and to speak out on related matters of public interest.*

3. *that community and provincial Chambers of Commerce and Boards of Trade urge local and provincial authorities to emphasize teaching in the schools the principles of democracy, of our economic system, and of freedom of the individual, and that maintaining these herit-*

ages depends on each individual's acceptance of social and civic responsibility.

4. *that member Boards and Chambers establish active Public Affairs Committees with a view to developing at the community level programs of study and action with respect to community, provincial and national problems.*

5. *that member Boards and Chambers place emphasis on liaison with educational authorities and teachers and that organized efforts be encouraged to assist young Canadians to gain a better understanding of economics and how our competitive enterprise system operates, to the end that students may better understand the economic as well as the cultural and political principles of freedom.*

6. *that the Federal Government, in consultation with other levels of government and various segments of the economy, concern itself with fostering an economic climate conducive to optimum economic growth.*

7. *that government confine its activities to areas which are not being or cannot be served adequately by private enterprise.*

6   The Role of Government in a Free Society*

Milton Friedman

A common objection to totalitarian societies is that they regard the end as justifying the means. Taken literally, this objection is clearly illogical. If the end does not justify the means, what does? But this easy answer does not dispose of the objection; it simply shows that the objection is not well put. To deny that the end justifies the means is indirectly to assert that the end in question is not the ultimate end, that the ulimate end is itself the use of the proper means. Desirable or not, any end that can be attained only by the use of bad means must give way to the more basic end of the use of acceptable means.

To the liberal, the appropriate means are free discussion and voluntary co-operation, which implies that any form of coercion is inappropriate. The ideal is unanimity among responsible individuals achieved on the basis of

*From: *Capitalism and Freedom* (Chicago, University of Chicago Press, 1962), Chapter 2 (reprinted by permission of author and publisher).

free and full discussion. This is another way of expressing the goal of freedom emphasized in the preceding chapter.

From this standpoint, the role of the market, as already noted, is that it permits unanimity without conformity; that it is a system of effectively proportional representation. On the other hand, the characteristic feature of action through explicitly political channels is that it tends to require or to enforce substantial conformity. The typical issue must be decided "yes" or "no"; at most, provision can be made for a fairly limited number of alternatives. Even the use of proportional representation in its explicitly political form does not alter this conclusion. The number of separate groups that can in fact be represented is narrowly limited, enormously so by comparison with the proportional representation of the market. More important, the fact that the final outcome generally must be a law applicable to all groups, rather than separate legislative enactments for each "party" represented, means that proportional representation in its political version, far from permitting unanimity without conformity, tends toward ineffectiveness and fragmentation. It thereby operates to destroy any consensus on which unanimity with conformity can rest.

There are clearly some matters with respect to which effective proportional representation is impossible. I cannot get the amount of national defense I want and you, a different amount. With respect to such indivisible matters we can discuss, and argue, and vote. But having decided, we must conform. It is precisely the existence of such indivisible matters—protection of the individual and the nation from coercion are clearly the most basic— that prevents exclusive reliance on individual action through the market. If we are to use some of our resources for such indivisible items, we must employ political channels to reconcile differences.

The use of political channels, while inevitable, tends to strain the social cohesion essential for a stable society. The strain is least if agreement for joint action need be reached only on a limited range of issues on which people in any event have common views. Every extension of the range of issues for which explicit agreement is sought strains further the delicate threads that hold society together. If it goes so far as to touch an issue on which men feel deeply yet differently, it may well disrupt the society. Fundamental differences in basic values can seldom if ever be resolved at the ballot box; ultimately they can only be decided, though not resolved, by conflict. The religious and civil wars of history are a bloody testament to this judgment.

The widespread use of the market reduces the strain on the social fabric by rendering conformity unnecessary with respect to any activities it encompasses. The wider the range of activities covered by the market, the fewer are the issues on which explicitly political decisions are required and hence on which it is necessary to achieve agreement. In turn, the fewer the issues on which agreement is necessary, the greater is the likelihood of getting agreement while maintaining a free society.

Unanimity is, of course, an ideal. In practice, we can afford neither the time nor the effort that would be required to achieve complete unanimity on every issue. We must perforce accept something less. We are thus led to accept majority rule in one form or another as an expedient. That majority rule is an expedient rather than itself a basic principle is clearly shown by the fact that our willingness to resort to majority rule, and the size of the majority we require, themselves depend on the seriousness of the issue involved. If the matter is of little moment and the minority has no strong feelings about being overruled, a bare plurality will suffice. On the other hand, if the minority feels strongly about the issue involved, even a bare majority will not do. Few of us would be willing to have issues of free speech, for example, decided by a bare majority. Our legal structure is full of such distinctions among kinds of issues that require different kinds of majorities. At the extreme are those issues embodied in the Constitution. These are the principles that are so important that we are willing to make minimal concessions to expediency. Something like essential consensus was achieved initially in accepting them, and we require something like essential consensus for a change in them.

The self-denying ordinance to refrain from majority rule on certain kinds of issues that is embodied in our Constitution and in similar written or unwritten constitutions elsewhere, and the specific provisions in these constitutions or their equivalents prohibiting coercion of individuals, are themselves to be regarded as reached by free discussion and as reflecting essential unanimity about means.

I turn now to consider more specifically, though still in very broad terms, what the areas are that cannot be handled through the market at all, or can be handled only at so great a cost that the use of political channels may be preferable.

Government as Rule-maker and Umpire

It is important to distinguish the day-to-day activities of people from the general customary and legal framework within which these take place. The day-to-day activities are like the actions of the participants in a game when they are playing it; the framework, like the rules of the game they play. And just as a good game requires acceptance by the players both of the rules and of the umpire to interpret and enforce them, so a good society requires that its members agree on the general conditions that will govern relations among them, on some means of arbitrating different interpretations of these conditions, and on some device for enforcing compliance with the generally accepted rules. As in games, so also in society, most of the general conditions are the unintended outcome of custom, accepted unthinkingly. At most, we consider explicitly only minor modifications in them, though the cumulative effect of a series of minor modifications may be a drastic alteration in the character of the game or of the society. In both games and society also, no set of rules can prevail unless most participants most of the time conform to them without external sanctions; unless that is, there is a broad underlying social consensus. But we cannot rely on custom or on this consensus alone to interpret and to enforce the rules; we need an umpire. These then are the basic roles of government in a free society: to provide a means whereby we can modify the rules, to mediate differences among us on the meaning of the rules, and to enforce compliance with the rules on the part of those few who would otherwise not play the game.

The need for government in these respects arises because absolute freedom is impossible. However attractive anarchy may be as a philosophy, it is not feasible in a world of imperfect men. Men's freedoms can conflict, and when they do, *one man's freedom must be limited to preserve another's*—as a Supreme Court Justice once put it, "My freedom to move my fist must be limited by the proximity of your chin."

The major problem in deciding the appropriate activities of government is how to resolve such conflicts among the freedoms of different individuals. In some cases, the answer is easy. There is little difficulty in attaining near unanimity to the proposition that one man's freedom to murder his neighbor must be sacrificed to preserve the freedom of the other man to live. In other cases, the answer is difficult. In the economic area, a major problem arises in respect of the conflict between freedom to combine and freedom to compete. What meaning is to be attributed to "free" as modifying "enterprise"? In the United States, "free" has been understood to mean that anyone is free to set up an enterprise, which means that existing enterprises are not free to keep out competitors except by selling a better product at the same price or the same product at a lower price. In the continental tradition, on the other hand, the meaning has generally been that enterprises are free to do what they want, including the fixing of prices, division of markets, and the adoption of other techniques to keep out potential competitors. Perhaps the most difficult specific problem in this area arises with respect to combinations among laborers, where the problem of freedom to combine and freedom to compete is particularly acute.

A still more basic economic area in which the answer is both difficult and important is the definition of property rights. The notion of property, as it has developed over centuries and as it is embodied in our legal codes, has become so much a part of us that we tend to take it for granted, and fail to recognize the extent to which just what constitutes property and what rights the ownership of property confers are complex social creations rather than self-evident propositions. Does my having title to land, for example, and my freedom to use my property as I wish, permit me to deny to someone else the right to fly over my land in his airplane? Or does his right to use his airplane take precedence? Or does this depend on how high he flies? Or how much noise he makes? Does voluntary exchange require that he pay me for the privilege of flying over my land? Or that I must pay him to refrain from flying over it? The mere mention of royalties, copyrights, patents; shares of stock in corporations; riparian rights, and the like, may perhaps emphasize the role of generally accepted social rules in the very definition of property. It may suggest also that, in many cases, the existence of a well specified and generally accepted definition of property is far more important than just what the definition is.

Another economic area that raises particularly difficult problems is the monetary system. Government responsibility for the monetary system has long been recognized. It is explicitly provided for in the constitutional provision which gives Congress the power "to coin money, regulate the value thereof, and of foreign coin." There is probably no other area of economic activity with respect to which government action has been so uniformly accepted. This habitual and by now almost unthinking acceptance of governmental responsibility makes thorough understanding of the grounds for such responsibility all the more necessary, since it enhances the danger that the scope of government will spread from activities that are, to those that are not, appropriate in a free society, from providing a monetary framework to determining the allocation of resources among individuals. . . .

In summary, the organization of economic activity through voluntary exchange presumes that we have provided, through government, for the maintenance of law and order to prevent coercion of one individual by another, the enforcement of contracts voluntarily entered into, the definition of the meaning of property rights, the interpretation and enforcement of such rights, and the provision of a monetary framework.

Action Through Government on Grounds of
Technical Monopoly and Neighborhood Effects

The role of government just considered is to do something that the market cannot do for itself, namely, to determine, arbitrate, and enforce the rules of the game. We may also want to do through government some things that might conceivably be done through the market but that technical or similar conditions render it difficult to do in that way. These all reduce to cases in which strictly voluntary exchange is either exceedingly costly or practically impossible. There are two general classes of such cases: monopoly and similar market imperfections, and neighborhood effects.

Exchange is truly voluntary only when nearly equivalent alternatives exist. Monopoly implies the absence of alternatives and thereby inhibits effective freedom of exchange. In practice, monopoly frequently, if not generally, arises from government support or from collusive agreements among individuals. With respect to these, the problem is either to avoid governmental fostering of monopoly or to stimulate the effective enforcement of rules such as those embodied in our anti-trust laws. However, monopoly may also arise because it is technically efficient to have a single producer or enterprise. I venture to suggest that such cases are more limited than is supposed but they unquestionably do arise. A simple example is perhaps the provision of telephone services within a community. I shall refer to such cases as "technical" monopoly.

When technical conditions make a monopoly the natural outcome of competitive market forces, there are only three alternatives that seem available: private monopoly, public monopoly, or public regulation. All three are bad so we must choose among evils. Henry Simons, observing public regulation of monopoly in the United States, found the results so distasteful that he concluded public monopoly would be a lesser evil. Walter Eucken, a noted German liberal, observing public monopoly in German railroads, found the results so distasteful that he concluded public regulation would be a lesser evil. Having learned from both, I reluctantly conclude that, if tolerable, private monopoly may be the least of the evils.

If society were static so that the conditions which give rise to a technical monopoly were sure to remain, I would have little confidence in this solution. In a rapidly changing society, however, the conditions making for technical monopoly frequently change and I suspect that both public regulation and public monopoly are likely to be less responsive to such changes in conditions, to be less readily capable of elimination, than private monopoly.

Railroads in the United States are an excellent example. A large degree of monopoly in railroads was perhaps inevitable on technical grounds in the nineteenth century. This was the justification for the Interstate Commerce Commission. But conditions have changed. The emergence of road and air transport has reduced the monopoly element in railroads to negligible proportions. Yet we have not eliminated the ICC. On the contrary, the ICC, which started out as an agency to protect the public from exploitation by the railroads, has become an agency to protect railroads from competition by trucks and other means of transport, and more recently even to protect existing truck companies from competition by new entrants. Similarly, in England, when the railroads were nationalized, trucking was at first brought into the state monopoly. If railroads had never been subjected to regulation in the United States, it is nearly certain that by now transportation, including railroads, would be a highly competitive industry with little or no remaining monopoly elements.

The choice between the evils of private monopoly, public monopoly, and public regulation cannot, however, be made once and for all, independently of the factual circumstances. If the technical monopoly is of a service or commodity that is regarded as essential and if its monopoly power is sizable, even the short-run effects of private unregulated monopoly may not be tolerable, and either public regulation or ownership may be a lesser evil.

Technical monopoly may on occasion justify a *de facto* public monopoly. It cannot by itself justify a public monopoly achieved by making it illegal for anyone else to compete. For example, there is no way to justify our present public monopoly of the post office. It may be argued that the carrying of mail is a technical monopoly and that a government monopoly is the least of evils. Along these lines, one could perhaps justify a government post office but not the present law, which makes it illegal for anybody else to carry mail. If the delivery of mail is a technical monopoly, no one will be able to succeed in competition with the government. If it is not, there is no reason why the government should be engaged in it. The only way to find out is to leave other people free to enter.

The historical reason why we have a post office monopoly is because the Pony Express did such a good job of carrying the mail across the continent that, when the government introduced transcontinental service, it couldn't compete effectively and lost money. The result was a law making it illegal for anybody else to carry the mail. That is why the Adams Express Company is an investment trust today instead of an operating company. I conjecture that if entry into the mail-carrying business were open to all, there would be a large number of firms entering it and this archaic industry would become revolutionized in short order.

A second general class of cases in which strictly voluntary exchange is impossible arises when actions of individuals have effects on other individuals for which it is not feasible to charge or recompense them. This is the problem of "neighborhood effects". An obvious example is the pollution of a stream. The man who pollutes a stream is in effect forcing others to exchange good water for bad. These others might be willing to make the exchange at a price. But it is not feasible for them, acting individually, to avoid the exchange or to enforce appropriate compensation.

A less obvious example is the provision of highways. In this case, it is technically possible to identify and hence charge individuals for their use of the roads and so to have private operation. However, for general access roads, involving many points of entry and exit, the costs of collection would be extremely high if a charge were to be made for the specific services received by each individual, because of the necessity of establishing toll booths or the equivalent at all entrances. The gasoline tax is a much cheaper method of charging individuals roughly in proportion to their use of the roads. This method, however, is one in which the particular payment cannot be identified closely with the particular use. Hence, it is hardly feasible to have private enterprise provide the service and collect the charge without establishing extensive private monopoly.

These considerations do not apply to long-distance turnpikes with high density of traffic and limited access. For these, the costs of collection are small and in many cases are now being paid, and there are often numerous alternatives, so that there is no serious monopoly problem. Hence, there is every reason why these should be privately owned and operated. If so owned and operated, the enterprise running the highway should receive the gasoline taxes paid on account of travel on it.

Parks are an interesting example because they illustrate the difference between cases that can and cases that cannot be justified by neighborhood effects, and because almost everyone at first sight regards the conduct of

National Parks as obviously a valid function of government. In fact, however, neighborhood effects may justify a city park; they do not justify a national park, like Yellowstone National Park or the Grand Canyon. What is the fundamental difference between the two? For the city park, it is extremely difficult to identify the people who benefit from it and to charge them for the benefits which they receive. If there is a park in the middle of the city, the houses on all sides get the benefit of the open space, and people who walk through it or by it also benefit. To maintain toll collectors at the gates or to impose annual charges per window overlooking the park would be very expensive and difficult. The entrances to a national park like Yellowstone, on the other hand, are few; most of the people who come stay for a considerable period of time and it is perfectly feasible to set up toll gates and collect admission charges. This is indeed now done, though the charges do not cover the whole costs. If the public wants this kind of an activity enough to pay for it, private enterprises will have every incentive to provide such parks. And, of course, there are many private enterprises of this nature now in existence. I cannot myself conjure up any neighborhood effects or important monopoly effects that would justify governmental activity in this area.

Considerations like those I have treated under the heading of neighborhood effects have been used to rationalize almost every conceivable intervention. In many instances, however, this rationalization is special pleading rather than a legitimate application of the concept of neighborhood effects. Neighborhood effects cut both ways. They can be a reason for limiting the activities of government as well as for expanding them. Neighborhood effects impede voluntary exchange because it is difficult to identify the effects on third parties and to measure their magnitude; but this difficulty is present in governmental activity as well. It is hard to know when neighborhood effects are sufficiently large to justify particular costs in overcoming them and even harder to distribute the costs in an appropriate fashion. Consequently, when government engages in activities to overcome neighborhood effects, it will in part introduce an additional set of neighborhood effects by failing to charge or to compensate individuals properly. Whether the original or the new neighborhood effects are the more serious can only be judged by the facts of the individual case, and even then, only very approximately. Furthermore, the use of government to overcome neighborhood effects itself has an extremely important neighborhood effect which is unrelated to the particular occasion for government action. Every act of government intervention limits the area of individual freedom directly and threatens the preservation of freedom indirectly. . . .

Our principles offer no hard and fast line how far it is appropriate to use government to accomplish jointly what it is difficult or impossible for us to accomplish separately through strictly voluntary exchange. In any particular case of proposed intervention, we must make up a balance sheet, listing separately the advantages and disadvantages. Our principles tell us what items to put on the one side and what items on the other and they give us some basis for attaching importance to the different items. In particular, we shall always want to enter on the liability side of any proposed government intervention, its neighborhood effect in threatening freedom, and give this effect considerable weight. Just how much weight to give to it, as to other items, depends upon the circumstances. If, for example, existing government intervention is minor, we shall attach a small weight to the negatice effects of additional government intervention. This is an important reason why many earlier liberals, like Henry Simons, writing at a time when government was small by today's standards, were willing to have government undertake activities that today's liberals would not accept now that government has become so overgrown.

Action Through Government on Paternalistic Grounds

Freedom is a tenable objective only for responsible individuals. We do not believe in freedom for madmen or children. The necessity of drawing a line between responsible individuals and others is inescapable, yet it means that there is an essential ambiguity in our ultimate objective of freedom. Paternalism is inescapable for those whom we designate as not responsible.

The clearest case, perhaps, is that of madmen. We are willing neither to permit them freedom nor to shoot them. It would be nice if we could rely on voluntary activities of individuals to house and care for the madmen. But I think we cannot rule out the possibility that such charitable activities will be inadequate, if only because of the neighborhood effect involved in the fact that I benefit if another man contributes to the care of the insane. For this reason, we may be willing to arrange for their care through government.

Children offer a more difficult case. The ultimate operative unit in our society is the family, not the individual. Yet the acceptance of the family as the unit rests in considerable part on expediency rather than principle. We believe that parents are generally best able to protect their children and to provide for their development into responsible individuals for whom freedom is appropriate. But we do not believe in the freedom of parents to do what they will with other people. The children are responsible individuals in embryo, and a believer in freedom believes in protecting their ultimate rights.

To put this in a different and what may seem a more callous way, children are at one and the same time consumer goods and potentially responsible members of society. The freedom of individuals to use their economic resources as they want includes the freedom to use them to have children— to buy, as it were, the services of children as a particular form of consumption. But once this choice is exercised, the children have a value in and of themselves and have a freedom of their own that is not simply an extension of the freedom of the parents.

The paternalistic ground for governmental activity is in many ways the most troublesome to a liberal; for it involves the acceptance of a principle —that some shall decide for others—which he finds objectionable in most applications and which he rightly regards as a hallmark of his chief intellectual opponents, the proponents of collectivism in one or another of its guises, whether it be communism, socialism, or a welfare state. Yet there is no use pretending that problems are simpler than in fact they are. There is no avoiding the need for some measure of paternalism. As Dicey wrote in 1914 about an act for the protection of mental defectives, "The Mental Deficiency Act is the first step along a path on which no sane man can decline to enter, but which, if too far pursued, will bring statesmen across difficulties hard to meet without considerable interference with individual liberty."[1] There is no formula that can tell us where to stop. We must rely on our fallible judgment and, having reached a judgment, on our ability to persuade our fellow men that it is a correct judgment, or their ability to persuade us to modify our views. We must put our faith, here as elsewhere, in a consensus reached by imperfect and biased men through free discussion and trial and error.

Conclusion

A government which maintained law and order, defined property rights, served as a means whereby we could modify property rights and other rules of the economic game, adjudicated disputes about the interpretation of the rules, enforced contracts, promoted competition, provided a monetary framework, engaged in activities to counter technical monopolies and to overcome neighborhood effects widely regarded as sufficiently important to justify government intervention, and which supplemented private charity and the private family in protecting the irresponsible, whether madman or child—such a government would clearly have important functions to perform. The consistent liberal is not an anarchist.

Yet it is also true that such a government would have clearly limited functions and would refrain from a host of activities that are now undertaken by federal and state governments in the United States, and their counterparts in other Western countries. . . . [A] few of these have been discussed above, but it may help to give a sense of proportion about the role that a liberal would assign government simply to list, in closing . . . , some activities currently undertaken by government in the U.S., that cannot, so far as I can see, validly be justified in terms of the principles outlined above:

1. Parity price support programs for agriculture.

2. Tariffs on imports or restrictions on exports, such as current oil import quotas, sugar quotas, etc.

3. Governmental control of output, such as through the farm program,

---

[1] A. V. Dicey, *Lectures on the Relation between Law and Public Opinion in England during the Nineteenth Century* (2d. ed.; London: Macmillan & Co., 1914), p. li.

or through prorationing of oil as is done by the Texas Railroad Commission.

4. Rent control, such as is still practiced in New York, or more general price and wage controls such as were imposed during and just after World War II.

5. Legal minimum wage rates, or legal maximum prices, such as the legal maximum of zero on the rate of interest that can be paid on demand deposits by commercial banks, or the legally fixed maximum rates that can be paid on savings and time deposits.

6. Detailed regulation of industries, such as the regulation of transportation by the Interstate Commerce Commission. This had some justification on technical monopoly grounds when initially introduced for railroads; it has none now for any means of transport. Another example is detailed regulation of banking.

7. A similar example, but one which deserves special mention because of its implicit censorship and violation of free speech, is the control of radio and television by the Federal Communications Commission.

8. Present social security programs, especially the old-age and retirement programs compelling people in effect (a) to spend a specified fraction of their income on the purchase of retirement annuity, (b) to buy the annuity from a publicly operated enterprise.

9. Licensure provisions in various cities and states which restrict particular enterprises or occupations or professions to people who have a license, where the license is more than a receipt for a tax which anyone who wishes to enter the activity may pay.

10. So-called "public-housing" and the host of other subsidy programs directed at fostering residential construction such as F.H.A. and V.A. guarantee of mortgage, and the like.

11. Conscription to man the military services in peacetime. The appropriate free market arrangement is volunteer military forces; which is to say, hiring men to serve. There is no justification for not paying whatever price is necessary to attract the required number of men. Present arrangements are inequitable and arbitrary, seriously interfere with the freedom of young men to shape their lives, and probably are even more costly than the market alternative. (Universal military training to provide a reserve for war time is a different problem and may be justified on liberal grounds.)

12. National parks, as noted above.

13. The legal prohibition on the carrying of mail for profit.

14. Publicly owned and operated toll roads, as noted above.

This list is far from comprehensive.

SUGGESTIONS FOR FURTHER READING

Burns, E. M., *Ideas in Conflict* (London, Methuen & Co. Ltd., 1960), chapter 10, "Twentieth Century Conservatism."

Cheit, E. F. (ed.), *The Business Establishment,* New York, John Wiley & Sons, 1964.

Cumming, A. A., "Are We Legislating Private Enterprise Out of Canadian Business?" in Litvak, I. A. (ed.) *The Nation Keepers: Canadian Business Perspectives,* Toronto, McGraw-Hill Co. of Canada Ltd., 1967.

Hayek, F. A., *The Road to Serfdom,* Chicago, University of Chicago Press, 1944.

Hayek, F. A., *The Constitution of Liberty,* Chicago, University of Chicago Press, 1960.

Hayek, F. A., "The Principles of a Liberal Social Order," in *Studies in Philosophy, Politics, and Economics* (London, Routledge & Kegan Paul, 1967), chapter 11.

Heilbroner, R. L., *The Limits of American Capitalism,* New York, Harper Torchbooks, 1966.

Ivens, D., and Dunstan, R. (eds.), *The Case for Capitalism,* London, Michael Joseph, Inc., 1967.

Jewkes, John, *The New Ordeal by Planning,* London, Macmillan & Co. Ltd., 1968.

Martin, The Hon. Paul, "Capitalism—An Agenda for the Next Half-Century," in National Industrial Conference Board, *The Future of Capitalism,* New York, The Macmillan Company, 1967.

Mason, E. S. (ed.), *The Corporation in Modern Society,* New York, Atheneum Publishers, 1966.

Mises, Ludwig von, *The Anti-Capitalistic Mentality,* Princeton, Van Nostrand Co. Ltd., 1956.

Monsen, R. J. Jr., *Modern American Capitalism: Ideologies and Issues* (Boston, Houghton Mifflin Company, 1963), particularly chapter 2.

Phelps, E. S. (ed.), *Private Wants and Public Needs* (New York, Norton & Company Inc., 1962), Part 1.

Pollock, Carl A., "The Case for Free Enterprise," in I. A. Litvak, (ed.) *The Nation Keepers: Canadian Business Perspectives,* Toronto, McGraw-Hill Co. of Canada Ltd., 1967.

Schriftgeisser, K., *Business Comes of Age,* New York, Harper & Row, 1960.

Schumpeter, Joseph A., *Capitalism, Socialism and Democracy,* New York, Harper & Row, 1950.

Sutton, F. X., *et al, The American Business Creed,* Cambridge, Mass., Harvard University Press, 1956.

Wright, D. McCord, *Capitalism,* Chicago, Gateway Publications, 1962.

PART TWO

The "Mixed" Economy

of Western Collectivism

INTRODUCTION

Apart from Karl Marx and the communists on the extreme left, the major ideological criticism of capitalism within the context of democracy has come from the socialists. The doctrines of socialism are at least as complex as the doctrines of capitalism; but socialism in theory and practice has been characterized fundamentally by three concepts. First, socialists have desired to substitute public ownership for private ownership of the principal means of production. Second, socialists have emphasized equality and have sought to establish equality of opportunity, which, they maintain, is neither present nor possible under capitalism. Third, since the 1930s, socialists have emphasized the concept of "economic planning" and have wished to substitute planning for the so-called "automatic," or "self-regulating," market.

Some of the arguments advanced by socialists have been accepted by capitalist society in a modified form, and some of the techniques advocated by the left have been adapted and applied to the free enterprise system. Even in countries such as Canada that have not abandoned capitalism nor elected socialist governments, there has been a growing tendency in the late nineteenth and early twentieth centuries to bring about sweeping changes and reforms in the prevailing capitalist economies. Most of these reforms have occurred in pragmatic response to practical problems rather than in response to socialist ideology. In the vast majority of Western countries, such changes have resulted in the so-called "mixed" economy or in what some scholars prefer to call "collectivism". It is collectivism, not socialism, that is our topic here.

Certainly one of the most striking general characteristics of Western civilization in the twentieth century has been the rise of the welfare state or Big Government. In almost all industrialized countries in this century there has been a rapid expansion in the functions of the state in economic life, and a shift from the passive or "negative" state toward the "positive" state. What has emerged in this century is a general acceptance of the view that the government should play an active role in regulating the capitalist economy. This view has eroded and substantially altered the orthodox concept of laissez-faire.

Even in Britain in the middle of the nineteenth century, where doctrines of laissez-faire found most favor, some considerable degree of government intervention in the market always existed. As early as the 1820s in Britain laws were passed to regulate the labor market and control the number of hours worked by women and children in mines and factories. By the middle of the nineteenth century, Britain and many other countries had passed innumerable acts to limit child labor, regulate conditions of work, and provide for one day's rest in seven. Eventually, after much conflict and even bloodshed, legislation was passed to legalize the formation of unions, collective bargaining, and the right to strike.

As collectivism spread, the movement away from laissez-faire and the expansion of government economic regulation took many forms. Many countries maintained or raised tariff barriers, and experimented with public subsidies to particular industries. The state took an active role in establishing public education throughout most of the Western world. Public health acts, and pure-food and drug acts, were passed in most jurisdictions. Britain was only one of several nations to experiment with public ownership in such public utilities as gas, electric power, and urban transportation facilities. Railroads, for example, came under public ownership in Australia by the end of the nineteenth century, and in Canada the Canadian National Railway was established as a crown corporation under public ownership by a Conservative government in 1917. Similarly, it was a Conservative government in the Province of Ontario that brought hydro-electric facilities under public ownership as early as 1906. In the twentieth century most industrialized Western countries implemented various welfare schemes and social insurance plans. Canada, for example, introduced old-age pensions in 1927, unemployment insurance in 1940, family allowances in 1944, and health insurance, or "medicare," in 1968.

Further examples of such collectivistic interventions in the market could be piled up almost endlessly, but the important point to be emphasized here is that all of these developments were particular rather than general. They involved no widespread or fundamental rejection of capitalism; instead, they were qualifications or adaptations of the market economy. The capitalist system based upon private property continued to flourish, but state intervention in the economy or state regulation of business became increasingly accepted as "normal". Many of these collectivistic acts, or techniques, were introduced by liberal or conservative governments of a pro-capitalist stripe in an attempt to improve upon, and compensate for, some of the weaknesses and shortcomings of the unregulated market. It cannot be over-emphasized that these actions were mainly pragmatic and *ad hoc*. Such government intervention was not usually based upon any particular doctrine or ideology. Certainly it did not represent any deliberate attempt to abolish the capitalist system. The movement toward collectivism was piece-meal, slow and gradual. It reflected empirical and generally non-doctrinaire attempts by governments to respond to particular and practical problems with particular and practical solutions involving state intervention. For the most part, the growth of collectivism has been pragmatic rather than ideological.

The British legal philosopher A. V. Dicey, in his important book *The Law and Public Opinion in England During the Nineteenth Century* says that if there was any one general viewpoint or underlying intellectual tendency implicit in the rise of modern collectivism, it was the Utilitarian doctrine of Jeremy Bentham. The expansion of state activity was often rationalized in vague, general terms of protecting the "public interest," or on simple humanitarian grounds of improving the lot of the poor, but the main intellectual thrust of collectivism in Britain can be traced to the influence of Bentham. From the Utilitarianism of Bentham, James Mill and his son John Stuart Mill, collectivism inherited three main principles. Usually these principles remained implicit rather than explicit, but they were important none the less.

First, the Benthamites gave to collectivism a general legislative idea: the principle of utility. Benthamism proclaimed as the goal of the state and society "the greatest happiness for the greatest number". The Utilitarians regarded man as a pleasure-seeking being who sought to maximize pleasure and to minimize pain. Utility would be maximized when pleasure was expanded throughout society and pain was reduced. The objective of the Utilitarian philosophers became the general objective of collectivism: the greatest happiness for the greatest number. The test of social legislation and state activity was whether it promoted this objective.

Second, collectivism inherited from the Benthamites a legislative instrument: the active use of parliamentary sovereignty. This was simply the assumption that the powers of parliament, particularly as parliamentary representation became more democratic, could be used to promote the general happiness. In other words, the power of parliament came to be regarded as something that could be used deliberately to promote the general welfare of society in an active way.

Third, collectivism inherited from Benthamite Utilitarianism a legislative tendency: the constant extension and improvement of the mechanisms of government. Unlike Adam Smith, the later Utilitarians believed that the state need not be neutral, but could actively intervene in the market on behalf of the poorer classes and might even be used to restrict the wealth and power of the rich and ease the lot of the poor. The mechanism of the state could be used more efficiently by improving the Civil Service and other agencies of government to make sure that social legislation was vigorously executed and enforced, and to ensure that the will of parliament was carried out. For example, the Factory Acts in the field of labor legislation could be more effectively administered if there was an expanded and efficient Civil Service including inspectors who would make sure the provisions of the legislation were enforced.

A. V. Dicey observed that:

> Somewhere between 1868 and 1900 three changes took place which brought into prominence the authoritative side of Benthamite liberalism. Faith in laissez-faire suffered an eclipse; hence the principle of utility became an argument in favour, not of individual freedom but of the absolutism of the State. Parliament under the progress of democracy became the representative, not of the middle classes, but of the whole body of householders; parliamentary sovereignty, therefore, came to mean, in the last resort, the unrestricted power of the wage-earners. [The] English administrative mechanism was reformed and strengthened. The machinery was thus provided for the practical extension of the activity of the State. . . .

Thus collectivism should be regarded as a general retreat from the doctrine of laissez-faire. In most countries, collectivism has been marked by a high degree of government intervention in the capitalist market without destroying private property or the market mechanism. Collectivism is a somewhat vague term generally used in contrast to the extreme individualism of nineteenth-century laissez-faire doctrines. It is, broadly, a term for a trend in social and political development, and a program for economic reform to supplement or offset the excesses and shortcomings of the market. The general goal of collectivism is the "welfare" of society and the greatest happiness for the greatest number, with society regarded as a totality or organism rather than as a simple aggregate of individuals. Collectivism involves deliberate and positive action by the state for the purpose of furthering certain broad objectives of social welfare, particularly the social welfare of the working poor rather than the capitalist middle class.

In his chapter on "Empirical Collectivism" in Recent Political Thought, F. W. Coker observes that collectivists usually aim at the reform and improvement of the capitalist system, although they reject the extreme dogmas of both the socialists and the advocates of extreme laissez-faire. Coker says that the collectivist seeks to understand the economic interdependence of all members of society and to find the proper adjustment of their economic and political relations to one another through the active use of the mechanism of the state. He suggests that democratic collectivists typically share the following views on certain basic social issues. On property: that neither private ownership nor public ownership should become a fetish. The collectivist believes in general that private ownership is to be preferred, but that there may be cogent arguments for public owner-ship of certain productive resources, particularly when monopolies or public utilities are involved. On labor legislation: the collectivist believes that state legislation is necessary and desirable to protect the interests of the workers in the industrial system through such means as minimum wage legislation and laws relating to the conditions of work. On regulation of prices: collectivists take the view that the state must intervene to regulate and set limits to profits and prices in certain industries that may be regarded as public utilities, utilities such as electric power and transportation. On taxation: collectivists tend to believe that state fiscal powers should be used to redistribute income in the interests of social justice, generally taxing the rich more heavily than the poor, and providing for certain welfare payments from the public treasury to the socially disadvantaged. On land and natural resources: collectivists believe that there is a legitimate role for the state to play in conservation policy, policies to assist farmers, provision of low rental or public housing, and the provision of parks and public recreational facilities.

If Bentham was the nineteenth-century source of most collectivist thought, a major fountainhead of mid-twentieth-century collectivist thinking has been the work of John Maynard Keynes. Certainly Keynes was the most influential English-speaking economist of this century, and certainly he was no socialist, but his ideas have had enormous force in the expansion of state economic activity and the reform of the market economy. Although Keynesian and post-Keynesian monetary and fiscal policy lie beyond the scope of these readings, it would be difficult to exaggerate the degree to which his ideas have permeated Western economic and political thought in recent decades. In an essay titled "The End of Laissez-Faire", written in 1926, Keynes laid bare the political assumptions that underlie his economic analysis of capitalism's ills in his book *The General Theory* written ten years later. He was particularly insistent that many of the old assumptions imbedded in traditional economic thinking had to be swept away.

> Let us clear from the ground the metaphysical or general prin-ciples upon which, from time to time, *laissez-faire* has been founded. It is *not* true that individuals possess a prescriptive "natural liberty" in their economic activities. There is *no* "com-pact" conferring perpetual rights on those who Have or on those who Acquire. The world is *not* so governed from above that private and social interest always coincide. It is *not* so managed here below that in practice they coincide. It is *not* a correct deduction from the Principles of Economics that enlightened self-interest always operates in the public interest. Nor is it true that self-interest generally *is* enlightened, more often individuals acting

separately to promote their own ends are too ignorant or too weak to attain even these. Experience does *not* show that individuals, when they make up a social unit, are always less clear sighted than when they act separately.

This statement illustrates the early rejection of purely market assumptions by many moderate liberals who wanted to reform capitalism, not to abolish it. In a frequently quoted paragraph from that same essay of 1926, Keynes argued for an empirical re-definition of the functions of government and an expanded economic role for the state.

We cannot, therefore, settle on abstract grounds, but must handle on its merits and in detail, what Burke termed "one of the finest problems of legislation", namely, to determine what the State ought to take upon itself to direct by the public wisdom, and what it ought to leave with as little interference as possible, to individual exertion. We have to discriminate between what Bentham, in his forgotten but useful nomenclature, used to term *Agenda* and *Non-Agenda,* and to do this without Bentham's prior presumption that interference is, at the same time, "generally needless and generally pernicious". Perhaps the chief task of economists at this hour is to distinguish afresh the *Agenda* of Government from the *Non-Agenda*; and the companion task of Politics is to devise forms which shall be capable of accomplishing the *Agenda*.

The state has always played a leading part in Canadian economic development, but our political scientists have sorely neglected the particular mechanisms of government intervention in the market. Perhaps this is because the active economic role of the Canadian state has been taken very much for granted and left to the economists to study. At any rate there is relatively little writing on the topic by students of politics. One of the most distinguished exceptions is Alexander Brady, Professor Emeritus at the University of Toronto. Professor Brady's essay, *Reading 7,* provides a lucid review of the Canadian experience, and stresses that "the role of the state in the economic life of Canada is really the history of Canada. . . ."

The three selections that follow elaborate this theme and illustrate the rather surprising degree of agreement among Canada's three main political parties on the amount of state intervention that is necessary under a "mixed" economy. A Liberal view is put by Senator Maurice Lamontagne, a former cabinet minister and an influential Liberal brain-truster. The late George Hogan, a former secretary and national vice-president of the Progressive Conservative Association of Canada, urges that public and private enterprise must be complementary, and the former Premier of Saskatchewan and recent NDP leader, T. C. Douglas, argues for an expanded role for government in the market place. There are differences between these three Canadian party spokesmen, but none suggests that the role of the state in the economy is, or should be, unimportant.

In a wider international context, the British historian E. H. Carr examines the general nature of the shift from laissez-faire to collectivism. Professor Carr's broad survey of the historical evidence leads him to assert in *Reading 11* that the Western world now has no real alternative, short of nuclear annihilation, to the maintenance of a "welfare state". If alternative choices of economic systems are still open to us, they are limited choices at best says J. M. Clark, the late Professor of Economics at Columbia University. All of the practical alternatives he canvasses in *Reading 12* involve significant levels of state intervention in economic life. The degree of "free enterprise" that remains may be defended on several grounds, Clark suggests, and he helpfully distinguishes reasons of greater and of lesser validity for preserving the institution of private property under a mixed economy.

Many writers have observed that with the spread of public enterprise and state regulation of industry, the traditional distinction between the private and public economic sectors is becoming less clear and less significant. Sir Eric Roll takes up this theme in *Reading 13*. He observes that few people are interested any longer in the old ideological debate over individual or state ownership of business' enterprise. In both the industrialized and the developing nations of the non-Communist world, says Roll, the real question is not *whether* the state should regulate business, but how and by what institutional means such regulation should be effected. Nor is that a simple question, as Andrew Shonfield makes clear in *Reading 14*, an excerpt from his book *Modern Capitalism: the Changing Balance of Public and Private Power*. Shonfield, who is Director of Studies at the Royal Institute of International Affairs, London, points out that government intervention in the market is increasingly designed to influence the quality as well as the quantity of economic production, and that such intervention requires the establishment by the community of explicit social objectives. Because, as Shonfield puts it, the free market "is a poor guide to the best means of satisfying the real wishes of consumers," we are driven to reliance upon considerations of social costs and benefits, or "cost-benefit" analysis, to aid us in the setting of economic and political goals. The danger, as Shonfield sees it, is that the determination of economic goals may be taken out of the political realm altogether and left to so-called "experts".

By the end of Part 2, thoughtful readers will be asking themselves some of the basic questions raised in these essays: in the general regulatory process by which the state either promotes of restricts commercial activity, does the state intervene enough, or too much, and does it intervene in the best ways? Sections Two and Three provide a factual framework for the analysis of these important questions.

7   The State and Economic Life in Canada *

Alexander Brady

In modern Canada the activity of the state has hitherto been shaped by the pioneer nature of the country, the physical structure of the half-continent, the imperial sweep of settlement after 1867, the influence of the interacting ideas and institutions of Britain and the United States, and the quick response of the whole society to the advance of western industrialism. State action is similar to that in the other Dominions or indeed to that of other northern countries with moving frontiers of settlement. The special distinctions that exist are rooted in differences of geographic position, physical environment, and cultural quality. Here there is space for only a brief sketch of the general theme. The role of the state in the economic life of Canada is really the modern history of Canada. . . .

Notable is the presence in numerous forms of protective or neo-mercantilist policies with both political and economic ends. From the establishment of the federal state in the 'sixties of the last century, the commercial, financial, manufacturing, labour, and even agrarian groups have exerted persistent pressure to transform a simple colonial economy into one integrated and national. This national aspiration has involved not merely protective tariffs, adopted in the 1870's and ever since maintained, but also bounties for struggling industries, prohibitions on the export of raw materials in order to stimulate domestic processing, the building and administration of canals, state aid to or direct participation in the construction of railways in order to exploit soils and forests and mines, the public generation and distribution of hydro-electric power, and the fostering of agriculture. Most of these state policies were concerned with creating and maintaining a continental economy wherein trade would flow east and west across the continent within the political boundaries of a growing nation.

Here we witness the familiar process whereby national economic policies are shaped in any modern democratic state, whether of Europe or of the New World. Special interests, conscious of their disadvantages and anxious for succour, argue their case before the public or directly exert upon governments such pressure as they can command. The organized groups of Canada are anxious to protect their economic identity against the formidable competition of rival groups in the United States. They are always conscious of a hard and unremitting struggle for survival in a continental environment wherein American industrialism, fed by rich natural resources,

*From: G. W. Brown (ed.), *Canada* (United Nations Series, University of California Press, Los Angeles, 1950), Chapter 15 (reprinted by permission of author and publisher). With the author's permission, some post-1950 material has been added by the editors.

is an imperial and ever-expanding power. The concept of Canadian nationality has lent coherence to the numerous claims of these interests for protection, and in public debate has given such claims a more attractive complexion.

Protection, however, has extended beyond the sphere of material interests. The establishment of the Canadian Broadcasting Corporation (1936), patterned in the main upon the British, was designed to afford protection and encouragement to many elements of cultural life. It has ambitiously but quietly sought to foster in the populace some sense of a national community and a national culture, both of which have seemed menaced by the power and success of the private broadcasting companies in the neighbouring country. While the proximity of the United States is only one of many influences, it is a major one, written clearly not merely in the fiscal but in all phases of state activity.

Varied circumstances have tempered the policy of fiscal protection. The agrarian interest, although weakened by regional fissures, has always had considerable weight in politics, and has been prompt to withdraw support from parties that seek what it regards as an extravagant protection of secondary industry. It has not been reticent in demanding protective duties for its own products, but large sectors of the rural community concerned with production for export have always supported freer trade, if not free trade. The growing political power of the wheat areas in the West during the early decades of the twentieth century strengthened such views in Ottawa, and in particular helped to revive interest in the idea of trade reciprocity with the United States.

The division of Canada into geographic and economic regions has also helped to modify the protectionist impulse, for rarely do all the regions obtain a similar benefit from a specific form of protection, and some regions disclaim ever receiving a major benefit from protective tariffs. A cautious policy that will appease as many sections as possible becomes politically imperative in order to ease the strains of the federation and save it from disruption. Such a policy has been dictated no less by the kindred need of maintaining a balance between Canada's commercial relations with the United States and those with Great Britain. Imperial preference, introduced in the 'nineties, was motivated not merely by sentiment for the motherland, or special economic interests shared with Great Britain, but by the necessity of exerting a bargaining influence upon the United States. From the 'seventies of the last century to the present, tariffs as an instrument in nation-building have been used with opportunism in performing a difficult task.

In Canada public ownership is closely related to protection in that most of it was undertaken in connexion with public utilities, such as railways and electric power, in order to quicken development in primary and secondary industry and to create an economy more integrated and diversified, able to stand on its own feet alongside the young, powerful economy of the neighbouring Republic. The factor of competition between American and Canadian transport routes has always been present, and helps to explain the fostering solicitude of government. Nation-building through the tying together of scattered settlements and the opening up of fresh territories has been the primary motive for railway subsidies or direct state construction. The unity of Canada has required railway lines no less than the Roman Empire required roads; they have been the main agency of colonization and industrial diversification. To the men who established federation in 1867, they were imperative to bind the Maritime Provinces to the St. Lawrence Valley and the western lands to the urban areas of the East, creating a continental market within which a national economy could be built.

But, in a new country, lines had to be pushed ahead of available traffic, involving hazards of heavy capital investment from which private enterprise shrank without state support. The Intercolonial Railway, completed in 1876 and built directly by the Government to connect Halifax with Quebec and Montreal, illustrates that combination of political and economic design which is implicit in all state-sponsored railways. Judged by the yard-stick of private business, it was never a commercial success. But it is almost irrelevant to assess it by the criterion of deficits or surpluses, since it was primarily a political achievement that served well the ends of a national government seeking to create an integrated community. Its administration was never brilliant and was always handicapped by competition with water-transport and shorter rail-routes through the United States, and by political interference, especially political patronage and the insistence of the Government on low rates in order to lessen the hostility of the Maritime Provinces towards other federal policies.

The transcontinental Canadian Pacific line was begun by the Government, but it was soon transformed into a private enterprise, much aided by public land-grants and capital. The land-grants were intended to make the railway no less responsible for colonization than the Government itself. The later transcontinental lines, the Canadian Northern and the Grand Trunk Pacific, were similarly assisted by the federal and provincial governments. The eastern branch of the Grand Trunk Pacific was built directly by the Government, and its route and terminus were in part determined by political considerations and regional claims. Generous public aid through land-grants, cash subsidies, and bond guaranties helped to double railway milage between 1900 and 1915, an increase which resulted in excessive capacity and created heavy overhead costs that could not be met from current revenues. The financial plight of these railways during the First World War brought them under the Government as the guarantor of their bonds, and between 1918 and 1923 the present Canadian National Railways took form, incorporating the Intercolonial with other lines. In this instance public ownership was virtually predetermined by the former lavish aid to private corporations, which in turn was derived from the perennial pressure exerted on the Government by commercial, industrial, and agrarian interests determined upon an expanding and continental economy. Historical cause and effect have here a singular lucidity.

What has been the record of the Canadian National Railways? It is obvious that the system suffers from serious disadvantages when compared over the last quarter of a century with the great private road, the Canadian Pacific: it had a larger mileage of light traffic lines; its equipment and property were at the outset in wretched physical condition; it faced throughout vast territories the task of creating goodwill among shippers and the public; as a government-owned railway it was subject to embarrassing pressures from various organized groups, which hampered effective management; and, finally, in 1922 it was simply a collection of different lines, built for competition, which had to be welded into a genuine unity. Inevitably, the Dominion was compelled annually to pay millions of dollars in deficits. But the Canadian National Railways are not to be judged merely by the test of profitable returns on investment, since, like other lines, they have been an instrument of nation-building, drawing together widely-scattered communities and making possible the exploitation of natural resources remote from the industrial heart of Canada. Credit, moreover, must be given for a notable improvement in their character. They became a distinguished railway system.

What happened within the national sphere happened also within the regions, especially in Ontario and Quebec. In Ontario the province constructed and operated the Temiskaming and Northern Railway, which was planned to quicken and integrate the development of a provincial economy and to bind the growth of the northern region, with its forests and mines, to the financial and industrial metropolis of Toronto. By 1913 the railway was extended to tide-water at Moosonee on an estuary of James Bay, and since then it has helped to open up the resources of the northland and to consolidate Ontario's industrialism.

Despite periodic flurries of opinion on the issue, the state-owned railway operates across the continent virtually side by side with the Canadian Pacific, accepting the same system of rates but in some degree competing in the quality of service. Thereby a giant railway monopoly is avoided. In times of economic adversity an amalgamation of the railways is advocated under either public or private management, but the powerful railway unions have hitherto resisted such a solution, fearing a reduction in staff. Other regional and group interests would also be sharply affected by amalgamation, and hence private enterprise and public policy continue to be mixed in the railway operations of Canada.

In the administrative organization of state railways Canadian experience may not afford so rich a variety as that found in Australia, but it has interest. Canada, on the whole, has discarded the direct operation of the lines by a department of the Government, a system which had exhibited the ills of political patronage in the days of the Intercolonial Railway. When the Canadian National Railways were established, provision was made for a public and independent board, appointed by the Government, resembling the organized directors in a private corporation, and fully answerable for administration. But while the Government did not attempt to control the day-to-day operations, it could not avoid a perennial interest in the performance of the management because of the profound importance of the railway to the public and because it paid the deficits. In 1932 the Duff Commission condemned the large board on the ground that it provided too much opportunity for regional pressures to assert themselves, and recommended instead a small body of three trustees. This institution in turn worked ill, and was replaced by a larger body, whose performance is under the annual scrutiny of a standing committee of Parliament.

State provision of electricity has a developmental role somewhat similar to that of railways, and the hydro-electric power system of Ontario easily holds pride of place. It represents the most impressive experiment in public ownership and is influential in other like ventures not merely within Canada but in the United States. Collectivism in the hydro-power of Ontario, in contrast to private enterprise in the hydro-power of the neighbouring state of New York, is a provincial complement to that national policy pursued by governments at Ottawa since the 'seventies: the public construction of canals, the building or subsidizing of railways, and the provision of protective tariffs and bonuses for secondary industry. It received its initial impulse from the small manufacturers, merchants, and municipal councillors of southern Ontario, who, in a province without coal, were zealous to exploit the sole major source of power in order to further a sturdy industrialism and a robust urban life. The insecurity of relying solely on American coal, periodically accentuated by stoppages and strikes in the mines of Pennsylvania, alarmed the public and influenced its action. In the early years of the century there was a prevalent fear that private companies financed in the United States might exploit the spectacular waters of Niagara and create a local aggregation of industry beneficial principally to American interests.

During the first decade of the century the urgent need of cheap power for industrial expansion was decisive in creating a drive for public ownership. The expanding market for goods on the new agrarian frontiers of Saskatchewan and Alberta impelled manufacturers in Ontario to support any measures that enabled them to lessen their costs and enlarge their output in the face of American competition. Heavy investment of capital in transmission lines was necessary in order to utilize in Toronto and other urban centres the water resource of Niagara; under government guaranty such capital was obtainable at relatively low rates. The chief creator of the public hydro-system, Adam Beck, always emphasized that cheap power was not to be had if private companies were permitted to command the situation and extract profit on watered stock. To be cheap, power must be sold at cost, and from the outset sale at cost has been the cardinal trait of the Ontario system. Public ownership was designed to eliminate profit-taking from the distribution of electricity. Such has been the interpretation placed upon the popular slogan that did such doughty service on many a political platform—"The water-powers of the province for the people of the province." In their more ebullient moods, politicians even spoke of making electric power as free as air, but this language was merely the customary hyperbole of a popular appeal.

The administrative instrument for this collective ownership of power is the Hydro-Electric Power Commission of Ontario, which since 1906 has existed as a body corporate of three members, appointed by the Lieutenant-Governor in Council and holding office during pleasure. From the outset the tie with the provincial government has been intimate. . . . Up to 1935 the capital used was advanced by the Government. After 1935 the Commission began to raise its own financial requirements. Adam Beck, the remarkable chairman of the Commission from its inception in 1906 till his death nineteen years later, was for part of the period a Minister of the Crown as well as chairman of the Commission. But Beck was always determined to make "the Hydro" as autonomous as possible in order to protect it from a political interference fatal to efficiency. Hence he emphasized that it was strictly a co-operative enterprise of the numerous municipalities in the province, existing only because these municipalities freely contracted to buy power from the Commission at prices fixed to cover the costs of generation and transmission. Through their payments for power the municipalities liquidated the borrowings made by the province for generating plants and transmission lines.

Yet in only a limited way is the actual administration of the system operated as a co-operative enterprise. The provincial Commission, under the authority of a provincial statute, exercises a decisive jurisdiction over the councils and commissions engaged in distributing electricity within their local areas. It controls wherever necessary the rates of municipalities which purchase power from the Commission, directs the use of profits in reducing rates, and insists on a uniform system of book-keeping. At every turn it makes them cling to its interpretation of the principle of power at cost, and more than once in the exercise of its authority it has clashed with the city of Toronto.

As a result of its essential nature the hydro-system was never remote from miscellaneous pressures, on the one hand from the provincial government and on the other from the municipalities. Adam Beck, through the weight of his personality and the skill of his leadership, created in all parties a strong following which shielded the administration and policies of the hydro-system from becoming a political football. Indeed, he was one of those men, rarely met with in political life, who, fortunately for Canada, was able to make his cause transcend the bounds of party. But soon after his death the management of the system came under intense political fire. The expanding consumption of electricity in the 'twenties, quickened by the growing industrialization in southern Ontario, began to strain the existing generating capacity, and a continued growth in the demand threatened to create an acute shortage of power. This threat drove the Commission to make contracts with private corporations in Quebec for the purchase of current generated in the Ottawa and St. Lawrence valleys. . . .

But on the whole no serious political interferences with the administration of the hydro-system have been revealed. Certainly, although mistakes have been made, no political corruption has reduced the quality of its performance. The engineer has generally been left with adequate freedom to perform his technical task. The Commission has been fortunate in securing distinguished engineers, whose utilization of the provincial water resources has made possible a steady industrial advance. The municipal distribution of the system increased from 2,500 horse-power in 1910 to 2,608,000 in 1945, and the number of co-operating municipalities from ten to more than nine hundred. Isolated generating stations have been linked by a vast network of transmission lines, and from hydro-power in country and town the economy of Ontario has received a remarkable stimulus.

Although the experiment of Ontario in public ownership profoundly influenced other provinces, the character and the pace of public policy in each province have varied greatly in accordance with physical, industrial, and cultural circumstances. Quebec for some decades shrank from entrusting the state with the electrical industry. In this province, industry was less diversified and there were fewer small manufacturers, merchants, and workers scattered in many towns and eager for cheap power. In Quebec, moreover, hydro-electric power at widely-distributed sites was developed incidentally by large companies concerned with other industries such as pulp and paper, asbestos, cement, and mining. Once firmly established in the production of electricity, these giant corporations were not easy to dislodge, and in any event the French electorate was not greatly stirred by the evangel of public ownership that was prevalent in the English-speaking community. In the early years of the century, public ownership was considered to be closely akin to socialism, and socialism was frowned upon by most of the Roman Catholic hierarchy as something sinister.

Yet in the 'thirties, under the sharp spur of new social discontents and a fresh upsurge of French-Canadian nationalism, a movement was launched for greater provincial control and ownership of water-power. In 1935 a commission of three members was appointed to co-ordinate the activity of power companies in the province and to supply electricity to the largest possible number of citizens. This was the first of a series of measures which culminated in 1944, in the creation of the Quebec Hydro-Electric Commission and the expropriation of the wealthy Montreal Light, Heat and Power Company, a supplier of electricity and gas in metropolitan Montreal. Behind such action was the mounting influence of a national and popular creed which declared that the humble French-speaking people of the province were being exploited by the wily English-speaking capitalists dominating the board-rooms of the power companies. Provincial autonomy and self-assertion, as well as the prospect of cheaper power, thus seemed to dictate the need of public ownership. Drifting away from old loyalties, Quebec tardily began to emulate the example of Ontario, [and by 1963 Quebec Hydro had absorbed almost all of the private electric companies].

In some of the other provinces, notably in Manitoba and Nova Scotia, public and private ownership of power exist side by side, but in the last twenty-five years the trend has been towards a wider jurisdiction by public bodies. [For example, British Columbia brought all of its hydro facilities under public ownership in 1961.]

The heavy taxation by the federal government of private power companies during the Second World War sometimes strengthened the case of the advocates for public ownership, since it was assumed that under provincial management the revenue which flowed to Ottawa could instead be used to extend the local consumption of electricity. The specious simplicity of this argument made it popular, and it harmonized well with the sentiments of those who were anxious to build up provincial institutions. But more important in the long run was the growing necessity in all provinces to integrate and simplify the generation and distribution of electricity and to extend its use to as many citizens as possible. In Manitoba and Nova Scotia, for example, the pressure for wide-spread rural electrification has tended to enlarge the activity of the public commissions, because they are best able to build lines into areas of low population density, where the development of an adequate load is inevitably slow. In this situation a public authority with public capital can meet the costs of service better than a private company.

Early in the present century public ownership in utilities other than electric power had already begun. The properties of the Bell Telephone Company in the three Prairie Provinces were purchased and administered by the governments. Here the special pressure came from farmers. Their amenities of life could be greatly enlarged by the telephone, but they were prompt to realize that a private company would shrink from providing service to a thinly-scattered rural population. Hence the risks of telephone service were made a collective responsibility. Within the same region other forms of assistance were offered: public elevators, credit facilities, debt-adjustment boards, the encouragement of co-operatives, and experimental farms.

Despite the individual organization of production on the typical prairie farm, successful growing of wheat on the great plains has always been peculiarly dependent on numerous aids from provincial and federal governments, including the provision of railways, the regulation of railway rates, the grading of grains, the supervision of marketing, and in the last generation the stabilizing and bolstering of prices for the product. It is little wonder that the western farmer is much more of a conscious and zealous collectivist than his fellow-agrarians of Ontario and Quebec. He opened up a hard frontier, which has remained hard. Through the state he has endeavoured to lessen or even to pool the risks of his highly-commercialized and precarious agriculture. In this endeavour he has often been encouraged by industrialists in eastern Canada, for to them a prosperous agrarian frontier in the West has been crucial. Significant, in addition to other forms of government aid, is the prairie farm rehabilitation programme, inaugurated under federal legislation in 1935 to rehabilitate farm lands in the dry and soil-drifting districts of the West; it constitutes one of the first attempts on a major scale to conserve agrarian resources by direct public action.

Labour legislation has been moulded by the peculiar influences of the social environment and the federal system. Until the last decade the growth of the Canadian labour movement, unlike that in its sister Dominions of Australia and New Zealand, has been delayed by regional fissures, racial divisions, the mobility of labour in the hopeful era of the open and accessible frontier, and perhaps most of all the agrarian nature of the economy for many decades after 1867, wherein the rural labour force has felt no urge to seek organization. Farm labour has been provided mainly by the farmer and his family. The hired man who may supplement the toil of the proprietary family has never been a suitable recruit for the ranks of organized labour. Where he is anything more than a temporary labourer on the land, his homely ambition is to possess a farm of his own, and hence his concern is less with his fellow-labourers than with the class of producers which he is anxious to join. In the Canadian country-side there has been nothing equivalent to that dynamic agent of pressure, the Australian Workers' Union; indeed, there has been no organization worthy of mention because no large units exist like the sheep-stations of the Australian outback, employing a rural proletariat.

Consequently, strong labour organizations have come only with the progress of urban industrialization, a progress much stimulated by the two world wars of the twentieth century, especially the second. Thus in 1937 the number of organized workers in Canada was 383,000, which was the largest figure of any year up to that date. By 1944 the number had almost doubled. [It increased to 1.7 million in 1968.]

Yet the ranks of urban labour are always weakened by the dispersal of the population in towns and cities across a continent, rendering organization difficult and exposing the movement to regional cleavages. The division into English-speaking and French-speaking groups impairs co-operation in central Canada, where the great metropolitan centres exist and where most of the industrial population is concentrated. The Roman Catholic unions of Quebec often have a different view of the goals sought through the state by the unions of the neighbouring Ontario. They are much less state-conscious, much less inspired by the secular philosophies of labour in North America, and, because of their Catholic leadership, much less militant. They are disposed to emphasize social collaboration rather than class struggle. But here again a fast-growing industrialism is introducing significant changes. The position of the Catholic unions is being challenged by the aggressive invasion of unions from English-speaking Canada and the United States, and the French workman in the industrial town is responding to social stimuli that differ from those traditional in rural Quebec.

The boundary between Canada and the United States is rarely a barrier to the migration of ideas, least of all in matters of labour organization and social pressures. The international unions of North America have created funnels whereby influences from the United States easily flow into the Canadian labour camp, sometimes with the effect of checking its national cohesion. British influence has always been present and often potent, owing to the fact that hitherto British immigrants provided much of the union leadership; but varied and pervasive influences from the United States are evident in the present active lobbying by labour and in its past tendency to avoid direct political action, a tendency now clearly on the wane.

Such circumstances, combined with the divisions of jurisdiction explicit in the federal system, determine the character of labour law. Most of the legislative power dwells with the provinces in virtue of their control over property and civil rights. Laws have been passed on the employment of women and children, minimum hours of work, wages, factory inspection, workmen's compensation in accidents, and conditions under which a stoppage in industrial work is legal. In brief, the Canadian labour code is mainly a complicated structure of provincial codes, but in substance it is similar to that found in other countries of the English-speaking world. The security of trade unions under the law came more slowly than in Great Britain; but the enactments, when made, tended to follow British models, with the most significant variations in Quebec, which through its Civil Code has a distinct legal tradition. The broad trend, most evident in the 'thirties and 'forties of the present century, is clearly towards protecting the unions as free associations, enabling them to exert their maximum power in industry and the state. Provincial legislation, much influenced by the National Industrial Recovery Act of the United States (1933) and by the Wagner National Labor Relations Act (1935), has been reasonably effective in protecting the right of workers to join unions and in compelling employers to negotiate with them.

Besides the provincial enactments, there were the Dominion amendments to the Criminal Code in 1939, making it illegal for an employer to dismiss or threaten to dismiss a workman simply because of his membership in a lawful trade union. With its increased powers during the emergency of the Second World War and under pressure of labour, the Dominion Government sought to strengthen trade-unionism and protect its personnel, notably in the War-Time Labour Relations Regulations of 1944, which proclaimed the rights of employees and employers, formulated rules for collective bargaining, and provided machinery for conciliation in industrial disputes. These Regulations set the pattern for post-war legislation in the Dominion and the provinces.

The most significant early federal legislation, which influenced all subsequent enactments, even when these go beyond it in scope, was the Industrial Disputes Investigation Act of 1907. This provided for compulsory investigation of disputes in industries in which stoppages of work diminish the welfare of citizens in general. But no attempt was made to compel parties to a dispute to accept the recommendations of the conciliation boards. Canada did not follow the precedents of Australia and New Zealand in providing for compulsory arbitration under the state. Underlying Canadian legislation was the assumption that conciliation would adequately serve the public interest by advancing a settlement. The statute was circumscribed by the limited jurisdiction of the Dominion Parliament in labour matters, but over the years it has had an important ameliorative effect on industrial struggles, and its essential elements are still retained in Dominion and provincial legislation.

Social services in their evolution have been affected by the same basic forces that shape the character of labour law. Only a few general observations are needed here. In Canada, as in the other democracies of the English-speaking world, notable spurts occurred in the rise of public social services as a consequence of three related events in the twentieth century: the First World War, the depression in the 'thirties, and the struggle against Nazi Germany. Of these, the depression was notable because it greatly enlarged the range of state action and made imperative heavy levies upon the Dominion treasury in Ottawa to aid the provinces and municipalities in providing relief payments.

Attempts in the national sphere to follow the example of the United States in its generous social-security measures and industrial regulation were, however, frustrated by the rigidity of the federal constitution. The draftsmen of the British North America Act had not envisaged national social services, which consequently remain limited by the letter of the law. In 1937 the enactments sponsored by the Bennett Government, the nearest equivalent in Canada to Roosevelt's New Deal, were in the main declared to be *ultra vires* of the federal Parliament. Nothing, therefore, was achieved comparable to the contemporary revolution in the social services of the United States or to the sweeping innovations embodied in the social-security legislation of New Zealand. Apart from any restraining influences within the community itself, the federal system of Canada was a barrier to drastic national change.

Yet expenditures on social services inclusive of education were steadily on the increase, costing the nation by 1939 more than a quarter of all public spending. The annual expenditures of Dominion, provincial, and municipal governments on public welfare and relief, excluding education, were in 1913 some $15,000,000; in 1930 they were $83,000,000; by 1937, $236,000,000. This increased public spending inevitably came to be reflected in taxation. In 1925 federal, provincial, and municipal governments were raising in taxes some 14.7 per cent of the national income. By 1938 that percentage had increased to 19.7 per cent [and by 1963 had reached 25 per cent].

The Second World War, through its economic and social consequences, created much public debate on the necessity for social reform, aroused public sentiment, and deepened the pressure for national action. Extensive publicity was given to the Beveridge Report and its implications. Democratic strategy, it was argued, required more effective social services. But more important than such general debate was the rapid emergence of a war economy which speeded the process of industrialization, still further enlarged the chief cities, and created a more powerful labour movement clamorous for social-security measures. The Rowell-Sirois Commission, whose monumental report was completed in 1940, prescribed a realignment of constitutional powers and financial responsibilities in order to place social services on a sounder basis; but attempts both during and after the war to implement its recommendations encountered stubborn opposition in the central provinces and some of the outlying provinces. Two important steps, were, however, taken during the war in the establishment of unemployment insurance (1940), patterned in the main upon the British system, and in the provision (1944) for the payment of monthly family allowances out of the Dominion treasury. [More recently two further developments in the field of health have been significant. The C.C.F. government of Saskatchewan established public hospital insurance in 1947 and medical insurance in 1962. As similar schemes were adopted in other provinces, national cost-sharing arrangements were instituted for hospital insurance in 1958 and "medicare" in 1968.]

The problem of state action in the sphere of social services inevitably becomes a constitutional issue, and that, in turn, a problem of achieving sufficiently wide agreement in a federal community. The major jurisdiction still dwells with the provinces, but most provinces are experiencing a decrease in their financial power to implement the far-reaching schemes of social amelioration demanded by advancing industrialism. While no province, least of all a province on the lean federal periphery, seeks to get sharply out of step with its fellows, there is an obvious lack of uniformity in the range and quality of services from province to province. The wealthy can afford to be generous, but the poor must be parsimonious. Ontario and to some extent Quebec, enriched by their industrial diversity, are strong enough to enact such social legislation as they deem suitable for their needs. [Since 1950, increased federal grants to the provinces and shared-cost programs have eased the situation somewhat.]

In social services, as in public utilities, Quebec in particular has its own distinctive views and peculiar procedures, determined by Roman Catholicism, its Civil Code, and its nationalist traditions. Here a well-established practice of activity by the religious orders in providing many services [at least prior to 1960] weakened the political impulse to look to the state and especially to Ottawa for assistance. Charity, inspired and organized by the religious communities, is regarded as a more desirable dynamic than the philosophy of state collectivism, and it provides hospitals, orphanages, and asylums. In the smallest social cell, the parish, the *curé* directs the application of local charity, and in the larger social units the bishops provide appropriate organization for social amelioration. The Church, an indefatigable upholder of private property as an agency for developing personality, looks suspiciously on the enlargement of state functions, especially those which threaten to draw away influence and responsibility from itself. It readily sponsors co-operative enterprise among all portions of the population, but it fears the growth of the secular Leviathan. Nevertheless, even in Quebec the role of the state grows ever larger, for with the march of industrialism private charity is inadequate to cope with the modern problems of social service, particularly during periods of depression. [In the 1960's, Quebec's expenditures on welfare and education increased dramatically.]

The conclusions are self-evident. Since 1867 Canada as a state has become more collectivist in character, owing mainly to those economic and social forces which explain collectivism throughout the Western world. There is nothing singular in this phase of her evolution, nothing in the role of her government that cannot be paralleled elsewhere, especially in countries, like the Dominions, with moving frontiers of settlement and development. She accepts as a matter of course that the state must become "the universal intervener", the chief instrument of economic co-ordination and direction, particularly in adverse times. She also responds to the urges of an industrial society, the incitements of nationalism, and the claims of democracy, but she responds with those subtle variations that derive from the quality of her community and the influence of geography. Much of her state intervention has been concerned directly with the building of a national economy over half a continent, alongside the United States, and with the aspiration to maintain independence and balance within that economy.

In recent decades the most distinctive and important trend pertains to welfare legislation and social services. Here as elsewhere in the Western world there has been a widening concept of welfare, an ever-growing sense of public responsibility for the ill-favoured individual or for the ordinary individual as a citizen. The change is profound from the simple colonial economy of 1867, with its reliance upon the capacity of the rural family to provide a livelihood and shelter for its members, to the complex economy of the present, with its accelerated tendencies to devolve upon the state the responsibility for personal security. Regions as well as individuals expect and demand security, and are subsidized by the national government through transfers of income from more affluent regions.

This collectivism is throughout empirical, shaped by the thinking of those who are concerned with the practical problem of the moment and the exigency of given situations. Hence all political parties in turn have furthered it, and in this matter the labels of Liberal and Conservative are almost irrelevant. Political leaders have responded to concrete necessities, mass pressures, and the inevitable reorientation in public sentiment with the expansion of an industrial civilization.

The rise since the 'thirties of the Co-operative Commonwealth Federation [since 1961 known as the N.D.P.], inspired by a socialist sentiment and determined to reduce private profit-making, has introduced more ideological discussion on the role of the state, but it is only a symptom of the new social forces that are beginning to change the programmes and actions of the older parties. The C.C.F.-N.D.P. has been nourished by intellectual food of mixed origin—the ideas of British liberal socialism, the aspirations of American reformers associated with some of the Protestant churches, and the traditions of agrarian democrats and trade unionists anxious to curb big business. Whatever its own future as a third party, its ideas and feelings will have an influence in this generation in helping to reshape the functions of the state into a more collectivist mould.

Finally, it is to be emphasized that, owing to the federal structure of the state and the bi-national character of the community, Canadian state collectivism is not highly centralized. The federal government at all times exercises powerful controls over the economy through the currency, tariff, and taxation, but, so long as the federal system survives, it is forbidden to operate directly in some spheres except in periods of national emergency and war, [although this tradition has been altered by numerous precedents and by judicial interpretation of the constitution since 1949]. Significant differences exist among the policies of the provinces. Each provincial government is held accountable to its electorate for the development of local natural resources and the provision of most social services, a circumstance which prevents a highly-centralized and top-heavy state.

But any growing trend towards collectivism in the next generation will increasingly be related to the strains of the federation. As the provinces, especially those on the periphery, enlarge the functions of their governments, they will inevitably look to the national treasury for financial assistance. Conversely, as the central Parliament endeavours to hold the national economy in balance, it will seek more controls over local policies and provincial incomes. What government does and how the federation works will continue to be two inseparable issues in the Canadian state.

8   The Role of Government *

Maurice Lamontagne

. . . We are now in a position to set out the main conclusions concerning the evolution of the role of government in Canada since Confederation.

---

*From: M. Lamontagne, "The Role of Government," in E. P. Gilmour (ed.), *Canada's Tomorrow* (Macmillan, Toronto, 1954), pp. 132-33, and 143-6. (Reprinted with the permission of publisher and of Canadian Westinghouse Co. Ltd.)

Past experience shows that the striking fact in that respect has not been so much the extension of government responsibilities as their changing character.

Up to the twenties, government played an active role in the field of a long-term economic development through its programme of direct public investments and of encouragement to private initiative. It was the real dynamic factor in industrial progress during that period. On the other hand, because of its long-term influence over the Canadian economy and because of other features of the industrial structure, short-term economic instability was not so much a problem; to a certain extent, this explains why the responsibilities of the public authority in that respect as well as in the field of social security were almost negligible.

Since the twenties, however, the role of government has followed a different pattern. Long-term economic development has been taken over by private initiative, while public authorities have assumed new and increasing responsibilities first in the field of welfare and social security and later, especially since the forties, in respect to short-term economic instability.

It is highly important to note the Canadian past experience, because it shows that there is no basic general trend pointing toward an increasing role of government in the same direction. It also reveals that political ideologies have not played a decisive influence in determining State responsibilities. On the contrary, the role of government has been primarily functional in character; it has been adapted, with certain lags, to changing economic and social circumstances, which, in the last resort, were determined by the recurrence and the impact of industrial revolutions. . . .

The recognition of the complementary relationship between private initiative and government action has been the dominant feature of our political history at least since 1867, and there is no evidence at present to show that this long-established tradition will be broken. On the contrary, all the facts indicate that it will be strengthened.

First, the attitude of a Canadian Liberal government in that regard is clear and has been re-stated on several occasions since the publication of the White Paper on employment and income. Only recently, the Prime Minister, the Right Honourable Louis St. Laurent, declared:

"I think all of us recognize the fact that there are some things which it is more appropriate to have done by public authorities than by free enterprise. But I think we are all most happy when free enterprise does what is required to be done and public authorities do not have to intervene."[1]

On another occasion, he said:

"I don't think that free enterprise requires that governments do nothing about economic conditions. Governments can—and I believe governments should—pursue fiscal and commercial policies which will encourage and

---

[1]*Debates,* Commons (Monday, May 4, 1953) , p. 4764.

stimulate enterprise and wise government policies can do a lot to maintain the right kind of economic climate."[2]

Secondly, the major political parties recognize this fundamental complementarity existing between private initiative and government action, although they differ slightly, especially during electoral campaigns, on the emphasis to be put on either of these forces. Basically, those parties, once in power, behave according to the same functional principles.

Finally, it is evident that there are differences of opinion among the various sectors of the Canadian population as to what government should or should not do. However, these divergent preferences have not developed into opposite ideologies. Slogans denouncing the Welfare State or creeping socialism or government controlled by wicked capitalists had to be imported from other countries and were soon found to be unfit for Canadian consumption.

Thus, it may be inferred that the Canadian situation in the future will continue to reflect the equilibrium position and that the basic complementarity between private initiative and government action will be recognized in fact as it is described by our functional theory. . . .

The normal implication to be drawn from this outlook is that private initiative will continue to play the dynamic and dominant role in the field of long-term industrial development in Canada during the next decades. The role of government will be auxiliary and conditioning. It will consist mainly in maintaining a favourable climate for private initiative and in adopting policies designed to ensure that the natural resources will be rationally utilized to the advantage of the Canadian population.

9   Free Enterprise*

George Hogan

We have said that Conservatism's main purpose is to preserve our national heritage. What is the Canadian heritage? In my view, the Canadian heritage is one of progress based on individual freedom and national independence. . . .

The second component of the Canadian heritage Conservatives uphold is our economic system based upon free enterprise. Like our Constitution,

---

[2]Statement by the Prime Minister at the Annual Convention of the Canadian Lumbermen's Association, (Montreal, February 9, 1953), pp. 9 and 10.
*From: *The Conservative in Canada* by George Hogan, reprinted by permission of the Canadian Publishers, McClelland and Stewart Ltd., Toronto (1963), pp. 54-61.

this system is not perfect; but it has one great proven advantage: it works. In terms of the individual standard of living of our citizens, in terms of the aggregate wealth of our country, and in terms of the position it holds in the world because of its material progress and strength, our economic system has shown itself at least as successful as that to be found in any other country.

An economy genuinely based upon free enterprise is characterized by three main features: private ownership, individual economic decision, and competition. When any one of these features is seriously weakened, the system cannot honestly be called "free." Naturally, in the complex conditions of a modern economy, no system can be applied or defended as a theoretical absolute. All parties today believe in some form of what is commonly called a "mixed economy." Any return to the uncontrolled economics of *laissez-faire* capitalism is a practical impossibility. Conservatives believe in an economic system based upon free enterprise, but this is as far as it can be taken. The differences among our parties today are not differences as to whether there should be a privately or publicly controlled economy, but rather as to the extent and manner in which both private and public enterprise should participate in a mixed economy.

Fifteen years ago, free enterprise seemed the chief Canadian institution to be defended, because it was the most openly under attack. At the end of the Second World War, socialism, as expounded by what was then known as the CCF, was a vociferous and ·growing philosophy in this country. Its avowed aim, as proclaimed in the CCF's Regina Manifesto, was to eradicate capitalism. In those years, there was a real public issue about the very existence of an economy based on free enterprise, and at least in Ontario, Saskatchewan, and British Columbia, some serious doubt about the outcome.

Conservatives defended free enterprise against this open frontal attack, on the grounds that it was the system which best gave expression to the two foundations of the Canadian heritage, progress and freedom. For the adoption of a socialist society would do violence to both concepts. The socialists claimed that they stood for a policy of "democratic socialism." But they forgot that you can maintain democracy and still lose freedom. The whole concept of socialism requires the replacement of individual decisions and individual initiatives by government decisions and government initiatives. It seems obvious that the more we surrender to government of our right to make decisions concerning our individual daily lives, the less freedom we retain to make such decisions for ourselves. And even if we retain the democratic right to elect the people who will make those decisions for us, this does not alter the loss of the freedom to make the decisions themselves. On the other hand, Conservatives pointed out, an economic system that removed the incentive provided by competition for improvement in prices and products, would greatly retard our rate of economic progress; and a system that, in addition, superimposed upon the economy a dead weight of restrictions and controls might well end up in a total throttling of all progress.

Today such issues sound as quaintly dated as a Second World War propaganda movie. The fact that these socialist theories, like the economic difficulties that gave rise to them, have now been left far behind in the wake of Canada's economic progress, is in itself an impressive example of that progress. The heirs to this socialist tradition now call themselves the NDP. They retain its old enmity to free enterprise, but they have lost both its reason for it and its alternative to it. The socialists don't talk much about socialism now; but they have certainly not espoused free enterprise. In this posture of baffled obsolescence, they remain a minor threat to the progress and freedom that result from free enterprise, and a major obstacle to the effective working of parliamentary democracy.

In their defence of free enterprise against socialism, Conservatives are careful not to equate socialism with social security, or social justice, as they usually call it. It is a common mistake, made by both the friends and enemies of socialism, to describe social welfare measures as socialistic. To do so is to give the socialists an easy patent on a vital field of public policy. Socialism requires a preference, in principle, of public ownership over private ownership; of a "planned economy" over individual economic decision; of state monopoly over competition. An acceptance, in principle (there will always be detailed exceptions), of any of these preferences is incompatible with a belief in free enterprise. But the acceptance of social justice measures is in no way incompatible with free enterprise. Indeed, free enterprise (and by this we still mean a mixed economy based upon free enterprise) is probably more compatible with social justice than any other system. For it is from the growth and progress free enterprise makes possible, and the revenues which flow from the profits of free enterprise, that the means to pay for social justice principally come.

. . . In purely economic terms, social justice measures such as old age pensions and unemployment insurance provide a constant element of purchasing power which help to level out the peaks and valleys of the business cycle. It does not provide equality, but it does help to provide equality of opportunity, by making sure that no Canadian family need fall below a basic standard of health and education. Conservatives have made major contributions to the growth of social justice in Canada. In so doing they have helped to strengthen the economic basis of free enterprise itself, and to make sure that its benefits were in some measure shared by all Canadians. . . .

The modern Conservative approach to free enterprise is based on the very old Conservative principle that free enterprise and government should be partners, not rivals, in economic progress. It was not *laissez-faire* capitalism that built the early St. Lawrence canals, or the Canadian Pacific Railway, but free enterprise in partnership with government. This same relationship can be, and must be, maintained if Canadians are to get the maximum benefit from their resources and their efforts.

Conservatives today believe, and I think unitedly believe, in an economic system in which free enterprise and government will work together for the economic betterment of Canada. They believe that wherever possible free enterprise should be left alone because progress and freedom are best ensured by its natural workings. But they also believe that government should create the environment in which free enterprise can be most productive; that government should establish conditions under which all Canadians will have a share in its benefits; and that government should, where necessary, take economic measures of its own for the general good where it can do so more effectively that can free enterprise. In this spirit of partnership, free enterprise and government will achieve the economic growth and national prosperity which Canada's natural wealth makes possible.

10   The Government and the Economy*

T. C. Douglas

In my view there is a clear and positive case today documenting the need for an expanded government role in the overall direction of the Canadian economy. The case rests upon the evidence of the long sweep in our social evolution, upon the contemporary experience and evident failure of our economy to measure up to its potentials, and upon the political and social goals which we set for ourselves as a Canadian people. Contrary to what is often asserted, the expansion of government need not at all imply a growth of restriction, an erosion of freedom, or a loss of initiative and enterprise. Rather, the people of this country, acting through democratically-elected governments, can broaden our freedom and opportunity, assure higher standards of living for ourselves, and impart a new dimension to national growth. But to do so we must have governments prepared to accept an enlarging role, inspired to meet new challenges and organized to carry out creative new responsibilities. . . .

It is clear, for example, that maintaining a rapid growth in employment, given the accelerating pace of labour-saving technology and automation,

*From: T. C. Douglas, "The Goverment and the Economy," I. A. Litvak (ed.) *The Nation Keepers: Canadian Business Perspectives* (Toronto, McGraw-Hill, 1967), pp. 45-50 (reprinted with the permission of author and publisher).

has become a very complex process. An indispensable adjunct to normal market forces is an array of labour market services embracing adequate information and forecasting of employment change, aids for geographic and occupational mobility on the part of workers, long-range manpower training and retraining, and effective adjustment programmes to meet technological and economic shifts in employment. The improvement in productivity advance calls for expanded investment in many forms of human capital and human skills, a great extension in public social capital, particularly in meeting the mushrooming needs of our cities, and a rapid expansion of industrial construction, machinery and equipment. A far greater effort in research and development, in the application of new technology, and in basic scientific investigation must be launched. We need to explore methods for increasing specialization in Canadian industry, for expanding foreign trade on a truly multi-lateral basis, and for effecting a sweeping rationalization of our industrial structure to make our economy more fully competitive in the international league. An important lift to growth in real production and consumption should be sought, on one hand, by the expansion of long-standing public services and the introduction of new public programmes. On the other hand, there is a pressing urgency to provide adequate consumer protection and information and to curtail wasteful production processes and inflated selling costs. These latter add nothing to the real level of output, and in fact impose a burden upon our economy equal in cost to many of our basic social services.

In all of these economic areas there is urgent need and wide scope for extending the role of government. But little will be gained if this extension takes place only on a makeshift, haphazard basis, with response to this pressure and that, usually at the last moment. The obvious result of the traditional sticking-plaster approach to the problems of a complex, integrated economic system has been confusion, inconsistency and conflict in public policy. Rather, as I have stressed, the expansion of the government's role must proceed in a planned, co-ordinated way, with a firm but flexible integration and consistency among strategic economic goals, specific operational targets, and applied action programmes.

In this planned approach it is essential to adopt new vigour, imagination, and a willingness to experiment and innovate in the whole range of traditional techniques of government intervention; for example, in fiscal, monetary and commercial policies, in the use of legislation and statutory regulation, in new forms of grants, subsidies and incentives to private enterprise, and in the broad revenue and spending powers of all levels of government. In the same way, if government is to effectively carry out its larger and more complex responsibilities in the period ahead, it must also be prepared to intervene directly in the economy. This includes recognizing the need for an expanded role for government enterprise whenever it is appropriate to the circumstances, the need for new vehicles to mobilize private savings for industrial investment, the possibilities for a productive partnership with private industry, and the long-range importance of direct participation in research and development. . . .

11 From Competition to Planned Economy *

E. H. Carr

Experience shows that the structure of society at any given time and place, as well as the prevailing theories and beliefs about it, are largely governed by the way in which the material needs of the society are met. In feudal Europe, as in most settled primitive communities, the unit of economic self-sufficiency was extremely small. Division of labour there was; but, apart from the famous traditional division between "those who fight, those who pray and those who work", it was confined mainly to the division of labour between man and woman and to the simple specialization of rural crafts. In the then conditions of transport, trade was conceivable only in luxury articles of high value for the benefit of a few privileged persons; where it existed, it was carried on by outsiders coming from afar, and did not enter into the life of the community as a whole. Through the centuries that followed improved techniques of production led to the growth of cities, bringing the decay of the small self-sufficient unit and a new division of labour between town and country, the development of international trade and the beginnings of international banking and finance, and then, in the so-called mercantilist age, the consolidation of large potentially self-sufficient national markets. Through the same centuries new conceptions of social relations and social obligations were growing up side by side with the old patterns and gradually driving them out—first the new and revolutionary conception of the enterprising individual who enriches himself in competition with other individuals by providing services useful to the community, and then the equally new and revolutionary conception of national loyalties replacing, on the one hand, the old loyalty to the local community and, on the other, the old loyalty to the universal church and empire.

It was only when the industrial revolution brought into operation the hitherto unsuspected and unimagined productive capacities of the machine age that cheap large-scale mechanical production and cheap mechanical transport ushered in a period of unprecedented specialization and division

*From: E. H. Carr, *The New Society* (Boston, Beacon Press, 1957), Chapter 2 (reprinted by permission of the original publisher, Macmillan and Co. Ltd.).

of labour, broke through the now constricting limits of national markets, and created for the first time in history a single world economy and single world market whose blood stream was international trade and international finance, and whose nerve-centre was the city of London. The last remnants of the old conceptions of social hierarchy were swept away. The new society was to be a society of free and equal individuals. The dictates of economic morality were henceforth summed up in obedience to the laws of the market; the individual pursuing his own economic interest was assumed to be promoting that of the whole society. Minor local and sectional loyalties were merged in the larger loyalty of the individual to his nation, of the citizen to the state. It was taken for granted that even this loyalty would soon be merged in a still larger loyalty to the whole community of mankind (which was the logical corollary of the single world market) and that the citizen of a single state or nation would be superseded by the citizen of the world.

The nineteenth-century economic society produced its own corresponding political order and political philosophy; and for a lucid and succinct summary of them one cannot do better than turn to Macaulay, that unrivalled expositor of the current ideas of his age:

> Our rulers will best promote the improvement of the nation by strictly confining themselves to their own legitimate duties, by leaving capital to find its own most lucrative course, commodities their fair price, industry and intelligence their natural reward, idleness and folly their natural punishment, by maintaining peace, by defending property, by diminishing the price of law, and by observing strict economy in every department of the state. Let the government do this: the people will assuredly do the rest.

Or as Bastiat, the French economist, put it, the two principles of personal interest and free competition, "which may be judged sceptically if they are considered in separation, together create by their mutual interaction the social harmony". In this society of free and equal individuals harmoniously competing against one another for the common good the state had no need to intervene. It did not intervene economically—to control production or trade, prices or wages; and still less politically—to guide and influence opinion. It held the ring to prevent foul play and to protect the rights of property against malefactors. Its functions were police functions. It was what Lassalle, the German socialist, contemptuously called the "night-watchman state".

There is no more fascinating theme in contemporary history than to follow the stages through which the *laissez-faire* "night-watchman state" of the nineteenth century has been transformed into the "welfare state" of today—at one and the same time its logical opposite and its logical corollary. The process was, of course, gradual and had begun long before the twentieth century or the first world war. While the industrial revolution was still in its infancy, Robert Owen had issued a warning against the danger of giving it its head and pleaded for state action to curb some of its consequences:

> The general diffusion of manufactures throughout a country [he wrote in 1817] generates a new character in its inhabitants; and, as this character is formed on a principle quite unfavourable to individual or general happiness, it will produce the most lamentable and permanent evils unless its tendency be counteracted by legislative interference and direction.

The humanitarian movement which led to extensive factory legislation to protect, at first the child worker and the woman worker, and later workers in general, against extreme forms of physical exploitation, were well under way in Britain in the 1840's. In the 1880's Herbert Spencer was already fighting a losing rearguard action in defence of the night-watchman state when he listed a number of recent enactments of the British parliament which contravened sound liberal and *laissez-faire* principles: these included measures prohibiting the employment of boy chimney-sweeps, imposing compulsory vaccination, and permitting local authorities to establish free public libraries paid for out of the local rates. About the same time Bismarck was sponsoring the introduction in Germany of the first system of compulsory social insurance for the workers, and thus helping to prevent, forty years later, a German Bolshevik revolution. The first social insurance measure in Britain came in the 1890's in the form of compulsory insurance of workers against industrial accidents.

Social pressures brought about these enactments in the most advanced and densely populated industrial countries before any widespread conscious departure from the *laissez-faire* philosophy could be discerned. But they were symptoms of a profound underlying refusal to accept the continued validity of that philosophy and of the presuppositions on which it rested. The conception of a society where success was, in Macaulay's terminology, the "natural reward" of "industry and intelligence", and failure the "natural punishment" of "idleness and folly", was not particularly humane. But it was clear-cut, logical and coherent on one hypothesis—namely that the free and equal individuals who competed for these rewards and punishments did, in fact, start free and equal. What ultimately discredited the philosophy which Macaulay had so confidently enunciated was the realization that the competitors did not start free and equal and that, the longer the competition continued, the less scope was left for freedom and equality, so that the moral foundation on which *laissez-faire* rested was more and more hopelessly undermined. How had this happened? How could the logic of *laissez-faire* lead straight to a system which seemed its opposite and its negation?

In Great Britain and in the chief European countries, the Industrial revolution broke in on a long-standing traditional order based on social hierarchy. The economic and social inequalities left behind by the *ancien régime* made impossible anything like the clean start between the competitors which was assumed by the exponents of *laissez-faire*. But this flaw, much less in evidence in the new world of America than in old Europe, was not very important. What was far more serious was that the revolution, which purported to wipe out the old inequalities and did in large measure wipe them out, soon bred and tolerated new inequalities of its own. The notion of a society in which individuals start equal on equal terms in each generation—the unqualified recognition of *la carrière ouverte aux talents*— is soon tripped up by what seems to be a deep-seated human instinct. How- ever firmly we may in theory believe in an equal start for everyone in the race, we have no desire that our children should start equal with the children of the Joneses—assuming that our greater wealth or more highly placed connexions enable us to give them the initial advantage of better nutrition, better medical care, better education or better opportunities of every kind. Twenty years ago a school was started in the Kremlin in Moscow for children of high party and Soviet officials. Nobody supposes that its function was to enable these children to start equal with other Russian children. And so, in every society, however egalitarian in principle, in- herited advantages quickly set in motion the process of building up a ruling class, even if the new ruling class has not the additional asset of being able in part to build on the foundations of the old. And so it happened in the industrial society of the nineteenth century; and the story of the industrious errand-boy who became the managing director and of the lazy son of the managing director who became an errand-boy was soon an agreeable myth which took little or no account of the facts of life. But, when this myth was exploded, it carried away with it whatever moral justification had existed for the non-intervention of the state in a society where industry and intelligence were automatically rewarded and idleness and folly auto- matically punished.

Nor did the trouble stop there. What was much worse than any inequality of initial opportunity was the fact that individuals engaged in the economic process obstinately refused to remain individuals. Instead of competing against one another on equal terms for the good of all, they began to com- bine with one another in groups for their own exclusive profit. Mr. Paul Hoffman, when he was Marshall Aid administrator in Europe, once re- marked in a broadcast that there was nothing like competition for keeping business men awake at nights. The picture of American business men tossing from side to side in sleepless beds and haunted by nightmares of competition may well be correct; according to British social mythology, British business men play golf and enjoy dreamless sleep. But Mr. Hoff- man told only half the story. For three-quarters of a century American as well as other business men have been thinking night and day about com- petition. They long ago decided that it was an evil to be got rid of as thoroughly as possible in the branches of industry or trade in which they earned their profits; and since they were intelligent and ingenious men, they have on the whole been remarkably successful in doing so. The nightmare of competition has been replaced by the dream of monopoly. During this long period the individual business man has been ousted by the company, the company by the cartel and the trust, the trust by the super-trust. In this process the sky is the limit; nothing short of monopoly, first national, then, in favoured cases, international, is the ultimate goal. The general pattern is hardly affected by the survival of a host of small men in out-of-the-way places or in other than key industries; these are now no more than the hangers-on of modern economic society, directly or indirectly dependent on the big concerns, tolerated in lines of business where no large profits are to be earned and debarred by their isolation from exercising any real economic power. The continuous and progressive replacement of the smaller by the larger unit has been the typical trend of economic organization in our time.

It is an illusion, still fostered by that select group of business men of whom Keynes once said that they "are generally the slaves of some defunct economist", that monopoly is wicked and inefficient. Every human institution has its share of abuses arising from human wickedness. But it would be hard to prove that the abuses of monopoly are more widespread or more wicked than the abuses of competition. Let me quote from a recent biography by a well-known American writer of perhaps the greatest of the American financiers and trust-builders—*The Great Pierpont Morgan,* by F. L. Allen:

> By instinct, if not by reason, most business men hate competition.
> . . . A man's competitor is the fellow who holds down his prices,
> cuts away his profits, tries to seize his markets, threatens him with
> bankruptcy, and jeopardizes the future of his family. . . . It is
> hardly an accident that most of the Americans who at the begin-
> ning of the twentieth century were charged with being monopo-
> lists had got a good look in their youth at competition at its savage
> and unbridled worst and had decided to do something about it.

I hold no brief for the Pierpont Morgan; but neither do I see anything particularly noble about unbridled competition, "red in tooth and claw". Nor is the choice today between monopoly and competition, but rather between monopoly and what economists call "oligopoly"—that fig-leaf which serves to temper the shock of monopoly to a prudish public and to evade ill-conceived anti-trust laws—the system by which two or three powerful groups flourish side by side in the same field on the basis of written or unwritten price-fixing and market-pooling agreements. Oligopoly offers most of the abuses of monopoly without its efficiency. The man who thanks God he is not a monopolist may easily be something worse.

This summary outline is enough to show that contemporary forms of economic organization, while they are in one sense a direct negation of the *laissez-faire* system, in another sense proceed directly from it. The result of free competition has been to destroy competition; competing individuals have replaced themselves by monopolistic groups as the economic units.

The further, however, this process advances, the more untenable becomes the conception of non-interference by the state. The philosophy of *laissez-faire* presupposed the free competition of individual employer and individual worker on the labour market. The capitalist system in its maturity offers the picture of a class struggle between two vast power-groups; the state must intervene to bring about that modicum of harmony which *laissez-faire* so conspicuously failed to produce, and to mitigate the harshnesses of a struggle which, carried to its extreme conclusion, would wreck the foundations of the existing order. Hence the development of factory legislation, social insurance, wage-fixing and legislation against strikes. But the philosophy of *laissez-faire* also assumed that the consumer would call the tune of the economic process, that his word would be law and his decision final. Capitalist reality shows the unorganized consumer, the typical little man of modern society, helpless before the battery of monopoly, price manipulation, salesmanship and mass advertising trained upon him by the highly organized and competent producer; the state must intervene, by price-fixing and quality controls, to protect the consumer against the overwhelming power of organized capital, sometimes supported on this issue by organized labour. Nowhere has state intervention been more widely solicited than by the small consumer seeking protection against the allegedly inflated prices and profits of the large producer. Finally, in times of extreme scarcity, the state must intervene to ensure an equal distribution of limited supplies to meet the minimum requirements of each and all.

Historically speaking, however, it was neither the need to mitigate the struggle between capital and labour nor the need to protect the consumer which drove the last nail into the coffin of *laissez-faire* capitalism and provoked massive state intervention in every function of the economy. This was brought about by the problem of mass unemployment. The final blow was struck by the series of economic crises culminating in the great depression of the early 1930's. . . .

. . . It has thus come about that after the second world war American policy was still publicly and privately committed to the defence of private enterprise and apparently oblivious of the immense inroads that had been made into it, even in the United States. A highly artificial attitude came to prevail. The defence of private enterprise became a required article of faith of an established church. Many professed, with varying degrees of sincerity, to believe in something they no longer really believed in; others sincerely believed in what they no longer practised; most of all repeated the creed without asking what it meant. The performance of these rites does not alter the fact that private *laissez-faire* capitalism, dead everywhere outside the United States for twenty years, has there too been mortally stricken. Today, in the aftermath of the second world war, the criteria of *laissez-faire* are no more accepted in the United States than in any other Western country as an adequate guide to economic policy. The principle of state intervention and control is tacitly admitted; the only difference is in the greater or less efficiency of the intervention and in the greater or less frankness with which the rôle of the state is admitted. During the first half of 1951 the major issues of American economic policy were price-fixing and wage-fixing; and controversy turned only on the question where to fix them, not whether to fix them. The principle was no longer contested.

. . . We have thus arrived at a paradoxical position. *Laissez-faire* individualist capitalism—the régime of private enterprise in the true sense of the term—has evolved by an inherent process of development into monopoly capitalism. Monopoly capitalism has provoked and made inevitable the intervention of the state as a more or less active directing force in the economic order. This is the system which in its fully developed form is known in English as "planning", in German as *"Planwirtschaft"*, in French as *"une économie dirigée"* and by Marxists as "state monopoly capitalism". But this system—which, whatever it is, is not socialism—is confronted by an unexpected difficulty.

The advantage of the *laissez-faire* philosophy of which capitalism in its heyday was the practical expression was that it dispensed with the need to formulate any aim of economic policy. The consoling assurance was offered to the individual that, in promoting his own economic interest, he was equally promoting that of the community. But once the practice and philosophy of *laissez-faire* were abandoned, some purpose had to be defined, or at any rate silently assumed, which would guide the intervention of the state.

Any kind of state control or state planning automatically raises a number of questions which cannot be dismissed with a vague appeal to efficiency. The questions, Efficiency for What? and Planning for What? became acutely practical; for the answers to them determine our policy. The nineteenth-century capitalist order has been transformed by a process of historical evolution into a system where state intervention and state planning are imperative. What is still uncertain and still controversial is the purpose for which the state intervenes and plans. It is a tragedy of our generation that the only purpose for which planning is yet universally admitted as necessary and legitimate is the contingency of war. This choice is obviously the simplest. Any kind of planning involves irksome controls; nearly everyone will accept the inconvenience of controls and restrictions in order to make his nation militarily secure and militarily powerful. It is the choice which is most likely to appeal to the largest and most powerful groups in industry. Hitler made it at a time when he was under heavy obligations to the big German industrialists and could scarcely have afforded to antagonize them. It provides full employment and can therefore be made acceptable to the worker. The dilemma of this choice is, however, its transient and impermanent character. It is not my task to discuss current rearmament policy. Nothing that I have to say is intended to support the view that Britain has at the present time reached the physical or psychological limits of her capacity. But, taking a long-term view, such limits obviously exist—for

Britain as for other countries. Neither a war economy nor a rearmament economy provides a conceivable basis for a lasting social order. War itself would not solve the problem—except for those whom it annihilated altogether. Whatever was left after the war would have to take up again the planning of a social and economic order directed to some other purpose, and judged by some other criterion, than that of efficiency for war.

If, therefore, my interpretation of history and my diagnosis of the present and future are sound—and I can claim to offer no more than my own interpretation and diagnosis and to show how they are intertwined with one another—we have reached a point in history where the process of transition from the nineteenth-century *laissez-faire* capitalist order offers us no alternative, short of annihilation in war, to a social and economic order which we can call the "welfare state", the "social service state", or simply "socialism". It has often been said that war is a forcing-house of socialism. The same is partly true even of rearmament, since the diversion of scarce resources to purposes of defence clearly involves a new emphasis on equal distribution of what remains—a policy of "fair shares for all". But the essence of socialism resides in the manner in which production is organized, in the purposes which inspire the public control and planning of the economy. You cannot in these days plan for inequality. Once you can no longer explain inequalities either as the salutary result of a natural economic process or as incidentals in an economic organization primarily designed to prepare for war, it must become a main purpose of economic policy to eliminate them. This is the political connexion between planning and socialism. In theory, they are separable; historically, they spring from different sources. But, once the historical evolution of the capitalism system has made a controlled and planned economy necessary, and once the temporary expedient of planning for war has become obsolete, to plan for socialism is the only available alternative.

This dilemma also provides the key to another disputed question—the relation between democracy and socialism. Both words are vague and susceptible of varieties of interpretation. But they are widely accepted as the embodiment of the political and of the economic aspirations of the modern world. It has often been said that the liberty and equality of political democracy are hollow unless they are completed by economic liberty and equality; Babeuf lost his head for saying it first in 1797. So long as democracy remained the political partner and counterpart of *laissez-faire* capitalism, responsibility for the workings of the economic system could be rejected as beyond the reach of the political arm. But, once state intervention in the economic process is accepted as legitimate and inevitable, political responsibility for economic ills can no longer be declined. We have reached a stage when the realization of Babeuf's dream has become imperative.

It is this task of combining political and economic goals, of reconciling democracy and socialism, which, after the second world war, inspired the social policies of Great Britain and of some of the smaller European countries. The possibility of the attempt to make political liberty compatible with planning for socialism has been challenged from both sides. It is denied by the communists—not indeed, explicitly, but implicitly in the practice of Soviet Russia. It is equally denied by those old-fashioned democrats whose conception of democracy is still rooted in the derelict philosophy of *laissez-faire*. The second challenge is rendered particularly insidious by the current international emergency; for those who denounce planning as incompatible with democracy when it is directed to social ends, readily accept planning when directed to preparation for war. A body of opinion is thus unconsciously created which justifies planning for war as essential for democracy while it condemns planning for socialism as incompatible with democracy. Yet, in so far as the issue turns on the prospects of democracy, the distinction is fallacious. Experience shows that, whatever the difficulty of reconciling democratic freedoms with socialism, many of these freedoms are immediately vulnerable to war or intensive preparation for war. To reconcile democracy with planning for socialism is a difficult task. It may have been undertaken too late. But it is the only course which may yet, if war can be avoided, enable democracy to survive.

12   Free Enterprise and a Planned Economy*

John Maurice Clark

What are the Real Alternatives

Some think that only two systems are possible: thorough-going *laissez faire* or complete collectivism. I shall contend that for this country no very close approach to either of these extremes is thinkable and that all our pertinent alternatives lie somewhere in the mid-range.

Absolute *laissez faire* or free enterprise is a myth; the nearest approach to it involves a good deal of control. One definition of free enterprise is a system of controls, in accord with people's sense of right, to which they have become so acclimated that they do not think of them as "controls." Another definition is: a system of controls mainly negative, telling people

---

*From: J. M. Clark, *Economic Institutions and Human Welfare* (New York, A. A. Knopf, Inc., 1957), Chapter 11 (reprinted by permission of publisher).

what they must not do, and leaving them free to choose within the limits thus set. Such a system has elastic limits, which may change with time. But goods in private hands—to the extent of what to produce and how much, it would, as a minimum, leave a majority of the work for creating economic at what price, and whom to employ on what terms. In most of these matters, except perhaps quantity produced and price, controls setting some minimum standards are accepted as consistent with free enterprise.

Planning implies that someone, somewhere, has power to act in pursuance of the plans, or else the plan is mere advice or pious wish. One plans what one administers. Business men plan for their enterprises; government plans its policies with a view to probable results; but under private enterprise no one plans the economy as a whole. A planned *economy* implies power to administer the economy as a whole, or power of control sufficient to determine the quantitative outcome to a roughly equivalent extent. On the other hand, planning need not include complete power to dictate the outcome— as every general knows when he plans a battle, or every farmer when he plants a crop. There are always conditioning factors one does not control. Business plans subject to the market, which it does not control. A planned economy would exert some conscious control of total amount of demand but not dictate its precise directions. In any economic planning we need contemplate, output of consumers' goods will be planned subject to demand arising from consumers' free choice; and wages and the allocation of employment will be planned subject to individuals' free choice of occupations. In these matters, planning will include inducements, not commands.

Private Enterprise

The system of private enterprise displaced the medieval system of relatively static technique and custom-sanctified status, with a system of rapidly changing techniques, in which status (with the possible exception of the landed aristocracy) was at the mercy of unmitigated competition. It had its theory, that competition made business the servant of the people in their capacity as consumers—roughly true as to physical supply, though advertising is a good deal more than an obedient servant, and standards of taste, ideals and morals are shaped by agencies we have little reason to trust for such social leadership. In these early days of dominant individualism the people, in their capacity as workers, were not so well served—to put it mildly.

The subsequent story has been, first, one of development of piecemeal controls to deal with particular abuses and blind spots of the system. These controls business has learned to assimilate, and for present purposes we may pass them over. Second, more pregnant for our purpose, is the fact that along with these piecemeal controls the history of the system has been the story of various methods of escape from the extremer rigors of competition—some generally approved and other not—until our system can no longer fairly be characterized as a competitive one, following economic laws tending to a definable competitive equilibrium; rather, it has become an indeterminate economy of organized groups, in which competitive forces act on the "business" sector, but spottily and unevenly.

It is indeterminate because these groups now have more than was contemplated by the original theory of *laissez faire*. These rival powers of business, labor, agriculture and others threaten the free system, bringing it face to face with the alternative of coercion or chaos, if the existing powers are used irresponsibly and without limit. It is perhaps a minor matter that they have ruined the determinate accuracy of those formulas with which economists defined the results which economic adjustments naturally tend to bring about, and which were called "economic principles." They have brought to the fore one overshadowing economic principle that had little recognition in the nineteenth century: the principle that the degree of freedom that can persist is determined and measured by the degree of responsibility with which group economic power is exercised. This may be a moral principle, but I believe it is also a statement of objective cause and effect, having as much claim to scientific standing as many traditional "economic laws." Irresponsible self-interest can no longer be accepted as a satisfactory basis for an economic system by people who know what is happening in the world they live in.

In the third place, in this setting we face the most currently-emphasized defect of the system of private enterprise—its failure to afford assured opportunity for employment to all who properly qualify. This is the problem that will give the dominant character to the continuing evolution of the system in the next decade or two—assuming that it develops by evolution rather than by catastrophic change, and that we are not caught in another great war. Ink has also been spilled, especially in British economic journals, over the issue of equality in distribution of incomes. In terms of income after taxes, this does not appear to be a dominant present issue, in Britain or the United States, except for really low incomes that have fallen behind the rise of prices. . . .

In the twenties we thought that credit policies aiming at stabilization, under the Federal Reserve System, were sufficient. We were disillusioned. Competitive flexibility of prices and wages is still thought, by a dwindling minority of economists, to be a sufficient anti-depression stabilizer. Since 1929, policy has, on the whole, been moving mainly in the opposite direction—toward stabilized wages and prices, and measures sustaining purchasing power. If these measures should prove insufficient to prevent another major depression, we shall be driven to go further, into measures to which private business has not acclimated itself, and which contain numerous possibilities of disappointing their advocates' expectations. The mildest are attempted stimuli, to which the response of business is uncertain. The ones that are more positive in their effect come under the lesser degrees of planning.

Degrees of Planning

1. Totalitarian control. This plans and directs not only the economy, but all other activities, including expression and, so far as possible, thought. Such control is inconsistent with democracy, since it negates the independent judgment of the citizen, on which democracy rests.

2. Complete economic collectivism. This need not extinguish personal liberties of thought, expression, political action, etc., but it would put obvious difficulties, for example, in the way of the preservation of a free press, since the press would consist either of government organs or co-operatives. Government as the sole employer would have opportunity to tyrannize over the citizen through its power over his job; and this would need to be guarded against by decentralization of hiring and firing, strict prohibition of any kind of blacklist, and a firmly established spirit of "eternal vigilance" with power to take action against abuses. It seems just possible that our British cousins might be able to preserve personal liberty under these conditions. Our larger and less coherent population would make it harder for us; so would our keener spirit of competition and determination to gain the immediate end. Personal freedom and freedom of business enterprise are not the same, and propaganda that confuses them should not be taken seriously. But complete collectivism would be a threat to personal freedom; and this seems to be the strongest single reason against adopting it at this time.

It could, if it would, provide substantially full employment. This would be due partly to planned and regularized capital outlays, including residential construction; and more, perhaps, to control of the distribution of income and of incentives to saving; but most of all because output need not stop when profits turn into losses. In short, it would be due, not mainly to planning per se—plans will miscarry even under such a system—but more to unified ownership and operation of industry. And a good enough result could probably be secured by less drastic means.

3. Mixed systems. These may be of two main varieties. First, predominantly collective, but with private enterprise in special sectors for special reasons (bearing the burden of proof) ; for example, in small-scale trade, agriculture, newspapers, magazines, and publishing generally. This would take into the collective area the industries that are primarily responsible for the fluctuations of capital outlays, which in turn are the main cause of general business ups and downs. This would be especially true if housing were included in the collective sector.

Second, those predominantly private but with government enterprise or co-operatives taking a considerable part in producing marketable goods and services, either displacing or competing with private enterprise in these sectors. These might include further extensions in the field of banking—already entered by government on a large scale—also natural monopolies, or other monopolies or imperfectly competitive industries where "yardstick" competition is sought as a regulator; or they might include industries selected mainly because the government is attempting to bring about an adequate and stable flow of capital outlays and finds it impossible to produce a sufficient effect without actually administering the capital outlays in a fair-sized sector of the field. In that case, industries would be selected involving large capital outlays of sorts that lend themselves to controlled timing. The socialized sector might exert regulatory effect over the private sector, either for expansion or, more positively, for restriction of booms, by limitation of basic supplies. The nature of this effect is highly conjectural.

4. A regimented economy, where nominal ownership and operation remains in private hands, but where policies are positively dictated, so that production, investment, and employment can be planned with some approach to the certainty that would characterize public operation. A totalitarian society could do this; whether a democratic one could do it successfully is a question open to considerable doubt.

5. Private economy with public or collective planning and management of aggregate demand. This might be called a "compensated economy" (Walter Lippmann's phrase, I think), especially where the emphasis is on stabilizing fluctuations, though the term might be equally appropriate for an economy that undertakes to compensate for an unbalance that chronically fails to spend all the income a prosperous people would make in active times, and therefore chronically fails to employ its resources fully. It would also, in principle, include the opposite kind of compensation—action to neutralize an excess of aggregate demand over supply, such as is responsible for the demand side of inflationary pressures when they occur. This represents the general kind of planning with which we shall probably be experimenting within the next decade. It is advocated as planning not to displace private enterprise but to preserve it by making it work.

The operation of this grade of planning is crammed with technical questions of feasibility, about which the specialists are busily disputing. What seems fairly established is, first, that policies coming under this category can have a good deal of stabilizing effect, but are far from being able to guarantee perfect stability. Second, they can do something to raise the long-run average level of production and employment, if it needs raising, but are far from being able to guarantee "full employment" without going beyond the limits of this type of program. Third, they can restrict demand —that is, they are technically capable of restricting it—if it is found to have reached unhealthy "boom" proportions, and thus they can have some effect in reducing inflationary pressures; but it seems virtually certain that this alone will not be sufficient to prevent price inflation without also checking employment substantially short of what would be regarded as a satisfactory level.

One new thing that has been added is the unprecedented power of organized labor. And while "new era" predictions are at a heavy discount, it seems highly probable that this has introduced a long-run inflationary bias into the price system. In that case, the problem is to keep this inflationary bias within tolerable bounds, which for this purpose might tentatively be defined as a long-run upward trend in the general price level at an average rate of 2 per cent per year, or possibly a little more—enough so that the real basic rate of interest would be reduced, by the shrinking buying power of the principal, to a nominal amount, but would not be turned into a minus quantity. Whether an inflationary tendency can be kept within this limit by this type of policy, no one can predict with certainty.

Real Reasons, and False Ones, for Preferring to Maintain Private Enterprise

1. False Reasons

(a) Uncontrolled private enterprise is the ultimate, correct system. This hardly needs disproof.

(b) It is in accord with human nature, because it builds on self-interest. Answer: it has done so too exclusively, and that phase of its development has outlived its usefulness. Under present conditions no system built wholly on individual selfishness can long survive. In fact, I doubt if the system could have survived to the present date if it had been based as exclusively on self-interest as some theories represented. Human nature has little-exploited capacities for responding to a sense of collective purpose. This is obvious in wartime, and needs to be extended to the crises of peace. It is obvious within trade unions, and needs to be extended to more comprehensive units.

(c) Business freedom is identical with personal freedom. This is implied more often than stated; and the foregoing discussion indicates why it is not true.

(d) Free choice of private buyers is always a truer guide to what is wanted or needed than is a governmental decision. Demonstrably false in many cases, despite the perversions to which governmental decisions are subject.

(e) Private enterprise is subject to impersonal economic law, which works correct results. Answer: under present conditions results are largely indeterminate and far from correct. Business has a margin of discretion as to prices; wages are set, not so much by economic law as by power politics and diplomacy, with mass coercion in reserve in an increasing share of cases.

2. Reasons Partly True

(a) Private enterprise is more efficient. True in part, as to ends that are well represented by market demand, not as to others. The efficiency is often misdirected; and unemployment and restrictions on output represent major failures.

(b) Private enterprise is more progressive and freer from bureaucratic tyranny, stagnation, and red tape. True only as a matter of degree, and of diminishing degree; but the difference is still of great importance.

(c) Private enterprise rewards talent and capable service. Answer: sometimes it rewards talent too liberally, by socially valid standards, and sometimes it rewards talent that is misdirected.

3. Reasons of Greater Validity

(a) It is wanted, not only by business interests and agriculture, but prevailingly (in this country) by organized labor. Why? Perhaps because organized labor feels it is better able to maintain its power and freedom, and can make business serve its interests better, than it could under collectivism. This is valid, in that we need free and strong unions as part of a balanced social structure; but it is obviously subject to serious abuse. Dictation over society as a whole by monopolistic special interests is an evil, whether they be the interests of capital or of labor.

(b) Finally, private enterprise as it now exists is an evolving thing and affords a basis for further evolutionary change of the most flexible sort available, with the most nearly voluntary methods of adjustment of conflicting interests and changing rights. This seems the most cogent reason for wanting it to continue. It represents an opportunity, which private enterprise may or may not be able to live up to.

Prevalent attitudes among average business men have, rather naturally, a one-sided emphasis on this matter. They want government to establish a "favorable climate" for business, and construe this largely in terms of letting business alone to work out its own problems, in the sincere belief that this will lead to a better record of performance. It may be true that such a policy would produce quicker revival from depressions than did the improvised "planning" of the New Deal; and it may, through long-run investment programs, make a real contribution toward forestalling or preventing such fluctuations. But the idea that its performance will be good enough to meet the tests of the coming generation—this is an act of faith. . . .

13 Individual Enterprise and the State*

Eric Roll

The tendencies toward an increasing role for the state in determining the direction and form of individual enterprise have already produced the term "mixed economy" commonly applied to the United States, Britain, and the

*From: *The World After Keynes: An examination of the Economic Order* (New York, Praeger Books, 1968), pp. 47-51 (reprinted by permission of publisher).

countries of Western Europe. The reference is to the coexistence of publicly owned and privately owned enterprise, and to the fact that private enterprise generally must operate within certain constraints imposed by public authority.

How novel the latter development really is can be argued at length but, I believe, fruitlessly. At best, the idea that there really was a golden age of free enterprise, when the last remnants of feudal restriction had finally disappeared and the interventions of the modern, democratic state had not yet made themselves felt, is an over-simplification; it could have had only limited validity for some countries during very short periods of their modern history. On the other hand, the Marxist, and neo-Marxist, concept of the inexorable march of industrial capitalism towards monopoly and increasing interdependence with "finance-capital" and the state "apparatus," with violent revolution to subjugate its overweening power the inevitable result, hardly provides any more useful an intellectual instrument. I am not persuaded that grand generalizations of this kind—relating to the proper way in which the institutional framework of the economic order should be constructed or to the question whether there is a clearly discernible historical process in which it evolves and changes—are necessary to a full understanding of the issues.

The significant fact is that in nearly all the major industrial countries the ideological contest over the ownership of business enterprise is now at a very low ebb. I find it hard to believe that it will break out again in full force in the foreseeable future, though this cannot be entirely ruled out. It seems more likely that questions of the most effective administration of the public and the private sectors (mainly in regard to particular areas, such as public utilities) will provide the primary source of intellectual debate and political controversy.

These issues will be sharpened by new scientific/technological advances. Forerunners may be seen in the application of atomic energy to the production of power; the aerospace industry providing new means of communication; new discoveries of already known sources of energy—oil, natural gas, etc.—all these raise anew old questions of the proper relationship between private enterprise and public authority. In all these instances characteristics of "natural monopoly" are present, and this has long been recognized as a factor calling for public regulation and "justifying" it against the canons of purely private enterprise economics. Moreover, in many, if not all, of these new developments the scale of the financial resources required is such that some recourse to public funds is virtually inevitable.

So it seems to me that in the next two or three decades the abstract issue of private versus public enterprise will give way to study and debate over precise methods of financial interrelation, pricing of products and services, proper rates of return on capital invested, and amortization. Although the problems will not be different in kind from those already encountered in relation to the existing range of "public" goods, the general area of the state's positive determination of the forms of enterprise is likely to be a very active one indeed—perhaps precisely because the simple black and white juxtaposition of public versus private ownership has ceased to be very meaningful.

In trade, in industry, and in finance, questions as to the regulatory functions the state should exercise have undoubtedly been increasing in complexity and will continue to do so, if only as a result of the much larger numbers involved and the consequently greater impact of any development in one sphere on the more closely interconnected network of economic relations. In all industrial countries, for example, the attitude to monopoly and restrictive practices is being looked at afresh. The historical experience and the current problems of different countries again show that no uniform set of theories or policies has yet been derived, nor can countries very easily be classified according to the degree to which they practice this or that form of regulation and intervention. Britain, for example, has only relatively recently followed the lead given long ago by the United States in pursuing an active policy of investigation and suppression of monopoly and restrictive practices. Yet, in a relatively short time, she has in some respects established an even more stringent antitrust regime—so much so that it is now often regarded as being an obstacle to the progress of industrial efficiency.

France, to take a different example, is not generally regarded as a country in which public regulation of enterprise is especially oppressive, despite the fact that she has under ownership all the usual range of public utilities. Yet her commercial banks are also, to all intents and purposes, fully nationalized, as is an important sector of the automobile industry. What is more important, a private capital market is practically nonexistent; and finance for the larger investment projects can be obtained only through the medium of state-controlled institutions. This, incidentally, . . . puts a powerful planning instrument at the disposal of the state.

In the United States, too, a country sometimes looked upon as the citadel of unfettered private enterprise, the relation between the federal—and sometimes state—government and business is far more intricate than appears at first sight. It is true that completely public-owned enterprise is much rarer than in Western European countries which have a roughly similar political framework and level of industrial development. But, as I have already noted, regulation of public utilities and control of monopolistic practices has a long history in the United States. Regulation of banking, the stock exchange, and the insurance industry in many respects goes much further than it does in Europe. Legislation relating to corporations—including provision for disclosure of information, prohibitions due to conflicts of interest, and the like—is also often more advanced than that in effect in many an otherwise more "planned" European economy.

Most important of all, perhaps, from the point of view of potential future developments, is the impact of great federal spending programs on certain areas of business enterprise. Outstanding in this respect is the defense effort, not only because of its size but because it relates to the technologically most advanced industries with the greatest potential for growth and for producing a revolutionary transformation of the industrial structure as a whole. This influence is spearheaded by the overwhelming impact of the expenditure of public funds on scientific, technological, and even economic, research and development. One has only to think of the electronic and aeronautical industries to realize how important these new defense-oriented enterprises are; and, although they are very different from tobacco monopolies or state-owned coal mines and railways, they are no less acutely significant in the consideration of public versus private ownership.

In the European countries, too, government expenditures have mounted for defense, for scientific research, and, in partnership with private enterprise, for technologically experimental new industrial ventures. Over the next two or three decades the politico-economic problems raised by this trend will require much study. Even if more peaceful international conditions lead to some relative decline of direct defense expenditures, the pattern already created will, because of its technological aspects, continue to be the active frontier of state/business relations.

It would, however, be rash to conclude from this that the scope for private enterprise, including ease of entry and mobility, would necessarily shrink. The growth of populations and the increasing mass market (due both to the emergence of new wants and to the enlargement of demand for known products as the level of prosperity increases) should leave much opportunity for enterprise and ingenuity. Here, the size of the market will be of great consequence. The larger the market, the less likely is it to become dominated by a few producers and distributors for any length of time. In the United States, the largest of the advanced industrialized countries, the scope for new products, new techniques for old products, or new methods of distribution, has remained consistently large in recent years; and it has not by any means invariably been exploited exclusively by the large corporations.

. . . A word might be said on how these issues present themselves in the perspective of the less developed countries of the world. Here, too, it is difficult to find a consistent pattern either by comparing groups of countries with one another or by seeking for analogies in the history of older economies. The evolution of business enterprise in England from the 16th to the 19th centuries is unlikely to be reproduced in, say, India, even in telescoped form. As regards scientific advance or technological know-how, it has long been accepted that the revolution in methods of communication has made it unlikely that the full sequence of earlier stages of economic development will be repeated. Phases are apt to be "skipped," as the railway age is likely to be, in part at least, in many developing countries. Also, in regard to the matters here discussed—namely, the most appropriate form of organization of business enterprise—learning from the experience of older countries may lead to the nonappearance of earlier controversies.

In the face of these hazards, one generalization may, however, be in order. In most developing countries economic advance is taking place under the close and continuous guidance of the state, even where development is not undertaken directly on public initiative. This is clearly inevitable. The pace of the reform of old social, political, and economic patterns has been greatly accelerated by rapidly changing relations between developed and developing countries; the virtually total disappearance of the colonial system; the enhanced political weight in international councils of the less developed world; the consequent change in trading relations even as regards the old "colonial" products; the stirrings of political pressure for material improvement within the countries concerned; and the development of a consciously directed flow of technical and financial aid from the richer to the poorer countries—all this leads to continued internal central direction and calls for highly centralized dealings between governments.

This pattern is bound to prevail for many years to come. But the resolution of the problems to which it will give rise (and which one may predict will form a major preoccupation for the rest of the century) will require, on the one hand, the deliberate creation of some scope within the developing countries for private business enterprise of the modern kind, and, on the other, control of private exploitation and enrichment in the major sectors of the economy, which must continue to be largely centrally directed. To suppress or avoid undesirable forms of relationship between government and large business will be a major problem not only for the developing world but also for the advanced countries that are aiding them to accelerate their growth.

14   The Approach to Planning *

Andrew Shonfield

. . . All that has to be shown in order to justify the effort of central planning is that it makes it more probable than it would be under a pure market system that complementary investments involving a long lead time will be carried out when they are required. There are more and more such investments in our rich and crowded societies. If foresight has any value at all,

*From: A. Shonfield, *Modern Capitalism: The Changing Balance of Public and Private Power* (London, Oxford University Press, 1965), pp. 226-36 (reprinted and abridged by permission of author and publisher).

a planned system will tend to work with a lower margin of underemployed capacity in any given productive sector. That is another way of saying that it will suffer from fewer bottlenecks. And it also implies that the capital-output ratio will be more favourable. This last is certainly one of the out-standing features of postwar France; and the French planners have, plausibly enough, claimed some of the credit for it.[1]

It would be wrong, however, to suggest that economic planning as it has developed in Europe to date is overwhelmingly concerned with making the total volume of national output increase faster than it otherwise would, regardless of how it is composed. It is true that this kind of approach is dominant in one or two countries, notably in Britain, but it is quite alien to the French view of the problem. In France the planners explicitly regard it as one of their tasks to ensure that the distribution of the anticipated increase in the nation's wealth over a period of years ahead is biased towards the attainment of certain social objectives. Again, one is struck by the Anglo-French contrast—the willingness of the French authorities to assume a tutelary role in the division of the prizes which result from a more efficient management of the economy, while British planning in the early 1960s was concerned exclusively with enlarging the aggregate volume of supplies; so far at any rate it has recoiled from any attempt to plan demand.[2] The French Fourth Plan insisted vigorously on its objective of achieving 'a more complete view of man'[3]—by which it meant that the additional resources becoming available between 1961 and 1965 must not be used merely to satisfy consumer demands which would find their normal expression through the market, but must be devoted to more profound purposes, for which the ordinary citizen might not opt spontaneously today but for which

---

[1]See the essay by Pierre Massé, *Revue du Marché Commun,* no. 55 (Feb. 1963), where he asserts that 'the Plan's . . . merit has been to reduce, thanks to better coordination of policies, overlapping and spare capacities, and thus to achieve the same growth target with a lower rate of investment' (p. 50). A report by the OECD in March 1962 puts this saving on investment at 2 per cent of gross domestic production—*Statistics of National Accounts 1950-61* (1964) shows that the rate of growth of French GNP from the mid-1950s onwards was slightly higher than the average of European OECD countries (4.7 per cent per annum against an average of 4.5 per cent), while the proportion of the French national product devoted to fixed capital investment was between 1 and 2 per cent below the OECD European average.

[2]The whole approach of NEDC was to discover from the various industries and other branches of the economy what each one of them would require in the way of resources, on the hypothesis that national output in the aggregate rose by 4 per cent a year. No attempt was made to argue systematically about the best way of distributing the national effort, so that the various increments of output—adding up to the national average of 4 per cent—would occur in the places where they would produce the greatest return, measured by some explicit criterion of social benefit. This is, of course, a political question and one that cannot be burked; but so far the British idea has been to keep planning out of politics. A national plan is thought of as the reflection of a tacit consensus, something that all right-thinking persons agree about implicitly. It is therefore only the practical detail which is worth discussing; the criteria are not.

[3]See e.g. Massé, *Revue du Marché Commun* (Feb. 1963), p. 51.

he will be grateful in the future—because by then he will be a different man. Specifically the French planners set their faces against a 'civilization of gadgets'.[4] The point of planning is thus in part an ethical one: it imposes choices about the use of resources other than those which the market would produce.[5]

This frank emphasis not on what people want now but on what they will want (or ought to be wanting) in the future is characteristically French in style. But leaving aside the transcendental overtones, it is in practice closely in line with the thinking of the growing body of planners elsewhere in the Western world. Increasingly the realization is forced upon us that the market, which purports to be the reflection of the way in which people spontaneously value their individual wants and efforts, is a poor guide to the best means of satisfying the real wishes of consumers. That is because market prices generally fail to measure either social costs or social benefits. In our civilization these grow constantly more important. Simply because some amenity—let it be a pleasant view or an uncongested road or a reasonably quiet environment—is not paid for directly by those who enjoy it, there is no measure of the cost of the disinvestment which occurs when a profitable economic activity destroys what already exists. Unless the state actively intervenes, and on an increasing scale, to compel private enterprise to adapt its investment decisions to considerations such as these, the process of economic growth may positively impede the attainment of things that people most deeply want.[6] Social benefits tend to be left out of account, or at best played down, in any hard-headed calculation of the return on any proposed piece of investment. It is the pride of hard-headed men, especially when they are accountants, to include in the arithmetic of prospective profit and

[4]See Cazes, *Planification en France,* and Massé's article, 'La France, le Plan et les gadgets', *Entreprise,* (Mar. 1962). Cazes admits (and laments) that the argument for social investment is not accepted by more than a small fraction of public opinion—which is why care is taken not to present the issue of social versus consumer goods as a straightforward matter of choice (p. 118).

[5]This is a fairly recent development. Pierre Massé has explained: 'We have, in the Fourth Plan, for the first time, emphasized social policy, which previously had been left completely out of the Plans . . . ' (see *Planning*—papers read at the Business Economists' Conference, Oxford, Apr. 1962). The new emphasis was reflected in the projected use of resources: personal consumption was planned to rise by 23 per cent between 1961 and 1965, while social investment was to rise by 50 per cent.

[6]The Swedish trade union organization LO urged its case for more planning on the government in 1961 on the ground that the 'price mechanism is becoming an increasingly unreliable indicator of real alternative costs because of . . . distortions of prices and through the divergence between social and private costs' (see Johnston, *Economic Expansion,* p. 165). The other side of the medal is that the classical capitalist system, which allowed the entrepreneur to pocket all the gains while meeting none of the social costs of any innovation, established, as Hirschman has pointed out, an exceptionally powerful incentive for business investment. Once these external costs become 'internalized', i.e. have to be taken into the calculus of profit and loss of those responsible for innovation, business may become less dynamic (see A. E. Hirschman, *The Strategy of Economic Development* (Yale UP, 1959) pp. 57 ff.

loss only those items which are sufficiently precise to be measured in monetary terms. The rest, the things that you do not pay for, may be thrown in
—where they are too obviously significant to be entirely ignored—as 'incidentals'; they may marginally add to the force of a conclusion emerging
from the monetary calculation, but rarely affect its substance.

It is instructive to observe how the slow advance in intellectual techniques, in this case the technique of measuring costs, may result in denying
to millions of people for several years the benefit of some desirable piece
of investment. A recent example is the building of the new underground
railway, the so-called Victoria Line, across the most congested area of central
London. The project was argued over, examined, and re-examined for well
over a decade from the time when it was first proposed, and always it was
turned down on the ground that it could not be made to pay its way. Then
in the early 1960s someone had the bright idea of bringing into the calculation the secondary benefits of having this extra channel of rail transport
across London—notably the saving in travel time and motor-vehicle operating costs which would result for people *not* using the new line, from the
reduction in traffic congestion in the central streets. When monetary values
were calculated for these and other savings, it was found that the true
return on the investment in the Victoria Line was over 10 per cent of the
capital cost of the project.[7] This answer, on the basis of which construction
of the railway has gone ahead, was arrived at by the technique of 'benefit
costing'—a method which has come into vogue since the war, as public
authorities have tried to struggle out of the windowless intellectual box
prepared for them by upright business accountants. There is nothing complicated or subtle about the method: it is merely a way of bringing into a
profit-and-loss account relevant but not immediately obvious products of an
investment which occur beyond the immediate confines of the investment
project itself. As such, it provides a handy weapon in an argument with
practical men who trust arithmetic above all else.

It is, however, a blunt weapon for any other purpose. The problem is
that the values imputed to the products of social investment usually include
a large element of the arbitrary. The gains are real enough—benefits like
time saved, less wear and tear on the nerves of people travelling in cities, a
smaller intake of motor exhaust fumes—but they do not lend themselves to
precise assessment in terms of shillings per man-year. The best that can be
done in most cases is to relate the item to be measured (e.g. wasted time)

---

[7]See C. D. Foster and M. E. Beesley, 'Estimating the social benefit of constructing an
underground railway in London', *R1. Statist. Soc. Journal,* Vol. cxxvi, pt. 1 (1963). The
answer, which is calculated on the basis of the discounted 'present value' of capital and
operating costs set against the future benefits of the project over the assumed 50 years'
life of the line, obviously varies with different assumptions about the level of interest
rates. If the rate of interest to be charged is 6 per cent, the estimated return on the
investment is 11.3 per cent; even with interest rates at 8 per cent, the return is 10.9
per cent—quite respectable by commercial standards.

to some activity which does actually produce or cost money; in this way the benefit-cost accountant is able to establish an upper and lower limit for the value of the service (or disservice) which he is trying to measure. The exercise sometimes calls for a great deal of ingenuity. If it seems at times to have a certain unreality, one has to remind oneself that the practical purpose of these intricate calculations of tenuous social returns is to supply an indication of a broad order of magnitude, which can be set against some conventional standard rate of return on capital as a means of judging whether a project is going to be wildly wasteful or not. But any attempt to determine an order of priorities by this species of arithmetical juggling is more difficult. In particular it provides little help in making a choice between competing social investment projects, each with a claim on public funds. The imputed magnitudes carry too large a margin of error to make any exact comparisons possible.

What this means is that public investment policy is less amenable to un-ambiguous answers derived from a scale of profit and loss than private investment is in its own sphere. Even an apparently straightforward issue like the return to be expected from public investment in education is sub-ject to very hazardous and various answers.[8] Some economists have dreamed of a world in which price tags of social as well as private costs and benefits are attached to all things, so that a large high-speed computer simulating the behaviour of a market would make its rational choices on behalf of society. But in the present and foreseeable state of the art of costing there seems little chance that the automaton will be able to replace the judgement of the planner. Computers will surely have a growing part to play in this too; but as auxiliaries not principals. . . .

As it is at present conducted, economic planning greatly reinforces the already powerful trend of 'the flow of power towards the executive'.[9] It is perhaps unreasonable to expect that at this early stage, when the techniques of planning are themselves still experimental and highly tentative, an answer should already have been found to the major political problems which they bring in their train. But the problems themselves urgently need to be identified. The worst danger to democratic institutions would be if it were pretended that there was nothing whatsoever to worry about—because a standing committee of the nation's major interest groups working in col-

---

[8]See Robbins Report, *Higher Education*, Cmnd 2154 (1963) for a summary of the various attempts that have been made by economists to measure the product of educa-tional investment. None of them is satisfactory, largely because it has proved impossible to isolate from among the various interconnected factors, which are together responsible for any given increase in productivity, the particular element that is due to the increased knowledge of the worker derived from additional tuition.

[9]The phrase is Professor Arthur Miller's (see 'Evidence before the House of Repre-sentatives Committee on Banking and Currency', 14 Apr. 1964) who was describing to the committee the resistance of the US to the trend—'in many respects the last country in the world that has not almost completely gone over to more of an executive type of government'.

laboration with a team of high-powered economic experts had succeeded in taking the issue right out of politics.

SUGGESTIONS FOR FURTHER READING

Burns, E. M., *Ideas in Conflict* (London, Methuen & Co. Ltd., 1960), chapter 6, "Democratic Collectivism."

Canadian Institute on Public Affairs, *Economic Planning in a Free Society?* Toronto, University of Toronto Press, 1963.

Coker, F. W., "Empirical Collectivism," in *Recent Political Thought* (New York, Appleton-Century-Crofts, 1934), chapter 20.

Dahl, Robert A., and Charles E. Lindblom, *Politics, Economics & Welfare*, New York, Harper & Row, 1953.

Douglas, T. C., "The Government and the Economy," in I. A. Litvak (ed.), *The Nation Keepers: Canadian Business Perspectives*, Toronto, McGraw-Hill Co. of Canada Ltd., 1967.

Durbin, E. F. M., *The Politics of Democratic Socialism*, London, Routledge & Kegan Paul, 1940.

Fabricant, Solomon, "Government and Economic Life," in *Thirty-fifth Annual Report*, New York, National Bureau of Economic Research, 1955.

Finer, Herman, *The Road to Reaction*, London, D. Dobson, 1946.

Ginzberg, E., Hiestand, D. L. and Reubens, B. G., *The Pluralistic Economy*, New York, McGraw-Hill, 1965.

Harrison, Anthony, *The Framework of Economic Activity* (New York, Macmillans, St. Martin's Press, 1967), chapter 6.

Keynes, J. M., Essays in Persuasion, *The End of Laissez-Faire* (New York, W. W. Norton & Co. Inc., 1963).

Myrdal, Gunnar, *Beyond the Welfare State*, New Haven, Yale University Press, 1960.

Phelps, E. S. (ed.), *Private Wants and Public Needs* (revised), New York, W. W. Norton & Co. Inc., 1965.

Reagan, Michael D., *The Managed Economy*, New York, Oxford University Press, 1963.

Roll, Eric, *The World After Keynes: An Examination of the Economic Order*, New York, Praeger Books, 1968.

Rostow, E. V., *Planning for Freedom: The Public Law of American Capitalism* (New Haven, Yale University Press, 1962), particularly chapter 2.

Samuelson, Paul A., "Personal Freedoms and Economic Freedoms in the Mixed Economy," in E. F. Cheit (ed.), *The Business Establishment*, New York, John Wiley & Sons, 1964.

Shields, Currin V., "The American Tradition of Empirical Collectivism," in *The American Political Science Review*, Vol. 46 (March, 1952), pp. 104-120.

Shonfield, A., *Modern Capitalism: The Changing Balance of Public and Private Power*, London, Oxford University Press, 1965.

Sirkin, Gerald, *The Visible Hand: The Fundamentals of Economic Planning*, New York, McGraw-Hill, 1968.

Tawney, R. H., *Equality*, London, George Allen & Unwin Ltd., 1952 and 1964.

Titmuss, Richard M., *Essays on "The Welfare State,"* London, George Allen & Unwin, Ltd., 1959.

Titmuss, Richard M., *Commitment to Welfare*, London, George Allen & Unwin, Ltd., 1968.

2

Policies to
promote competition
and regulate monopoly

PART THREE

Structure and Competitiveness

of Canadian Industry

INTRODUCTION

How competitive is business in Canada? This is not a simple question to answer, partly because there may be uncertainty about what we mean by "competitive" and also because it is difficult to generalize about the conditions under which the great variety of business enterprises in a modern industrial economy operate.

When the economist uses the term "competitive" he has in mind the concept of "perfect competition" or some tolerable approximation to it. That is, he is thinking in terms of a situation in which individual sellers or buyers are unable to exercise any perceptible control over market supply or price for the commodity concerned. This condition will be expected to obtain when there are enough independent sellers or buyers in the market that no one seller or buyer accounts for a noticeable part of the total supply of the goods or services in question. To the extent that this condition is not fulfilled, the economist recognizes some element of "monopoly" in the market. This could include the extreme of pure monopoly where a single seller or buyer (a monopsonist) accounts for the total amount of the goods or services supplied or demanded in the market. Within the two extremes of perfect competition and pure monopoly, sellers and buyers have some degree of power over total output and the price established in the market. How effectively this power can be exercised depends upon the size of the individual seller's or buyer's contribution to total market supply or demand.

Thus, firms that account for most of the sales of a commodity are likely to have considerable market power. This is why economists studying the organization of industry are interested in measuring the "degree of concentration" of sellers (or buyers) in an industry or market, that is, the proportion of output or sales accounted for by some proportion of the firms in the industry.

Surprisingly little statistical evidence concerning the degree of concentration in Canadian industry has yet been accumulated. But what there is, combined with more general observation, indicates a considerable variation in the degree of concentration from one industry to another. Agriculture and some of the service industries provide good examples of extremely low concentration, with a great many producing units supplying the total output of the industry. Such an "atomistic" market structure confers little, if any, market power on individual firms, leading to a situation approximating the ideal of "perfect competition". The public-utilities industries (including transportation, communications, electric power, gas, and water) and the financial industries (notably banking and insurance) are all highly concentrated with a small percentage of the firms accounting for a high percentage of the total output. Other industries present a more complicated picture. Manufacturing, the only type of industry extensively studied with regard to structure, is an example of such a complex situation. Some of the evidence, with an analysis of it, is presented in *Reading 15*.

It will be seen from this reading and the selections that follow it in this part, that there is reason to believe industry in Canada tends to be more highly concentrated than industry in the United States, and that one probable reason for this is the small size of Canadian markets relative to the efficient size of individual producing units. Some other reasons seem to be closely related to the peculiar situation of Canada in relation to the giant United States economy. One characteristic of our "branch plant" economy, as Professor Watkins has referred to our situation, is that, as shown in *Reading 16*, there is a correlation between concentration and degree of foreign control in Canadian industries. This is not to say that foreign control has caused Canadian industry to be as concentrated as it is, but the evidence does suggest that foreign direct investment has not made our industry more competitive. It also suggests that to the extent that concentration confers economic, social, and possibly political power on the oligopolists who dominate particular industries or markets, much of this power is in the hands of the foreign owners of these firms.

Other economic, social, and political implications of industrial concentration are discussed in the remaining selections in this part. Professor Rosenbluth analyzes a number of the economic and political problems created by high industrial concentration in *Reading 17*. The social aspects of economic power are identified by Professor Porter in *Reading 18*.

To this point the emphasis has been on the problems created by the way our real world economy differs from the economist's ideal of a competitive market economy. We have seen how these go beyond the narrowly economic problems of efficiency in resource use, spreading into the social and political spheres of our lives as well. This should not be surprising, for as we saw in Section One, the concept of a competitive market economy is only part of a larger system of social and political ideology. We might expect from this that it would be a relatively simple matter to frame policies that would move our real world situation closer to this ideal simply by restructuring markets, eliminating obstacles to competition, and breaking up concentrations of economic power. Were this so, we could pass immediately to Part 4 in which such policies are discussed. But the problem is not so simple.

The major complication arises from the possibility that important benefits may be derived from the lack of competition and from the concentration of economic power. A prevalent defence of monopolistic market structures is that the size and profitability of such firms enable them to make a greater contribution to the growth of the economy through their ability to make large investments in research and in the development of new products and techniques. Should this be so, the policy implications would be obvious. As a community, we would perhaps be willing to accept some of the inefficiencies of resource use and other problems associated with the lack of competition in industry as the price of obtaining a higher rate of economic growth and progress. This question is analyzed by Professor English in *Reading 19*.

Readers interested in pursuing the great debate on the merits of monopoly will find some of the main contributions listed in the bibliography for Part 3.

15   Firm Size and Concentration*

G. W. Wilson, Scott Gordon, and S. Judek

It is estimated that there are over half a million separate business firms in Canada (c. 1960) which vary in size from less than $25,000 in assets and employing only 2 or 3 persons to giant corporations with assets exceeding $100 million and employing several thousand workers. A very large propor-

*From: George W. Wilson, Scott Gordon, Stanislaw Judek and Albert Brown, *Canada: An Appraisal of Its Needs and Resources*. (Twentieth Century Fund, New York, 1965), pp. 336-41 (reprinted by permission of publisher).

tion of business assets in Canada is, not surprisingly, concentrated in the largest firms. Rosenbluth has estimated roughly one hundred firms have assets in excess of $100 million each and that 57 of these are non-financial corporations (i.e., those whose main assets are physical means of production).[1] In 1956 these 57 non-financial giants owned about 38 per cent of the total value of real assets (land, buildings, equipment, and inventory) of all non-financial corporations and about 20 per cent of all real business assets including those of unincorporated firms.[2]

US data suggests that the 100 largest firms in manufacturing, mining, and distribution (i.e., non-financial enterprises) owned approximately 30 per cent of all industrial assets in 1958. Thus, the degree of asset concentration in the US is less than in Canada in the sense that 100 largest US firms control a smaller proportion of total corporate industrial assets in the US than the 57 largest Canadian firms in Canada.[3] Although there are many statistical pitfalls in such international comparisons, the two sets of data regarding asset concentration appear to be sufficiently comparable to warrant the conclusion of significantly greater concentration in Canada.[4]

Indeed, the figures for Canada even tend to understate the degree of concentration since they treat subsidiaries as separate entities. An attempt to take account of subsidiary-parent relationships suggests that in 1956, 44 privately owned non-financial firms "accounted for 44 per cent of the value of 'real' assets held by all privately owned non-financial corporations." Thus, concentration in terms of assets may be very much higher than in the United States.

If we examine concentration in terms of the proportion of output or employment in any industry accounted for by the largest four, six, or eight firms, similar conclusions emerge. The largest firms in Canada are heavily concentrated in manufacturing, transport, finance, mining, and utilities. These sectors together accounted for about half of GDP in 1961 or close to 60 per cent excluding government administration and defence. Earlier evidence for manufacturing suggests that the degree of concentration in terms

---

[1]G. Rosenbluth, "Concentration and Monopoly in the Canadian Economy" in M. Oliver, ed., *Social Purpose of Canada* (Toronto, 1961), p. 198.

[2]*Ibid.*, pp. 198-200. Four of the 57 firms are crown companies. Excluding these, the 53 remaining privately owned corporations owned about 29 per cent of all real, privately owned assets of non-financial corporations, one-quarter of the real assets of all corporations and roughly 14 per cent of the entire Canadian business economy.

[3]US data from N. R. Collins and L. E. Preston, "The Size Structure of Industrial Firms," *American Economic Review* (Dec. 1961) Table 1, p. 989.

[4]Rosenbluth's calculations are outlined carefully in the Appendix to "Concentration and Monopoly in the Canadian Economy," pp. 244-45 and, as far as the corporate sector is concerned, are comparable to those of Collins and Preston. One difficulty is the different coverage. The latter exclude utilities, services and so on while Rosenbluth's estimates include these. But, except for utilities, the degree of concentration of non-financial corporate assets is generally lower outside of the sectors included by Collins and Preston: hence, the different coverage is not apt to make the estimates sufficiently non-comparable to reverse the above conclusion.

of output or employment is much higher in Canada than in the US for virtually all industries for which comparable data are available.[5]

* * *

The reasons for this degree of concentration relate primarily to two main factors. As already mentioned the size of the Canadian market in particular product lines clearly restricts the number of "optimal" sized firms. . . . But beyond the relationship between efficient firm size and market size, which is a very difficult thing to pinpoint with much accuracy, there is the institutional fact that antitrust enforcement in Canada has been much weaker than in the US. This is especially true as regards mergers. Indeed, it is probably not too much to say that the Canadian approach to the so-called monopoly problem has been so weak as to have had an imperceptible effect upon market structure and little more influence upon market practices. The amendments in this regard during the Diefenbaker administration have further weakened Canada's anti-monopoly legislation and enforcement.[6]

There are, of course, great numbers of small firms in such sectors as trade, services, and agriculture (including forestry and fishing) as in the United States. But, in general, the evidence suggests that the degree of concentration of assets, output, and employment is higher in Canada than the United States. To some extent the presumed monopolistic consequences of this situation in Canada are reduced by the fact that in several areas governmentally owned and operated firms are important forces. This is particularly noteworthy in transportation and communication, where the Canadian National Railways represents over half of the railway industry and is an important force in trucking as well. Air Canada is the largest airline in Canada while the Canadian Broadcasting Corporation is the largest radio and television broadcasting corporation. In addition to such dominance in these areas, the Polymer Corporation, which produces synthetic rubber products, Eldorado Mining and Refining Limited, which mines and refines uranium and produces nuclear fuels, and the Central Mortgage and Housing Corporation, which provides a large variety of services in the mortgage market as well as owning and managing rental housing units for war workers and veterans, are all government-owned enterprises of a business type which may be used as instruments of public policy and, in their respective areas, offset to some extent, the possible consequences of private concentrations of economic power. It should be stressed, however, that these government-owned enterprises have been established to operate much like private companies. Indeed, it is a point of some pride to the government

---

[5]G. Rosenbluth, *Concentration in Canadian Manufacturing Industries* (Princeton, 1957), chap. iv.

[6]For a brief review of Canadian antitrust laws see George W. Wilson, "How Effective Are our Antitrust Laws?" *Business Quarterly* (fall 1959), pp. 169-74. A more recent and extensive survey has been made by G. Rosenbluth and H. G. Thorburn, *Canadian Anti-Combines Administration* (Toronto, 1963).

to have these companies operate efficiently and show levels of profits as high as or even higher than in the private sector. It is not so much their existence *per se* that may offset the undesirable aspects of private concentrations as their *potential* in this regard should abuses of power become evident. For the most part, these crown companies are reluctant to deviate from business practices pursued by large private corporations. It is doubtless the case that, thus far at least, the real restraint in transportation comes less from the existence of the Canadian National Railways and Air Canada than from regulation by the Board of Transport Commissioners and the Air Transport Board.

Despite these important areas of government ownership and regulation, it seems to be a valid judgment that "problems due to 'bigness' . . . to extreme inequality of firm size, and . . . monopolistic control of markets by a small number of sellers are . . . of major importance in the Canadian economy."[7] Especially is this the case where the industries enjoy the benefits of tariff protection and have little to fear from anti-combines investigations —which seems to be the typical situation.

16   Foreign Ownership and the Structure of Canadian Industry*

Task Force on the Structure of Canadian Industry

An attempt has been made to assess empirically the role of non-resident firms in the Canadian economy, with respect to size of firms and contribution to industrial concentration. It is widely believed that foreign-controlled firms in Canada are larger than domestic firms. This impression is confirmed by data compiled under CALURA.[1] Well over half of the assets of foreign-controlled firms—the criterion used being foreign ownership of 50 per cent or more of the voting stock—is, in 1963, in companies each having net assets of over $50 million and over two-fifths are in companies each having net assets of over $100 million. By contrast, among domestically-owned corporations, only just over one-third of the assets are in corporations

---

[7]Rosenbluth, "Concentration and Monopoly in the Canadian Economy," p. 204.
*From: *Foreign Ownership and the Structure of Canadian Industry*, (Ottawa, Queen's Printer, 1968), pp. 138-49 (reprinted by permission).
[1]Corporations and Labour Returns Act (eds.).

each having net assets of over $50 million and just over one-quarter are in corporations each having net assets of over $100 million. Among the larger corporations, well over half the assets are in foreign-controlled corporations, while among smaller corporations the proportion of foreign-controlled firms is much smaller: the proportion of assets in foreign-controlled corporations rises with the size of the corporation until the latter reaches $25 million, but not much thereafter. Balance of payment statistics on foreign ownership and control—which, unlike CALURA, consolidate related companies in Canada—show much the same results. In 1960, about two-thirds of the capital of foreign-controlled enterprises is in large firms with more than $25 million capital each. The proportion is considerably higher for firms in petroleum and natural gas as well as mining and smelting, and considerably lower for firms in the merchandising, financial and service sectors. Well over half of the manufacturing activity in large enterprises is foreign controlled, and not much less than one-half is United States controlled. This striking difference in size between domestic and foreign firms is not entirely a matter of "industry mix", that is, it does not appear to result simply because foreign firms happen to predominate in industries characterized by large firms for reasons other than nationality of ownership. Of 81 narrowly defined manufacturing industries in 1963, 66 show a larger average firm size for foreign-controlled firms than Canadian firms, 13 show a larger average firm size for Canadian firms and in 2 industries average firm size is about the same.

Using CALURA and other data, an attempt has been made to classify the ownership of 743 of the largest Canadian corporations. It is estimated that 380 are foreign controlled and 363 Canadian controlled. Slightly more than half of the pre-tax profits of these companies accrued to the foreign-controlled companies. Of the 380 foreign-controlled firms, 99.9 per cent to 100 per cent of the profits accrued to non-residents for 221 of these firms. Of the 743 firms, non-residents derive 50 per cent or more of the profits for 381, or more than half of them. Of the 74 of these firms in mining, quarrying and oil wells, 47 are foreign controlled; of the 351 firms in manufacturing, 221 are foreign controlled. In contrast, of the 155 firms in finance, 106 are Canadian controlled.

There is a correlation, when different industries are compared, between the proportion of an industry's business that is foreign controlled and the degree to which output is concentrated in a few firms. In terms of broad sectors of the economy, it is known that agriculture, construction, services and trade have predominantly low concentration and a low proportion of foreign control, while manufacturing, mining, smelting, and oil refining have both high concentration and a high proportion of foreign control. But there are exceptions to this correlation at the sectoral level, with both utilities and railways having high concentration and a low proportion of foreign control. A more detailed analysis made for eighteen of the twenty largest manufacturing industries, compares the ranking of industries according to degree of foreign control (from balance of payments data for 1961) with the ranking of concentration ratios in Canada (1948) and the United States (1963). In both cases the rankings are correlated, that is, foreign ownership in Canada tends to be associated with a concentrated industrial structure in both Canada and the United States. When industries are grouped according to the degree of foreign control and matched with their relevant median concentration ratios, there is a tendency for the medians to fall with declining foreign control. Both high concentration and a high proportion of foreign control are characteristic of motor vehicles, petroleum refining, smelting and refining, and industrial chemicals. There are, however, exceptions to this association between foreign control and concentration, of which the most important are iron and steel mills, and slaughtering and meat packing, both of which have high concentration and low foreign control. A correlation between industrial concentration and degree of foreign control has also been found for other countries. In sum, foreign control tends to concentrate in the leading firms in Canadian industries. This is not to say that industries are concentrated simply because of foreign control. Rather it may be that foreign direct investment goes substantially into industries which are concentrated because of economies of large scale and absolute cost advantages.

The relationship between concentration and foreign control can also be examined by defining foreign control not in terms of the proportion of an industry's total business carried on by all foreign-controlled firms but by the number of foreign firms among the industry's largest firms. On the basis of CALURA data for manufacturing, the degree of concentration has been measured by.the percentage of the industry's sales in the eight largest firms. Where the eight firms accounted for 90 per cent or more of sales, on the average 4 were foreign controlled and 2 were United States controlled. The corresponding figures for 70 to 89 per cent of sales were 5 and 4; for 40 to 69 per cent of sales, 4 and 3, and for under 40 per cent of sales, 4 and 3. Thus, the incidence of foreign control of the largest firms is exceptionally high with "medium-high" concentration of 70 to 89 per cent, while, in the most highly concentrated industries, the incidence of foreign control is no higher than in the industries with low concentration. For United States-controlled firms among the leading eight, their number is exceptionally low in the most highly concentrated industries and, again, exceptionally high in the industries with "medium-high" concentration. When other sources of data are utilized to correct the deficiency of CALURA in not consolidating parent and subsidiary, what is evident is a great deal of variety in the role of foreign-controlled firms among the Canadian giants (mostly firms with assets of $100 million or more). Foreign firms have over 90 per cent of the assets of all leading firms in petroleum products, tobacco, rubber, aircraft, and automobiles, and between 50 and 90 per cent in chemicals, mining and smelting, and electrical products. In contrast the percentage of foreign control is very low among the leading firms in cotton goods, structural steel, cement products, transportation industries, utilities, banks, trust and mortgage companies, and is a little higher, but still very low in food industries, insurance, alcoholic beverages, steel, and telephones. One inference from these findings is that, while foreign control tends to concentrate in the leading firms of those industries in which foreign direct investment is substantial, this tendency does not depend on the relative share of total output controlled by the leading firms. Furthermore, the correlation between concentration and foreign ownership does not preclude the existence of leading firms, and giant firms, which are Canadian-owned.

While no clear trend is discernible over time with respect to the concentration ratios, as was noted above . . . there is a predominant, though not a very pronounced trend, towards a decrease in the relative importance of foreign-controlled firms among the leading oligopolists. As measured by the proportion of foreign-controlled assets among the assets of the leading 4 firms and the leading 8 firms, respectively, there is a decrease in the relative importance of foreign control in 9 industries, no significant change in 9 others, and an increase in only 3 cases. Decreasing foreign control among the oligopolists is found both in the industries in which concentration is increasing and the industries in which concentration is decreasing but, on the basis of a count of industries, it is slightly more important in the industries in which concentration is falling. The industries in which there is no significant change in concentration are typically also industries in which there is no significant change in the importance of foreign control among the leading firms.

The acquisition of firms through merger is a means by which dominant firms emerge and then maintain their position, and hence keep concentration ratios high, and also a means by which direct investment can take place, that is, the take-over of a Canadian firm by a foreign firm. While not much is known about mergers in Canada and, in particular, no empirical study exists on the causes and consequences of foreign take-overs, an attempt has been made to investigate whether foreign-controlled firms have a greater tendency to acquire others through merger than domestically-controlled firms. (Comprehensive information on mergers for the years 1945 to 1961 was collected under the Combines Investigation Act. Merger activity on the part of acquiring firms is measured by the total assets of the acquired firms. To determine whether merger activity is disproportionately high or low, it is related to capital invested, as used in the statistics on Canada's international investment position, by foreign and domestically controlled firms respectively.) On the basis of tentative findings, it would appear that, for the period as a whole, Canadian firms were responsible for a disproportionately low amount of merger activity and foreign firms as a whole for a disproportionately high amount of merger activity. Since it does not appear that United States-controlled firms were responsible for an exceptionally high proportion of merger activity, the inference is that firms controlled overseas have been responsible for a disproportionately high share of merger activity. In manufacturing the proportion of merger activity by Canadian-controlled firms is about equal to their relative importance in the economic sector, that by United States-controlled firms lower, and that by firms controlled overseas higher. In the petroleum and natural gas industries, mining, and merchandising, the Canadian share of merger activity is low, and the United States share is high. The overseas share is disproportionately low in mining and high in merchandising.

As industries expand, there might be expected to be a tendency towards an increase in competition through the entry of more firms of efficient size. But this will not happen to the extent that there are high barriers to entry because of the advantages, real or contrived of established oligopolistic firms or to the extent that merger activity by the oligopolists reduces the number of firms. Since foreign control is correlated with oligopoly, industries in which foreign control is important might be expected to show less of an increase in the number of firms than other industries as markets expand. On the other hand, to the extent that the direct investment firm has superior access to capital, technology, et cetera, than domestic firms, and insofar as there is a tendency for all of the leading firms in a particular industry in the United States to move into Canada, thereby making barriers to entry virtually irrelevant, it might be expected that industries that have attracted foreign direct investment would show a greater increase in the number of firms for a given expansion of the market than other industries. The examination of very unsatisfactory evidence suggests that there is no significant difference between industries in which foreign control is important, and those in which it is not, with respect to the response of the number of firms to changing industry size. A possible explanation for this tentative finding is that factors making for a high rate of entry of foreign-controlled firms in the Canadian market have been balanced by the tendency of foreign-controlled firms to engage in merger to a greater extent than domestically-controlled firms.

Two main points emerge from the analysis of foreign control and industrial concentration. First, many oligopolistic firms in Canada are foreign controlled and many foreign-controlled firms in Canada are oligopolists. Second, foreign direct investment appears to have had both positive and negative effects on the degree of competitiveness of the Canadian economy. It has not clearly increased competitiveness. The first point, while widely known, has implications less widely appreciated.

The economic and political effects of foreign control depend on the market position of the controlling groups. Oligopoly means power—a freedom to determine goals that is not possessed by small and perfectly competitive firms. Because foreign control in Canada is substantially embodied in firms with economic power, it involves a diminution of decision-making within Canada that it would not have if it were embodied entirely in many firms actively engaged in price competition and fully subject to the discipline of the market.

17   Problems of High Industrial Concentration*

Gideon Rosenbluth

A. Monopolistic Business Policies

When markets are controlled by a small number of firms and entry of new firms is difficult, the way is open for monopolistic price and output policies. The general characteristics of such policies—though not the details—can be deduced from simple economic models on the assumption that firms seek profits. This is . . . a reasonable assumption. Concrete examples of such policies in Canada come to light in the reports under the Combines Act, and sometimes in other government investigations. On the whole, however, the secrecy surrounding the operation of modern private business forces us to deduce the nature of these policies from the basic characteristics of the business system, and the circumstantial evidence of concentration data, entry conditions, characteristics of prices and price changes, and so on. In the paragraphs that follow, a few leading types of monopolistic policies will be discussed.

Price Agreements

The most basic and best known type of monopolistic policy is the price agreement. Firms selling the same or related commodities agree on the prices they will charge, thus preventing a competitive bidding for business. Price agreements are not likely to be effective when there are many small firms and entry is easy, unless there is an elaborate apparatus for "enforcement". The reason is that a small firm or a new entrant has strong incentive to gain business by slightly undercutting the agreed price. On the other hand when the market is substantially in the hands of a small number of large firms, an agreement can be effectively maintained without much administration, since each firm knows that an undercutting of the price would have a substantial effect on the business of its rivals and would therefore be followed by immediate retaliation. Such agreements are therefore often maintained by conversations and telephone calls, leaving no documentary evidence that the Combines Administration could take to court.

The majority of the cases reported upon under the Combines Investigation Act have been price agreements under conditions of moderately high concentration, where enforcement of the agreement was sufficiently difficult to result in documentary evidence. For example the Canadian National Millers' Association maintained a system of price control in Eastern Canada

---

*From: G. Rosenbluth, "Concentration and Monopoly in the Canadian Economy," in M. Oliver (ed.), *Social Purpose of Canada* (Toronto, University of Toronto Press, 1961), pp. 212-24 (reprinted by permission of author and publisher).

described as follows: "Briefly, the system of control over prices has been exercised by the establishment of separate selling structures for Ontario, Quebec and the Maritime Provinces. This involved, within each structure, agreement upon prices and terms of sale, price differentials for the various grades of flour, price differentials for the different types of packaging and classification of customers. . . . In addition . . . indirect methods have also been agreed upon to prevent individual mills from reducing prices. . . . Agreements of this nature . . . related mainly to terms of sale and discounts. They have also included such matters as cash discounts, time limitations on shipments, non-repricing and non-cancellation of contracts except under certain conditions, cartage charges, legitimate storage points and storage allowances, carrying charges on undelivered balances and the effective dates of price changes. . . . Similar agreements were in force in Western Canada."[1]

In recent years there have also been reports under the Combines Investigation Act on price agreements in the sale of rubber goods, paper products, wire and cable, and in other industries.

Monopoly and oligopoly

When a market is substantially controlled by one firm or a very small number of firms, monopolistic prices can be maintained without agreement or any communication among firms. Such situations have not become the subject of combines investigations, except in a few cases where a deliberate policy of establishing a monopoly position was involved. There are, however, many important industries in Canada where the degree of concentration is so high that monopolistic prices can be maintained without agreement.

Price Discrimination

When competition is restricted by high concentration and obstacles to entry, price discrimination flourishes. This term denotes establishment by a seller of price differentials between different classes of customers, differentials which do not correspond to differences in cost. A firm can make higher profits if it charges each class of customers "what the traffic will bear" than it would if all customers paid the same price, but this practice cannot be maintained if the customers can shop around in a competitive market or can buy from one another. Discrimination between different classes of customers is very often a feature of price structures established by agreement. Discrimination in favour of a large buyer also frequently serves the purpose of giving this buyer an advantage over his business competitors in the markets in which he sells. In the groceries trade, for example, it is urged by representatives of small retailers that the competitive strength of the large chains is due in part to discrimination by suppliers. A Combines Branch inquiry showed that in 1954 chain stores and "voluntary chains"

---

[1]*Flour Milling Industry*, Report of Commissioner, Combines Investigation Act (Ottawa, 1949), pp. 16, 17, 49.

received "special discounts and allowances" amounting to 2.1 per cent and 2.3 per cent of their purchases, while wholesalers and other accounts received 0.9 per cent and 0.6 per cent.[2]

Policies designed to change the market structure

Since profits are to be gained from a market position that permits monopolistic practices, a great deal of the skill and energy of businessmen is directed to the establishment and protection of monopolistic business positions and the suppression of competition. Much of the business conduct that looks at first sight like failure to seek maximum profit is in fact directed at the development and protection of monopoly positions.

Where imports are freely available even a highly concentrated business structure does not permit monopolistic pricing. Much energy is therefore devoted to the suppression of import competition. In many cases, of course, import competition is controlled by the fact that the Canadian producers are subsidiaries of United States or other foreign parent companies. In other cases Canadian producers are themselves the chief importers and thus control the price of imports. Often strenuous efforts are made to ensure that tariffs are kept high enough to permit monopolistic pricing. Imports of radios, television sets and other electronic equipment are prevented by the operation of a patent pool,[3] which has become the object of US anti-trust action against the parent companies of the participants. In other industries Canadian producers have participated in international cartels which have generally assured for the producers of each country a monopoly of their home market.[4]

A major way in which the number of competitors has been reduced, or its expansion slowed down, has been the merger of two or more existing firms. There is hardly a firm among today's giant corporations that has not grown to a significant extent by merger. In many mergers, of course, the improvement of market control is not the main object, and often it plays no part at all in the motivation of the merging firms. There are, however, many instances where a reduction in competition is at least one of the objectives, and still more where it is the result. The merger of the Toronto and Dominion Banks in 1956 significantly increased concentration in commercial banking (and the merger, announced in 1961, of the Imperial Bank and the Bank of Commerce, raised it further). Canadian Breweries was formed in 1930, with the purpose, according to a document found in the company's files "of ultimately acquiring the ownership or control of a sufficient number of selected brewing corporations in the Province of

---

[2]*Discriminatory Pricing Practices in the Grocery Trade* (Ottawa, 1948), Table 5-1, p. 115.

[3]See *e.g.*, Royal Commission on Canada's Economic Prospects, *The Electronics Industry in Canada* (Ottawa, 1956), pp. 24, 25.

[4]*Canada and International Cartels,* Report of the Commissioner, Combines Investigation Act (Ottawa, 1946).

Ontario to establish itself as a dominant factor in the brewing business within that province." After a number of mergers had been completed its founder wrote: "I am sure that we now have the power to control prices and sales practices of the industry, and while it may be necessary for us to start local price wars here and there to discipline a small competitor, I am sure the profits will prove most gratifying to the shareholders."[5] Many postwar mergers have involved the acquisition of Canadian companies by United States or British firms and have thus further increased the importance of foreign control in the Canadian economy.

Price wars, local price cutting and other restrictive practices have been used to prevent new firms from getting a foothold, to drive out existing competitors, or to soften them up for a profitable merger. Thus, a merger of zinc oxide firms was preceded by a price war that had the specific objective of eliminating competition. Similarly the record of the Eddy Match Company shows that it maintained its monopoly by repeated local price cutting followed by absorption of independent firms. These price wars usually involved price discrimination. For example, "when . . . independent manufacturers quoted lower prices, Eddy Match generally met their competition, not by lowering the price of its standard products, but by introducing special brands, sometimes called 'fighting brands,' at reduced prices. These were sold only in the areas affected by the new competition, and only in limited quantities and for limited periods."[6]

Advertising and other promotional activities are of course a common method of competition, but they often serve the purpose of building up or defending a protected market for a particular product or brand. As has been pointed out, in some industries, such as cigarettes, the heavy advertising expenditures of existing firms raise the capital requirements of a new competitor far beyond those called for by technological conditions, and thus greatly increase the barriers to entry of new firms.

Numerous legal devices designed for other purposes have been used to restrict the number of competitors or to regulate competition. The use of patents to bar imports has already been mentioned. Patents have also been used to restrict the number of domestic producers, to control their selling prices, to control resale prices, and to control the use of unpatented articles in conjunction with the patented one. While the purpose of patents is often interpreted as the stimulation of invention by granting a temporary monopoly to the inventor, in practice patent monopolies have been extended far beyond the period of validity of a single patent, and patent rights have been

---

[5]*Report of the Director of Investigation and Research, Combines Investigation Act, 1956* (Ottawa, 1956), p. 10. In a recent court decision the company was acquitted of the charge of having violated the combines legislation. The acquittal was based on the grounds that the merger had not achieved a virtually complete monopoly, and that the price of beer was under some degree of provincial control. See section IVB.

[6]*Matches,* Report of Commissioner, Combines Investigation Act (Ottawa, 1949), p. 124.

used to restrict the supply and raise the price of patented and unpatented articles.

Close ties between existing firms and their suppliers have on occasion provided these firms with the support of their suppliers in their attempt to eliminate competitors. Thus the Zinc Oxide Company of Canada was given secret price concessions by its supplier of zinc, Hudson Bay Mining and Smelting Company, in support of its price war which ended in the elimination of one of its competitors by merger.

Monopolistic pricing policies and attempts to restrict entry are not confined to conditions of high concentration or giant firms. Small firms, particularly in retailing services, and contracting, have attempted to control prices through trade associations or by inducing suppliers to enforce minimum resale prices. The entry of competitors in a given locality is often obstructed by licensing requirements which may have had the original purpose of safeguarding the quality of the service rendered or sold (for example, skilled trades). Finally there are the well developed arrangements for eliminating competition in the sale of farm products many of which operate under provincial marketing legislation.

B. Inequality and Inefficiency

Monopolistic business policies have important effects both on the distribution of income and on the efficiency with which the economy operates. Receipts of the firms that benefit from such policies are higher than they would be under more competitive conditions and these higher receipts are mainly reflected in higher profits and higher incomes of corporate executives. Higher profits benefit the stockholders, either in the form of dividends or in the form of retained profits that raise the values behind the shares. We have already seen that stock ownership is highly concentrated in the top income groups, apart from the ownership of Canadian stocks by foreign corporations and individuals. The benefits derived from monopolistic policies therefore both in the form of profits and in the form of executive salaries, tend to increase the inequality of the income distribution, to raise the proportion of income going to the top income groups and to United States and other foreign owners. In some cases a part of the benefits of monopoly income can be shared by the employees of the monopolistic firm if, for example, they have a strong union.

The effect on the distribution of incomes is what is usually in the critic's mind when monopolistic practices are condemned. Similarly, the defences made of monopolistic pricing usually involve the argument that it is socially desirable or just to raise the income of a particular group by this device. What is often not realized is that monopolistic policies also render the operation of the economic system inefficient. First, they permit and therefore tend to promote technical inefficiency in the firms enjoying monopoly profit. Under competitive conditions, when profit margins are narrow, technical inefficiency is punished by the disappearance of profit in the backward firm.

Under monopolistic conditions, however, a certain degree of inefficiency will reduce but not eliminate profit, and the fear of lower profits is a much weaker incentive to efficiency than the fear of losses.

Secondly a good deal of the advertising and promotional activity which is fostered in oligopoly situations represents a socially wasteful use of labour, materials and capital. It is of course useful and indeed necessary, in any complex economy, to spread information about the goods that are available and their prices. A good deal of advertising and promotional activity is, however, not designed to convey information, but rather to change the buyers' tastes or to induce irrational behaviour. Generally speaking the pursuit of either one of these objectives does not represent a socially useful employment of labour and resources. Moreover, a good deal of advertising expenditure does not even succeed in influencing buyers' tastes, since to a considerable extent the competitive promotional efforts of rival firms neutralize one another.

Finally, monopolistic policies lead to *economic* inefficiency. An efficient economic system requires not only that goods and services be produced without waste of resources, in the technically most efficient manner, but also that the relative quantities that are produced be responsive to "what people want". The precise meaning of this requirement has been the subject of much discussion by economists. It is customary and useful to separate the question of economic efficiency from the question of the distribution of incomes by assuming that "what people want" corresponds to what they are willing to pay for. On that basis the high profit margins or inflated costs of the monopolized industries indicate that the system is producing too little of the monopolized output in relation to the output of more competitive industries. The prices people are willing to pay for additional supplies of the monopolized items are much higher in relation to the cost of the labour and resources required to produce them, than is the case in competitive industries. The system would therefore be more efficient if it allocated more of its labour and resources to supplying the goods presently monopolized and less to those produced under competitive conditions.[7]

Inequality and inefficiency must therefore be expected in an economy in which monopolistic conditions are widespread, as is the case in Canada.

---

[7]A reader of the manuscript has objected to this conclusion on the grounds that the demand for monopolized goods may be "inflated" by advertising so that in the absence of monopoly *and advertising* the efficient output might be *less* than the monopoly output. However, the criterion of efficiency based on "what people want" is violated by monopolistic market structures, regardless of whether these wants are conditioned by custom, education, government propaganda, advertising or anything else. Moreover, the view that demand for a particular product is "inflated" by advertising implies a judgment that the influence of advertising on consumer tastes is undesirable. I would agree with such a judgment in some particular cases, though on the average there is no reason to suppose that the quality of consumers' tastes is either damaged or improved by commercial advertising. Even if it were damaged, however, it would not follow that to deprive consumers of what they want through monopoly is a suitable remedy.

Monopolistic conditions are not, of course, the only source of inequality and inefficiency, and it is doubtful whether they are the most important. We do not, in fact, know "how much" inequality of incomes or inefficient use of resources is to be attributed to monopoly. Recently it has been suggested that the problem is not serious. Suggestions to this effect have been made by the economist J. K. Galbraith in two successive books that have received much publicity.[8] In the first he suggested that both the inequality and the inefficiency due to monopoly are reduced by the development of "counter-vailing power". A monopoly on one side of a market leads to defensive organization on the other, and when both sides of the market are monopo-lized, the result of bargaining will be more like that emerging from competi-tion than the result of one-sided monopoly would be. Certain historical trends seem to be in agreement with Galbraith's theory. Monopolistic organization of big business was followed by the development of co-operative marketing and finally government controlled marketing in agriculture, and by the growth of labour unions. It is, however, hardly realistic to suggest that the power of such organizations rivals that of big business. Much propa-ganda to the contrary notwithstanding, a labour union cannot control the supply of labour. Its only real bargaining weapon is the strike, and its financial resources are slight indeed compared to those available to large corporations. A union's leadership cannot "order" a strike; it can strike only if a large number of workmen, with insignificant individual savings and small collective savings, individually vote to sacrifice their livelihood tem-porarily in the uncertain expectation of a longer-run gain. A large corpora-tion, by contrast is centrally directed by its board or an even smaller group and the major beneficiaries of its operation, executives and stockholders, have, individually and collectively, high incomes and considerable wealth which render their livelihood independent of temporary interruptions in the firm's operation.

Moreover, the theory of countervailing power breaks down completely when it comes to the consumer. Particular groups of workers or farmers may be sufficiently strongly organized to gain a share in monopoly profits, but in their capacity as consumers, all members of the public are exploited by monopoly.

The great majority of individuals participate in the economic system as sellers of their labour and as buyers of "consumer goods". Hence anything that raises the price of goods relative to their labour cost is against the interest of the majority of the public, though it may benefit a particular minority. Monopolistic business policies and inefficiency clearly have this effect.

Galbraith further suggests that economists lack a sense of proportion in emphasizing the inefficiency and waste due to monopoly, since output can

---

[8]*American Capitalism* (Cambridge, Mass., 1952); *The Affluent Society* (Cambridge, Mass., 1958).

be raised much more effectively by stimulating innovation, increasing the rate of capital investment, and reducing cyclical unemployment than by curbing monopoly. This judgment cannot be put to an empirical test at present, but even if it is correct, it would not furnish reasonable grounds for complacency about the problem of monopoly. Moreover, as indicated in subsequent sections, there are reasonable grounds for the view that the prevalence of large corporations and high concentration in an economy renders the stabilization of employment more difficult and does not promote technological progress.

C. Depression and Inflation

The prevention of serious cyclical unemployment has become a generally accepted goal of government policy in Canada and the United States. Fiscal and monetary policies by which governments can pursue this aim all involve an increase in government-induced spending when serious unemployment threatens, in order to prevent or reverse a decline in total spending. If such policies are to be effective, an increase in spending must be promptly reflected in an increase in output and employment. They are rendered ineffective to the extent that the business response to increased spending is an increase in prices while substantial unemployment remains.

In a flexible and competitive economy substantial price increases will not occur until the volume of unemployment is very low. Where large firms predominate and concentration is high, however, firms have substantial control over their prices and can raise them in response to the pressure of increased demand instead of expanding output.

The behaviour of the "administered prices," controlled by large firms under conditions of high concentration, attracted considerable attention in the thirties. The evidence available at that time suggested that such prices had a tendency to be "rigid"—to fall less than other prices in the downswing of the business cycle and to rise less in the upswing. The behaviour of "administered prices" in the last decade, however, suggests a different pattern. They have shown a tendency to rise more than others when business is improving, and to fall less when conditions are relatively slack. Table 1 shows recent United States price increases for steel, machinery and "motive products" (automobiles, railway rolling stock, etc.) compared with price increases for other industrial products. This evidence suggests the possibility that the behaviour of administered prices has changed, because businessmen now expect the government to stabilize demand and underwrite reasonably full employment, whereas before the war they had to contend with violent fluctuations in demand and employment which rendered "price rigidity" a sensible defensive strategy. Thus, where "administered prices" are a major factor in the price structure, government policies to raise or maintain employment are likely to operate in an inefficient manner and to achieve their objective only at the cost of persistent upward pressure on the price structure.

Where a strong union exists it may secure for its members a share of the gains resulting from rising administered prices. Indeed, it has frequently been suggested that the pressure for higher wages is the main *cause* of the rise in prices. Strong unions have, however, developed only in response to high concentration in business and the greater-than-average wage advances have been secured in highly concentrated industries in which, typically,

Table 1

Changes in "Administered" and Other Prices in the United States

| | Percentage price increase | | |
	1947-51	1951-55	1955-58
All commodities other than farm and food products	22	1	8
Iron and steel products	37	14	20
Machinery and motive products	29	8	17

SOURCE: O. Eckstein and G. Fromm, *Steel and the Postwar Inflation*, Joint Economic Committee (Washington, 1959), p. 5.

profit margins too have risen.[9] Thus, high business concentration may reasonably be considered as the basic factor in the inflationary pressure from administered prices.

D. Political and Social Implications

A small firm has relatively little scope for influencing the technological, economic, political and social environment in which it operates. In most respects it will either be impossible for the firm to exert such influence, or else the cost involved will exceed the financial benefit to be expected. As a firm grows, however, the range of aspects of the environment over which it can profitably exert an influence increases.

Economists have analysed the difference in the firm's power to influence price, and in the profitable extent of its "selling costs" (expenditure on advertising, salesmen, etc.) that comes with a difference in firm size in relation to the market. The analysis can, however, be extended to many other aspects of the environment. Large firms find it worth while to engage in research, to devote a considerable expenditure to "public relations" and "employee relations", to operate training programmes, to influence governments, educational institutions and media of mass communications. These are aspects of the firm's environment where no influence can be exerted unless the expenditure is large, and where such expenditure is not worth while unless the benefit to the firm is applied to a large output. The employment of specialized personnel for functions of this type is only worth while for firms operating on a large scale or for co-operating groups of firms.

---

[9]O. Eckstein and G. Fromm, *Steel and the Postwar Inflation,* Joint Economic Committee (Washington, 1959), pp. 14-21, 32-33.

The distinction we are making between the range of functions of small firms and large firms is essentially a matter of degree. Even quite small firms find it worth their while to exert political influence at the municipal government level but a firm has to be larger before it can profitably perform this function at the federal level. Firms that are large in relation to the government of Newfoundland may be small in relation to the federal government, and firms, domestic and foreign, that are large in relation to the federal government may be small in relation to the government of the United States.

A good case can be made for the view that all the functions of business firms that are directed at influencing the environment are either socially undesirable or better performed by other agencies. In the case of monopolistic practices—those operations on the business environment that are commonly considered "economic"—the undesirable features have been adequately discussed in the literature, and we have referred to them in the preceding section. Here we shall select certain other aspects of business policy for more detailed review.

Political influence

There is no doubt that the activities of government have become a major factor in influencing the fortunes of business firms. Correspondingly the function of influencing government activity must be an increasingly important aspect of business policy. With the increase in government expenditure at all levels, taxes have become a dominant element in the business cost structure, and government contracts an increasingly important market for firms in a growing range of industries. In other industries—such as residential construction—the indirect effects of government expenditure and the government's monetary and fiscal policies have become major determinants of market conditions. Governments are called upon to help businessmen in securing foreign markets and to protect them from foreign competition. Government legislation and regulation establishes the legal framework in which business operates and many industries are subject to a good deal of regulation.

Little is known in detail about the way in which governmental processes are influenced in the interest of business firms. Corporate contributions to the campaign funds of both major parties appear to be standard practice, and are commonly divided in the ratio of 60 to 40 between the government and the opposition.[10] These contributions form the background for the use of techniques of persuasion that range from formal briefs and argument before commissions, committees, etc., to the most informal personal contacts.

The official attitude of governments and politicians to these activities is variable and often not clearly defined. Personal gifts of money or in kind

---

[10]R. M. Dawson, *The Government of Canada* (Toronto, 1957), p. 567.

designed to secure favourable action are generally considered improper, but contributions to party funds are fairly openly solicited. Politicians seem to differ in their evaluation of the use of stock options or inside information permitting favourable operations on the stock exchange. "Lobbying" and other persuasive techniques not coupled with offers of personal advantage are generally regarded as justifiable business activity.

How far is the exercise of political influence by business firms compatible with the values underlying democratic government? No serious student of politics would suggest that the citizen's attempt to influence government should be confined to the ballot box. In the modern theory of democracy the attempts of various interest groups to *organize* in order to gain favourable political action is recognized as part of the democratic process. The underlying value judgment remains, however, that expressed in the principle, "one man one vote"; political power should be approximately equally distributed.

If concentration were low and business firms small, the exercise of political influence by business firms would not be in conflict with this principle. When, however, economic power is highly concentrated in large corporations, as it is in Canada, those in control of these corporations exercise political power far out of proportion to their number. Hence highly concentrated private economic power conflicts with political democracy. This conflict is probably a far more serious consequence of the rise of great corporations than the economic inefficiency and inequality of incomes discussed above.

It should be stressed that the exercise of political influence does not reflect any "sinister machinations" on the part of corporate interests, but is simply the result of the rational pursuit of profit, within the bounds set by law and current moral standards, in an age when legislation and government activity are important features of the business environment. In fact, it often does not require any political activity at all, on the part of the corporation, beyond the standard contribution to campaign funds. Since the party machines are in fact dependent on large business contributions, the interests of large corporations are bound to be very influential in both legislation and administration. Politicians must constantly strive to achieve a balance between the aspects of legislation and administration that appeal to a large number of voters, and those that appeal to the sources of campaign funds.

In federal politics the influence of concentrated business power is probably a somewhat less serious problem than in provincial politics, since a greater variety of business interests is involved and the government is financially stronger in relation to the financial power of large corporations. Provincial governments on the other hand, are in many cases financially much weaker than individual giant corporations. At the same time their control over natural resources combines with their financial inability to exploit these resources themselves to render them most profitable targets for the exercise of influence by large international corporations. In this respect they are in fact in exactly the same position as the Middle East oil kingdoms.

Public relations

Political influence is exerted not only directly but also indirectly by influencing the views of the electorate. Such influence is an important aspect of the increasingly important public relations activities of large corporations. More generally, public relations activity has the objective of rendering the public sympathetic to the corporation concerned and to business in general, as well as to policies favoured by business groups. Public relations includes the guidance of the conduct of the corporation's employees and the performance of corporate good works. A great deal of it, however, is concerned with influencing the public through the media of mass communication—newspapers, periodicals, television and radio. Here again, the influence of the large corporation is to a considerable extent indirect. Its advertisements are generally confined to selling its goods, but since this advertising constitutes the major source of revenue for newspapers, periodicals and broadcasting stations, these media must strive to satisfy the advertisers in their choice of material for publication and broadcasting.

The efficiency of public relations activity is increased by the fact that the mass media themselves are a highly concentrated industry. Over the years mergers of newspapers have brought matters to the point where in most areas there is only one local paper. Moreover, many papers are linked by common ownership in a "chain". Radio and television stations are local monopolies or duopolies, often under common ownership with the local newspaper. Public ownership of the CBC constitutes an exception of major importance to the concentration of private control over the mass media.

Independent and critical views can reach the public only through a few periodicals of limited circulation or on some of the CBC programmes. On any controversial issue, large sums will be spent to put the view favoured by large corporations before the public through monopolized channels of communication, and other views get only a very limited hearing. A good example is the current tendency of communications media to impress on the public an unfavourable picture of labour unions.

The public relations interests of large corporations present formidable obstacles to the efficient operation of the democratic process. On major issues of public policy the public does not get a balanced presentation of alternative views. Some slight counterbalance to the corporate point of view is provided by the socialized element in broadcasting (although here, too, as has recently been shown, the presentation of "controversial" points of view is severely limited) and by a few periodicals with very small circulation.

Social services and education

In Canada governments do not accept full responsibility for social services and higher education. Hence funds required for the operation of "charitable institutions" and universities must be laboriously collected from private individuals and corporations. The undistributed profits of large corporations constitute a major source of such funds. The "charitable contributions" of such corporations are almost negligible in relation to their total profits, but constitute an important element in the revenues of universities and social service agencies.[11] Naturally enough, this situation is reflected in the control of these institutions; the large corporations and their executive staffs are well represented on the governing boards of universities, hospitals and charitable institutions. Naturally also, the activities of these institutions are influenced by the corporate scale of values. Funds are more readily available for facilities and fellowships in the natural sciences, engineering, and commerce than in the humanities and social sciences.

Thus, as governments have refused to accept what should be their responsibility, the large corporations have in some measure become "private" government agencies. They levy their own private "sales tax" which is included in the controlled price of their product and apply the proceeds to the provision of social services, education and research. They differ from government agencies only in one respect, but it is of major importance: there is no social control over their activities.

18 Dominant Corporations and the Economic Elite*

John Porter

The economic élite is here defined as the directors of the 183 dominant corporations [in Canada]. Many of this group hold more than one directorship in the dominant corporations, and at the same time hold directorships in the principal financial institutions. The group would seem to be a reservoir of men who are able to assume these roles because they have demonstrated skills in the handling of economic resources. It may be that

---

[11]In 1958 corporate grants to universities and colleges constituted only 0.36 per cent of corporate profits, but were 7.2 per cent of the capital and operating expenditures of these institutions (*Financial Post*, September 12, 1959, p. 13, quoting a report by the Industrial Foundation of Education).

*From: John Porter, "Concentration of Economic Power and the Economic Elite in Canada", *Canadian Journal of Economics and Political Science*, Vol. XXII, no. 2, (May 1956), pp. 199-220 (reprinted by permission of author and publisher).

some of these directorships are honorific, but it is also likely that each person is active in at least one of them. Whether their roles in the economic system are active or honorific they are recognized legally as the trustees of large economic resources.

The directors of 13 of the 183 dominant corporations could not be identified. Ten of these 13 corporations are wholly owned American subsidiaries. In the 170 examined there are 1,613 directorships, 243 (or 15 per cent) of which are held by American residents who are assumed to be American citizens. Fifty-three (or 3 per cent) are held by residents of the United Kingdom who are assumed to be British citizens.[1] The remaining 1,317, or 82 per cent of all the directorships of the 170 corporations, are held by Canadian residents, but it cannot be assumed that all of them are Canadian citizens. No doubt a few of these 1,317 directorships, perhaps no more than 100, are held by American citizens who are resident officer-directors of those firms in Canada which are wholly owned subsidiaries of American parent firms. It must be remembered, however, that by migrating to the "land of opportunity" the individual can achieve upward mobility. For this reason what might have been temporary Canadian residence will change after a time into Canadian citizenship. Professor Brebner has pointed out how Canada has been a halting-place for "birds of passage".[2] Many of the present economic élite who are now Canadian citizens were born outside Canada, and had Canada not provided opportunities they too might have flown on. It seems reasonable to consider the Canadian residents who hold the 1,317 directorships as the economic élite. It is hoped that further studies will clarify the effect of migration on social mobility in Canada.

The economic élite, then, consists of the 922 individuals who hold the 1,317 directorships. Of these, 203 individuals, about 22 per cent, hold more than one directorship in the dominant corporations. Most of them of course hold directorships in other corporations which are not classified as dominant. The 203 who hold more than one directorship hold altogether 598 (or 45.3 per cent) of all the directorships. The largest number of directorships held by one person is ten.[3] Table 1 . . . shows how the 1,317 directorships are distributed among the 922 individuals. Table 2 . . . contains comparable data for the United States for 1935, although it includes directorships in financial corporations. In both countries a small percentage of the total number of individuals hold a large percentage of the total number of directorships. If the interlocking director is characteristic of developed industrial systems, it would seem that in this respect also Canada has reached the position of the United States.

---

[1] It has beeen pointed out above that a further 119 directorships of American subsidiaries and 11 of United Kingdom subsidiaries could be considered as representing influence outside Canada. However, these Canadian residents are here included in the economic elite in Canada.

[2] J. B. Brebner, *North Atlantic Triangle* (New Haven, Conn., 1945), 227.

[3] This distinction is Mr. E. P. Taylor's.

Table 1

Distribution of 1,317 Directorships of 170* Dominant Corporations among 922 Individuals, Canada, 1951*

No. of director-ships held by one person	Total no. persons	Total no. directorships	Cumulative			
			Directors		Directorships	
			No.	%	No.	%
10	1	10	1	.1	10	.75
9	1	9	2	.2	19	1.43
8	2	16	4	.4	35	2.7
7	3	21	7	.7	56	4.3
6	7	42	14	1.5	98	7.2
5	13	65	27	2.9	163	12.3
4	20	80	47	5.0	243	18.47
3	43	129	90	9.7	372	28.1
2	113	226	203	22.0	598	45.3
1	719	719	922	100.	1,317	100.
TOTALS:	922	1,317				

*183 dominant corporations less 13, the directors of which could not be established.

Table 2

Distribution of 3,544 Directorships in 200 Largest Non-Financial and 50 Largest Financial Corporations among 2,722 individuals, United States, 1935*

No. of director-ships held by one person	Total no. persons	Total no. directorships	Cumulative			
			Directors		Directorships	
			No.	%	No.	%
9	1	9	1	.03	9	.2
8	3	24	4	.1	33	.9
7	6	42	10	.3	75	2.1
6	6	36	16	.5	111	3.1
5	19	95	35	1.3	206	5.8
4	48	192	83	3.	398	11.2
3	102	306	185	6.8	704	19.8
2	303	606	488	17.9	1,310	36.9
1	2,234	2,234	2,722	100.	3,544	100.
TOTALS:	2,722	3,544				

*Adapted from *Bureaucracy and Trusteeship in Large Corporations*, Table 2, p. 6.

The relationship between the non-financial and financial corporations in Canada can be seen by examining the directors of life insurance companies and the chartered banks. For this purpose the nine chartered banks[4] listed in Table 3 . . . and the ten largest life insurance companies listed in Table 4 have been selected. The chartered banks had a total of 203 directors, 5 of whom were United States residents and one British. Of the 197 Canadian directors, 118 together held 297 directorships in the dominant corporations, that is, the banking group held 22.6 per cent of those directorships in the dominant corporations held by Canadian residents. Conversely, the directors of the dominant corporations held 118 out of 203 (or 58 per cent) of the directorships in the chartered banks. It is necessary to keep this converse relationship in mind since it is frequently heard that bank directors are on the boards of other corporations because they are bank directors. It might equally be said that they are bank directors because they are directors of dominant corporations. The banks are no doubt crucial in determining the place of the individual in the economic élite, but their exact function in that respect is not clear. Bank directorships might be honorific posts, but undoubtedly there are advantages for both corporations and banks in having directors in common.[5] None of the bank directors interlock as bank directors.

Like the banks, the life insurance companies are linked through director-ships to the dominant corporations. The ten largest life insurance companies in Canada, arranged in order of gross assets in Table 4 had insurance in force of $9,046,100,000 in 1950.[6] This sum was 56.1 per cent of the total insurance in force of all the 59 companies operating in Canada. The two large American companies, the Metropolitan and the Prudential, are not included in this study. If the insurance in force of these two American firms is added to that of the ten largest Canadian firms, the remaining 47 in Canada share about 23 per cent of the business. The ten Canadian companies have a total of 134 directors, 78 of whom hold 188 (or 14 per cent) of the directorships in the dominant corporations and 55 (or 27 per cent) of the directorships in the nine chartered banks. Conversely, the directors of the dominant corporations held 78 (or 58 per cent) of the directorships in the life insurance companies, and the directors of the chartered banks held 55 (or 41 per cent). These ten life insurance companies are not linked with each other by interlocking directorships, nor are the banks. Thus the positions which many of the economic elite hold on the boards of both life insurance companies and banks confirm their selection as an economic élite.

Another feature of the economic élite in Canada is its regional distribution. Although a majority of its members are from Montreal and Toronto,

---

[4]The Bank of Canada has not been included. The directors of several Crown corporations and other publicly owned economic organizations have been omitted from the economic elite, but are to be included in the bureaucratic elite on the grounds that they work more as officials than entrepreneurs.

[5]Berle and Means, *The Modern Corporation and Private Property*, 231.

[6]*Financial Post* (April 7, 1951).

the centres of economic power, those who belong to other cities tend to hold more than one directorship in corporations whose head offices are located in those other cities. Accordingly, firms in a region such as British Columbia have a large number of directors in common. Furthermore, firms which are national in their operations, particularly if they have branches across the country, have on their boards representatives of the regional élite. No attempt has been made to analyse this process in the dominant corporations but a cursory glance at those which are national, as well as at the banks and insurance companies, will confirm this impression. Regional representation, a characteristic of so many Canadian institutions, is a feature of economic life also. No doubt many of the directorships which are awarded to satisfy this requirement of the social system are honorific, but the fact that they are awarded to certain individuals, that is, the regional élite, and not to others, is further confirmation of the existence of this élite. Many of the 1,317 directorships are no doubt honorific for various reasons, but if all these were eliminated, the economic élite would be the same by virtue of those active directorships which its members hold.

Elite groups are always changing, losing some members and acquiring others, but the present analysis has been concerned with a segment of a complex social structure, during one period of time. Further studies will aim at the more dynamic aspects of social circulation, principally the conditions of entry to the élite.

Table 3

Directors and Gross Assets of Nine Chartered Banks

Bank	No.* directors	Directorships in dominant corps.	Directorships in insurance companies†	Gross* assets 1951 ($ million)
Royal Bank of Canada	29	71	7	2,516
Bank of Montreal	29	73	12	2,222
Canadian Bank of Commerce	35	56	15	1,734
Bank of Nova Scotia	25	21	6	874
Imperial Bank of Canada	19	25	8	535
Bank of Toronto	18	16	1	489
Banque Canadienne Nationale	14	17	2	464
Dominion Bank	20	16	3	458
Provincial Bank of Canada	14	2	1	186
TOTALS:	203‡	297	55	

*Financial Post Survey of Industrials, 1952.
†The 10 Canadian companies listed in Table 4.
‡Includes 5 U.S. residents and 1 U.K. resident. Only 118 of the 203 hold the 297 directorships in the dominant corporations.

Table 4

Directors, Gross Assets, and Insurance in Force, Ten Largest Canadian Life Insurance Companies*

Company	No. of directorst	Directorships in dominant corps.	Insurance‡ in force ($ million)	Gross Assets§ ($ million)
Sun	15	39	1,641	1,597
Manufacturers	9	11	572	414
Canada	15	12	854	388
Great West	13	16	906	385
Mutual of Canada	15	32	1,151	366
London	9	2	1,972	345
Confederation	16	36	650	260
Imperial	15	8	427	168
North American	14	16	459	144
Crown	13	6	414	135
TOTAL:	134"	188	9,046	
Percentage of 59 companies in Canada	—	—	56.1	
Metropolitan*	—	—	2,508	
Prudential*	—	—	1,072	
TOTAL 12 companies			12,626	
TOTAL 59 companies in Canada			16,099	
Percentage, 12 companies of 59			78.4	

*The two American companies, Metropolitan and Prudential, are not included in this study. Their amount of insurance in force is included in the table for comparison only.
†From *Best's Life Reports* (New York), 1950.
‡*Financial Post* (April 7, 1951). Data refer to 1950, Canadian operations only, and include ordinary life, group, and industrial insurance.
§Mainly 1951 and 1952, *Financial Post Corporation Service*.
"Including 1 U.S. resident. Only 78 of the 134 hold the 188 directorships in the dominant corporations.

19   Industrial Organization and Technical Progress*

H. E. English

The Role of Industrial Organization — Theoretical Aspects

In economic analysis, passing judgment on the organization of markets, and of sellers or producers in particular, consists in answering the question: how well do they respond to the revealed preferences of consumers (leaving aside for the moment all consideration of exogenous factors which may affect the quality of those preferences in questionable ways through the distribution of income and the flow of information)? The decision made by sellers as to what to offer in the market place—the main feature of the allocation decision—is really a result of two processes, cost reduction and demand manipulation.

Price theory, in explaining cost and demand circumstances, involves a sort of successive approximation of reality, beginning with the theory of price competition and its substantial normative properties, moving to monopoly theory, logically at the other end of the range, and concluding with the theories of monopolistic competition and oligopoly, which cover the middle ground incorporating most of the real world. We classify industries by various combinations of structural characteristics, of which the following are most important:

(a) number and relative sizes of producers,

(b) degree of differentiation of product,

(c) barriers to entry of new competition, and

(d) special institutional considerations—a catch-all category covering ownership arrangements, etc., which may affect market behaviour in ways not covered by the three former categories.

In the theory of the behaviour of industry we speak of the short run and long run, where the short run is defined as the interval during which no change occurs in the resources supply available to the individual producer, and in particular his capital equipment. A distinction is drawn between static and essentially dynamic aspects, the latter being exclusively concerned with the long run as just defined. Static elements in industry behaviour include pricing and non-price behaviour, with the latter being more important the fewer the producers (so long as there are more than one), and the greater the importance of product differentiation and other barriers

---

*From: H. E. English, "Industrial Organization and Technical Progress," in T. N. Brewis (ed.), *Growth and the Canadian Economy* (Toronto, McClelland and Stewart, 1968), pp. 114-24 (reprinted by permission of author and publisher).

to new competition. Essentially, dynamic behaviour relates to the investment decision as well as to longer-run aspects of pricing policy. The investment decision is in part an extension of product policy, though it also includes process changes and simple capital expansion. It is the nature of the investment decision to which we shall devote our chief attention.

But before turning to this, it should be noted that economic performance of the private economy may be judged in terms of several interrelated standards which focus on the microeconomic impact of industrial organization:

(a)   The efficiency with which resources are used at any time (sometimes referred to as technical efficiency) —purely a cost consideration.

(b)   The effectiveness with which resources are allocated among uses preferred by consumers at any time—the static allocation norm.

(c)   The extent to which the time allocation, the distribution of resources between current and future use, corresponds to consumer preferences.

There are of course other aggregative standards by which the performance of the market economy is judged—the stability standard (substantially full employment without substantial inflation) and the welfare standard (the distribution of real income which will maximize consumer satisfaction). The industrial structure affects both of these through its effect upon profit levels and investment behaviour. But even though the appropriateness of the growth rate at any time is judged primarily by its effect upon the stability of the economy, these effects may *per se* be disregarded because they are derivative, and closely related to our analysis of growth.

To examine the impact of industrial organization upon economic growth, one must study the investment decision under different industrial structures. How does the response to new market opportunities and to technical challenges differ from one industrial situation to another? One can be more confident about market expansion than about technological progress. An increased market is the result of new population growth domestically, or the opening up of new international markets. Under any industrial structure, firms will respond by expanding productive capacity, assuming they are already operating near capacity.

There are, however, certain distinctions between purely competitive firms and oligopolists or monopolists. In the first place, because of their pricing practices the latter would not be as likely to require production units of larger scale (relative to the market size) and they may be hesitant to expand output unless the increased market is enough to enable them to attain an efficient level of operations in a new or extended plant.

There are also more subtle considerations. Since oligopolists or monopolists benefit from barriers to new competition in the form of established brands, owned-resource supplies and privileged positions based upon government legislation (for example, the use of oil resources) they are likely to hesitate over any move which might involve the sacrifice of such a barrier, and in this sense would be anxious to maximize their profits in the long run. I shall attempt to demonstrate later that such considerations affect Canadian industry in important ways.

Turning to the technological challenges, one encounters much more difficult theoretical problems. It is useful, if somewhat artificial, to distinguish between invention and innovation. Invention can be described as the development of new ideas out of research, while innovation can be described as the introduction of such ideas into use. Under pure competition, invention by definition would have to be financed largely through the capital market. Successful financing in this way would depend upon the size of the research expenditure required in relation to the size of the firm and in relation to the security of its marketing position. However, once the invention has been made, the purely competitive firm would be likely to introduce it at once into use, for if it did not do so, a new firm would be likely to enter the market. It was on this motivation to innovation that the classical economists based their belief that competition was the source of progress.

Under less competitive conditions, invention is more likely to be internally financed. Furthermore, given the size of the market, monopoly and oligopoly situations will probably involve larger firms and, in many cases, more secure market positions. All of these considerations favour a higher rate of invention under imperfectly competitive market situations. However, the rate of innovation (introduction into use of these new processes or products) may under non-competitive conditions be delayed by the desire of the firm in a secure position to exploit fully its existing capital before making technical changes. Of course the barriers to entry of new competitors will differ in degree and kind from industry to industry.[1]

Apart from the fact that pure monopoly is rare, there are other important differences between pure monopoly and oligopoly. In the case of oligopoly, there is less security for the individual firm and it will therefore be inclined to innovate more rapidly. However, in circumstances in which product differentiation is general, there will be a tendency for the oligopolist to favour product variations which bring returns in the short run, and these are likely to involve selling practices or style changes as often as real product improvements.

The crucial question is the relation between rates of innovation under oligopoly and more competitive industry. Of course the question can be treated as involving only the imperfection of the capital market, and remedies may be discussed in this context. However, the most important reason for the imperfection of the capital market is the fact that oligopoly

---

[1]It is difficult to assess the implications of this difference between the rate of invention and the rate of innovation, though in the theory of natural resources one can do so conceptually by endeavouring to calculate the rate of return to resources conserved. See A. D. Scott, *Natural Resources: The Economics of Conservation* (Toronto, Toronto University Press, 1955).

has in most cases an important technological basis. There are only a few firms in most industries because plant size needs to be quite large, and there are also some economies of firm size. Before endeavouring to remedy the faults of the capital market *per se,* therefore, one should attempt to discover in what ways the oligopolists affect the character of technological development.

Economic theory provides little assistance here. It tells us that because highly competitive industry is more responsive to consumer preferences, investment decisions, like those affecting current operations, should be more representative of consumer wishes under these circumstances. However, even the crudest empirical observation indicates that both in private markets and through public policy, consumers have been satisfied with many of the technological advances which non-competitive industry and also public enterprise have introduced. This may not, of course, be interpreted to mean that the efforts of imperfectly competitive industry have been ideal, and we are left with the necessity of examining critically the performance of such industries on standards which are very difficult to apply empirically.

Empirical Evidence

In searching for empirical evidence on the question of the progressiveness of non-competitive industry, one necessarily begins with the views of two prominent Harvard economists, Joseph Schumpeter and John Kenneth Galbraith. In introducing his concept of creative destruction, Schumpeter justly criticizes economists for stressing "how capitalism administers existing structures", and argues that the important problem is how it creates and destroys them. He then goes on to claim that history provides ample evidence of the creative power of non-competitive industry. He argues that monopoly profits are a necessary return for bearing the risks of innovations.

If for instance a war risk is insurable, nobody objects to a firm's collecting the cost of the insurance from the buyers of its products. But that risk is no less an element in long-run costs, if there are no facilities for insuring against it, in which case a price strategy aiming at the same end will seem to involve unnecessary restriction and to be productive of excess profits. Similarly, if a patent cannot be secured or would not, if secured, effectively protect, other means may have to be used in order to justify the investment. Among them are a price policy that will make it possible to write off more quickly than would otherwise be rational, or additional investment in order to provide excess capacity to be used only for aggression or defense.[2]

But however good this argument, it is certainly not empirical. Furthermore, this passage clearly implies that the development is fully justified, though it may not necessarily reflect consumer preferences.

John Kenneth Galbraith pays homage to Schumpeter and goes on to

---

[2]Quoted in Edwin Mansfield, *Monopoly Power and Economic Performance* (New York, Norton, 1964), pp. 32-33.

develop his argument. He also makes rather casual references to general empirical observations, which others have criticized as lacking much substance. For example, he argues that the fact that bituminous coal in the United States is produced under relatively competitive conditions is the reason why the industry is so technically backward, while the petroleum industry has made many advances because it is oligopolistically organized.

The British economist John Jewkes, who made more effort than Galbraith to discover empirical evidence on technical progress, has pointed out that the bituminous coal industry in the United Kingdom was no more progressive before its nationalization, even though it was anything but competitive. Jewkes also cites examples of leading firms, in such industries as steel, aluminum and automobiles, which have not been the principal innovators in those industries. More generally, he concludes that, "for the very slightly concentrated industries (say those where the three largest firms account for twenty per cent or less of the total output) interest in research has been slight and technical advance slow, but . . . in industries with a higher degree of concentration than this the conditions vary greatly."[3]

The principal empirical work in this area, however, has been done more recently, and primarily in the United States under the auspices of the National Science Foundation and the National Industrial Conference Board. One of the most important studies has been done by Professor Edwin Mansfield.[4] The bulk of his work has been on the iron, steel, petroleum refining and bituminous coal industries, though he has also examined the chemical and other industries. Not surprisingly, he finds that generalizations are risky in this area. The scale of research and development programmes required is much greater in some industries than in others. Given these differences, the relation of scale required in research and development to the size of the firms which dominate the industry is of essential importance. In both petroleum and coal industries he finds that the largest firms were the principal innovators, yet one (oil) is an industry in which both the size of firm and the size of research and development programme required are large, while in the other (coal), both are relatively small. In the steel industry, on the other hand, the largest firms have contributed a smaller percentage of the major innovations than they have of sales.

Mansfield arrives at a number of other interesting conclusions:

1. In the industries he has studied, among firms that do research, he found that the larger ones spent on research no more than the smaller ones as a percentage of their sales. Except in the chemical industry, there appeared to be no great economies of scale in research and development among firms engaged in research. He does not appear, however, to have

---

[3]*Ibid.*, pp. 51-52.

[4]*Ibid.*, pp. 57-64. The results of Professor Mansfield's work have also appeared in "Size of Firm, Market Structure, and Innovation," *Journal of Political Economy* (December, 1963), and other articles.

studied industries producing missiles and those producing some of the more advanced electronic equipment used for defence purposes.

2. He found that smaller firms were more efficient in their use of research and development expenditures of a given size. This evidence has more recently been borne out by a study conducted by Arnold C. Cooper of Purdue University.[5] He reported that this is a result partly of such factors as greater flexibility and sensitivity to market demands, and is partly due to the fact that employees of a small company work harder and care more about their work because they are more directly involved in the success of the business. Men interviewed by Cooper who had managed development in both large and small companies believe that the large companies spend up to ten times as much as small organizations to develop a similar product. Furthermore, men who managed rapidly growing companies had found that the efficiency of product development declined by 10 to 30 per cent as their companies grew from fifty employees to five hundred.

3. Mansfield also finds that there was no consistent group of leaders in innovation. However, he does discover that the largest firms tend to innovate more quickly, and attributes this to the lower risk, larger engineering departments, closer association with the equipment manufacturers, and similar advantages. Companies with a wider range of operating conditions are also more likely to have units requiring replacement.

In conclusion, on the basis of Mansfield's findings (to date), one can say that the larger firms have some advantage in research and development, but that this advantage is much greater in some industries than in others, and many relatively small firms have been very successful in their research programmes.

Certain other evidence on the American economy is also relevant for Canada. This concerns the absolute size of firms engaged in research and development and the role of government support. The research programme of American industry is often cited in Canada with admiration. In fact, in 1960 the $10 billion research and development (R&D) expenditure by American industry was financed primarily by the federal government—to the extent of 60 per cent of the total. Although the comparable Canadian figure was 50 per cent in the mid 1950's, it was only about 20 per cent by 1959. As indicated in the tables from a Conference Board study (Table 1),[6] American industrial research expenditures are concentrated in aircraft and missiles, and electronic and electrical equipment, both closely related to defence and supported by government (to the extent of 88 per cent and

---

[5]Arnold C. Cooper, "R & D Is More Efficient in Small Companies," *Harvard Business Review* (May-June, 1964), pp. 75-83.

[6]National Industrial Conference Board, *Research and Development: Its Growth and Composition* (New York, 1963).

Table 1

Distribution of Research and Development Activities
by U.S. Manufacturing Industries, 1960*

	Total Expenditures on R and D ($ millions)	% by First 4 Companies	% by First 20 Companies	Average size of R and D ($ millions) First 4	Average size of R and D ($ millions) Last 12 of First 20
Aircraft and Missiles	3,621	50	95	452.6	75.4
Communication Equipment and Electronic Components	1,249	62	90	193.6	12.5
Other Electrical	1,184	82	92	242.7	4.9
Industrial Chemical	664	60	90	99.6	8.9
Drugs and Medicines	171	41	83	17.5	4.3
Other Chemicals	165	52	79	21.5	2.2
Machinery	949	50	71	118.6	7.9
Transportation Equipment	852	88	97	187.5	3.6
Scientific Instruments	215	78	94	41.9	1.6
Other Instruments	184	63	94	29.0	2.3
Petroleum	298	48	92	35.8	5.2
Primary ferrous products	93	60	96	14.0	1.1
Non-ferrous and Other	69	59	96	10.0	1.1
Rubber Products	119	86	96	25.6	0.5
Fabricated Metal Products	112	51	76	14.3	0.9
Food and Kindred Products	104	40	81	10.4	2.2
Paper and Allied Products	54	31	69	4.2	0.9
Textile and Apparel	32	53	77	4.3	0.4
Lumber and Wood Products	13	54	82	1.8	0.1
Total	10,148				

* Source: National Industrial Conference Board, *Research and Development: Its Growth and Composition*, Tables 24 and 25.

66 per cent respectively). Canadian government support for research has gone mostly to the aircraft industry. . . . Although 86 per cent of the total cost of industrial research is performed by companies with more than 5,000

employees, it must be remembered that this figure is very much influenced by the defence-supported research of a few major corporations.

As shown in the table on size distribution (Table 2), there was an over-all correlation between company size and the size of research budgets, but there was also a wide dispersion in the amounts spent for R&D by companies of a given size. The nature of the industry was highly important. The Conference Board study concludes that there was only a weak correlation between companies' assets and the size of their R&D staff.

Another interesting table (Table 3) from the Conference Board study indicates the distribution of R&D expenditures between three categories or stages of such activity—development, applied research and basic research. It is generally said that development activity requires a large scale of operations, and it is in the defence industries, the electrical equipment industry, the machinery group, and industries producing professional and scientific equipment that development expenditures are the largest share—between 75 per cent and 85 per cent of the total of R&D. In other industries the percentage is often less than fifty, whereas applied research and basic research are of greater importance.

A further feature of Conference Board studies is an enquiry into the ways in which companies plan and control research and development activities. The Board reports that "Most of the participating companies determine the aggregate size of their research budget either as a percentage

Table 2

Size Distribution of R&D Programmes in U.S. Industries, by Company Size, 1960*

Size of R&D programme (in thousands)	All companies performing R&D	Number of companies with employment of		
		under 1,000	1,000-4,999	5,000 or more
Less than $10	4,842	4,800	37	5
$10-$99	4,910	4,700	187	23
$100-$999	1,522	1,000	427	95
$1,000-$9,999	455	100	174	181
$10,000-$99,999	92	2	10	80
$100,000 or more	23	0	0	23
Total number of companies	11,844	10,602	835	407

*Source: The Conference Board, op. cit., Table 61.

This tabulation includes all firms which reported conduct of R&D in 1960, both in manufacturing and non-manufacturing. Estimates for companies with less than 1,000 employees and with funds for R&D performance of less than $10 million and related totals were rounded to the nearest 100.

Table 3

Composition of R&D Work Performed, by Stage of Research Process in Selected Industries, 1960*

Industry	Per cent of industrial R&D in:		
	Development	Applied Research	Basic Research
Total, all industries	76.8%	19.6%	3.7%
Aircraft and missiles	85.2	13.6	1.2
Electrical equipment and communication	84.4	12.3	3.2
Communication and electronic components	84.3	11.2	4.5
Other electrical equipment	84.6	13.5	1.9
Machinery	84.2	13.5	2.3
Professional and scientific instruments	73.7	23.8	2.3
Fabricated metal products	69.6	29.5	0.9
Lumber, wood products, and furniture	53.8	46.2	0.0
Primary metals	50.0	44.4	6.2
Chemicals and allied products	46.1	42.1	11.7
Industrial chemicals	44.7	43.5	11.7
Drugs and medicines	30.4	52.0	17.5
Other chemicals	67.3	26.7	6.1
Food and kindred products	42.3	50.0	7.7
Petroleum refining and extraction	41.3	40.3	18.5
Percentage of expenditures in companies with 5,000 or more employees	88	82	82

*Source: The Conference Board, *op. cit.*, Table 15.
Percentages may not total 100 per cent due to rounding.

of estimated sales or as required by individual project needs." There is apparently some tendency for such expenditures to fluctuate with cash flows—a not surprising finding. However, there is considerable lag in this relationship, since it may be costly to cut off research programmes in mid-stream. The tendency to allocate a given percentage of sales revenue to R&D activities does not inspire confidence in the standard employed to evaluate investment in this area. However, the Conference Board also reports that,

... *most companies require advance justification of proposed expenditures for each new research project. Often, the person or department who originates the project, or who assumes responsibility for it, must complete a special form which provides information on the project and formally requests approval for it. These project approval forms frequently cover such factors as the purpose of the project, its chance of success, its market potential, anticipated cost savings, facilities required, time schedules, anticipated costs, and estimated return on investment.*[7]

Individual studies of returns to R&D activities, like those studies relating to the returns on educational investment, frequently do suggest that a high rate may be expected from R&D expenditures. However, such studies rarely cover all related expenditures which have not produced results, and they leave unanswered the question as to the means of assuring the best allocation of resources for such purposes.

SUGGESTIONS FOR FURTHER READING

Adelman, M., "The Measurement of Industrial Concentration," *Review of Economics and Statistics,* November, 1951.

Bain, J., *Barriers to New Competition: Their Character and Consequences in Manufacturing Industries,* Cambridge, Mass., Harvard University Press, 1956.

Baran, P. A., and P. M. Sweezy, *Monopoly Capital: An Essay on the American Economic and Social Order,* New York, Monthly Review Press, 1966.

Berle, A. A., *Power Without Property: A New Development in American Political Economy,* New York, Harcourt Brace & World, 1959.

Brecher, I., "The Flow of U.S. Investment Funds into Canada Since World War II," in *The American Economic Impact on Canada,* Durham, Duke University Press, 1959.

Canadian Bank of Commerce, *Industrial Concentration in Canada,* a study prepared for the Royal Commission on Canada's Economic Prospects, Ottawa, Queen's Printer, 1956.

Caves, R., *American Industry: Structure, Conduct, Performance,* Englewood Cliffs, N.J., Prentice-Hall, 1964.

Caves, R. E. and R. H. Holton, *The Canadian Economy: Prospect and Retrospect,* Cambridge, Mass., Harvard University Press, 1959.

Drummond, I. M., *The Canadian Economy: Organization and Development,* Homewood, Illinois, Irwin Inc., 1966.

Economic Council of Canada, "Scale and Specialization in Manufacturing," chapter 6 in *The Canadian Economy From the 1960's to the 1970's,* the Fourth Annual Review, Ottawa, Queen's Printer, 1967.

---

[7]The Conference Board, "Getting Maximum Returns from Research Expenditure," *Business Record* (April, 1961), p. 10.

Fowler, R. M., "The Future of Competition in Canada—A Businessman's View," in J. J. Deutsch (and others), *The Canadian Economy: Selected Readings*, Toronto, Macmillan Co. of Canada Ltd., 1961.

Galbraith, J. K., "Monopoly and the Concentration of Economic Power," in H. S. Ellis (ed.), *A Survey of Contemporary Economics*, Homewood, Illinois, Irwin Inc., 1952.

Heilbroner, R. L., *The Limits of American Capitalism*, New York, Harper & Row, 1966.

Kaplan, A. D. H., *Big Enterprise in a Competitive System*, Washington, Brookings Institution, 1964.

Kefauver, E. and I. Till, *In a Few Hands: Monopoly Power in America*, Baltimore, Md., Penguin Books Inc., 1966.

Kilbourn, W., *The Elements Combined: A History of the Steel Company of Canada*, Toronto, Clark Irwin & Co. Ltd., 1960.

Machlup, F., *The Political Economy of Monopoly*, Baltimore, Md., John Hopkins Press, 1952.

Main, O. W., *The Canadian Nickel Industry*, Toronto, University of Toronto Press, 1955.

Mansfield, E., "Size of Firm, Market Structure and Innovation," *Journal of Political Economy*, December, 1963.

Mason, E. S., "The Apologetics of 'Managerialism'," *Journal of Business*, January, 1958.

Means, G. C., "A Contemporary View of Industrial Concentration," in D. Grunewald and H. L. Bass, *Public Policy and the Modern Corporation: Selected Readings*, New York, Appleton-Century-Crofts, 1966.

Nossiter, B. D., *The Mythmakers: An Essay on Power and Wealth*, Boston, Mass., Houghton Mifflin Company, 1964.

Phillips, W. G., *The Agricultural Implement Industry in Canada: A Study of Competition*, Toronto, University of Toronto Press, 1955.

Raynauld, A., "Industrial Organization," chapter 7 in *The Canadian Economic System* (Toronto, Macmillan Co. of Canada, Ltd., 1967), pp. 133-147.

Rosenbluth, G., *Concentration in Canadian Manufacturing Industries*, National Bureau of Economic Research, Princeton, N.H., Princeton University Press, 1957.

Royal Commission on the Automotive Industry, *Report*, ("The Bladen Report"), Ottawa, Queen's Printer, 1961.

Royal Commission on Banking and Finance, "The Use of Foreign Capital," chapter 5 in *Report on Banking and Finance* (Ottawa, Queen's Printer, 1964).

Safarian, A. E., *Foreign Ownership of Canadian Industry*, Toronto, McGraw-Hill Co. of Canada Ltd., 1966.

Safarian, A. E., "Foreign Ownership and Control of Canadian Industry," in A. Rotstein (ed.), *The Prospect of Change,* Toronto, McGraw-Hill Co. of Canada Ltd., 1965.

Safarian, A. E., "Country of Ownership and Performance of the Firm," *Economic Record,* March, 1968.

Safarian, A. E., "Commentary: The Task Force Report on Foreign Ownership," *Journal of Canadian Studies,* August, 1968.

Stigler, G. J., "The Economist Plays with Blocs," *American Economic Review,* May, 1954.

PART FOUR

Anti-Combines Policy

INTRODUCTION

If we begin with the ideal of a self-regulating market economy operating within a framework of law and go on to see that in its real-world application the basic regulating force of competition is weak or non-existent, perhaps the most consistent remedy would be to incorporate measures into the legal framework to prohibit business practices that weaken competition.

Certainly this has appeared to be a very important part of economic policy in the United States. The Sherman Anti-Trust Act passed in 1890 declared succinctly: "Every contract, combination in the form of trust or otherwise, or conspiracy, in restraint of trade or commerce among the several States, or with foreign nations, is hereby declared illegal." The Clayton Act of 1914 made a number of specific acts illegal if they would "substantially lessen competition or tend to create a monopoly". In England, the Common Law has for centuries reflected a strong prejudice against private agreements to restrict trade. In Canada, too, there has been a long tradition of legal provisions relating to competition and monopoly. The legislation of 1889 in this country made it a misdemeanor to conspire, combine, agree or arrange unlawfully "to limit the production or movement of commodities or to unduly lessen competition in the production, trade or movement of commodities". The Combines Investigation Act of 1910 established procedures for investigating alleged combines and added to the sanctions against monopolistic practices the possibility of denying tariff protection to offending businesses. The main weapon against combines, however, was to be the unfavorable publicity arising from a conviction under the legislation.

At first sight the existence of this legislation, as subsequently amended and elaborated, would suggest that public policy toward business in Canada

143

was founded upon a clear commitment to competition as the preferred means of regulating business activity in the public interest. Such is not the case, as Professor Skeoch makes clear in *Reading 20*. He, in fact, argues strongly that there never has been such a commitment to a general rule of competition in this country.

Why this should be so is suggested by the point of view represented by the Canadian Manufacturers' Association in *Reading 21*. That association, like many other organized interest groups in this country, can be seen to accept the ideal of a private-enterprise, free-market economy as the preferred model and to recognize "the great importance and value of effective competition" as a corollary of it. But, and here is where the issues involved grow complicated, the CMA urges that competition must not be allowed to become an end in itself and that pursuit of it must not be allowed to inhibit the achievement of our "national economic objectives". Because these objectives are determined politically, once introduced they invite unlimited debate among interested parties who have their own views as to what these objectives should be and how they should be attained. Consequently a form of collective decision-making replaces the automatic functioning of competitive markets as the ultimate determinant of the economy's functioning. The policies decided upon in this way, it would seem, must reflect the relative political power of the various groups involved.

The content and the scope of anti-combines law itself will of course be influenced by this same process and it is with this that Professors Rosenbluth and Thorburn are concerned in *Reading 22*. They contend that because there is no strong political group in Canada concerned with promoting the effective application of the anti-combines laws, this legislation has been used in a way more symbolic than effective. The legislation represents a recognition of the principle of competition, but it may not have much direct impact on the conduct of business in Canada.

Apart from the ambivalent attitudes toward competition reflected in the absence of any widespread insistence upon it as a fundamental objective of policy, the effectiveness of Canadian anti-combines measures has also been limited by the difficulties encountered in trying to translate economic principles into legal ones.

This problem can be illustrated by reference to the provisions of the Canadian legislation applying to mergers. This is a particularly important matter in Canada where the small size of most of our markets means that there is room for only a few firms and plants of a technically efficient size. Under these conditions it seems that a strong practical justification may be found to support a policy of "rationalization". This would mean reducing the number of firms in an industry to the point where those remaining are large enough to produce efficiently, that is, at low costs.

Leaving aside the question of whether these efficient firms could be expected to pass on these efficiencies through lower product prices rather than simply increasing their profits, the problem arises of distinguishing between such potentially beneficial concentration and concentration arising from a simple quest for monopoly power on the part of a particular firm seeking to grow beyond the point where any further efficiencies could be realized. Section 33 of the Combines Investigation Act, as amended in 1960, states: "Every person who is a party or privy to or knowingly assists in, or in the formation of, a merger or monopoly is guilty of an indictable offence and is subject to imprisonment for two years." ("Merger" and "monopoly" are defined in section 2 (e) and (f) of the Act.) Yet, as J.C.H. Jones shows in his analysis of the 1960 case of R. v. Canadian Breweries (*Reading 23*), the Ontario Supreme Court has interpreted this in such a way that a merger apparently does not create an economic problem, so far as the courts are concerned, unless it results in a "monopoly" situation. Thus, although to the economist it would seem that the company in this case had deliberately set out to eliminate competition and to expand its share of the market beyond any reasonable extent justified by scale considerations, the legal understanding of "monopoly" was apparently such as to force the court to reject this interpretation of the facts. The effect, as Professor Jones concludes, has been the complete emasculation of the sections of the Canadian legislation dealing with mergers.

The relative weakness of Canadian anti-combines policy is thus seen to be partly a consequence of our uncertain commitment to competition, upon which such policy must ultimately be founded, and to problems of application, especially those arising out of the uncertain meshing of legal and economic principles relating to monopoly and competition. It is conceivable that these problems of application may be resolved as legal concepts become more informed by economic analysis, as methods of investigation are improved, and as a consequence of other reforms in anti-combines procedures. But the scope for such improvements is limited. The more fundamental problem of deciding how much competition public policy should insist upon remains. If it is true that technical efficiency in producing for small Canadian markets can only be obtained at high levels of concentration in certain industries, we must look for means of protecting the public interest by public regulation of imperfectly competitive business enterprises. This alternative approach is the subject of Part 5.

20   The History of the Legislation *

L. A. Skeoch

Private agreements and combinations in restraint of trade were matters for concern very early in the history of the English common law. Until the

*From: L. A. Skeoch (ed.), *Restrictive Trade Practices in Canada* (Toronto, McClelland and Stewart, 1966), pp. 2-5 (reprinted by permission of author and publisher).

early years of the eighteenth century, the law's ban was stringent, if not absolute. At the same time the state, in varying degree with different rulers, made use of combinations and monopoly organizations to develop the domestic economy, to cater to private interests, and to promote external trade. Mercantilism saw the state emerge, in Professor M. M. Knight's phrase, as "a combination of combinations." The combinations had become an essential element in the statecraft of the time. With the decline of mercantilism and the rise of *laissez faire,* emphasis shifted to reliance on a "natural law" scheme of individual competition to increase the wealth of nations. Combinations in Adam Smith's universe were objects of suspicion and derision.

Somewhat paradoxically, as public attitudes and policies towards combinations and monopolies were hardening, judicial attitudes towards private agreements in restraint of trade under the common law were becoming more benign. With the passage of time individuals were permitted to enter into agreements to promote their business interests without being required in any significant sense to justify the arrangements as conforming to the public interest. The same freedom to combine was allowed to labour only after a long lag. Technological and institutional changes reinforced the trend to the formation of "private governments of economic interest." *Laissez faire* came to mean the freedom of powerful groups to avoid competition, an interpretation that was in many respects the antithesis of the Smithian concept. It may be observed in passing that this same interpretation of *laissez faire* is still sometimes invoked by both labour and business groups in defence of their claims to be free from government "interference."

Uncombined economic interests reacted to the superior economic power of the combinations and ·monopolies by demanding government action against such groups and by themselves forming new combinations. Governments enacted legislation of a regulatory character to deal, often ineffectually, with the so-called "natural monopolies" (railways, public utilities, and the like) and to give protection to certain weaker groups (as in factory acts, minimum wage laws, and the like). Some governments also attempted to overcome the shortcomings of the common law by directly prohibiting the formation of combinations which operated "to the detriment of the public."

It can be argued that these broad forces have gradually pushed the state towards a form of neo-mercantilism: a new "combination of combinations" in which the role of competition is restricted and in which combinations attempt to influence the public authority to advance their interests, and the state attempts to develop a working compromise among the combinations which is more political than economic in orientation. This hypothesis raises very broad issues which it is not the intention to expore here. However, it may be interjected as a personal view that even though the natural law version of individual competition no longer plays a vital role in our thinking about economic organization, impersonal market forces are still so valuable for their contribution to economic efficiency and to freedom as to justify strenuous efforts to maintain them and even to extend their scope.

Perhaps the most striking aspect of the history of the legislation dealing with restraints on competition in Canada is the mixed character of the economic beliefs and policies it discloses. For example, the early debates in the House of Commons on the Combines Investigation Act—and the more recent debates, for that matter—display no broad support for a general policy of competition. There was opposition to monopolies and combinations which behaved in ways that were detrimental to the public. But this view differs fundamentally from that which would require the rigorous enforcement of a rule of competition. In fact, the sponsor of the combines legislation had many favourable things to say about the advantages to be derived from monopolistic organizations in the setting of modern industry. The subsequent history of the legislation, with the repeated attempts to undermine the rather modest restraints which, in practice, it imposed on the elimination of competition, suggests a wavering and uncertain belief in the advantages to be derived from a competitive economy. It is difficult to understand the development of anti-combines policy without taking account of the mixed, and perhaps confused, attitudes towards competition that have prevailed in Canada.

These attitudes are revealed not only in the limited range of activity under the combines legislation but also in the general exemptions specifically written into that legislation and by other statutes and types of government policy which tend to promote monopolies and nourish and support restraints of trade. The combines legislation, for example, applies only to combinations having relation to "articles" or "commodities" which may be the subject of trade or commerce.[1] This has been interpreted in such a manner as to exclude from the reach of the legislation large and increasingly important categories of services, many of which, in an economic sense, are functionally "related to" commodities which are the subject of trade or commerce. Banking services and services relating to the purchase and sale of real estate are obvious, but by no means the only, examples. Other categories of services which may not be "related to" commodities and thus are exempted from the legislation may, nonetheless, be important to the efficient functioning of the economy. A concern for efficiency, if not for equity, would suggest that such sectors should not be permitted to flirt with —and certainly not to live "in open and notorious cohabitation with"— restrictive practices.

The combines legislation also exempts from its reach combinations of workmen and employees where they combine "for their own reasonable protection." In view of the great changes which have occurred in the structure and power of labour organizations in recent years and of the importance

---

[1] To this there is one minor exception, since section 32 (1) (c), as it is now numbered, includes "the price of insurance upon persons or property." However, no action has, as yet, been taken under this particular division of the section.

of union policy for economic expansion and stability, there may be grounds for reviewing the latitude of immunity which this exemption is considered to confer. To do nothing more than prohibit labour organizations from participating in the collusive fixing of prices of "commodities"—as Canadian policy tends to do—is to adopt a narrow and inadequate interpretation of the economic consequences of some collusive or structural aspects of union power and policy.[2]

Outside the ambit of combines legislation, the range of possible exemptions from the rule of competition is wide: government approval, and even enforcement, of certain restrictive types of marketing schemes; restraints on entry and on competitive practices imposed by public regulatory bodies; licensing requirements exercised by government from the federal to the municipal level for everything from banks and breweries to local construction firms; government purchasing practices; and so on through a long list. All can be, and are, used, incidentally or expressly, in support of restrictive practices.

It may involve some exaggeration to claim, as Adams and Gray do that:

We seem to be afflicted with internal tension, ambivalence, confusion, and contradiction. We appear to have no clear-cut notion of what kind of economic system we want or how to get it. In an effort to achieve "Lockean entrepreneurial unanimity" we tend to placate particularized, vocal, contentious, and powerful interests—giving only ancillary thought to social consequences. Lacking an essentially consistent philosophy, we tend to rationalize particular policies as best we can in pragmatic terms of short-run expediency.[3]

At the very least, however, it is clear that there is no Canadian public policy commitment to a general rule of competition. To assume that there is (or has been) is to misread the history of combines legislation and to simplify out of all relation to reality the vagaries of government policy and administration.

The time is long overdue for a reappraisal—some would say for a first appraisal—not so much of combines policy in the narrow sense as of the role of competition in the totality of the economy. If we are to opt for an attenuated role for competition, then something approaching consistent and rational grounds for determining the nature and extent of the permissible restraints for all groups in the economy will be clearly required. If we choose the course of liberating and strengthening the general role of competition, it will not be sufficient to rely on combines legislation, even if it is revised and extended; there will also be required a new awareness and

---

[2]It is of interest to note the following questions and replies in the 1965 Chase Manhattan Bank Opinion Survey of (U.S.) College and University Economists: "Do you think the Federal government should set up a system of compulsory arbitration to settle major labor disputes? Yes—26%. No—74%. Should anti-trust laws apply to labor unions? Yes—52%. No—48%."

[3]Walter Adams and Horace M. Gray, *Monopoly in America* (New York, The Macmillan Company, 1955), p. 164.

acceptance of the problems involved in promoting adjustment and adaptability in the economy.[4] Positive programs to promote competition (or economic adaptability, if that term be preferred) will be as necessary as programs to prohibit interferences with competition. The haphazard and arbitrary meddling with competition that now characterizes so much of Canadian public policy has no place in either approach—that of attenuating or that of liberating the forces of competition.

21   Free Competition*

Canadian Manufacturers' Association

When we look into the history of the Combines Investigation Act and of the former Section 498 of the Criminal Code, and their interpretation by the courts, it becomes apparent that the main object of the legislation has generally been regarded to be the preservation and protection of the interest of the public in free competition. Thus, in the Container Materials case, Chief Justice Duff said, "The enactment before us, I have no doubt, was passed for the protection of the specific public interest in free competition."

Mr. S. F. Sommerfeld has described the philosophy behind Canadian combines legislation as follows:

> "We may sum up our view of the Canadian anti-trust legislation in the light of the decided cases, as follows: The interest of the public, which it is the purpose of Section 498 of the Criminal Code and of the Combines Investigation Act to protect, lies in the preservation of free competition. Assuming the existence of a combine to have been established, the ground upon which the members of such a combine can be convicted is that it has operated to destroy competition. The other grounds contained in Section 498 and in the Act, while they may exist concurrently with suppression of competition (largely because they are a result thereof), cannot exist independently as grounds for conviction. It is the suppression of competition, apart entirely from any effect on prices or, in fact, any objective injury to the public interest, that brings a combination under the ban of Section 498 and the Combines Investigation Act."[1]

---

[4]For a discussion of some of the issues involved in a program "to aid and speed" the process of adjustment, see L. A. Skeoch and David C. Smith, *Economic Planning: The Relevance of West European Experience for Canada* (Montreal, 1963), *passim*.
*From: "A Submission to the Economic Council of Canada on Combines, Mergers, Monopolies and Restraint of Trade", (August 1967), pp. 4-10 (reprinted by permission).
[1]See L. A. Skeoch, *Restrictive Trade Practices in Canada* (1966), p. 44.

While the theory of competition has clearly been established as the basic economic mainstay of the present combines legislation, it is noteworthy that in other areas competition has steadily been losing ground. There has been an increasing tendency by governments to eliminate the operation of competition in many fields and to establish more and more monopolies or quasi-monopolies. For instance, transportation, communication, and many public utilities are largely under the control of government owned or regulated monopolies. Under marketing legislation many farm products are sold by monopolistic sales agencies which effectively prevent competition. Many services as well as all trade unions and similar combinations of employees are exempt from the combines legislation. The confusion of public policy in the area of combines and restrictive trade has been aptly described as follows:

"To an increasing degree, one gets the impression that the right hand of public policy is not aware of what the left hand is doing. Confusion, contradiction, short-run expediency—these are terms that most accurately describe much of public policy in the area of restrictive economic behaviour. Important areas of the economy—such as services—are excluded from the reach of combines policy altogether. Government, at both the federal and provincial levels condones or enforces certain highly restrictive types of marketing legislation. And so one could go on through a lengthy list. There is no broad rationale to relate these measures to a general policy of promoting economic adaptability and economic growth. Rather, they amount to nothing much more than a haphazard and arbitrary meddling with the forces of competition."[2]

The courts, in their decisions, have tended to regard competition as being synonymous with price competition. They have overlooked the significant fact that effective competition is provided by developing technology, by the availability of competitive or alternative products, and by the provision of services in relation to products. We recognize that competition, properly defined, plays an important and essential role in the economy. The problem lies with the definition of competition. The narrow concept of competition adopted by the courts is, in the Association's view, clearly unsound and outmoded by the realistic facts of everyday commercial and industrial life in the market place. The existing law continues the notion that a dissimilarity of prices and terms is evidence of competition. This strikes us as a narrow and short-term view since in many cases similarity of price is a clear indication of vigorous competition. Competition fulfils its functions if it contributes to a dynamic business climate where new products replace old products in volume and at reasonable prices (having regard for labour and material content and the need for manufacturers to make a reasonable

---

[2]L. A. Skeoch, "The Case for Changes in the Combines Law," *Industrial Canada* (July 1966), p. 220.

profit) ; where the diesel locomotive can replace the steam locomotive for the benefit of all.

There is no doubt that a change is required in anti-combines legislation which will permit the achievement of Canada's economic objectives and in so doing provide a realistic approach to the problem of competition.

In 1950 the Minister of Justice established the Committee To Study Combines Legislation, headed by Mr. Justice MacQuarrie. Its Report issued two years later contained important recommendations for changes in combines laws, much of which was subsequently enacted. Of particular interest at this time are the views expressed by the Committee on the economic background to the Canadian combines legislation.

The basic justification for combines legislation, in the opinion of the Committee, was its function in maintaining a competitive system of free enterprise. The Committee contended that competition operates as a controlling device in such a way that it promotes economic efficiency and general welfare. No other standards or criteria for the evaluation of combines legislation were advanced. A glance at the economic discussion in the Report makes it clear that the Canadian economic climate has undergone profound changes in the last fifteen years.

The present-day reader, although in agreement with the importance of competition in a free-enterprise economy, will look in vain in the 1952 Report for any references to such national economic problems as your Council in recent years has so ably dealt with in its annual reports. Thus, for instance, we find no mention of employment and unemployment, the need for increased productivity, the problem of curbing inflation, exports and international balance of payments. Economic objectives are ignored. In a word, most of the basic economic problems of the day which are currently debated in Parliament or in the press are not even referred to.

Today, perhaps as a result of the economic research carried out by many organizations, and notably by your Council, it is widely accepted that legislation affecting business and industry should be in accord and not in conflict with the national economic needs and objectives. There is general realization that economic problems, such as combines, mergers, monopolies and restraint of trade, cannot be treated in water-tight compartments, but must be considered in the light of and in relation to other national economic problems.

The Association, while recognizing the great importance and value of effective competition, submits that competition should be regarded as a means to an end rather than a national goal in itself. We suggest that your Council look beyond the narrow concept of competition held by the courts, for sound criteria which should be incorporated into Canadian combines legislation in order to assess the economic effect of any allegedly restrictive practices. Competition must not be permitted to overstep its ancillary but important role and to usurp a place among the national basic economic and social goals.

Directing our attention to "the Government's long-term economic objectives", we note that four of them, viz., full employment, a high rate of economic growth, a reasonable stability of prices and a viable balance of payments, demand an increasing rate of national productivity. It therefore follows that wherever the present combines legislation either directly or indirectly inhibits the evolution of Canadian business and industry toward higher productivity, such legislation is prima facie not in the national interest and should receive the most exhaustive scrutiny.

The GATT negotiations recently concluded, the effects of which have not yet been fully assessed by Canadian business, have added to the already difficult problems of Canadian producers facing competition from abroad. They have also added to the range of world markets accessible to firms where costs of production are in a favourable relationship with those of foreign competitors. These effects must not be overlooked in determining the kind of combines law you ultimately find desirable to meet Canadian needs.

It is submitted that the present legislation with its acceptance essentially of the single test of a narrow form of competition, and with its rigidity made, if possible, more inflexible by the judicial interpretation which it has suffered, does not—indeed, cannot—in the concept of a progressive and dynamic economy achieve or assist in achieving any of the above-described economic and social objectives. If this is so, then the present legislation does not serve the national interest and there is no warrant for its continued existence.

This is not to suggest that there ought not to be legislation of the nature of combines or anti-trust legislation, but it should be legislation dedicated to the fulfilment of the national interest and constructed so as to aid in the achievement of a progressive and dynamic economy which alone is capable on a continuing basis of achieving the major national economic and social objectives. This will, of course, require flexibility and the adoption of criteria devised to test actions on the basis of whether such actions aid, or prejudice or inhibit, achievement of the national economic objectives. Your council may wish in this respect to refer to the relevant provisions of the Treaty of Rome. And, in the interests of the essential flexibility required, there is no compelling reason why criteria once adopted could not be altered or expanded to conform to the possibly changing requirements of the national economy, provided only that new criteria or changed criteria should not on the ground, at least, of equity be capable of retroactive application.

This proposal may well require for its implementation a form of tribunal or body differing from the courts which are concerned with these matters under present legislation. Such a tribunal or other body must of necessity be prepared and qualified to consider economic problems and to assess economic implications, a field in which courts now considering these matters have fully disqualified themselves. There is, we submit, no reason to suppose that such a form of tribunal or other body cannot be constituted in Canada.

22 Canadian Anti-Combines Administration 1952-1960 *

G. Rosenbluth and H. G. Thorburn

The Combines Investigation Act furnishes an excellent example of the kind of political tight-rope walking that is necessary in a modern industrial democracy. Governments try hard to avoid antagonizing large blocks of voters, and at the same time to maintain the support of substantial business interests, not only because political campaigns are expensive, but also because, in a multitude of ways, the environment in which government operates is influenced by the actions and attitudes of the major business groups. Very often, particularly in non-economic areas, there is no conflict between these objectives, and, even in the economic field, important aspects of government policy may not involve conflict. Everybody favours prosperity. Where conflict arises between the interests of these two elements, the government is compelled to work out a "compromise"; the effect of such a policy on the public interest can only be ascertained by the study of particular examples.

Anti-combines policy is an instance of this kind of conflict. One has only to read the Combines Investigation Act (in any of its versions since 1923) to realize that it is bound to arouse the opposition of major business groups, while it will appeal to the mass of farmers and employees and to individual businessmen, particularly small businessmen, who are the victims of monopolistic restrictions.

In a period of general prosperity, the damage to the public interest arising from monopolistic structures and practices is generalized and not felt acutely by any one section of the population. The economic inefficiencies in the production and allocation of goods introduced by monopoly reduce the real national output, but other forces are pushing it up. The transfer of income to the monopolistic groups is hidden by the general rise in incomes. It follows that there is no significant political group that has any strong interest in checking the effectiveness with which combines legislation is enforced. Political leaders find, therefore, that the interest of the mass of voters in

---

*From: G. Rosenbluth and H. G. Thorburn, *Canadian Anti-Combines Administration 1952-1960* (Toronto, University of Toronto Press, 1963), pp. 96-106 (reprinted by permission of authors and publisher).

combines legislation is satisfied by action which is symbolic and dramatic, though it may not be particularly effective.

In such a situation, the compromise between the requirements of mass support and the requirements of business support is likely to take the form of limited enforcement activity with the emphasis on a few flagrant cases of price agreements which will produce spectacular judicial decisions. This leaves the activities of the leading corporations substantially untouched.

There is one qualification, however. When general prosperity is accompanied by inflation, the attention of the public turns to the determinants of prices at the retail level. In such a situation, a government may attempt to reduce public criticism of its policies by directing the attention of the public to monopolistic arrangements, particularly at the retail level.

These general considerations help to explain the revision of the combines machinery and the selective implementation of the recommendations of the MacQuarrie Committee. Under the St. Laurent—Howe administration, the backgrounds and personalities of the government leaders, their natural desire for financial support from business interests for campaign purposes, the remoteness from the electorate caused by the duration of the Liberal regime, and the general economic prosperity all favoured a certain solicitude for the interests of large corporations. In the field of combines legislation, the logical development of government policy would have been towards reduction in emphasis upon activities that might disturb major business groups.

The administrative structure under the Combines Investigation Act was, however, such that the activities of the commissioner could not be controlled by the government, and he did, in fact, follow a policy that was the direct opposite of that suggested by the considerations above. His twenty pre-war reports had dealt mainly with small business: retailers of coal, wholesalers of fruit and vegetables, bakers, building contractors, manufacturers of fruit baskets, and so on. After the war, however, he launched investigations into international cartels, the pulp and paper industry, the rubber industry, wire and cable, matches, flat glass, and so forth. Large manufacturing corporations were therefore attacked, and in many cases large international interests were involved. Seen in this context, the dispute over the flour milling report was clearly the last straw. In view of the conflict between the Commissioner's policy and that of the government, it was desirable from the government's point of view that the Commissioner should resign. It was also desirable that the administrative structure should be altered in such a way as to reduce the independent power of the commissioner. Business interests had always urged that the commissioner should not combine the powers of "judge and prosecutor," and the government was now extremely receptive to this idea. The change of personnel was therefore followed by the splitting up of the functions of the commissioner, as recommended by the MacQuarrie Committee. However, most of the MacQuarrie Committee's recommendations, which might have led to more effective action against the monopolistic tendencies of large corporations, were rejected. These included the recommendation of large-scale research into problems of industrial organization and monopoly, the search for more effective remedies than criminal prosecution, and the integration of other aspects of government policy with combines policy.

How does the prohibition of resale price maintenance fit into this picture? Such a ban had long been advocated by the Commissioner, and the Royal Commission on Prices in 1949 made a similar recommendation.[1] The government does not appear to have developed a strong interest in this issue until 1951, when it asked the MacQuarrie Committee to submit its views on resale price maintenance "at an early date."[2] It is probable that inflation caused by the Korean war was a major factor in the government's sudden sponsorship of this cause. It was politically important that the government take some action against high retail prices, and the ban on resale price maintenance was a dramatic move of this kind. It did not, of course, deal with the basic inflationary forces, but in the political arena it could be represented as a move against inflation.[3] It is also significant that resale price maintenance has not in general been strongly supported by large manufacturing interests, but rather by small retailers and other distributors.

The administration of the Combines Investigation Act since 1952 has on the whole followed the lines of the foregoing analysis. With the new administrative structure, the staff was considerably increased, but since then it has not kept pace with the growth of the economy. The proceedings against major manufacturing groups, planned and launched by the preceding Commissioner, have not been dropped, but most of the new cases have been price agreements involving small or medium-sized firms. Monopolistic situations that have not been investigated or whose investigations have been dropped at an early stage have remained large in comparison with

---

[1]*Report of the Royal Commission on Prices* (Ottawa, 1949), vol. I, pp. 27-28, 41; vol. II, pp. 238-39, 256-59.

[2]MacQuarrie *Report*, p. 55.

[3]In public discussion preceeding the legislation, the contemplated ban on resale price maintenance was generally linked with the inflationary situation. Thus a *Financial Post* editorial on October 13, 1951, stated: "The government's avowed intention of legislating on resale price maintenance is not impressive. It's true that the high cost of living is the problem uppermost in the popular mind. But it looks very much as if the government is going to make a big show of 'doing something' about the high cost of living by tilting against resale price agreements."

In the House of Commons, Mr. St. Laurent linked the ban on resale price maintenance with the inflation, while at the same time suggesting that it was not likely to have much effect as an anti-inflationary move: "As regards immediate additional measures to curb inflation . . . the only one we are prepared to submit at this time is the one that will arise out of this report of the combines committee with respect to resale prices, because I do know that there are some instances where the spread between what the consumer has to pay and what goes to the primary producer seems to be inordinately large." *Debates, (Commons)* (1951), Second Session, pp. 41-42.

those that have been effectually dealt with. A few merger cases have been investigated, but only two, the Canadian Breweries and Western Sugar cases, have been tested in court. In both cases the government failed to secure convictions, and the judicial interpretations suggest that a merger can be attacked under the legislation only if it eliminates virtually all competition. The government has not appealed these judgments.[4] There has thus been no effective action in relation to mergers. Nor has there been any serious attempt to deal with the problem of discrimination, except for the new provision relating to promotional allowances.

The trend in administrative policy is also evident in what may be considered more minor aspects of administration. The colour and layout of the covers of the published reports have been changed so as to make them even less attractive than they were before, and press releases have been reduced to the point where they reveal nothing of the contents of the reports. Thus Mackenzie King's policy of using publicity, or the threat of publicity, as a deterrent, has been quietly abandoned in favour of a policy of minimizing embarrassment to the parties concerned.

The amendments of 1960 represent a further step in the direction of minimizing interference with monopolistic business structures and practices. The ban on resale price maintenance has not been removed, but has probably been rendered virtually unenforceable. The change in the wording regarding price agreements has undermined the doctrine that they are illegal *per se* and has provided psychological encouragement for agreements that take the form of a concern with statistics, product standards, and so on. Price agreements in the export field have been explicitly permitted.

We have suggested that the ineffective administration of the Combines Investigation Act is an aspect of the compromise between the power of the vote and the power of the dollar that is a feature of Canadian democracy. This does not mean, however, that the government and the civil servants who administer the act are engaged in a conspiracy to fool the public. On the contrary, the evidence suggests that the staff of both branches of the combines machinery are conscientious and hard-working. To some extent, of course, ineffective administration is the result of inadequate budgets and inadequate staffing. But on the whole, neither the director nor successive ministers appear to have been conscious of any substantial inadequacies in the size of the staff. Their conception of the combines problem and of the role of the combines machinery has made them unaware of any serious inadequacy.

The administration's view of the proper role of the combines machinery has been described as a "cops and robbers" concept. Combines officers are viewed as a species of specialized policemen who enforce a particular statute

---

[4]The wording has been changed slightly in the 1960 amendments, but the change is not such as to invalidate the judicial interpretations. The government's decision not to appeal the Sugar case was announced on January 27, 1961.

by looking for violators, investigating their activities, and bringing them to justice before the courts. For this kind of job, competent investigators and lawyers are needed. Other types of personnel, for example, research economists, are merely "frills." The branch seems to estimate its success by its record of convictions. The professional staff of the combines branch comes by this view naturally since its leading members are lawyers. For the Cabinet ministers who have appointed the key personnel of the combines branch, this is also a natural view since any other, such as that put forward by the MacQuarrie Committee, would render the necessary political compromise more difficult.

The "cops and robbers" attitude has led to concentration on the investigation of a particular kind of case: *per se* offences, especially price-fixing conspiracies. These were cases in which the law was clear and the job of the director was simply to collect evidence.[5] Evidence that will stand up in court is not always easy to obtain. If the price agreement involves only a small number of firms, it is probable that no documentary evidence exists. This has led to the dropping of some cases where other indications pointed to serious infractions of the act. Some, at least, of these cases have involved very large firms, such as the producers of heavy electrical equipment. However, when the price fixing agreement involves a very large number of firms, it is more likely that written records will have to be kept. These cases are therefore more likely to be prosecuted. They also tend to involve medium-sized or small firms rather than the largest corporate giants. No serious attempt has been made to adapt the combines machinery to cope with this problem.

Concentration on the goal of successful prosecution also meant that cases where the application of the law was doubtful were not developed. Thus the courts were not given a chance to clarify the meaning of all sections of the act, and the act was not given its full application. Price agreements were generally prosecuted under the Criminal Code and their status under section 32 of the Combines Act was not clarified.[6] The application of the law to mergers was tested only at the end of the period under review and the clause on price discrimination remains unexplored.

Neglect of the research function is also a consequence of the "cops and robbers" attitude. Instead of the establishment of a research division, as recommended by the MacQuarrie Committee, only one senior research officer was appointed in 1951, and no further research staff was added. This

---

[5]Our comments on the conduct of operations under the act apply to the situation preceding the 1960 amendments. In particular, the statement that "the law is clear" no longer applies.

[6]The Director's annual reports stress the point that "a recent case, under the Act, in the British Columbia Court of Appeal" suggests that conviction under section 32 of the Combines Act requires "proof of some immediate and specific harm" instead of the rule established under the Criminal Code cases, that price agreements are illegal *per se* (*Annual Reports,* 1958 and 1959) , p. 8. Yet the government, although given an opportunity for a new trial of this case (Vancouver Gasoline) decided to drop it.

research officer subsequently left the branch and has not yet been replaced, so that for all practical purposes no specialist research personnel were employed at the end of our period.[7] Owing to the neglect of research, no body of knowledge has been built up about the structure of industry in Canada to form the basis for policy-making in the combines field.

The problem of the legalistic orientation of senior combines personnel and the neglect of research, has been compounded because conviction in a court of law has been the only remedy employed. Thus the evidence collected is the type to which courts are accustomed. The practice of turning prosecutions over to lawyers in private practice has emphasized the legalistic bias, which avoids cases involving monopoly, merger, and price discrimination, where economic analysis is essential.

The neglect of the research function in the office of the Director of Investigation and Research has apparently been accompanied by a similar neglect on the part of the Restrictive Trade Practices Commission. The time of the Commission has been largely taken up in acting as a sort of court of first instance, reviewing the factual evidence presented by the director in price agreement cases, and presenting it to the minister and the public in a lengthy report. Curiously enough, the Commission has adopted the practice of avoiding specific recommendations to the minister about prosecution. As a result, it is not clear exactly what contribution the Commission makes to the consideration of per se cases.

In the few cases involving merger or price discrimination, the Commission's discussions have been narrow and legalistic and have not adequately explored the basic economic issues. Like a court, it has generally confined itself to the consideration of the evidence presented by the director and the opposing parties.

Our objective here has been analysis, not prescription. Certain recommendations for legislative and administrative changes, however, follow fairly clearly from our review and are summarized below. They are based on the assumption that the "cops and robbers" concept of combines administration is mistaken. In the Canadian economy, monopolistic practices are not the infrequent acts of a criminal minority. Monopolistic market structures and practices are widespread and constitute the typical business environment. We believe that these elements of monopoly seriously impair the economic and social health of the country, and that combines legislation should be effective and should be enforced.

Clearly the MacQuarrie Committee's recommendation that a research organization be set up should be implemented. The simplest way would be

---

[7]The Director's *Annual Report* for the year ended March 31, 1961, states that the Combines Branch was reorganized as of that date, and that a Research Section was established, the functions of which are described as the planning of research inquiries, liaison with other government departments, and the study of anti-trust practices in the international field. There is also a new Merger Section for the investigation of mergers and monopolies (pp. 42-43).

to establish two divisions under the director, one to conduct investigations (as at present) and the other a new research division. The latter, under an experienced research economist, should have *carte blanche* to study any aspect of the structure and functioning of business firms and industries, and it should prepare reports on its findings. It would have to be given the power to examine the records of firms and to require that they provide information as directed. Only with such powers can the actual conditions of business in Canada become known. Such information is essential if the government is to frame appropriate and effective legislation. Indeed, the research division could be asked for studies of areas in which the government is contemplating legislative or administrative changes. Naturally this would include such beclouded areas as merger, monopoly, and price discrimination.

The almost exclusive reliance on the criminal law is a serious shortcoming of Canadian anti-combines methods. Other remedies, such as legislation under the federal "trade and commerce" power, should be explored. The 1960 amendments, providing for a court order to dissolve a merger or monopoly without a conviction, providing for the institution of proceedings by "information" as well as by prosecution, and providing for cases to be heard in the Exchequer Court are examples of more direct effective remedies.[8]

Modification of tariff or patent protection in order to promote competition is provided for in the act, but these provisions have hardly ever been used. The MacQuarrie Committee recommended that the act be amended so that such action would not have to wait on a finding that a combine exists, but could be taken whenever "the requirements of the public interest" made it desirable.[9] This recommendation was never implemented, but the change should be made and the government's power over tariffs and patents should be used to promote competition.

More generally, as the MacQuarrie Committee pointed out, the interaction between combines administration and other aspects of government policy should be constantly kept in mind by governments at all levels, and possible effects on competitive conditions should be considered in planning and administering government policy in various fields. For example, some aspects of the tax structure may promote mergers and concentration, while others may encourage the formation of new firms. Procurement by competitive tender will encourage competition and give a fair chance to aggressive small firms. Procurement by negotiated deals will usually benefit the larger firms, regardless of efficiency, and promote concentration. The promotion of low interest rates by the Bank of Canada and the provision of credit through such agencies as Central Mortgage and Housing and the Industrial Development Bank will tend to encourage new businesses and small firms, while a

---

[8]The provision for cases to be heard by the Exchequer Court is greatly weakened by the proviso that no case can be tried there without the consent of the accused.

[9]MacQuarrie *Report*, pp. 41-42.

"tight money" policy and restriction of government credit will tend to favour large firms with adequate internal sources of finance. Government trade promotion policies and government research activities, and the manner in which research results are made available to business, government licence policies (for instance, for television stations) and resource development policies, all these have important implications for competition, particularly in new industries.

The administrative arrangements currently employed in combines cases could be improved. The Commission normally considers all cases before they go to court. Since most are routine price fixing conspiracies, there is really nothing to be gained by the Commission's review, and the accused businessmen are understandably disturbed at having their arrangements and practices reported in public before an action has been brought in the courts. Such routine cases should go directly to the courts for disposal. The Commission would then be free to examine in detail those cases in which the elucidation of the public interest is more complex; and if its staff were increased by the addition of research personnel, it could develop an approach to these neglected areas of the combines problem by hearing and reporting on such cases.

The Commission's reports should contain specific recommendations relating to prosecution, and should discuss fully the policy issues involved. This would help to take the decision regarding prosecution out of politics, as the minister would be inclined to follow the Commission's recommendation. If he chose to reject it, he would have to satisfy Parliament that he had legitimate reasons for so doing. The minister would thus be relieved of pressure from the private interests involved, and, by making his action formal only, provide both the appearance and probably the substance of greater impartiality.

Our main plea is for a change in the approach of the responsible authorities to the problem of combines. We must escape from the "cops and robbers" concept.

23 Mergers and Competition: The Brewing Case *

J. C. H. Jones

In 1960, the first major decision of any doctrinal importance concerning mergers under section 32 of the Combines Investigation Act was handed down in the Supreme Court of Ontario.[1] This decision established that there is no merger problem under the Act unless the fusion of firms creates a monopoly situation. Such a test, aside from being incomprehensible in economic terms, is based on a narrow legal premise (that may or may not be legally correct) which, taken together with the decision in *R. v. British Columbia Sugar Refining Co. Ltd.*[2] and the inexplicable decision of the Crown to appeal neither case, has resulted in complete emasculation of the merger section of the Act.[3] In effect, mergers have ceased to become an economic problem.

* * *

The essence of the economic problem associated with mergers is that they may give rise to increased market power and/or increased efficiency. Therefore, from the point of view of public policy, it is necessary to separate those mergers which, on balance, may increase market power from those which realize significant real economies. However, once we move from the extremes of merger under conditions of perfect competition or duopoly into the realms of oligopoly, we are confronted with a vast range of uncertainty within which there is no precise and simple way to establish probabilities as to the effects of mergers, because value theory *per se* provides few informative insights into the problem. Therefore, any legitimate treatment of mergers must avoid quantitative cardinality and proceed on a case-by-case basis

---

*From: "Mergers and Competition: The Brewing Case", *Canadian Journal of Economics and Political Science*, Vol. XXXIII, no. 4 (November 1967), pp. 551-68 (reprinted by permission of author and publisher).

Note: J. C. H. Jones wishes it clearly understood that the statements which appear in this edited version of his article are fully substantiated in the original.

This article is based on the author's doctoral thesis at Queen's University. The author would like to express his thanks to his supervisor, Professor L. A. Skeoch, and to the Combines Branch who eased his access to the trial record. For the present paper helpful comments were made by Professor Skeoch and by Professor G. R. Elliott of the University of Victoria. The intention of the paper is not to challenge the legality of court decisions with respect to brewing, but to apply the rather different criteria of economic analysis to the brewing industry.

[1]*R. v. Canadian Breweries, Criminal Reports*, vol. 33, 1960. Prior to 1960 the only other merger cases to come to court were *R. v. Canadian Import Co.* (1933), *R. v. Staples* (1940), and *R. v. Eddy Match* (1952). None of these cases provided any clear criteria by which merger could be judged under section 32.

[2]See *R. v. British Columbia Sugar Refining Co. Ltd. et al.* (1960) *WWR (NS)* 577.

[3]The 1960 amendments to the Act make no real difference to the substance of the offence or the criteria by which it is judged.

revolving around considerations of market power and the concomitant ordinal assessment process involving structure, conduct, and performance variables.

Essentially, market power involves some degree of freedom from constraint: the freedom for the firm (or group) to select a price-output policy and arrive at a market position which other firms in the market find difficult to erode. For the purpose of this paper, market power may be defined as a situation in which the firm (or firms) can behave persistently in a manner different from that which a competitive market would enforce on firms facing similar cost and demand conditions. As so defined, market power has two pronounced characteristics. First if it is based on "real" (as opposed to pecuniary) economies, such power may be considered "reasonable." Second, *persistent* market power raises questions of market dynamics, the appropriate question being whether such power is a temporary aberration which can be destroyed by the elements of change inherent in any market. Therefore, the criterion adopted is that mergers which enhance market power to an unreasonable degree, without the offsetting benefits of real scale economies, are not in the public interest.

In accordance with this criterion the conclusion of this study is that "unreasonable" market power of both an "individual" and "joint" nature exists in brewing. Individual power is held by Canadian Breweries, Molson, and Labatt, and these companies form the group that possesses joint power. However, the joint power involves more than a promotion of symmetry because, although a tight oligopolistic structure prevails, implicit bargaining over the competitive variables has been replaced by extensive overt joint control. The major factor establishing this joint dominance was the extensive series of mergers in which all three engaged. The key elements in reaching the conclusion revolve around the behaviour of the "big three" with regard to price determination and advertising and the absence of real scale economies.

With regard to price, the brewers defend uniformity on the basis that it is fixed by provincial authorities, thus implying that market power at the producer level is irrelevant because such *regulation* protects the public interest. Even if this proposition is unsubstantiated, it is possible that provincial authorities could exercise a "big buyer" function[4] and so protect the public interest by *negotiation* over price. It is the contention here that neither regulation nor the "big buyer" concept is realistic in this industry. Price is covertly set on a joint profit-maximization basis by the brewers.

With prices fixed and uniform, the competitive emphasis has been placed on advertising. Because of the relationship between transportation costs and resale value, the market for beer is regional. However, as the mergers gave the "big three" a national multiplant base and since "national" advertising

---

[4]See J. B. Dirlam and A. E. Kahn, "Antitrust Law and the Big Buyer: Another Look at the A. & P. Case," *Journal of Political Economy*, 60 (1952).

appears the most effective in this industry, regional brewers are placed at a competitive disadvantage by conditions unrelated to regional markets. With respect to entry barriers, the emphasis on advertising means that an unnecessarily high overhead is placed on potential entrants, a fact which in turn puts a premium on the scale at which they can enter. Added to this are the facts that excess capacity exists and demand is relatively static. Therefore, both from within and without the market, the positions of the big three are relatively impregnable.

Such impregnable positions are not justified on the basis of real scale economies. On the one hand, the possible economies which could accrue would do so only to Canadian Breweries' operating divisions, not the firm as such. On the other hand, it appears that even here the existence of such economies is debatable. Certainly if the profit figures of the small brewers are any guide such economies are not overpowering. . . .

SUGGESTIONS FOR FURTHER READING

Allen, G. C., *Monopoly and Restrictive Practices,* George Allen & Unwin Ltd., London, 1968.

American Economic Association, *Readings in Industrial Organization and Public Policy,* Homewood, Illinois, Irwin Inc., 1958.

Andrews, P., *Fair Trade: Resale Price Maintenance Re-examined,* New York, The Macmillan Co., 1960.

Bladen, V. W., *Competition and Monopoly and Their Regulation in Canada,* submission to the Royal Commission on Canada's Economic Prospects, Toronto, January, 1956.

Bork, R. H., "Goals of Anti-Trust Policy," *American Economic Review,* Papers and Proceedings, Vol. 57 (May, 1967).

Brecher, I., "Combines and Competition: A Re-appraisal of Canadian Public Policy," *Canadian Bar Review,* Vol. 38, 1960.

Britnell, G. E., V. C. Fowke, M. F. Timlin, and K. A. H. Buckley, *Workable Competition and Monopoly,* submission to the Royal Commission on Canada's Economic Prospects, Ottawa, March, 1956.

Canadian Institute of Chartered Accountants, *The Combines Investigation Act and Management,* Toronto, 1965.

Clark, J. M., "Toward a Concept of Workable Competition," *American Economic Review,* Vol. 30 (June, 1940).

Cohen, Maxwell, "Towards Reconsideration in Anti-Combines Law and Policy," *McGill Law Journal,* Vol. 9, 1963.

English, H. E., "Competition and Policy to Control Restrictive Practices," chapter 2 in T. N. Brewis (and others), *Canadian Economic Policy* (revised edition), (Toronto, Macmillan Co. of Canada Ltd., 1965).

Forster, D. F., "The Politics of Combines Policy: Liberals and the Stevens Commission," *Canadian Journal of Economics and Political Science,* Vol. 28 (November, 1962).

Gosse, R., *The Law on Competition in Canada,* Toronto, 1962.

Jacobs, D. M., "The Application of Anti-Trust Legislation in North America," *International and Comparative Law Quarterly,* Vol. 15, (April, 1966).

Jones, J. C. H., "The Economics of the National Hockey League," *Canadian Journal of Economics,* Vol. 2 (February, 1969).

Kaysen, C., and D. F. Turner, *Anti-trust Policy: An Economic and Legal Analysis,* Cambridge, Mass., Harvard University Press, 1959.

Lincoln, J. A., *The Restrictive Society: A Report on Restrictive Practices,* George Allen & Unwin Ltd., London, 1967.

Lyon, R., "Recent Canadian Anti-Combines Policy: Mergers and Monopoly," *University of Toronto Law Journal,* Vol. 15 (1963).

Organization for Economic Co-operation and Development, *Guide to Legislation on Restrictive Business Practices,* Paris, annual.

Phillips, W. G., "Canadian Combines Policy—The Matter of Mergers," *Canadian Bar Review,* Vol. 42 (March, 1964).

Report of the Committee to Study Combines Legislation and Interim Report on Resale Price Maintenance (The MacQuarrie Report) Ottawa, Queen's Printer, 1952.

Report of the Director of Investigation and Research, Combines Investigation Act, Ottawa, Queen's Printer, annual.

Reynolds, L. G., *The Control of Competition in Canada,* Cambridge, Mass., Harvard University Press, 1940.

Skeoch, L. A., "The Consumer Interest in Anti-Combines Legislation," *Canadian Consumer Problems, Proceedings of National Conference of Consumers' Association of Canada,* Ottawa, 1962.

Skeoch, L. A., "The Abolition of Resale Price Maintenance: Some notes on Canadian Experience," *Economics,* Vol. 31 (August, 1964).

Skeoch, L. A., (ed.), *Restrictive Trade Practices in Canada, Selected Readings,* Toronto, McClelland & Stewart Ltd., 1966.

Stocking, G. W., "On the Concept of Workable Competition as an Anti-Trust Guide," *Antitrust Bulletin,* Vol. 2 (September, 1956).

Stykolt, S., *Economic Analysis and Combines Policy,* Toronto, University of Toronto Press, 1965.

Stykolt, S., "Combines Policy: An Economist's Evaluation," *Canadian Journal of Economics and Political Science,* Vol. 22 (February, 1956).

Thorburn, H. G., "Pressure Groups in Canadian Politics: Recent Revisions of the Anti-Combines Legislation, *Canadian Journal of Economics and Political Science,* Vol. 30 (May, 1964).

Whitley, A. E., "Some Contrasts and Similarities in Canadian, American, and British Procedures for the Examination of Monopolistic Situations," in R. M. Clark, *Canadian Issues,* Toronto, University of Toronto Press, 1961.

Wilson, G. W., "Anti-Combines and Injury to the Public," *Canadian Journal of Economics and Political Science,* Vol. 23 (February, 1957).

Yamey, B. S. (ed.), *Resale Price Maintenance,* London, Weidenfeld and Nicolson, 1966.

PART FIVE

Public Regulation and Ownership

INTRODUCTION

Where it is not feasible to have more than one or a few firms operating in a particular industry, the free-market economy's principal regulating device, competition, is not available to insure that these firms will produce an optimum amount of product at a price equal to the cost of production. They may, instead, limit output in quantity (and perhaps in quality, too) and charge prices high enough to yield monopoly profits.

Two important alternatives to competitive controls in such situations are public ownership and public regulation of privately-owned firms. Both have been particularly important in Canada, where, in this respect, the practice differs noticeably from that in the United States. It is interesting to speculate on the reasons for this. One, which has already been alluded to, is that the relative smallness of Canadian domestic markets has limited the extent to which competitive forces have been available. Another is the apparently greater political and legal acceptability of public regulation and ownership in this country. One important political consideration here has been the objective of developing national unity and independence from the United States. Public ownership and regulation of business enterprise in Canada have often been accepted, it would seem, on these "nationalistic" grounds. The national policy respecting railroads, broadcasting, and financial institutions would be examples. Legally, the important consideration has been the constitutional competence of Parliament to bring private business under government control—whereas the courts in the United States have traditionally emphasized the sanctity of private ownership and business profits as forms of private property.

A broad sampling of the issues and principles associated with the Canadian experience with public regulation and ownership is provided by the readings selected for this part; but it must not be read as more than a sampling. The inexhaustible variety of practices and issues associated with this topic can be attributed in part to the complexities of a federal system of government. Electricity, gas, water, urban transit, and telephone services are publicly owned and regulated at the provincial-municipal level of government. Railways, airlines, broadcasting, and banking are subject to Federal regulation and, in some cases, ownership. These jurisdictions overlap in many instances, with provincially-owned railways, for example, being subject to a Federal regulatory agency.

The situation is further complicated by the absence of any particular pattern separating public ownership of industry and public regulation as alternative forms of control. Some firms in an industry may be publicly owned whereas others are privately owned. Both may be subject to a public regulatory board or commission sitting in judgment on their rates and services.

These complications create a difficult problem of taxonomy, although anyone with a penchant for organization and a large sheet of paper could probably produce a reasonably accurate depiction of the institutional complexities involved here. More challenging are the intellectual difficulties that arise when the self-regulating competitive market determination of price and output is replaced by some form of administered decision-making to determine these values.

How should the prices charged by public utilities companies be determined? Should public monopolies operate at a profit? How competitive should government-supported crown corporations be with privately-owned firms in the same industry? These are some of the questions raised when public regulation and control has to be used to replace or to supplement spontaneous market forces.

An illustration of the kind of vexing problem that arises when administrators take over from markets is provided in *Reading 24*. This extract from a longer article is concerned with the way public regulatory bodies go about establishing a rate structure for a private public-utility company such that its owners will receive a "fair" rate of return on their investments.

The foregoing is one of the problems that, it might appear, could be overcome simply by the state taking over ownership of the company concerned. Under public ownership there would be no group of private investors to worry about. But public ownership creates its own problems, of course. Perhaps the most fundamental of these is the problem of ensuring that the publicly-owned business conducts itself in the way the public (or economists) think it should, and not in the way some politically influential pressure group thinks it should. A publicly-owned business cannot be expected to meet simultaneously the criteria of economic efficiency—producing the desired level of output at the minimum economic cost—if it is also to be used as a device for channelling hidden subsidies to its customers or suppliers in order to promote some political objective.

The interesting issue concerning the extent to which this type of organization is compatible with the maintenance of private enterprise is dealt with in the succeeding selection by Professor Musolf. He advances the hypothesis that the extensive use of public ownership in Canada, compared with that in the United States, is the consequence of a pragmatic approach to peculiar Canadian economic problems rather than to any ideological preference for public ownership as such.

As noted earlier, a fundamental peculiarity of the Canadian situation is our proximity to the economically and politically most powerful nation in the world. Many examples could be found of economic policies in Canada that reflect the problem of developing and preserving some degree of national autonomy under these circumstances. Among them is the use of public regulation and public ownership to develop or to control certain industries in the national interest. Consideration of such policies, it might be suggested, would be better deferred to Section Three where policies to restrict competition and to interfere with market forces are discussed. It happens, however, that the key national industries, such as the transportation, broadcasting, and banking industries used as illustrations here, are also industries in which the problems of regulating monopolistic situations arise in particularly acute forms in this country. Thus it is impossible to separate the use of regulation and public ownership for "political" purposes of national development, unity, and independence, from their use to overcome deficiencies of competitive private ownership as a means of ensuring the economic efficiency of these industries.

The particularly close interconnection of these purposes in the case of the Canadian transportation industries is well documented in the perceptive study of these industries in *Reading 26* from the report of the 1961 Royal Commission on Transportation.

In the case of radio and television broadcasting, the political aspects of public control over the industry are particularly important and contentious. The technical and, to some extent, economic characteristics of this industry make a measure of public regulation necessary. Some sort of central control is needed to maintain order in the use of radio frequencies and television channels. The allocation of these limited facilities to particular broadcasters creates, however, an inherently uncompetitive market structure consisting of local broadcasting monopolies. Yet, as the Royal Commission on Broadcasting reveals in *Reading 27,* some difficulty is experienced in reconciling state control of broadcasting with the maintenance of certain types of free political institutions.

Public regulation of banking in Canada has long been accepted as a necessary public responsibility. Few industries have been so closely regulated, the relevant legislative controls being embodied in the decennial bank act under which most Canadian commercial banking business is carried on. As in the case of broadcasting, but perhaps to a lesser degree, this regulatory activity has the side effect of limiting the number of firms in the industry.

Having to obtain a bank charter, like obtaining a license to broadcast, constitutes a restriction on entry to the industry, a condition that, however unavoidable or necessary, has the effect of lessening competition. Yet this is not the intention of the policy of regulating banking. On the contrary, as Professor Slater shows in his review of the most recent Canadian banking legislation, public policy in Canada is designed to promote competition— if not among chartered banking companies—at least among the banks and other financial institutions in the country. Again it will be noted that, as in the cases of transportation and broadcasting, public policy toward the regulations of banking in Canada includes elements designed to protect national independence, in this case by limiting foreign ownership of banking in this country.

24 The Determination of the Fair Rate of Return for Public Utilities*

A. B. Jackson

Nearly all the boards and commissions in the United States and Canada that regulate public utility rates do so on the basis of allowing a public utility a "return" on the "value" of the public utility property. The return that must be allowed is usually referred to as the "fair return," but it is often designated as a "fair and reasonable" or "just and reasonable" return. Annual revenues are allowed that enable the utility to meet its operating expenses, including income taxes and other taxes, to provide for depreciation and then to have for the benefit of investors a "fair return." The utility uses the "return" it earns to pay interest and dividends and to hold or re-invest any balance on behalf of shareholders.

The fair return is vitally important. It often may amount to more than one-third of the total revenues required for a public utility. Yet almost no one considers it capable of precise determination.

Public utility rate regulation is often described as both a science and an art because, although much of rate regulation can be carried out by applying fairly well-accepted and definite rules to recorded figures and other

*From: "The Determination of the Fair Return for Public Utilities", *Canadian Public Administration*, Vol. VII, no. 3 (1964), pp. 343, 357, 358 (reprinted by permission of author and publisher).
Note: A. B. Jackson wishes it clearly understood that the statements which appear in this edited version of his article are fully substantiated in the original.

definite data, the job cannot be carried out by this process alone. Engineers and accountants can settle in a more or less "scientific" way most of the questions as to the amounts of revenue required for operating expenses and depreciation but their professional skills do not enable them to give a definite answer to the question, "What is fair?," in determining a "fair" return.

*   *   *

After reviewing the development of the idea of "fair return" in the United States and its application there and in Canada, perhaps the most obvious conclusion is that the exercise of "good judgment" in deciding the fairness of a rate of return is inescapable and is of crucial importance.

It must be noted that, although there is general agreement on the tests of a fair return as expressed in general terms by economists and by the Courts (e.g. comparability of earnings, capital attraction, maintenance of financial integrity), the kind of evidence that is given is necessarily so indefinite and inconclusive that reputable expert witnesses draw widely differing conclusions from it.

Analyses and formulae have been applied to the problem of the fair return in determined attempts to reduce the element of judgment to manageable proportions. Thus there has been a tendency to break the over-all fair return down into components comprising (1) the cost of debt and preferred share capital, (2) the cost of common share capital, and (3) other necessary allowances.

Nearly all Commissions that make a break-down of the fair return use the historic cost of debt and preferred share capital and thus reduce the element of judgment to a minimum in this very large item.

Until fairly recently, earnings-price ratios of somewhat more than 10 per cent seemed fairly reliable evidence of the cost of common share capital and had fairly widespread acceptance as the measure of such cost. But more recently investors have priced common stocks according to optimistic future expectations rather than current earnings so that earnings-price ratios have gone down, sometimes even to a level below the rate of interest on first mortgage bonds. The result has been that, from being sometimes treated as the equivalent of the current cost of common share money, earnings-price ratios are now usually received with some suspicion along with much other evidence and are seldom used very directly in a finding of cost of common share capital. Thus, although it seemed for a while to some that the element of judgment could be almost entirely removed from the determination of the cost of common share capital, it is now generally recognized that any such hope is futile and that what is fair to allow to common shareholders of a particular utility can be arrived at only in a rather general way by applying judgment to a mass of evidence bearing indirectly on the question. Commissions now seem to avoid making any specific finding of a fair return on common share capital and, at most, merely test possible over-all rates of return by deriving therefrom corresponding rates of return on common share capital and testing these rates by considering in a fairly general way all the relevant evidence.

All that remains to be said about the break-down of the fair return is that there are some elements which are usually recognized as separate items and are often even treated separately from the allowance for common share capital. These elements are almost never given a precise valuation but are usually considered altogether in arriving at an over-all rate of return. They include allowances for such things as efficiency of management, prospective increases in the proportion of common share capital, the likelihood of early approaches to the money markets for substantial amounts of new capital, and "attrition" or "regulatory lag," and some allowance at least in the common share component of the rate base for inflation and for unusual risks. In some way or other the income tax benefit obtained by a public utility that uses accelerated depreciation for tax purposes but provides for normal tax in its operating accounts is usually reflected in the amount of the fair return. How this is done is such an important and unsettled subject that it can be examined properly only in a separate study of income tax and accelerated depreciation.

To sum up the whole subject in a few words, it may be said that the mass of inconclusive evidence that Commissions consider makes the determination of a fair return a vague process. But this is necessarily so, because no ingenious formula can take the place of a sense of fairness or justice applied to all the aspects of the particular case.

25 The Boundaries of Public Enterprise*

Lloyd D. Musolf

The operational area for government enterprise is bounded at its extremes by two familiar Canadian landmarks: (1) the tradition that the national government should act aggressively to establish and maintain national economic unity; and (2) the tradition of an economic system anchored on private enterprise. The first factor argues for the creation of sufficient government enterprise to assure accomplishment of the national goals; the second signifies the absence of an ideological drive to place industry in the government's hands.

The vital part played by the state in developing Canada has been noted often by the country's economists. "The role of the state in the economic

*From: Lloyd D. Musolf, *Public Ownership and Accountability* Cambridge Massachusetts, Harvard University Press, 1959), by the President and Fellows of Harvard College, pp. 4-11 (reprinted by permission of publisher).

life of Canada," Professor Alexander Brady has remarked, "is really the modern history of Canada."[1] Confederation itself, another economist has argued, "can be interpreted as a political adaptation to the unfavourable impact of the first industrial revolution on Canada."[2] At the very least, the Confederation document—the British North America Act—obligated the national government to undertake a commercial venture in order to bind the Maritime Provinces to Quebec and Ontario. Soon after satisfying this obligation by building the Intercolonial Railway, the government heavily subsidized the Canadian Pacific in order to reinforce British Columbia's links to the nation and to provide the first transcontinental railroad. The government also built canals, provided protective tariffs and bonuses for secondary industry, and opened the western lands to settlement. These actions performed the vital function of supplementing the inadequate efforts of private capital. Generally speaking, they were popular, as Sir John A. MacDonald's "National Policy" in particular demonstrated.[3]

The stimuli which made the state take an active role—"the pioneer nature of the country, the physical structure of the half-continent, the imperial sweep of settlement after 1867, the influence of the interacting ideas and institutions of Britain and the United States, and the quick response of the whole society to the advance of western industrialism"[4]—retain much of their force today. Partly this is so because it has been characteristic of Western society, in whose dynamic nature Canada shares, to advance constantly its concepts of minimum requirements. Thus, an old field of concern for the state—transportation and communication—has continued to challenge the government as new inventions have come along. In the case of transcontinental aviation and radio broadcasting, for example, the government chose to create public corporations in the 1930's to operate these services rather than to allow chaotic private development. As examples of relatively recent actions designed to bind the nation together, the reasoning involved is worth considering briefly.

The swift advance in the commercial possibilities of air travel—as demonstrated by private air lines in the United States—had caught Canada by surprise. Private enterprise, in the opinion of the Liberal government, was not up to the task of providing the nation with efficient transcontinental air service. Lamenting the fact that a "score or more" of private companies

---

[1] "The State and Economic Life," in *Canada*, ed. George W. Brown (Berkeley, 1950), p. 353.

[2] Maurice Lamontagne, "The Role of Government," in *Canada's Tomorrow*, ed. G. P. Gilmour (Toronto, 1954), p. 122.

[3] The term was popularized by MacDonald and the Conservatives in the campaign of 1878. Its meaning is generally restricted to the institution of the protective tariff, but cogent arguments have been made for subsuming the entire group of policies named above under the title. See V. C. Fowke, "The National Policy—Old and New," *Canadian Journal of Economics and Political Science*, XVIII (August 1952), 271-286, and Brady, "The State and Economic Life," in *Canada*, pp. 358-59.

[4] Brady, in *Canada*, p. 353.

had ended on the financial junkheap, C. D. Howe, minister of transport, told the House of Commons in 1937: "Our task in Canada is to set up this service without all the lost motion that has been expended during the past ten years."[5] The creation of Trans-Canada Air Lines, a corporate subsidiary of Canadian National Railways, followed. At a later date, in reviewing the airline's remarkable progress, Howe tied T.C.A. into the tradition of national development in the following words: "Facilities for transportation and communication have been among our most powerful tools in the fashioning of Canadian unity . . . T.C.A. serves in the same high tradition . . . Canadian distances have already lost much of their old significance . . . and a new sense of nationhood is being fostered by Canada's new accessibility to its citizens. In particular, Canadian industry and business have received a major stimulus from air transport."[6]

The creation of the Canadian Radio Broadcasting Commission (predecessor of the Canadian Broadcasting Corporation) in 1932 demonstrated that government ownership for the sake of national development was not a monopoly of the Liberal party. Radio broadcasting had to be under government auspices for three reasons, Conservative Prime Minister R. B. Bennett told the House:

> First of all, this country must be assured of complete Canadian control of broadcasting from Canadian sources, free from foreign interference or influence . . . [so that] national consciousness may be fostered and sustained and national unity still further strengthened . . . .
>
> Secondly, no other scheme . . . can ensure . . . equal enjoyment of the benefits and pleasures of radio broadcasting. . . .
>
> [Thirdly] . . . the air itself . . . is a natural resource over which we have complete jurisdiction . . . I believe that there is no government in Canada that does not regret today that it has parted with some of these natural resources for considerations wholly inadequate and on terms that do not reflect the principle under which the crown holds the natural resources in trust for all the people.[7]

The years since the onset of World War II have witnessed a merger of the national development theme with that of national defense. Each reinforces the strength of the other. Does it aid defense or development more when, for example, public corporations mine and refine uranium or build transportation and electric power systems in remote, primitive areas of the country? The pace of events still outruns the capabilities of private interests in conquering Canadian geography alone, even if business wished to devote its efforts to relatively unprofitable projects. In view of world events and Canada's own ambitions, it is evident that continued government action of this sort will be needed in the foreseeable future.

The second familiar Canadian landmark that affects the scope of public

---

[5]*Debates* (Commons) (1937), p. 2215.

[6]*Debates,* 1945, 2d sess., p. 1358. A member of the opposition responded with further words of praise "for what they [T.C.A.] have done in helping to develop the country" (p. 1359).

[7]*Debates,* 1932, pp. 3035-36.

enterprise is the prime role of private enterprise in the economy. The logic which gave an active economic role to the state has never been extended (except in platforms of the Cooperative Commonwealth Federation, the democratic socialist party) to the nationalization of industry. No huge existing industries have been taken over by the government, unless one includes the acquisition of the bankrupt railroads during World War I.[8]

In the instance of the railroads, not only was the prosperous Canadian Pacific left intact, but the reasoning by which the other private railroads were acquired demonstrates the limited role of sentiment favoring public ownership. The onset of war had abruptly shut off the flow of immigration and of foreign capital, a situation which immediately threatened the solvency of several railroads that had just reached a period in their development when earnings might offset the heavy initial expenditure of capital and begin to repay extensive government loans made in the developmental period. The *Debates* of the House of Commons reflect the shock of the members at the grim turn of events—a shock made all the greater because of the rosy vision of Canada's future entertained especially by members from the prairie provinces. Although much time and energy were spent in recriminations and attempts to fix the blame for the "needless duplication" and "costly overbuilding" of railroads, the problem of what to do remained. Public ownership was arrived at only after a painful canvass of various alternatives. To let the railroads go into receivership was not considered a viable alternative because foreign investors had relied on the guarantees given by the national and provincial governments in connection with bonds issued by the railroads.[9] Default on the guarantee, it was felt, would affect Canada's credit adversely at the very time it was fighting a great war. Further loans to the railroads were out of the question because it was suspected that public opinion would not tolerate them, a feeling summed up by the Conservative Minister of Finance when he declared: "If the public does the financing, the public should enjoy the ultimate reward."[10] Government leaders were certain that public opinion would not allow the bankrupt roads to fall into the hands of the gigantic and prosperous Canadian Pacific.[11] Finally, once a segment of a transcontinental road was acquired from a bankrupt company, it was financially necessary to take over the rest of the line.[12] Thus, the acquisition of the Canadian Northern was followed by that of the Grand Trunk and the Grand Trunk Pacific.

---

[8]In 1950, under the stimulus of an agreement concluded by the Commonwealth countries, the Canadian Overseas Telecommunication Corporation did expropriate (under the direction of the Governor in Council) the facilities of two private companies engaged in external telecommunications. See the corporation's first *Annual Report*, dated March 31, 1951.

[9]*Debates*, 1917, p. 4218.

[10]*Ibid.*, p. 4015.

[11]*Debates*, 1919, p. 1741.

[12]*Ibid.*, 2d sess., p. 1054.

In emphasizing that the Canadian government more or less "backed into" ownership of the railroads, it is not intended to imply that public ownership sentiment was non-existent. As a matter of fact, the *Debates* contain considerable evidence that the House was well aware of popular sentiment, especially in Ontario and the West, favoring government ownership.[13] Nevertheless, it is apparent that this sentiment did not govern the situation. The Borden government drew a sharp line between taking over bankrupt railroads and wholesale nationalization, rejecting the latter as highly detrimental "to the credit of the Dominion and to our prospects for future financing."[14]

Just as pragmatic considerations outweighed public ownership sentiment in the acquistion of the bankrupt railroads, so they have prevailed in subsequent ventures in public enterprise. In fact, freed of the elements of surprise and reluctance manifest in the railroad situation, the government has appeared to weigh practical aspects even more deliberately. One of the best illustrations is found in a debate on the government's proposals for liberalization of credit to small businessmen, farmers, and fishermen in 1944. The flexibility of the Liberal government's approach was demonstrated by the fact that an Industrial Development Bank was proposed to handle loans to small businessmen, while the commercial banks were to be agents in making government-backed loans to farmers and fishermen. Highly practical reasons were offered for employing public enterprise in one instance and rejecting its use in the other.[15] In the course of debate government spokesmen were called upon to defend their stand against nationalization of all commercial banks, which had been demanded by the Cooperative Commonwealth Federation. The Minister of Finance took the position that: "The question of nationalization of an industry or a specific firm should not be one of ideology. We should neither shrink from nationalization because of an economic philosophy based on fear, nor embrace it rashly . . . We should

---

[13]*Debates,* 1917, pp. 4275, 4384; and 1919, 2d sess., p. 1057.

[14]*Debates,* 1917, p. 4015. It is true that the M.P.s' awareness of public ownership sentiment produced an almost ludicrous jockeying to gain credit for public ownership measures while denying a doctrinaire bias toward the principle (see pp. 1811 and 2115.) Furthermore, several prominent Conservatives seem to have expected public ownership to play an increasingly important role as the industrialization of Canada proceeded.

[15]J. L. Ilsley, the minister of finance, argued as follows. "The house will appreciate, however, that unlike the industrial development bank, which will operate with a relatively few offices and a comparatively small but highly skilled staff, a similar agency to provide intermediate credit for agriculture could do its job effectively only with literally thousands of branches or offices throughout rural areas readily accessible to farmers. Some of the United States farm credit organizations were considered as possible models, but . . . the same objective could be attained more speedily and effectively and at a fraction of the cost by a comparatively simple extension of existing lending facilities. Moreover, a new set of institutions would have taken years to build up and to equip with competent and experienced staff." *Debates,* 1944, p. 2558.

use it only where it alone can serve the public interest or can serve it better than any alternative form of organization. Commercial banking, I am convinced, is not one of those cases."[16] In his rebuttal, M. J. Coldwell, the C.C.F. leader, recited a number of alleged inadequacies in the banking system and emphasized that "It is on these grounds then, that we call for the national ownership and control of the financial system, and particularly the banks; not, as the minister suggested, on some doctrinaire theory that their socialization will destroy the present system." [17] This denial of a doctrinaire approach, it may be noted, came from a source usually identified as one of the most doctrinaire on the subject of public enterprise.

A highly pragmatic attitude, then, has consistently demonstrated its usefulness in any situation where the traditions of national economic development and private enterprise may come into conflict. This attitude has probably been able to emerge more easily because business and government are constrained by the circumstances toward moderation. Business cannot easily boast of an exclusive role in building the economy, as it tends to in the United States, for it is faced not merely with a history of government enterprise dating back to Confederation, but with an even more vital present. Furthermore, under the brand of Keynesianism practiced by the Canadian government, it has a close working arrangement with the government in the promotion of prosperity and industrial development.[18] Probably it is also restrained by a consciousness of its own limited strength, its vulnerability to a charge that subsidiaries of American corporations are prominent in its midst, and, less importantly, a fear that a reactionary stand might strengthen the hand of the C.C.F. and bring on nationalization. The government, for its part, has not exhibited—under either the Conservatives or the Liberals— any inclination to push public enterprise for its own sake; in this it has but mirrored its recognition and approval of private enterprise as the foundation of the economy. Although it has not shrunk from taking action necessary to attain the goal of economic unity, even if this has meant launching a commercial venture, it has done so only in response to demonstrated need.

---

[16]*Ibid.*, p. 2547.

[17]*Ibid.*, p. 2718.

[18]See the "White Paper" issued by C. D. Howe, the minister of reconstruction and development in 1945 (*Employment and Income, with Special Reference to the Initial Period of Reconstruction*, Ottawa, 1945); an article by Owe, "Industrial Development in Canada," *Public Affairs*, XI (December 1948), 207-213, in which the author lists "four principles underlying our industrial development program"; and O. J. Firestone, "Investment and Economic Development in Canada," *The Statist* (Canadian Supplement, May 31, 1952, pp. 18-20). For an indication of the extent to which business regards itself as a partner of government, see John T. Bryden, "Government and Business," in *Canada: Nation on the March* (Toronto, 1953), pp. 67-74, and Howard Gamble, "The Road to Tomorrow," *Canadian Business,* XXVII (January 1954), pp. 22-24, 50ff. Gamble asserts, "There is in Canada probably a greater genuine liaison and rapport between government and business than in any other country" (p. 50).

26   Limitations of Competition in Transportation *

Royal Commission on Transportation

The nature of competition in transportation in Canada being what it is and trending in the direction which it appears to be, we recognize the fact that market forces cannot be relied upon absolutely to achieve the objective of the most efficient allocation of resources in transportation.

There are a number of reasons which force us to this conclusion. Some are associated with the historical role of transportation in the national development, the relative sizes of firms in the various modes which have developed, the minimum amounts and length of commitment of capital necessary to operate, the divided nature of regulatory powers in Canada, the unequal contribution of public investment, and other assistance to the various modes at all levels of government. Of these factors, some are amenable to change by public action if there is developed a greater degree of uniformity in public policy at all levels of government. Others, however, are the results of the economic and institutional structure of the various modes and are not susceptible to significant alteration by public action without the creation of instability and inefficiency.

Reliance on the efficacy of competition to bring about total transportation efficiency must be limited for some less obvious but equally cogent reasons. In any industry where a few firms are supplying the total product or service the condition of imperfect competition occurs. This condition can be sustained wherever other firms find it difficult to enter the industry, either because of the large amount of investment required in relation to the total market, or because of artificial regulatory control over entry. Whenever conditions exist which limit entry, prices may tend to become regulated by tacit or explicit arrangement. If these arrangements are private they will be primarily in the interests of revenue stability for the few firms, and at prices higher than would otherwise prevail. If the controls are public, the regulatory authority has the double, and often conflicting, task of attempting to limit monopoly or oligopoly price while trying to maintain revenue requirements and acceptable service standards. In the instances of a market small in relation to necessary investment (a condition sometimes referred to as a natural monopoly), the only solution for public policy is to limit the number of firms. If accompanied by rate control, such limitation is consistent with the objectives of National Transportation Policy, in these special circumstances. If such regulatory arrangements do not exist at all, pricing in imperfect competition may be so disorganized that severe instability will result.

This is the dilemma which faces those responsible for creating a policy

*From: *Report,* (Queen's Printer, Ottawa, 1961), Vol. II, pp. 13-20 (reprinted by permission).

and administering it. Where a given mode of transport has a clear-cut cost advantage (which, to be effective, is reflected in rates) over all other modes in the movement of certain commodities, and conditions occur which limit the number of firms, the central problem is the public regulation of the firms in that mode to provide "reasonable" rates. Public policy in that case has the task of deciding, through applying standards of reasonableness, what the rates must be. This is public utility regulation and the theory and practice of it is sufficiently developed to need no treatment in this Report.

The instances of clear-cut, over-all cost advantage pertaining to a given mode of transportation are becoming fewer. More and more, new techniques are making the movement of goods by alternate modes possible. Each mode has a range of costs at which it can provide its particular services and, if competition were pervasive enough, these costs would parallel with fair accuracy the prices charged. But the more competition is limited, the more the pricing of any individual movement will tend to be opportunistic, unrelated to the costs properly associated with the service performed. This, as a matter of course, finds its effects in the misallocation of resources in transportation, and distorts to a greater or lesser degree resource allocation in the rest of the community.

Public action, therefore, in developing a National Transportation Policy, must seek to encourage competitive forces where the structure of the industries permits pervasive and effective competition to operate, and to regulate where it does not. In practice this amounts to developing agencies of regulation which recognize that freedom of pricing will bring efficiencies in those sectors of the transportation industry where the firms can be numerous and achieve satisfactory economies with commitments of capital small in relation to the total market. Trucking is the obvious example. Regulation in this situation should be firm, uniform, clearly stated and adequately enforced, confined to maintaining standards of safety and performance. This applies particularly in Canada at the provincial level where co-ordination needs to be developed to achieve uniform standards and to be able to resist pressures, in the interests of those firms already established, for stricter control of entry. Stability within the industry, as defined by some proposals, is not synonymous with the provision of service at lowest real cost to the community.

For those parts of the industry where efficiencies in operation are obtainable only by very large capital commitments, the number of firms will be small in relation to the total market. The railways are the classic case in point. Here competition cannot be totally relied upon to regulate price in the interest of lowest real cost. It is here that public action must acknowledge the necessity of control comparable to any utility regulation but with one important complication. These large firms, for a large and growing portion of their business, are within a cost range which is competitive with the trucking industry. Thus the unique situation exists, and will likely persist, of a few large railway companies being the sole practical movers of a few types of commodities important to Canadian development, but competitive with one another and with a lively and growing host of trucking firms offering specialized local and long-distance road hauling. Therefore, the development of a National Transportation Policy must on one hand attempt to exercise limits on individual rates where evidence of monopoly exists. On the other hand a consistent National Transportation Policy must do nothing to inhibit the growing free play of competition, nor cushion the rough blows of competition in that segment of the whole transportation industry where a large number of firms will bring efficiency and flexibility.

Fortunately, this apparent dilemma can, we believe, be resolved by policies which are adapted to the present transportation environment and acceptable within the Canadian constitutional framework.

The policy which we believe should be adopted will not guarantee longevity to any specific firm offering a transportation service nor guarantee the long-run continuity to any given mode of transport as we now know it. The facts of competition and the national demands for efficiency eliminate such guarantees. The policy should provide a climate in which any firm providing transportation by means of a mode, or modes, shall have the opportunity to reap the rewards of flexibility and efficiency or take the consequences of rigidity and inefficiency. We conclude, therefore, that efficient transportation should be the objective and measure of public responsibility for the nation's transportation system.

Basis for Regulatory Control

Whatever may have been the rationale behind transportation pricing policies in the past, the evidence set before this Commission, and the analysis we developed in arriving at conclusions, make clear that the emergence of competition inevitably throws the ratemaker into sharper contact with the whole problem of costs of movement. Whether it is the costs associated with a particular movement by his own firm, or the costs of movement by a competitor, the orientation is evident. He must be in a position, before he can attempt to place an evaluation upon the quality of service of the movement by his firm, to know the minimum rate, determined by costs, below which he cannot go. And the relevant costs are determined in considerable part by the volume, speed and periodicity requirements of the traffic. The development of rapid and accurate costing methods is essential to all modes competing for traffic.

As the range and intensity of competition spreads, and individual *ad hoc* rate adjustments become less and less useful in maintaining or capturing traffic, broad and general revisions of the traditional rate structures are needed to bring them more in line with cost patterns. Only thus will each mode be in a sufficiently competent position to move the traffic most suitable to it.

The development of costing techniques is particularly vital for railways, and we have been impressed by the degree of sophistication already displayed. The submissions made to this Commission on the costs associated with the movement of grain and grain products from Western Canada to export positions is evidence that the science and art of cost finding have made significant strides. The determination of the degree of competence in costing principles and practice was the reason why so much time was taken up dealing with the cost studies on the movement of grain. It was an excellent test case. This knowledge will, under the pressure of competition, be continually refined and improved with the expectation of increased accuracy in the results. However, we wish to acknowledge that several of the most important decisions respecting any costing operation are matters of judgement and not of technique, and are likely to remain so.

The unique position occupied by railways in the total transport picture makes railway costing of significant importance to the regulatory authority, the Board of Transport Commissioners for Canada. The same conclusion may be drawn for any mode of transport where the capital investment of the firm is significant in relation to the total volume of traffic moved. Where this phenomenon exists, regulation of rates, particularly minimum and maximum rates, becomes essential. . . . It is sufficient to state here that, for these reasons, the development of adequate and accurate cost and traffic data becomes of vital interest to all rate regulatory authorities. At the moment, we do not have, in sufficient detail for all modes, the total volume of traffic handled or its composition or the nature of movements or the significant reasons for the choice of a given type of movement. Without such information, any adequately broad and composite picture is unavailable to the regulatory authorities which would enable them to judge specific regulatory decisions in perspective. Even more serious, those responsible for policies of public investment in transportation are unable now to judge accurately the influence of their decisions upon the mode concerned or on other modes. No accurate universal assessment of cost measured against benefit can possibly be made without the necessary statistical series. A serious aspect of this limitation has been the probable effects of public investment on those modes most completely dependent upon private sources for capital funds. The end result of the lack of sufficient data has been the inability to assess proper user charges for the use of public investment in transport, or to be able to use the instrument of the user charge to direct activity toward that mode making the most efficient use of resources.

Without accurate and sufficient statistical evidence wasteful public expenditure is a constant probability. If the objective of the National Transportation Policy is the creation of an efficient transportation system this involves the encouragement of the various modes, separately or in combination, to the extent of their economic capabilities. This involves, without question, cost and traffic compilations by the carriers and inevitably by the regulatory and the policy-making authorities. Accurate collection of such data and co-operative development of costing techniques are basic to an effective transportation policy and practice.

27   Is Regulation of Broadcasting in Canada Necessary?*

Royal Commission on Broadcasting

Before considering the problem of regulating our broadcasting system and suggesting how it might be done, it may be well to consider if regulation is necessary at all. After our hearings and full consideration of this question we are satisfied of the need of regulation, not only as to the technical control of frequencies and power but also as to programme content and station performance. We are satisfied that for Canada this is a legitimate and proper function of the state, and under our constitution it is a function of Parliament.

Probably the simplest basis for this conclusion is that it was supported by the great majority of witnesses who dealt with the subject before us. There was considerable difference of opinion as to the methods and procedures by which such regulation should be exercised, but the fact of control and regulation by an agency of the state was almost universally recognized as desirable and necessary in Canada.

It might have been expected that the Canadian Association of Radio and Television Broadcasters, speaking on behalf of most of the private radio and television stations in Canada would have had basic objections to public regulation. Indeed, they did at our opening sittings submit a brief (Exhibit 16) which contained a somewhat inconclusive argument as to the nature of broadcasting, suggesting it was a form of publishing and not a public utility or within the public domain. Again, in the final rebuttal hearings another document was filed (Exhibit 308) consisting of various newspaper editorials in which it was argued that government regulation of broadcasting should be limited to technical controls. This exhibit was not discussed at our hearings and no argument was based on it; nor were we able to find out what we were supposed to do with it[1]. However, in the original submission[2] it was clearly stated by CARTB that "we do not advocate that there should be no specific delegation of these functions (of Parliament or the Government) to a regulatory body having essential minimum regulatory powers over radio and television broadcasting in Canada". Then, in our final hearings, we endeavoured to discover what CARTB envisaged as the proper scope and degree of government regulation and control, and answers were given by counsel in the presence of the president, executive vice-president and some ten or twelve directors of the association[3]. They stated clearly that their pro-

---

*From: *Report*, (Ottawa, Queen's Printer, 1957), Vol. I, pp. 81-87 (reprinted by permission).

[1]Evidence, p. 7447.
[2]Exhibit 16.
[3]Evidence, p. 7226.

posals for a change in the machinery of regulation represented "no less control from the point of view of the public than is going on at the present time"[4], that their intention was "that the control would be the same as today on the operator but the method of control would be different"[5] and they specifically agreed that there should be control of such matters as programme content[6], import of programmes[7] and the use of Canadian talent[8].

In the face of the overwhelming weight of evidence approving the need in Canada of government control and regulation of broadcasting, it is probably unnecessary to labour the theoretical arguments in favour of such regulation. But we will make a brief reference to one or two of the points which were discussed in our hearings and on which there can easily be some public confusion.

It was suggested that broadcasting is a form of publishing and that broadcasters are entitled to raise the cry of "freedom of the press", when faced with state control of their programmes and performance. Those putting forward this suggestion seemed unwilling to push the analogy with the press to the point that they opposed all such controls. But let us examine the basic question as if it had been boldly asked:—What is the need and justification for regulation of the performance of radio and television stations when other forms of public information and communication such as newspapers and magazines are left free from regulations of performance other than general laws against sedition, obscenity, libel and the like?

Freedom of the press is one of the basic freedoms in a democratic society. But the principle can be, and is at times, used in an attempt to protect private rights and privileges which have nothing to do with the essentials of this freedom. Freedom of the press is not, except in an incidental or secondary sense, a right of the publisher to be left free from government interference or control. The essential freedom is that of the individual citizen to publish, to resort to the written and the spoken word, to communicate his ideas and proposals to his fellow citizens without prohibition or interference so long as the laws of the land are not broken. It is the right to use, and have access to, a pulpit, a press or a soap box.

This kind of right is for technical reasons not fully available in broadcasting. Up to the present time at least, the science of communicating by wireless signals has not developed to the point that every citizen can own a radio or a television transmitter. It is only possible to have, at the most, a certain number of people in Canada—possibly a thousand—broadcasting at any one time. If there were more than that number there would be the

---

[4]Evidence, p. 7096.
[5]Evidence, p. 7154.
[6]Evidence, p. 7146.
[7]Evidence, p. 7141, 7147.
[8]Evidence, p. 7142.

confusion of Babel. To avoid this confusion there must be control by the state which goes at least as far as allocating radio frequencies and television channels and prohibiting unauthorized persons from broadcasting over the air waves. No one has ever seriously argued against this type of technical control by the state.

But the point is important because the need of a licence necessarily results in broadcasting becoming somebody's monopoly. The decision as to who shall speak over the radio or be seen on television rests with the operators of the 189 radio stations and 38 television stations in Canada. There is nothing that any individual Canadian can do to gain access to these broadcasting media except with the permission of this handful of licensees.

The analogy with the press breaks down because of this power in a few to control the access to broadcasting facilities of the many. The freedom of the press is sometimes discussed as if it were an exclusive right of the publishers of daily newspapers. It is much wider than this. It may well be that, for economic reasons, the establishment of a new daily newspaper in any particular community is virtually impossible. But if a Canadian with a story to tell or a cause to advocate finds it impracticable to establish a daily newspaper, he may perhaps find it possible to have a weekly newspaper, or a monthly magazine, or, at least, to rent a duplicating machine and circulate his ideas and proposals in print. The right of access to the printed word may take many forms, some more effective than others, but access in some form is open to anyone and does not depend, as in broadcasting, on the decision of some one of the licensees of the relatively few available frequencies in Canada.

Even within the narrower comparison with the daily newspaper, the operation of a radio or television station may be distinguishable because of the newness of the broadcasting media and the fact that they have not yet developed an established body of tradition. Had they done so the case for regulation and control would be weaker. We asked, for example, a number of private radio station operators if they attempted to sell all their available time and were told that this was their objective. This, in the analogy with the newspapers, is to put them in the category of a "shopping news". For all reputable newspapers there are some portions of the paper that are not for sale and some attempt is made to preserve a balance between non-paid and advertising content. There is no such established tradition in private radio. All portions of the programme are open for advertising sponsorship; little, if any, time is specifically reserved for public service and non-commercial broadcasts, and what public service is done usually finds its place in time that could not be sold to sponsors. In these circumstances it is not suprising to find that, as a general rule, the amount of public service broadcasting by a private station is inversely proportionate to its commercial success. We would not want to minimize or ignore the substantial amount of public service that is in fact performed by many private stations in Canada and which we discuss elsewhere in this report. The present point is that it is not regarded as a primary function with accepted priorities and beyond interference.

Control by the state over the various media of communications would appear to be more acceptable for newer media and less necessary where a body of tradition and self-regulation has had time to develop. For newspapers and magazines, which have been developing a tradition for several centuries, the degree of public control is slight and is exercised by laws of general application. For moving pictures, which are a newer medium, some detailed control by the state of programmes and performance is generally accepted and applied; but here also, as a tradition of self-regulation developed, the degree of public control tended to become less. For the still newer media of radio and television, regulation and control of performance is justified until recognized standards of performance have been developed and applied. This type of distinction is not unique; it applies in other branches of economic life. In the older professions, such as law and medicine, where a body of professional tradition has grown up, regulation by the state is at a minimum, and control is exercised by self-regulation within these professions. With newer professions and other businesses a greater measure of public control is exercised and is accepted. But where worthy traditions of performance develop, public controls tend to recede.

Economic forces may also have an influence on the need of control and regulation. So long as there is a substantial element of commercial sponsorship in our broadcasting system, there may be a need for public control to restrain commercial forces from the excesses to which they may go. In a later section of this report, we discuss the legitimate and positive role that advertising plays in our broadcasting system. We believe that the values of commercial activities should be recognized and retained. But they can have an undesirable influence on programme performance which should be restrained. This influence is not an obvious and direct interference with programme content which is rare indeed and if attempted would be quickly resented and effectively resisted. It is rather the indirect influence on the programme schedule of the demands for time by commercial sponsors. It is not that private broadcasters are less public spirited than other people. Many of them may have a desire to produce good programmes and may attempt to do what they can. But they are faced with a conflict of interests and motives. Like other businessmen they must have a profitable business, and they make profits by selling time. Even the most public spirited broadcaster is constantly faced with an uncomfortable conflict between his desire to render a public service and his sound business instincts. His problem is further complicated when he is not the sole owner of a station and has a fiduciary responsibility to its stockholders. The demands of advertisers for time, especially for the more popular or desirable hours of the broadcasting day, can result in a monotonous similarity of programmes of immediate popular appeal or in a total advertising content which is excessive or in a form of advertising which in its insistence and blatancy is offensive.

Against such advertising practices the public can, in the absence of regulation, have little defence. It is true that, in the extreme case, public reaction can be violent and the operator of a station must always attempt to weigh public opinion and public acceptance of the station's performance. But within a fairly wide range, it is much easier for an operator to assess and attempt to please his commercial sponsors than to measure and meet the contradictory views of his scattered and largely inarticulate audience. These commercial demands may even be individually unexceptionable but cumulatively they may be excessive. They cannot be left to be resisted either by the force of public opinion or by the exercise of self-restraint by private station operators. If broadcasting is to serve the public interest as it should, we believe there must be some externally enforced standards of public interest to strengthen the instincts of public service that many private broadcasters feel.

Such regulations may well be a restraint on the freedom of a private station to accept an unlimited number of spot announcements or the unbridled promotion of detergents, laxatives and deodorants. However, it is not the freedom of the private station operator or the commercial sponsors that is important; it is the freedom of the public to enjoy a broadcasting system which provides the largest possible outlet for the widest possible range of information, entertainment and ideas. In recognizing that advertising has a value and a place in our broadcasting system, it is a legitimate exercise of public control to see that a limit is placed on the results of commercial pressures.

Another form of economic pressure on private stations may justify other kinds of programme regulation and station performance in Canada. The proximity to the United States and the comparative ease and cheapness with which American prógrammes can be acquired by Canadian radio and television stations could result in their becoming no more than outlets of American networks. If we want to have some Canadian content in our broadcasting fare and some development of Canadian talent in radio and television, a degree of regulation and control to overcome these forces of economics is inescapable. There must either be creation of Canadian programmes by a public agency and regulation to require that such programmes be carried on private stations; or there must be a requirement for the production of a certain proportion of Canadian programmes by the private stations themselves.

Possibly these theoretical justifications for the regulation of broadcasting in Canada are unnecessary. Perhaps the simple fact is that radio and television are powerful forces of widespread public influence, and in a complex world where life is hazardous any instrument that affects all of us cannot be allowed to get out of our control. The Canadian public has the right to expect a high standard of service from those few citizens to whom radio and television franchises are granted. It has the right to make sure that the service is well rendered.

28   The 1967 Revision of the Canadian Banking Acts*

David W. Slater†

The main message of the new banking legislation in Canada[1] is the astonishing degree to which competition within the banking community and between banks and other financial institutions has been embraced as the official policy, following the direction set by the Porter Commission.[2] Canadians and their governments have been led to the belief that a safe, equitable, efficient, adaptable financial system can be achieved by a vigorous overlapping system of private competition in banking and finance. Such competition is expected to be partly a natural phenomenon, given the environment, but it is also to be actively promoted by government legislation and administration. At the same time Canadians have been led to the belief that a satisfactory standard of management of monetary and financial policy can be achieved by a limited range of indirect, general instruments in the hands of the governmental monetary authorities, operated by altering the environment within which the private banking and financial system works. A second notable feature is the attempt to bring off, through deposit insurance systems and in other ways, a federal-provincial compromise of regulation and privilege for those provincially chartered institutions which engage in banking-type activities rather than to deal directly with them through exercises of the unqualified federal jurisdiction over all banking matters in Canada. The third outstanding feature is the adoption of a piecemeal approach towards limiting the foreign ownership of banking operations in Canada—an approach which promises a difficult and uncertain course in the future in international banking affairs both inside and outside Canada. And fourthly, the new legislation offers a major improvement in the comparative advantage of the banks in relation to other financial intermediaries, more in relation to some than others; the squeeze seems likely to be most severe for small trust companies, for a wide variety of loan companies and credit unions and for insurance companies.

*From: David W. Slater, "The 1967 Revision of the Canadian Banking Acts, Part I: An Economist's View", *Canadian Journal of Economics*, Vol. I, no. 1, (February 1968), pp. 79-91 (reprinted by permission of the author and publisher).

A paper presented at the Ottawa meetings of the Canadian Economics Association and the Canadian Political Science Association, June 1967.

†The author wishes to acknowledge the assistance of Mr. Colin Crisp, the comments of Mr. J. Harvey Perry, Mr. R. M. McIntosh, and Mr. D. B. Marsh, and access to a helpful paper by Dr. H. H. Binhammer.

[1]*An Act to amend the Bank of Canada Act, An Act respecting Banks and Banking, An Act respecting Savings Banks in the Province of Quebec*, all assented to on 23 March 1967; and the *Canada Deposit Insurance Act of 1967*.

[2]*1964 Report of the Royal Commission on Banking and Finance* (Ottawa, 1964).

I / Constitutional and jurisdictional issues: Near-banks and deposit insurance

The Porter Commission proposed a single uniform core of federal regulation of and privileges for all institutions engaging in banking-type activities, regardless of the governmental source of the initial charter of the institutions. Banking-type activities were to be identified by the short-term nature of the debts of a financial institution, by their transferrability and liquidity, and by their utilization in the payments mechanism of the country. Both the chartered banks and the federally and provincially chartered near-banks would be identified in this way as engaged in banking-type activities. The banking operations subject to the regulation were to be measured proximately by the amount of short-term "deposit" indebtedness of the institutions; cash reserve requirements were recommended for all banking operations, cash to be uniformly obligations of the Bank of Canada. Though the Commission could not be held to the view, their recommendations seemed also to imply that, if secondary reserve requirements were imposed on any banks, they should be imposed on all, and that lender-of-last-resort and clearing facilities would presumably also be available for all banking operations on the same terms.

The basis of the Porter Commission's recommendations, a basis which is completely correct, in my opinion, turns on four propositions. The first is the exclusive legislative authority of the Parliament of Canada over all matters coming within the enumerated clauses in the BNA Act[3] concerned with currency and coinage, banking, incorporation of banks and the issue of paper money, savings banks, bills of exchange and promissory notes, interest and legal tender.

The second is that the scope of this authority has been and must continue to be determined by those things which perform from time to time the main monetary functions for the nation; that is, the things which constitute the principal media used in the payments mechanism and which have "store-of-value" characteristics of the highest order of liquidity. The media which perform these functions change from time to time, owing to shifts in custom and technical and institutional developments. They have shifted historically from coins to government and private paper money and later to various book deposits of various institutions. The scope of the responsibility which the sovereign has exercised over things which are money has had to shift accordingly. The concern of the government has to be at least as much with the *quality* of the monetary unit as with its *quantity*, though both have been and continue to be surrounded by an unusual public (as opposed to private) interest. To allow private institutions to create monetary units offers great power and opportunity for abuse; it must be assured by the highest authority that the management of the institutions allowed this privilege does protect the holders of their debts.

[3]Clauses 14 to 16 and 18 to 20.

The third proposition is that an institution's banking operations are to be judged by what it does and not by the original source or intention of its charter. While an institution's banking business depends on the customs of, and its acceptability by, the public, its operations also depend on the institution *choosing* to engage in banking. An institution may not be able to make itself a bank by choice, but it cannot be made into a banking institutition without exercise of its choice. It has to accept short-term deposits, to provide liquidity, to participate in the payments mechanism, and to adapt its other operations accordingly. The institution might combine banking operations with other functions, and the combination may influence the ease of participation or management of its banking business; but the decision to carry on the central core of banking operations *per se* is essential to the participation by an institution in banking on any significant scale.

Fourthly, if institutions opt into banking operations by their own choice, they come under the jurisdiction of the federal banking authority. That federal jurisdiction embodies both the regulation and extension of rights under federal responsibility. Banking-type regulations would thus apply to "near-banks," but near-banks would also become entitled to banking-type privileges, such as lender-of-last-resort and clearing facilities.

In my judgment the argument of the Porter Commission setting out the basis and range of federal jurisdiction over banking and near-banking operations in Canada is sound. But there is room for somewhat different approaches from those Porter recommended for the exercise of this jurisdiction. In my own view the case is strong for defining banking operations and for designating the fundamental basis of federal government responsibility over all banking institutions in Canada. But various alternative methods for discharging these obligations may be worked out, some in co-operation with the provinces and some in which banking, near-banking, and other financial operations are treated together. But the federal government should set out its fundamental responsibility clearly and negotiate from a definite position with respect to its rights *and* responsibilities.

In the 1967 Canadian banking legislation, the issue of direct federal government responsibility for the regulation and privileges of the near-banking operations in Canada was postponed. An indirect approach was taken to some aspects of the issue, through the development of the federal deposit insurance[4] operation. By this scheme the federal government requires a broad group of deposit-taking institutions which it has created— chartered banks, federally chartered trust and loan companies (within the meaning of the Loan Companies Act) —to insure the individual customer's deposits. Provincially created deposit-taking institutions of the same types are given the opportunity, with the consent of the provincial governments, to enter into the same deposit insurance arrangements on the same terms. *Caisses populaires* and credit union central organizations are not given the

---

[4]*Canadian Deposit Insurance Act of 1967,* clause 9.

privilege of federal deposit insurance. It was hoped that most of the provinces would force or persuade their banking-type and trust and loan institutions into the federal scheme (as most of them have done), and that any separate provincial schemes could be effectively harmonized with the federal scheme and any other provincial schemes.[5] The Quebec system is the only one which is quite different in pattern[6]; it includes *caisses populaires* and could include some deposit-taking institutions other than banks, trust, and loan companies; it contemplates a narrower range of remedial action for institutions; it is to be financed by the government rather than an insurance premium. The harmonization of this system with the federal and other provincial schemes is yet to be completely worked out.

The important feature of deposit insurance is not the likely use of insurance settlements after a financial institution is in peril; rather it is that banking-type inspection will be required continuously to detect trouble before it becomes serious, and banking-type remedial action is to be taken before it becomes unlikely that the institution can discharge its deposit obligations. A federal or some sort of joint federal-provincial inspection service is therefore implied for the provincially chartered near-banking institutions which are insured. Inspection is a central feature of the Quebec scheme too, and interesting questions arise concerning Quebec licensing and inspection of chartered banks.

Another related issue concerns the extension of lender-of-last-resort facilities and improved clearing facilities to the insured deposit-taking institutions other than the chartered banks. Arrangements about both these facilities are in an unsatisfactory state at present, and the new legislation leaves both issues in limbo. It is possible that some stand-by or emergency lending facilities for the insured near-banks could be worked out through the deposit insurance corporation, but if too great reliance on this corporation is made, the deposit insurance corporation would be assuming a central banking function without clearly adequate resources. Indirect arrangements for clearing and emergency credits could continue to be worked out for the near-banks through the chartered banks, but this arrangement would have the unsatisfactory features of making the near-banks dependent on the grace and favour of their principal competitors and of the contingent obligations being large in relation to chartered banks' capital and reserve capacities. Some lending arrangements might be worked out through the money market dealers, with these dealers in turn being given enlarged facilities at the central banks. But all of these arrangements are second-best; and all of them raise further controversial issues in federal-provincial government relations.

---

[5] *An Act to establish the Ontario Deposit Insurance Corporation*, Bill 24, 5th Session, 27th Legislature, Ontario, as amended by Bill 97, same session.

[6] *Quebec Deposit Insurance Act*, Bill 51, First Session, 28th Legislature, Legislative Assembly of Quebec, 1967.

The near-banks are multi-faceted institutions, as are the Canadian banks. If banking and non-banking functions are combined in the near-banks, it may be difficult to have the federal government applying regulations of the banking operations and other governments regulating separately the other functions when some aspects of the functions are intertwined. Thus even though the federal jurisdiction over banking is undoubted, it may be best to apply a co-operative federal-provincial regulation of these institutions which mix banking and other functions. The alternative is to force every institution which engages in banking to any significant degree to obtain a federal banking charter. A provincially chartered institution which now combines banking and other functions would have to separate out the banking from the other functions, but not necessarily divest itself of the banking functions. An institution might be permitted to own a bank, but the bank itself would be subject to the full panoply of federal regulations, facilities, and privileges. The present approach through deposit insurance and a pragmatic approach to the other aspects of banking regulations and privileges is a half-way house that will not be satisfactory in the long run. There have been indications that this unsatisfactory state has been recognized,[7] and there have even been indications that the federal government will in due course attempt to enact bills setting out a broader applicability of certain banking-type regulations and let or invite a test of the constitutionality of such bills take place before the Supreme Court. If such acts were upheld, then the basis would arise for the more systematized and clear-cut extension of federal banking-type regulations, responsibilities, and privileges. Such developments may also be related to federal-provincial co-operation and stronger federal initiatives in security regulations and the regulation of other financial institutions and practices.

II / Banks as borrowers and lenders

The new legislation affects the scope and terms on which banks may borrow from and lend to the public, and relates the one activity to the other.[8] The most notable changes in lending operations are the raising (initially to $7\frac{1}{4}$ per cent) of the interest ceiling on ordinary bank loans and a commitment to complete its removal (the trigger has been already fired;[9] the ceiling lapses 1 January 1968), and the granting to the banks of extensive privileges to engage in both conventional and NHA-insured mortgage lending. With respect to banks as borrowers from the public, the outstanding change is the additional bank privilege of selling their own debentures. In the

---

[7]*Minutes*, (Commons Standing Committee on Finance, Trade and Economic Affairs, no. 42, Feb. 2, 1967), submissions and evidence by the Hon. Mitchell Sharp, Minister of Finance. Cited hereafter as *Minutes*.

[8]The following discussion is mainly of provisions of the Bank Act and of those provisions of the amendments to the Bank of Canada Act that affect directly the banks.

[9]The conditions set out in Section 91 of the new Bank Act for a definite future removal of the interest rate ceiling to be removed effective 1 January, 1963 unless the legislation is altered before that date.

coupling of borrowing and lending opeartions by banks, the main changes are the reduction to 4 per cent in the minimum cash reserve ratio required for all deposit and certificate obligations except current chequing accounts, and the raising of the minimum cash reserve ratio formally to 12 per cent for current chequing accounts, following the Porter recommendations. The effect of these two changes is to reduce significantly (from 8 to about 6.6 or 6.7 per cent by the time the new act came into force) the over-all minimum cash reserve ratio required of the banks against the totals of all deposit and certificate obligations, as well as to differentiate the reserve requirements betwen different types of accounts. No longer will the central bank have the power to vary minimum cash reserve ratios. The new cash reserve ratios together with the broadened range and more flexible terms on which banks might engage in "lending" encourages the development of a differentiated structure of deposit arrangements betwen the banks and the public. Technically the banks could still continue their schemes of compensating balances recently associated with many of their loan contracts. Service charges are to be justified in the future by provision of services rather than as ways of getting around the interest rate ceiling. In any case, compensating balances related to a loan or advance can henceforth be required only with the express consent of the borrower. A new legal requirement is for the banks to hold secondary reserves against their deposits, this reserve ratio being alterable within limits by the central bank. The banks are permitted, even while the interest rate ceiling continues during 1967, to maintain their present consumer instalment loan schemes, by which they effectively obtain *gross* interest charges of between 9.5 and 11.5 per cent depending on the bank and the particular contract. When the interest rate ceilings on bank loans lapse in 1968, the banks can charge any interest rates or service charge which they competitively determine for business and consumer loans, subject only to new strict rules of disclosure of true interest charges, and the consent of the customer.

What is the significance of these changes? First, the banks are being permitted to engage in a wider range of intermediation functions on a more favourable set of terms. Canada has taken several *more* steps in the direction of the "department-store-of-credit" concept of banks. Secondly, the two-rate structure of minimum cash reserves, dependent on the type of deposits, provide attractions for banks to persuade customers to shift deposits away from current accounts, particularly when the banks are under a cash squeeze. Thirdly, even while the interest ceilings persist but at higher levels, and certainly after the ceilings are removed in 1968, the question naturally arises about protecting the general public against excessive charges if and when opportunities arise for lenders to take advantage. Disclosure and competition as protection for the public are considered below. Fourthly, the banks may, at the discretion of the Bank of Canada, be brought under a fortnightly averaging scheme for meeting the minimum cash reserve ratio instead of the monthly averaging scheme as at present; notice has been given that fortnightly averaging will be required.[10] The effect of this would be to raise the average cash reserves which banks will actually have to work to, or else encourage the development of inter-bank arrangements for exchanging excess and deficient cash reserves of individual institutions, either directly or by increased utilization of money-market arrangements. Fifthly, the temptation for the banks to borrow by selling debentures will be very strong, both because no cash reserves are required behind a bank debenture liability, and because banks would have the opportunity of borrowing longer-term funds in sympathy with the developments of longer-term lending operations, particularly in mortgage finance and perhaps also in longer term government and industrial bonds.

III / Competion among banks: Competition between banks and other financial intermediaries

The central basis of the Porter Commission's conclusions was reliance on and promotion of competition among the chartered banks, between the chartered banks and near-banks, and among financial intermediaries generally as the means to a safe, efficient, equitable, adaptable, socially responsive banking and financial structure. The record of improvement through private action during the last three decades provided the underpinning to the Commission's recommendations. The function of legislation then becomes enhancement and improvement in the competitive mechanisms. With few exceptions, the most notable relating to foreign banking, the new Canadian legislation adopts the general competitive strategy recommended by the Porter Commission. It is a moot point, however, whether or not the tactics of execution are yet entirely satisfactory.

Consider first the changes influencing competition *among* the chartered banks. The most important issue concerns the number of such banks which will exist. Under the new Act it will be neither easier nor more difficult to incorporate new banks. The minimum authorized capital stock has been modest under recent acts and it is not increased by the new Act. Various provisions about limiting the proportion of shares held in one set of hands are to be waived for generous periods of time for newly incorporated banks. The crucial feature of government policy is not the legislation *per se* but rather the willingness of the government to permit a new bank to obtain a charter and to commence business. The present Minister of Finance has also indicated[11] the desirability of more banking competition. Though the development of the new legislation was considerably complicated thereby, charters were granted to the Bank of Western Canada and to the Bank of British Columbia *before* the new bank acts were passed. The House of

---

[10]The Governor of the Bank of Canada has already given the banks written notice that the fortnightly basis would be adopted at the end of the transition period.

[11]For example, by his statement at the resolution stage of Bill C222, introduced 7 July 1966.

Commons Standing Committee on Finance, Trade and Economic Affairs in its final report on the Bank acts recommended:

Noting the desirability of increasing competition in the banking industry through the establishment of more chartered banks, your Committee recommends that the rules of the House be amended to make it possible for the House to come to a prompt decision on applications for banks charters after reasonable debate, provided that before a final decision is made the applications be referred to the Standing Committee on Finance, Trade and Economic Affairs for detailed study.[12]

What do the acts say directly or imply about competition *among* the chartered banks? Agreements among banks with respect to the rate of interest on deposits or the rate of interest or the charges on a loan are prohibited (Bank Act, section 138). "Collection charges" on cashing out-of-branch and out-of-town cheques continue to be permitted (section 93) up to a maximum scale set out in the Act, but presumabily these charges are to be set by the individual bank rather than being subject to inter-bank agreement. The new Act requires and specifies the measurement and disclosure of the cost of borrowing to each individual borrower (section 92). This section was added to the bill by the Minister of Finance when it was under consideration by the Trade, Finance and Economic Affairs committee.

What are the significant changes dealing with relations between the banks and other financial intermediaries? The first important one limits very severely, to a maximum of 10 per cent of the equity share, the ownership which a bank may have in a trust or loan company (sections 76(1)(*b*)); and prohibits, in due course, a person from being a bank director if he is a director of a deposit-receiving trust or loan company (section 18). The *second* important change is the availability of deposit insurance on very favourable terms (the same as to the chartered banks) to certain other deposit-taking institutions, a change, which *ceteris paribus* improves the competitive position of some of those near-banking institutions in the deposit-taking business. The third is that a bank is prohibited from owning more than 50 per cent of the common shares of a Canadian corporation, other than a trust or loan company (note above, the 10 per cent rate for them) "in any case where the total amount paid or agreed to be paid by the bank for such of the shares of the corporation as have voting rights attached thereto, is five million dollars or less. . . . (section 76(1)(*a*)). This provision was inserted at the Committee stage of the bill to permit the continued participation by a bank on a substantial scale in such financial satellites as Roynat, Kinross, or UNAS, though the provision is not restricted to the ownership and effective control of financial satellites; nor does it keep these satellites necessarily to a small size. Limited use of this provision is probably in the public interest, but a broad or intensive development by banks of multitudes of "small" specialized financial satellites would be contradictory to the competitive spirit of the new Canadian acts, and

[12]*Minutes,* (28 Feb. 1967) , p. 3592.

possibly a dangerous pyramiding of the burdens on the bank's capital and liquidity position.

A fourth provision bearing on competition is the prohibition of beneficial ownership of banks shares by the federal or provincial governments (section 53(3) and (4)). Presumably this is to keep an arm's length between governments and what is intended as a private chartered banking system, though a provincial government could obtain a considerable leverage over a small bank if it concentrated its banking business there. Fifthly, a potential change that might have altered the competitive position in favour of the competitors of banks, namely the explicit formal granting of clearing house facilities to them, was not included in the legislation, but was recommended by the Committee for future action: "Your Committee recommends that the Canadian Bankers' Association Act be amended to permit those financial institutions who presently have access to the clearing system only through the intermediary of a chartered bank to participate directly in the system on an equitable basis."[13]

IV/Foreign Ownership and Control

Perhaps the most controversial aspect of the new limitations on competition in banking and finance concerns the treatment of foreign banking. One frequently hears that the efficiency and technological development of the Canadian banks is "twenty years behind" that of the large institutions in the main financial centres in the United States. A suggestion is that Canadian banking would be improved greatly by an infusion of competition in Canada from foreign, particularly American, banking institutions. The general provisions of the new acts limit to 25 per cent the ownership by foreign residents of the voting shares of a Canadian bank, and limit to 10 per cent the ownership of the shares of a bank by a single shareholder, foreign or domestic. The Act also has other provisions which are general in terms but in effect apply to the Mercantile Bank. The effect of these is to exempt the foreign owners of that bank from meeting the 25 and 10 per cent clauses, but to limit the ultimate size of the total liabilities of that institution if they use that exemption. As the Act was eventually passed the permission of the bank to have liabilities in excess of twenty times its paid up capital and yet to be free of the 25 per cent rule, can apply up to 1972, subject to the discretion of the Governor in Council. The essential point is that Mercantile will have to demonstrate to the satisfaction of the Governor in Council, from time to time, progress toward meeting the 25 per cent rule by 1972, or else be subject immediately thereafter to the restriction on the size of the total liabilities of the bank, i.e., to a total of liabilities of about $200 millions.

The government appeared to be much more concerned to limit the foreign ownership and control of Canadian banking and financial institu-

---

[13]*Ibid.*

tions (banks, trust companies, insurance companies) than of non-financial businesses. Presumably this is due to a belief that the main financial corporations are a relatively concentrated set of institutions which occupies a commanding position over Canadian business and economic activity and through these on social and political life. If one accepts these premises and adds a judgment that a major incursion of foreign ownership and control of Canadian financial institutions was imminent, then the conclusion follows that a line must be drawn. The Mercantile affair was the drawing of the line so far as banks were concerned. Some say that the action will turn out to be ineffective, as foreign financial institutions can acquire ownership and control of provincially chartered trust and loan companies, which in turn can increase their near-banking activities, becoming banks in most, but not all, respects. For federally chartered trust and loan companies such an event is not likely, as the relevant acts limit the transfer of share ownership to foreign residents.[14] For provincially chartered trust and loan companies, the possibility of increased foreign ownership and control still exists, but the ease or the likelihood of such a development remains to be determined.

It has been frequently suggested that Canada should permit the establishment of foreign banking agencies, a specific range of agency functions being permitted, subject to appropriate regulations. At present Canadian banks have agency privileges in *some* American states, notably in New York under privileges granted by New York State banking laws. Canadian banks own banks in some other states, notably in California. One favourable argument is that some of the benefits of infusion of foreign banking expertise would be made available in Canada without the alleged drawbacks from general foreign ownership and control of Canadian banks. Another argument is that such an agency privilege would be an act of reciprocity for Canadian agency and other banking privileges abroad. Some argue that Canada's attitude to foreign ownership and control prejudices the continued operation of the foreign agency and other banking by Canadian banks, and that this prejudice would be overcome by making agency privileges available in Canada. No action was taken along these lines in the new banking bills, but the Committee made recommendations for future development: "Your Committee has commenced some studies with regard to the desirability or otherwise of the establishment in Canada of agencies of foreign banks. However, it has not been able to complete these studies in the time available and requests authority to pursue these studies further."[15]

Increased foreign participation in banking and near-banking in Canada would probably increase competition, and lively effective innovation can be promoted in other ways. The risks of foreign banking in Canada seem to me to have been exaggerated; and the capacity of Canadian banks to compete effectively in and out of Canada to have been underrated. The

---

[14]Chap. 40, *Statutes of Canada* (1964-65).
[15]*Minutes,* (28 Feb. 1967), p. 3592.

issues are not in any case completely settled by the new legislation; nor is the Mercantile Bank issue finally resolved.

V / Evaluations, prospects, and conclusions

Will the share of the chartered banks in financial intermediation in Canada increase in the future, reversing the trend of the last two decades? Will the new legislation work in this direction for all types of intermediation now carried on or made accessible to the banks? Has the legislation put the right weight on the right side of the scales in these respects? The share of a set of financial institutions in financial intermediation depends on the acts and regulations under which they operate, but also on the preferences of the public for various types of intermediary functions and the efficiency and innovating management of the institutions themselves. The new legislation may strengthen the participation of some near-banks in operating in the payments mechanism and the bank share of these functions (which is now overwhelming) may tend to decline a little as a result. On the other hand, the new legislation increases the scope and improves the terms on which the banks can carry out many other types of intermediation, particularly savings-investment functions; in this way the share of the banks should be increased. In so far as the comparative advantage of the banks in one type of business is interdependent with comparative advantages in others, the improvement of the bank position in savings-investment intermediary functions may also strengthen the position of the banks in other financial functions. The development of new types of deposit accounts, new procedures, improved management, and attractive new specialized lending activities in recent years, particularly during the last two years, leads one to expect good things for the banks in improving their share of the market in the future. As to tastes of consumers for the intermediary services provided by banks, there is quite a considerable attraction to integrating one's financial transactions and asset and liability positions within a single institution (e.g., by doing one's mortgage financing, some of one's long-term saving, one's financing of purchases of consumer durables, and one's ordinary week-to-week transactions, perhaps one's trustee business, in a single institution or set of related institutions), providing that one can shift the whole package to another institution if there is a suspicion of unfair dealing, a belief in better management, or other cause. This too should strengthen the position of the chartered banks, because, except for trust services, they combine nearly all of the financial services which individuals, families, and modest-sized businesses desire. Regarding the inter-institutional equity, it was generally conceded that the preceding legislation and regulations discriminated against the chartered banks, by imposing more costly cash reserve requirements, by limiting interest rates, by restricting bank mortgage lending, and in other ways (though the banks had advantages too, particularly in interest-free borrowing from the public by demand deposit accounts and control of the clearing system). The new acts have improved the position of the banks. Only with further study, and with clarification of the operations of deposit insurance, lender-of-last-resort privileges for deposit-taking institutions other than the chartered banks, and modifications of trust company regulation, will it be possible to judge whether the banks have been given too much of a competitive advantage.

Will adequate competition emerge among the chartered banks and between the banks and other financial intermediaries? In some respects competition among the banks appears to have been inhibited in the past, e.g., in types and interest on deposit accounts, in service charges, and in the type and availability of banking services. Competition was intense in other respects: in money market activity, latterly in deposit certificate rates, in bidding for large customer business, and in some aspects of the consumer instalment loan business. The new acts should promote more active competition among the banks in the deposit business and in some aspects of the lending business. The prohibitions on agreement regarding interest or on terms of loans are particularly relevant here, as is the requirement for clear disclosure of the interest and other charges on loans. There are signs revealing a possible breakdown of a classic oligopoly in the increases in interest rates on, and the devising of new types of contracts in, savings deposits, and in advertising and new promotion activities. So long as the number of competing banks and closely related near-banking competitors is small, however, one should expect that after a period of transition a new equilibrium will emerge in which competition will be quite limited in some directions but active in others. Nobody can really be certain about the effectiveness of the new competition which the legislation seeks to promote. It is a promising experiment which will have to be watched with some care and scepticism and in which further legislative and administrative steps to promote effective competition in all the important directions may well be required. I personally hope that the wasteful advertising programs do not eat up very much of the improved gross revenues of the banks.

Several aspects of the competition in banking will bear careful review. The first is that, in attempting to promote Canadian ownership and control of Canadian financial institutions, we do not inhibit unduly the foreign operations of Canadian banks, and protect too severely our own banks from the fresh winds of foreign ideas, skills, energy, and innovation. The second is that adequate opportunity be given for the creation of new banks, including those which choose to specialize somewhat by region or type of mix of intermediary functions. Providing that regional or specialist banks are integrated into the national banking system, providing that they compete at arm's length for deposit business, and providing that they can evolve viable cost-revenue relations, they can be attractive additions to the competitive structure of Canadian banking. Thirdly, the loophole of permitting the banks to own and control "small" satellite financial institutions must not be abused. Canada has recently had some shocking lessons in the misrepresentation, mismanagement, and fraud that can all too easily be introduced with complicated hierarchies of financial holding and operating companies. Also the competitive goals of banking developments in Canada imply that sharp limits should be set on the ownership and control of financial satellites by banks. Fourthly, the links between trust companies and banks are to be reduced; but these changes require a further careful consideration. Associations of trust and banking functions are very attractive: if trust companies are to be able to combine both and if the trust companies are to expand their banking functions, should the banks be permitted to develop trust departments? Also, may the acquisition or establishment of provincially chartered trust companies be a way around the limitations of foreign ownership and control in banking? May this be encouraged by the difficulties banks can have in divesting themselves of trust company shares to meet the rule of maximum holding of 10 per cent of the voting shares of a trust company? May it be necessary to improve the clearing and lender-of-last-resort facilities open to the deposit-taking institutions (other than the chartered banks) to give them a good opportunity to compete with the banks in the banking business? Should trust companies be given the opportunity to make general business loans?

Will the new banking structure be sufficiently responsive to changes in monetary management and to special credit needs, especially in times of tight money? The ineffectiveness of operation of the big "levers" of monetary management in Canada has not been attributed in any significant way to the inability of the monetary authorities to obtain prompt vigorous responses by the banks and other financial institutions, taken together.[16] The exercise of that management has been primarily through altering the cash reserve positions of the banks and altering the portfolio balance of the banks, other financial institutions, and the general public. These abilities are not fundamentally altered by the new legislation. As to the on-going provision for special credit needs, such as for farmers, for new, small, risky ventures, and for post-secondary education and training, the principal approach in Canada has been to develop special legislation directed to the special purposes, leaving the general run of credit allocation otherwise alone.[17] Frequently these special arrangements have been worked through the banks. These arrangements continue. Also, there is some hope that the removal of the interest rate ceilings will permit the banks to tailor loan contracts to variations in risk, administrative cost, and repayment schedules more effectively than in the past, and thus to serve special needs more effectively in the ordinary course of banking business. The same hopes hold for the treatment of special needs in periods of tight money—but only performance will tell that tale. Finally, there lies ahead the resolution of the constitutional issues regarding the regulation, priviliges, and responsibilities for banks and near-banks in Canada.

---

[16]*1964 Report of the Royal Commission on Banking and Finance,* chaps. 6, 18, 20, 21, 22 and 27.

[17]*Ibid.,* chaps. 12 and 14.

SUGGESTIONS FOR FURTHER READING

Anderson, F. W., "Research and Public Policy Issues: Some Canadian Comparison," in *Transportation Economics,* A Conference of the Universities —National Bureau Committee for Economic Research, New York, Columbia University Press, 1965.

Ashley, C. A., *The First Twenty-Five Years: A Study of Trans-Canada Air Lines,* Toronto, Macmillan Co. of Canada Ltd., 1963.

Ashley, C. A., and R. G. H. Smails, *Canadian Crown Corporations,* Macmillan Co. of Canada Ltd., Toronto, 1965.

Balls, H. R., "The Financial Control and Accountability of Canadian Crown Corporations," *Public Administration,* Vol. 31 (1953).

Black, E. R., "Canadian Public Policy and the Mass Media," *Canadian Journal of Economics,* Vol. 1 (May, 1968).

Blakeney, A. E., "Saskatchewan Crown Corporations," in W. Friedmann, (ed.), *The Public Corporation: A Comparative Symposium,* Toronto, Carswell Co. Ltd., 1954.

Corbett, D. C., "Liquor Control Administration in British Columbia: A Study in Public Enterprise," *Canadian Public Administration,* Vol. 2 (March, 1959).

Corbett, D. C., *Politics and the Airlines,* Toronto, University of Toronto Press, 1965.

Currie, A. W., *Canadian Transportation Economics,* Toronto, University of Toronto Press, 1967.

Currie, A. W., "Rate Control of Public Utilities in British Columbia," *Canadian Journal of Economics,* Vol. 10 (August, 1944).

Currie, A. W., "Rate Control on Canadian Public Utilities," *Canadian Journal of Economics and Political Science,* Vol. 12 (May, 1946).

Dales, J. H., "Land, Water, and Ownership," *Canadian Journal of Economics,* Vol. 1 (November, 1968).

Dales, J. H., *Pollution, Property and Prices: An Essay in Policy-Making and Economics,* Toronto, University of Toronto Press, 1968.

Denison, M., *The People's Power,* Toronto, McClelland & Stewart Ltd., 1960.

Drummond, I. M., "The Regulation of Broadcasting," in T. Lloyd and J. T. McLeod, (eds.), *Agenda 1970,* Toronto, University of Toronto Press, 1968.

Friedmann, W., *The Public Corporation,* Toronto, Carswell Co. Ltd., 1954.

Grove, J. W., *Government and Industry in Britain,* London, Longmans, Green & Co. Ltd., 1962.

Hanson, A. H., *Public Enterprise and Economic Development,* London, Routledge & Kegan Paul, 1959.

Hodgetts, J. E. and D. C. Corbett, *Canadian Public Administration*, Toronto, Macmillan Co. of Canada Ltd., 1960.

Hull, W. H. N., "The Public Control of Broadcasting: The Canadian and Australian Experiences," *Canadian Journal of Economics and Political Science*, Vol. 28 (February, 1962).

Innis, H. A., "Government Ownership and the Canadian Scene," in M. Q. Innis (ed.), *Essays in Canadian Economic History*, Toronto, University of Toronto Press, 1962.

Katzarov, K., *The Theory of Nationalization*, The Hague, Nijhoff, 1964.

Lessard, J. C., *Transportation in Canada*, a study prepared for the Royal Commission on Canada's Economic Prospects, Ottawa, Queen's Printer, 1957.

McIntosh, R. M., "The 1967 Revision of the Canadian Banking Acts, Part II: A Banker's View," *Canadian Journal of Economics*, Vol. 1 (February, 1968).

Main, J. R. K., "An Outline of the Development of Civil Air Transport in Canada," *Canada Year Book* (1967), pp. 838-843.

Neufeld, E. P., *Money and Banking in Canada*, Toronto, McClelland & Stewart Ltd., 1964.

Roberts, L., *The Life and Times of Clarence Decatur Howe*, Toronto, Clarke-Irwin & Co. Ltd., 1957.

Robson, W. A., *Nationalized Industry and Public Ownership*, Toronto, University of Toronto Press, 1960.

Royal Commission on Government Organization, "The Organization of the Government of Canada," Vol. 5 of the *Report*, Ottawa, Queen's Printer, (1963). (See pp. 58-72 concerning public corporations).

Shanks, M., *The Lessons of Public Enterprise*, A Fabian Society Study, London, Jonathan Cape Ltd., 1963.

Stevens, G. R., *Canadian National Railways*, Toronto, Clark-Irwin & Co. Ltd., 1962.

Stigler, G. J. and Friedland, C., "What Can Regulators Regulate: The Case of Electricity," *Journal of Law and Economics*, Vol. 5 (October, 1962).

Ward, Norman, *The Public Purse*, Toronto, University of Toronto Press, 1962.

Wheatcroft, S. F., *Airline Competition in Canada: A Study of the Desirability and Economic Consequences of Competition in Canadian Transcontinental Air Services*, Ottawa, Queen's Printer, 1958.

Policies to Limit
and to Counteract
Market Forces

PART SIX

Policies to Promote
Manufacturing in Canada

INTRODUCTION

The most conspicuous and time-honored policies to restrict competition are the tariff and other measures to protect domestic producers from foreign competition in home markets.

The logic of the private-enterprise, free-market model upon which the Canadian economy is commonly held to be based makes no provision for tariffs or other impediments to free international trade. David Ricardo, one of the nineteenth-century architects of the system, wrote: "The sole effect of high duties on the importation, either of manufactures or of corn or of a bounty on their exportation, is to divert a portion of capital to an employment which it would not naturally seek. It causes a pernicious distribution of the general funds of the society—it bribes a manufacturer to commence or continue in a comparatively less profitable employment." (*The Principles of Political Economy and Taxation,* London, Everyman's Library Edition, 1911, p. 210)

The relevance of these principles of free-market economics to the situation of a young developing country could, of course, be challenged. The principal intellectual attack of this kind was that mounted by Friederich List in his book *The National System of Political Economy*. Classical economists such as Smith and Ricardo, he argued, quite neglected the causes of national wealth, that is, the process by which the "productive forces" of the state came to be developed. In order to get established, he contended, the state should protect newly-created industries from foreign competition.

Such a policy of protection had much to commend it in the eyes of manufacturers operating in a country such as Canada struggling to industrialize under difficult conditions in the late nineteenth century.

The "National Policy" implemented by Sir John A. Macdonald's Conservative government in 1879 marked the official declaration of Canada's rejection of free trade and the adoption of protectionism as part of the grand strategy for Canadian development. The Liberal Party, the Opposition, vigorously denounced the principle of protection.

At the Liberal Convention in 1893, Sir Wilfred Laurier eloquently denounced the Canadian tariff as "a servile copy of the American system of protection," and as a "fraud and robbery under which Canadians suffer," depicting it further as a means of "levying tribute upon the people . . . for the benefit of a private and privileged class". Let it be well understood, he declared, "that from this moment we have a distinct issue with the party in power. Their ideal is protection; our ideal is free trade." Anticipating some difficulties in implementing reform, he observed: "Nothing is more difficult . . . than to wipe away protection, because under it interests have been established which every man who has at heart the interests of all classes must take into consideration." [Note: These declarations and proceedings are reported at length by Edward Porritt in *Sixty Years of Protection in Canada, 1846-1912*, second edition, Winnipeg, Grain Growers' Guide, 1913, pp. 311-14, from which these, and the following, quotations are taken.] Another prominent speaker at the same convention elaborated by declaring: "You can have no true liberty under a protective system; you can have no true liberty under a system the function of which is to create a privileged class, and to concentrate an undue proportion of the wealth of the community in the hands of a few individuals." Note was taken of the political power such beneficiaries of protection could wield by contributing to "corruption funds" . . . "sharing with their masters the plunder which they have been enabled to take from the people".

Once in power, however, the Liberal Party appeared to develop more sympathy with the protectionist point of view and the student of subsequent Canadian tariff history is hard pressed to correlate changes in tariff policy with changes in governments. The debate on free trade versus protectionism in this country subsequently has been between Canadian manufacturers in central Canada and spokesmen for the Western and Maritimes hinterlands, with the latter finding allies in the ranks of academic economists.

The selections chosen for this part are representative of some of the "classic" issues and points of view in this debate. The traditional manufacturers' arguments are succinctly expressed by the Canadian Manufacturers' Association in *Reading 29*. One of the strongest appeals of this argument is the suggestion that if we abandoned protection, virtually all Canadian manufacturing would be obliterated by imports from the United States. In *Reading 30*, Professors Paul and Ronald Wonnacott examine the economic implications of Canada and the United States entering into a free-trade-area agreement. Finally, in *Reading 31*, the Economic Council of Canada reports on the impact of the tariff on different regions in Canada.

It will be noted that the effects of tariffs are pervasive and far reaching. They influence the allocation of resources among alternative uses in the economy; they influence the distribution of income; they affect the rate of economic growth, the competitiveness of business enterprise, and the level of employment. These effects in turn influence, and are in some degree themselves influenced by, social, political, and cultural institutions and practices. On all of this, most authorities would probably agree. But there are sharp differences of opinion about the extent, significance, and even the "direction" these and other effects of tariffs have on the life of the country. The bibliography for this part suggests further reading that will be of help to the student interested in pursuing some of these issues, particularly as they relate to the Canadian situation and experience.

Another well-established way in which governments have traditionally aided particular business interests is by purchasing goods and services from them. While there is certainly nothing new about government purchasing as such, the volume and variety of it have increased greatly in the last several decades. Although the quantitive aspects of this have been the subject of a good deal of frequently anguished criticism and discussion, surprisingly little has been said about the way it affects the structure and performance of the economy. Perhaps this has been because governments have been expected to behave like rational consumers and businessmen and to follow the simple policy of buying at the lowest price goods and services of the required kind and quality. But there is reason to believe that they do not.

One of the established techniques political parties have of getting their candidates elected is by offering implicitly or explicitly to reward party workers and other supporters once they are in power. Patronage is part of politics in our system; but the extent to which it influences the purchasing policies of governments in practice is impossible to assess. Politicians are extremely sensitive about publicizing this aspect of the political process. Nor is it a simple matter to discover patronage by studying the public accounts or by examining the detailed operations of government purchasing and other departments. Certainly most governments in Canada today have purchasing codes and tendering procedures to minimize the "misuse" of public buying power. But these procedures are complex and, in some cases, secret. Even today not all tendering for government contracts in this country is done publicly. For these and other reasons, then, there is much we do not know about the economic and political effects of government purchasing policies. What is known relates mainly to openly declared policies to promote some particular industry or business as a matter of deliberate public policy.

A number of such policies are described and analyzed by Professor Albert

Breton in *Reading 33*. A particular example of the point of view that leads to such "discriminatory" government policies is provided in *Reading 34* in which the Canadian Manufacturers' Association urges that domestic suppliers should be preferred to foreign suppliers of goods required by government in Canada. Similar arguments are also advanced by provincial, municipal, and other local producers and suppliers who seek to escape the full force of competition from firms operating in other jurisdictions.

Of particular interest because of its absolute size and its political implications is the practice of the Federal government in procuring military equipment and supplies. This has been carefully studied by Professor Rosenbluth, and his findings are summarized in *Reading 35*. Again a statement by the Canadian Manufacturers' Association on this subject is included to illustrate the case made by Canadian manufacturers for a nationalistic defence procurement policy. It will be noted that an important element in this argument is a concern with promoting industrial research and development in Canada.

Interest in the contribution the commitment of resources to research and development can make to economic growth and progress has increased greatly in recent years in all the developed industrial countries. This is the subject of *Reading 36* in which Professor English assesses the need for government policies to promote invention and innovation in Canada. He concludes that such policies may not be as effective a means of improving the efficiency of Canadian manufacturing industry as would changes in our commercial (trade) policy. Specific measures for directly stimulating invention and innovation discussed in this selection are patents, tax incentives, and subsidies. The former are also assessed in *Reading 37*.

This part surveys a number of public policies toward the manufacturing and related industries. All these policies more or less deliberately seek to protect these industries or to accelerate their development. To the extent that they are effective, these measures must cause more resources to flow into these lines of production than would otherwise be the case. We have no way of measuring the extent to which the structure of the Canadian economy has been altered in this way, but the policies themselves are probably more numerous and comprehensive than most of us realize. Although it makes rather tedious reading, the catalogue of specific Federal policies to assist Canadian manufacturers reproduced as *Reading 38* may be instructive in this respect. For an even more detailed picture it would be necessary to add all the provincial and municipal programs to promote manufacturing in their specific jurisdictions. Sources of information on these other programs will be found in the bibliography for this part.

29   Tariff Policy for Canada *

Canadian Manufacturers' Association

A sound tariff policy for Canada is of vital importance to the prosperity and welfare of every Canadian citizen. A healthy domestic economy will enable Canada to continue to advance and develop and will result in the expansion of Canadian industry with more and better employment opportunities for all. Our goal is to foster the development of a strong and vigorous Canada. In order to accomplish these objectives, we should encourage and support private initiative, fair competition, and a rapidly expanding domestic market.

History has shown that no country has been able to create a well-balanced and prosperous economy without establishing and maintaining a tariff policy which provides for Customs tariff rates and duty valuations designed to develop and maintain its agricultural and industrial production, as well as to protect the people and capital engaged in various forms of enterprise. We are firmly convinced that no people will ever achieve and sustain such a position without a policy of adequate tariff protection. However attractive the principles of free trade amongst all nations may appear, it is an impractical policy for any one nation to follow under the conditions prevailing throughout the trading world today.

The foundation of our tariff policy must always be the development and maintenance of well-balanced and diversified primary and secondary industries, capable of providing a growing population with profitable and stable employment opportunities now and in the future.

The Canadian Manufacturers' Association has the utmost faith in the industrial potential of this nation. It is convinced that the present and future welfare and prosperity of the Canadian people are predicated on Canada's continuing to be one of the leading industrial nations of the world.

However, if this postion is to be maintained, if stable employment is to be achieved, if improved products are to be provided, and more efficient production methods are to be used, the manufacturing industry which is Canada's largest employer of labour, must have access to ever-widening markets. This is essential if Canadian industry is to avoid a situation where rising costs of production and distribution result in its pricing itself out of not only its foreign markets but also the domestic market, and in all policies this must be a major consideration.

In the opinion of the Association it is essential that an adequate Customs Tariff structure should be established which is fair, just, reasonable, balanced, impartial, and in the national interest. As conditions of trade are

---

*From: *Canadian Manufacturers' Association*, Submission to the Canadian Tariffs and Trade Committee, (May, 1964), Appendix "A" (reprinted by permission).

not static but forever changing, the need for a certain amount of flexibility in our Customs Tariff rate structure is apparent. Efficient Canadian manufacturers should always have an opportunity to sell in the domestic market on a fair competitive basis with imported goods.

Specific rates of duty and maximum duties should be re-examined and replaced where necessary with more realistic rates. It is generally acknowledged that ad valorem rates or compound rates of duty are more equitable, and therefore require less adjustment whenever changes in business conditions occur.

Materials and products should, wherever justifiable, be processed to an increasing extent in Canada thus affording more employment.

The valuation for duty provisions of the Customs Act and the anti-dumping provisions of the Customs Tariff should be designed to effectively prevent the Canadian domestic market being used as a dumping ground for the surplus production of manufactured and agricultural products of other countries.

30   U.S.-Canadian Free Trade*

Paul and Ronald Wonnacott

In the past, free trade with the United States has been dismissed in Canada on the grounds that, in such a situation, U.S. industrial giants would merely increase their output by 10 percent and eliminate manufacturing activities in Canada. How does this contention stand up under analysis? On the one hand, there does seem to be a substantial prospect of such an outcome in declining industries. A firm closing up plants is likely (although by no means certain) to close its Canadian plant in preference to curtailing U.S. operations, since the former would in most cases be less efficient until it had been subject to rationalization, which U.S. plants would not require. On the other hand, in the majority of industries with expanding markets, our assessment suggests that the Canadian location becomes much more attractive with free trade. The issue here is where a firm expands next. And many firms, given the option of building a new plant in Michigan or reorganizing an existing plant in Ontario, would be likely, according to the evidence we have found, to choose the latter.

It is not just the vested interest in existing plant that would serve to help Canadians retain such activities. From the point of view of present or

---

*From: Paul and Ronald J. Wonnacott, U.S.—Canadian Free Trade: The Potential Impact on the Canadian Economy, Canadian-American Committee, Private Planning Association of Canada, (Montreal and Washington, 1968), pp. 45-47 (reprinted by permission of the publisher).

potential U.S. and Canadian investors, Canada also enjoys a substantial cost advantage in the form of lower wages—an advantage which is generally only moderated, but not offset, by other cost differences. For this reason one would expect some firms, faced with the option of building a new plant in Michigan or a new plant in Ontario, to choose the Canadian location.

This brings us to a second assertion that has often appeared in Canadian debate: "With free trade, Canadian wages would automatically jump to the U.S. level, and with this one source of advantage gone, Canadian industry would collapse." The argument in this form is fallacious and is tangled in internal contradictions; the labour market does not work that way. No one (the unions included) could or would institute this sort of wage boost in the face of a collapsing demand for labour. If Canadian wages rose towards the U.S. level—as would seem likely in the long term—then it would be because of expanding demand for labour. But such a development could occur only where Canada proved to be a good place to produce goods efficiently.[1]

However, while labour unions cannot reverse economic trends, they can play a key role in modifying them. This is the argument for temporary wage restraint, as a means of keeping Canada as attractive a location as possible during the initial period during which industry patterns were being sorted out. Otherwise there could be a real danger that the period of reorganization would prove very painful for Canada.

It must be emphasized that wage restraint is by no means the only requirement for successful Canadian reorganization. Our relatively favourable projections are based on several other key assumptions. The first is that labour is inherently as productive in Canada as in the United States and can perform similar tasks with the skill and energy of U.S. labour. On the management side, it is assumed that Canadians are equally competent—and equally willing to put forth the imagination and effort to sell in the U.S. (as well as the Canadian) market. Indeed, during the temporary period of reorganization, extra efforts by both management and labour may be necessary to "catch up" with U.S. industry.

The limited available evidence suggests that labour in Canada is inherently as productive as in the United States. On U.S.-Canadian management comparisons, there is little to go on, aside from the observation that Canadian businessmen who have emigrated to the United States have done well there in direct competition with Americans.

---

[1]"Wage parity" is likely to be a bargaining device by Canadian unions in the future, whether or not there is free trade or protection. The conditional free trade agreement in autos has apparently strengthened union insistence on this point. However, this is not a free trade precedent because this agreement provides protection for auto employment in Canada, and the union knows it. Under the current agreement, the possibility of job losses is not a restraining influence on wage demands. The union knows that wage increases will be reflected primarily in lower profits rather than in some uncertain combination of lower profits and potentially lower employment.

If these assumptions are valid—even approximately—then Canada would be a satisfactory location for manufacturing industry. Hence Canadians would not become "hewers of wood" but, instead, would undertake a broad range of activities, including manufacturing—as they have done in the past. The big difference is that they would do it a good deal more efficiently. They would concentrate on specialized lines: because the Canadian economy is much smaller than the American, Canadians would not have to compete all along the line but rather could select specific products in which they enjoyed a special advantage.

Tariff elimination would introduce a greater degree of competition—with all its rewards and discipline. It would provide a stimulus for the efficient and pressure on the inefficient. The implied shift of labour and capital from less efficient to more efficient activities would be reflected in a rise in Canadian real income—but this change might take time. In the initial period, free trade benefits might be partially (perhaps even fully) offset by adjustment costs. Moreover, there might be some loss of population because the labour market is not perfect and because some Canadians would be faced with the option of switching countries or jobs—and not all of them would, one supposes, necessarily choose to remain in Canada. It is, therefore, only as regards the long-run effects that our conclusion is unambiguous: the net benefits of free trade may be conservatively estimated at 10 percent of Canadian income; and this rise in income would be above and beyond the normal increase in income that might be expected over time. Hence the U.S.-Canadian income gap would be narrowed. (And, with more equal job opportunities in Canada, the historic loss of population to the south would presumably be reduced.)

Finally, there are reasons to believe that the growth in income and more efficient use of capital equipment in Canada with free trade would combine to advance the date at which Canada ceased to be a net importer of capital and became a net exporter.

31   National Tariff Policy*

Economic Council of Canada

Of all the major instruments of national economic development, perhaps none has proved to be a more potent source of interregional tension than the system of protective tariffs and related commercial policy devices. It is a time-honoured and enduring ritual at federal-provincial conferences on

*From: Economic Council of Canada, *Fifth Annual Review: The Challenge of Growth and Change*, (Ottawa, Queen's Printer, 1968), pp. 154-56 (reprinted by permission).

fiscal and economic problems for Ontario to remind the country that it provides about 45 per cent of the total direct tax revenues flowing into the national treasury, and for the Atlantic and western provinces to rejoin that, among the various burdens they carry, the tariff provides Ontario with its sheltered market while most of their own producers must sell abroad at competitive world prices. Over the years regional unevenness of the cost of the protective tariff has been regularly used to support arguments for providing an elaborate structure of regional and national transportation subsidies, special assistance to primary producers in agriculture, fisheries and mining, tax concessions of particular regional interest, and revenue equalization payments to the lower-income provinces.

As we have already indicated, the initial purpose and effect of the protective tariff, together with a national transportation system, was to establish an east-west trading relationship, involving a considerable degree of regional economic specialization. The manufacturing and industrial core of the country developed in Ontario and Quebec, with a strong primary resource orientation in the other regions. The expectations of the Atlantic Provinces that they would also perform an important national manufacturing and service function were frustrated both by changing technology and by the westward shift of North American population and activity. How much this broad historical picture of regional patterns might have been altered by a basically different commercial policy cannot be known. But it is relevant for our purposes to look at the regional effects of the tariff in the present day, and to suggest how the problem of regional balance might be affected by freer trade.

In broad terms, we can distinguish two major influences upon the various regions resulting from the imposition of a tariff on imported goods—one from the side of consumption and the other from the side of production.

The broad structure of the tariff and the traditional view of its national and regional impact are generally familiar. One of the main effects of tariffs is that purchasers of goods pay higher prices for certain commodities than they would pay for the same goods at duty-free import prices. The amount involved is what has been called the "cash cost" of the tariff. Earlier studies have suggested that this "cash cost" of the Canadian tariff is substantial. Not only do Canadian consumers pay substantially more for many finished products as a resutlt of the tariff, but most Canadian producers pay more for a wide variety of materials, machinery and components as a result of the tariffs on these items; and these higher costs of production are reflected in the prices of goods produced in Canada. All Canadian consumers and producers share in the cash cost of the tariff to the extent that tariffs affect the price of the goods they buy. But the impediments that tariffs impose to access to some cheaper source of supply in adjacent areas of the United States tend to result in a somewhat larger cash cost in the Atlantic Region and the western provinces than in Central Canada.

But a far more important effect of tariffs is that they tend to depress the levels of output per employed person in Canada. In particular, tariffs shelter or cause inefficiency in contemporary Canadian industry by encouraging product diversity over a wide range of protected products, limiting efficiencies that could otherwise be gained from scale and specialization. This was one of the major conclusions in Chapter 6 of our *Fourth Annual Review,* in which we indicated that the effects of Canadian and foreign tariffs combined are reflected in higher prices for machinery and other material inputs, and in the basic structural pattern of large net imports of manufactured products[1]. Recent studies have concluded that this "production effect" of the tariff (both Canadian and U.S.) may be very substantial —indeed that the economic costs to Canada may be significantly higher than the "cash cost" of the Canadian tariff—and that these combined economic costs may constitute a very significant element in the large and persistent gap in productivity levels and in the average levels of real standards of living between Canada and the United States. In fact, this element could well be even larger than that arising from the educational disparities between the two countries discussed in the *Second Annual Review.*

In summary, the consumption aspect of the national tariff suggests important relative gains in real income for the Atlantic, Prairie and British Columbia regions if the tariff were reduced or eliminated. There would be little net change in Quebec, and some relative decline in Ontario. But if the production aspects of the tariff are even more important than the consumption aspects, large, new and difficult questions arise about tariffs— questions which cut across many traditional views. For example, is it perhaps the main manufacturing regions of Central Canada, rather than the Atlantic Region or the western provinces, that are now bearing the main economic costs of tariffs? Also, is it possible that substantial tariff reductions, even though they would benefit Canadians in all parts of the country, may have the effect of *widening* rather than *narrowing* regional income disparities—particularly between Ontario and the Atlantic Region? And have the tariff reductions over the past two decades in fact been tending to offset other forces working towards the narrowing of inter-regional disparities (thus helping to explain the stubborn persistence of the wide disparities in Canada)? The Council does not have answers to such questions at this time, but these and related questions raise important issues requiring further examination.

---

[1]See also D. J. Daly, B. A. Keys and E. J. Spence, *Scale and Specialization in Canadian Manufacturing,* Staff Study No. 21, Economic Council of Canada, (Ottawa, Queen's Printer, 1968).

32 "Made-in-Canada" Considerations in Purchasing *

Canadian Manufacturers' Association

"MADE-IN-CANADA" CONSIDERATIONS IN PURCHASING

It is believed that it is in the national interest for purchasers at every level to specify "made-in-Canada" products in preference to imported ones whenever it is practical to do so. This principle has been enunciated in Association publications and addresses, has been supported by labour and consumer organizations and, we believe, is generally accepted by the Canadian Government.

Government purchasing in itself, and by its example, exerts an important influence on the market for manufactured goods. At the same time its purchasing selections are not motivated by personal taste preferences as is the consumer, nor by the short term pressures of business considerations. In consequence we submit that purchasing operations by all departments of government should be subject to the wholehearted application of the "Made-in-Canada" principle, and that the public interest so demands. Government purchasing policies should also give due consideration to the desirability of geographical diversification of industry.

The Association recommends that all government purchases and contracts be subject to a standard clause similar to that which is already in use in some departments, i.e.:

"To the full extent to which the same are procurable, consistent with proper economy and the expeditious carrying out of this contract, Canadian labour, parts and materials shall be used in the work."

It is further urged that this requirement be made clear at the time of issuance of tenders and that appropriate measures be taken to ensure adherence by sub-contractors as well as contractors. Tenders should, in all cases, require that the origin of the goods be stated.

In the determination of what is consistent with "proper economy" under the standard clause suggested above, the Association suggests that there be taken into account the fact that manufacturers, their employees, and their suppliers are substantial taxpayers and that a sizeable proportion of every dollar they earn from government purchases returns to the public purse by way of direct and indirect taxes. It is difficult to state a specific percentage as representing this effective cost reduction on government purchases of Canadian goods, but the Association submits that it would not be unrealis-

---

*From: Canadian Manufacturers' Association, *Representations to the Royal Commission on Canada's Economic Prospects,* Toronto, December 1955, (pamphlet) , p. 10 (reprinted by permission) .

tic to allow a price differential of from 10 per cent to 20 per cent in favour of Canadian goods versus imported ones on these grounds.

The Association urges that all Canadian business constantly review their purchasing policies to ensure that Canadian-made alternatives to the products they are now importing are given a fair opportunity.

33   Purchasing Policies *

Albert Breton

. . . I distinguish between expenditure and purchasing policies, leaving the first expression to cover decisions related to the type and quantity of goods entering governmental budgets, and using the second expression to cover the effective carrying out of expenditure decisions in the market place. In addition, I further limit the term "purchasing policy" to purchasing activity which is not carried out in the lowest-price market. Under these definitions, if a government buys in the lowest-cost markets all the goods and services it needs, it will have an expenditure policy but not a purchasing policy.

The number and type of devices which comprise purchasing policies are difficult to identify completely because most governments prefer not to be too explicit about the particular devices they use; they may even declare (sometimes in good faith) that they do not implement a purchasing policy when they do. For this reason, in the following discussion I will not endeavour to describe the details of such-and-such a government's purchasing policy, since this would in all likelihood be incomplete and most certainly unsystematic. Instead, I will focus on a number of devices which, taken together or separately, are important constituent elements of any purchasing policy. In fact, it is probable that other constituent elements could be analyzed as subcases of the ones discussed in this chapter.

The following discussion is based on information from a variety of sources. Civil servants and former civil servants in the federal government in Ottawa and in the governments of Ontario, Quebec, and Saskatchewan were among the principal of these sources.[1] We did obtain information from other governments, but it was much less systematic than that from

---

*From: Albert Breton, *Discriminatory Government Policies in Federal Countries*, Canadian Trade Committee, Private Planning Association of Canada, (Montreal and Washington, 1967), pp. 5-20 (reprinted by permission of author and publisher).

[1]In the illustrations and discussion below, governments will sometimes be identified by name. This should never be construed to imply that the governments not mentioned do not have purchasing policies or that they do not use the devices that are being discussed or illustrated.

the four governments listed above. Information was also gathered from a number of business firms who are, or were, suppliers of governments or government agencies. Finally, some public documents were studied, as well as a number of private ones to which we were permitted access; we also looked at a cross-section of "requests for tenders" taken from a relatively large roster of newspapers from across Canada.

Although it is probable that purchasing policies—as here defined—have always been used by governments, one gets the impresson that with the growth in the size of their budgets, governments have come to realize that purchasing policies can be used to pursue some objectives which were previously more clumsily pursued. Consequently, the entire field may be subject to rapid evolution.

The following discussion is divided into two main parts. Part A deals with the mechanics of purchasing policies, describing in some detail the devices and procedures which constitute these policies; Part B is more analytical and is intended to bring out the economic meaning and implication of these policies. Part A is subdivided into four sections. The first deals with the system of priorities used by governments in their purchases. The subject matter is often referred to as the "preference policies" of governments. However, since other practices are also preferential, I have decided to adopt a slightly different language to describe these policies. In the second section, I discuss some aspects of qualification systems adopted by some governments to determine whether a firm is eligible to supply them or their agencies. In the third section, I consider how purchasing policies have come to be used in conjunction with other policies for the purpose of achieving higher rates of growth of some parts of total output, or some other objective. Finally, I discuss briefly the consequences for governments of buying on the basis of specification instead of on the basis of brand.

Before taking up each of these topics, it is essential to underline the distinction between "procurement" and "contracts." The former refers to the purchases of goods by governments, while the latter is restricted to construction of roads and bridges, or of buildings, such as schools, hospitals, and office space. Both procurement and contracts for a given department are generally under the authority of that department's head. However, in certain cases, such as in Quebec and Saskatchewan, procurement is centralized in one agency.[2] Sometimes a department head by-passes the Central Purchasing Agency by signing, for the construction of a hospital, for example, a contract which contains orders for beds, operating tables, and other required hospital equipment, all items which are technically under the authority of the Purchasing Agency. In most cases, however, department

---

[2]In the federal government, procurement is under the authority of each department's head (Royal Commission on Government Organization, Vol. II, pp. 77-142). Recently plans have been made, and are currently being carried out, to transform the Department of Defence Production into a Department of Supply, which would be a central purchasing agency. According to present plans, this transformation should be completed by 1970.

heads are not free to do what they want; a number of orders-in-council exist which specify the framework within which decisions must be taken. To be able to bid on procurement orders below a certain value, firms must usually have their names on a mailing list and be classified as selling the products wanted by the government. A request for tender is then mailed to them. If the procurement exceeds a certain sum, a request for tender will be published in a number of newspapers. The value of the procurement below which a letter is sent and above which a request is placed in the newspapers is not determined by law or by order-in-council. It has not been possible to ascertain what this amount is, but it apparently varies according to whether there are many or few suppliers and whether the product is required immediately or not. A little later, under the heading of qualification systems, the conditions which a firm has to meet to be on the mailing list for governmental procurement will be discussed.

In the case of contracts, the practice is to place a request for tender in a number of newspapers, giving some details as to who can bid for the contract. These details generally refer to requirements that suppliers must satisfy to qualify as bidders. The report of the Royal Commission on Government Organization describes the steps to be taken after publication of requests for tender by the federal government; in some cases the number of steps to be carried out is as high as thirty-eight. However, this is a problem of government efficiency which has only indirect relevance to the analysis of purchasing polices. . . .

A. Description of Purchasing Policies

1. The System of Priorities

A government that is implementing a purchasing policy does not treat all suppliers in the same way, even though all suppliers may have identical production and transportation costs for their products. Some suppliers, having certain special characteristics, are given priority in the sense that the government will buy from them even if their prices are higher than those of their competitors. Possibly these characteristics vary from time to time and from place to place, but the two most frequently encountered in the investigation for this study were region and ethnicity, with the frequency of the former far in excess of that of the latter. Indeed, it can be said that the system of priority is dominated by region. Most governments (certainly all of those considered herein) rank suppliers according to region. Preference is usually given to suppliers of the province, then to those of the country, and finally to foreigners. In the case of one province,[3] we were told that foreigners were also ranked, those from the United States and the United Kingdom coming first, and then those from Japan; for some reason the ranking did not allow for Western Europe!

_____

[3]When the information we have was made available to us "unofficially," we will refrain from naming the province or the region.

The classification of suppliers according to region operates in one of two ways. First, the supplier from outside the province (or from a foreign country) may be allowed to bid for a contract, but if his price does not fall below the price of the local supplier by more than a given margin, he will not get the order. This is the system of override prices. Alternatively, the supplier may simply not be allowed to bid, as was the case in the example of requests for tender cited above. Both systems are widely used by governments (including the federal government) [4] in Canada.

For some large firms with a number of branch plants, it is not obvious to what region they should be assigned. Consequently, in some cases rules have been devised to classify firms according to regions. In Quebec, for example, the concept used is that of the "principal place of business." It is defined negatively in the following way: "A firm does not have its principal place of business in a region if, first, its headquarters are not in the region and, second, if its management (top, middle, and lower) and the buildings where its materials are usually kept are not in the region."[5] Such a definition does not cover all cases, but it should be remembered that requests for tender are not restricted to the suppliers of a particular region when a supplier cannot be found there; the definition of the principal place of business therefore determines when the system of regional priority will be used and when it will not.

In some cases, regional priority is not applied to the firm but to the inputs and/or some production processes. In this case, inputs are ranked on a regional basis. Sometimes a Canadian-content rule is applied, sometimes a provincial-content rule, and at other times a local-content rule. Again, it appears that whenever local inputs are physically available, the local-content rule is applied; if local inputs are not available, then the

[4]This can be documented by the following quotation:

Hon. Marcel Lambert (Edmonton West): Mr. Speaker. I wish to direct a question to the Minister of Defence Production. In the light of reports that Canadian defence contractors may face a reduction in the preference granted in orders placed by his department, would the Minister advise the House whether there has been a change in that if Canada gets larger defence orders from the United States he must reduce the preference granted to Canadian contractors?

Hon. C. M. Drury (Minister of Defence Production): I am not sure, Mr. Speaker, that I quite understand the full import of that question. There is no question that there will be any reduction in the preference now granted to Canadian contractors. *Debates,* (Commons) First Session, Twenty-sixth Parliament, (June 21, 1963), p. 1429. I have not performed a complete analysis of Hansard; a rather close examination of a relatively short period has brought out a number of declarations similar to the one above.

[5]The original text is: "Un entrepreneur n'a pas sa principale place d'affaires dans une région, dans une zone ou dans la province, s'il n'y a pas le principal bureau d'où ses affaires sont dirigées de même que le principal établissement où son personnel de maîtrise et son materiel se trouvent ordinairement." (Order-in-Council No. 1997 of October 21, 1964, modifying Order-in-Council No. 2372 of December 20, 1960.)

provincial-content rule is applied; and if inputs are not available at the local level or at the provincial level, the Canadian-content rule is applied.

It should be observed in this context that the federal government follows a Canadian-content rule.[6] Procurements and contracts exceeding fifteen thousand dollars are reviewed by the Treasury Board, which gives a priority of approximately 10 percent (it can be as high as 12 percent) to Canadian products.[7] This rule is applied in all projects where the federal government shares the costs with junior governments. This, of course, is likely to be a source of conflict whenever provincial governments want to give priority to provincial suppliers. In this context, it is noteworthy that Ontario, for example, does not seem to have a system of priorities like that of the governments of Quebec, Saskatchewan, Alberta, or the Canadian government; the preferences Ontario extends must be found, in the case of road building at least, in the qualifying rules it has adopted. Qualification systems are discussed in the next section. . . .

2. Qualification Systems

. . . Qualification requirements take a variety of forms, which differ as between procurement and contracts. In the present section I will discuss the qualifications required in both cases and, in some detail, the system which has been adopted in Ontario by the Department of Highways to rate potential suppliers.

In the case of procurement, suppliers who want to sell to the government must get the name of their firm on a list. Only when the amount to be purchased is large—a term which is administratively defined—is a request for tenders published in newspapers; otherwise the list is used. To be on the list, an entrepreneur must fill out a relatively simple form about the operations of his firm; space is provided on the form for a listing of the products manufactured, or stored and sold, by the firm. Once the form has been filled out, an inspector for the government is sent to the firm. If the inspector accepts the firm, it is put on the list. When letters are sent out to suppliers requesting them to bid, the decision as to who should receive

---

[6]Formally, this ruling seems to go as far back as 1921. Indeed, on July 23rd of that year an order-in-council (No. P.C. 2648) directed all departments of the Canadian government to "make purchase of goods of Canadian manufacture only, for departmental and other requirements, except in cases where such action would result in the purchase of articles or goods of so inferior a quality as to make this action undesirable." (Quoted in *Debates*, (Commons) , Fourth Session, Twenty-fourth Parliament, Ottawa, 1961, p. 1512.)

[7]*Debates*, (Commons) , Fourth Session, Twenty-fourth Parliament, 1961, pp. 1512 and 1514. In the same speech from which the above is taken, Mr. E. J. Broome states: ". . . at a cabinet meeting on March 8, 1955, the coal situation was considered, and it was decided that Canadian coal would be used in all government coal-burning installations where the laid-down cost of such coal did not exceed the competitive cost of other coals by more than 10 per cent. This decision was reviewed at a cabinet meeting on February 18, 1958, and because of the difficulties facing the Canadian coal industry, this price preference, on the recommendation of the Dominion Coal Board, was increased to 20 per cent of laid-down cost."

the letter is made after consideration of the list; only if a firm manufactures or sells the product will a letter be sent to it.

It has been extremely difficult to establish whether this procedure is adhered to in practice. We have heard of cases where being on the list did not really mean that one could bid for a contract. Sometimes a firm was simply not asked to bid. On other occasions, the product specifications or, more often, the factor and production process requirements were such that it appeared as if only certain preselected suppliers could bid. Such cases are extremely difficult to document; but witnesses and, in one case, a reliable "victim" assured us that such practices, though perhaps not common, did in fact exist. There is a case, not much more documented, which was brought up in the Canadian House of Commons and is consequently reported in Hansard. It relates to the cancellation of tender calls by the Department of Defence Production (which in terms of purchases is a large department) after the defeat of the Progressive Conservative Party on April 8, 1963. A question was asked in the House by a member of the opposition as to whether it was true that all tender calls had been canceled. After interventions of all kinds by front benchers on the government side, and a few assists from the Speaker of the House, the question went unanswered.[8] Although one cannot be sure that the requests for tender were in fact concealed, Hansard clearly gives the impression that they were.[9]

In considering qualification systems for contract, we must distinguish between prequalification and postqualification. Briefly, the distinction between the two rests on whether one is declared eligible to bid before or after submitting a bid. Getting one's name on a list, therefore, is a case of prequalification. Putting an ad in newspapers or trade magazines, which allows everyone who so desires to bid, is a case of postqualification. Of course, postqualification can be modified by asking bidders to post bonds of various kinds or by asking them to meet other requirements. Consider the procedure involved in the case of a contract when no prequalification is required. A department of government puts an ad in newspapers or trade magazines requesting submission of tenders but requiring that bidders post a "bid bond" equal to some percentage of the bid or to some prestated amount and stating also that the successful bidder will have to deposit a "performance bond" and/or a "labour, material, and services bond" equal

---

[8]*Debates*, (Commons), Vol. I, (1963) pp. 770-71.

[9]Another case reported in Hansard is of relevance. It has to do with the employment of Liberal and Conservative lawyers after the Liberal defeat of 1958. Part of the debate went as follows: Mr. Howard: ". . . So far as prosecutions under the Opium and Narcotic Drug Act are concerned, it seems that the most competent lawyers or firms of lawyers are Conservatives. This may be coincidental. It appears also that none of the lawyers or firms of lawyers who were retained for prosecutions prior to the Minister's (Mr. Fulton—Conservative) party taking office are now considered to be competent. Co-incidentally again, these firms and lawyers are Liberals . . ." Mr. Fulton answered: "I will be quite frank and say that we do not exclude from the list of those qualified those who happen to be our own friends."

to 50 percent or even to 100 percent of the value of the contract. The adver-
tisement, of course, is addressed to the prime or general contractor and
usually does not specify anything about subcontractors. The required procedure for prime contractors vis-à-vis subcontractors is well specified by
trade associations such as the Canadian Construction Association, which
requires the utilization of bid depositories—a system in which the prime
contractors, instead of using the telephone or face-to-face contacts to
negotiate subcontracts, in effect request submission of tenders from
subcontractors.

Labour, materials, and services bonds and performance bonds can be
obtained from specialized financial institutions that make these available
to contractors. The rates at which these bonds can be obtained vary from
time to time and are generally relatively low.[10] A contractor is eligible for
bonds if his credit rating is good, if his performance in the past has been
satisfactory, and, generally, if he is a bona fide entrepreneur.

Whenever bonds are requested, that is, whenever a modified postqualification system is used, only those who can secure bond are, in fact,
allowed to bid. This system, however, generally produces different results
from the prequalification system. The latter system is well developed in
the Ontario Department of Highways. Since some other provinces[11] are
at present considering adopting the Ontario system, it will be discussed in
some detail.

Since October, 1957, the Ontario Department of Highways, in requesting
tenders, has been using a prequalification system. Only those who meet
certain qualifications are allowed to bid. The system was last modified in
January, 1965, and this revised version will be described here. Officially the
system is designed to ensure that only contractors who are "financially and
technically capable of satisfactorily performing the work within the specified
time"[12] are allowed to bid. The system applies to all capital contracts, to
large maintenance contracts, and to re-surfacing and hot-mix patching
contracts. Each contractor who desires to bid for contracts must, within
three months of his fiscal year end, submit a certified financial statement to
the Department of Highways. This statement is used to rate the contractor.
The rating so obtained is called the *basic rating* and is equal to four times
the net current assets of the firm plus three times the sum of the standard

---

[10]At the time of our investigation (early August, 1965), a 50 per cent performance
bond could be had at a per annum rate of .35 per cent of the contract price; a 50 per cent
labour, materials, and services bond at a rate of .25 per cent; and bid bonds at ten
dollars each, whatever the amount, at one large insurance company doing that business
in Montreal.

[11]On June 2, 1965, the Department of Roads in Quebec declared in a press release that
Ontario's system would be adopted in Quebec with due consideration given to the par-
ticular conditions of certain regions and to the existence of smaller firms operating in
Quebec.

[12]Ontario, Department of Highways, *Revised Procedures Governing the Qualification
of Contractors*, (January, 1965).

depreciation value of machinery and equipment and the net book value of all other fixed assets. This basic rating is then used to establish the *adjusted rating* through modification of the basic rating for quality of past work as well as for past performance, that is, failure to maintain schedule, to discharge liabilities, to maintain public relations, etc. Maximum reduction is 100 percent. The basic rating is also adjusted for experience; lack of experience will bring about a reduction in rating. Experience is defined by a total of six criteria; for each criterion a minimum percentage reduction is specified. The criteria are the following:

a) never worked in Ontario—minimum reduction—   80 percent

b) worked in Ontario but not for Department of Highways—minimum reduction—   70 percent

c) worked only for subcontractor for Department of Highways—minimum reduction—   60 percent

d) worked for Department of Highways in one work classification only—minimum reduction in all other classifications[13]—   50 percent

e) worked only in "M"—minimum reduction—   80 percent

f) worked only in "G"—equivalent experience in "M" required.

In other words, a contractor from outside Ontario with a basic rating equal to that of an Ontario contractor will have an adjusted rating equal to between 80 percent and 100 percent less than the Ontario contractor. Since bidders are required to have a given rating to bid, the contractor outside Ontario will in all likelihood not be allowed to bid.

Once the adjusted rating is established, an *available rating* is calculated by subtracting from the adjusted rating the total tender value of all the work the contractor has on hand, defined as contracts on which he has been "read out" as a low bidder and contracts which have already been awarded to him. He must add to his adjusted rating the total of all progress-payment certificates submitted on contracts plus 20 percent of the tender value of those contracts on which the contractor has submitted at least one progress-payment certificate. This establishes the available and final rating, the necessary value of which is specified for each work classification when requests for tender are made.

It is our understanding that some trade associations strongly believe in prequalification systems and that they try to persuade departments of government to adopt prequalification systems. Because these systems give

---

[13]There are five classifications: "G"—Grading, "P"—Paving, "C"—Concrete paving, "S"—Structures, "M"—Miscellaneous.

the appearance of being more "liberal" than systems of priority, they will probably be adopted in one form or another by various governments.

3. Incentive Systems

Even though it is often asserted that provincial (or, more generally, junior) governments use purchasing policies to induce firms to locate in their jurisdictions, few cases can be documented. Upon reflection it seems obvious that purchasing policies can be used for that purpose, but only in conjunction with other policies. If a firm's profitability depends on the government's demand for its output, then, presumably, the company would need a guarantee of some kind that the government will continue to purchase that firm's output for some period in the future. This is not easily done.

In one case that was brought to our attention, the guaranteeing procedure was as follows: The president of a company sent a letter to the premier of the province stating his case and asking that the government satisfy all its need for the given product from his firm. The premier's answer could have been interpreted (and was later interpreted by members of the cabinet) as if no commitment had been made. It was interpreted by the president of the company as if one had been. In practice, the government bought everything it needed from that firm.

The specific technique by which the government ensured that the company would be awarded the contracts was to accept the list price submitted by the firm as the lowest possible price that could be obtained. Any firm submitting below the list price was viewed with suspicion and its bid disregarded. Among the firms bidding at the list price, the local firm was favoured, since its price was not higher than that of other "eligible" firms. The procedure implied that the government forewent all discounts.

It should, however, be added that, in view of the relatively short secured life of any government in a democracy, one should not expect guaranteed purchases to occur very often. Only when regional systems, like the one prevalent in Quebec, exist could one expect purchasing policies to act as an incentive that would attract industry because only in such cases are the policies built into the system to a sufficient extent that businessmen can expect them to have some degree of permanency. This may be one reason why the Quebec scheme is attracting interest elsewhere.

4. Specification Versus Brand Buying

Everyone buys certain products more by specification than by brand name; this is the case for houses (most certainly new houses), for some furniture, and for a number of other products. But often consumers buy by brand. Governments, on the other hand, do everything possible to buy by specification—that is, by stating how the product should be built, of what type of material it should be made, etc.

Requests for tenders ask bidders to call at a given address to get the exact specifications of the product demanded. Based on these specifications, the potential suppliers then estimate the price which they will have to ask for the product. A number of suppliers claim that governments often change specifications after contracts have been awarded. We have not been able to document this, nor to establish for which product the specifications are most often changed. One thing seems to stand out, however, namely, that changes in specifications are usually very costly for governments.

Furthermore, in the case of smaller items, the paper work involved in specification buying is larger than it would be in brand buying. The official justification for incurring these additional costs is that specification buying does not carry with it the stigma of political favouritism: the produce is bought—whatever its origin—only if specifications are met. In practice it would seem, however, that specification buying can be used as a more elaborate, if less obvious, type of political instrument. Indeed, it is possible to use specification buying as a most effective instrument of purchasing policy by imposing demands on the nature of the inputs or processes (both of which restrict supply unnecessarily) ; by determining what the origin of the suppliers should be; or by altering the specifications once the contracts are awarded or even after the work is under way.

B. Analysis of the Effects of Purchasing Policies

The various policies described above can be grouped into three major classes. The analysis for each of these classes will be presented separately.

Broadly speaking, all the policies described in Part A are subsidization policies of one type or another. In some cases the subsidy may seem more obvious because the price paid by the government is higher than the price it would have to pay for the same product in the market place. In other cases it may be less apparent, but the policy will also result in higher than necessary purchasing prices because the government imposes restrictions on the available supply. In the first class of policies, override price buying is certainly the most important, since some suppliers are thereby able to sell at non-competitive prices. In the second class, I include price increases resulting from changes in the requested specifications for a product after the contract has been awarded; such practices usually involve subsidization because, once the contract is secured, the entrepreneur is in the position of a monopolist capable of obtaining a monopoly price for that part of the contract which is respecified. The difference between the weighted average of the monopoly price and the price at which the contract was originally awarded, on the one hand, and the price which would have prevailed if specifications had been changed before the contract was awarded, on the other, measures the size of the subsidy; the weights should be based on the fraction of the contract that is not respecified for the contract-awarding price and that part which is altered for the adjusted "monopoly" price.

In the third class of policies—those akin to quantitative restrictions—I include the disallowance from bidding imposed on some suppliers who are not from the "proper" region or of the "proper" ethnic background. I also include here the exclusion from bidding of those firms whose factor inputs do not meet certain specifications related to origin or to some other factor. A special case of this, of course, arises in specification buying when it is known that some specifications which are not necessary for the product can be met by one or, at most, a few entrepreneurs; this would be the case if, for example, it was specified that a given building should be built with stones from a given area while similar and less expensive stones were available from elsewhere. Such practices restrict the number of suppliers who can bid for a given contract. Finally, I include in this class the prequalification policies referred to earlier, whenever the criteria for prequalification are not related to the job to be done. The best example of this is the adjustment made to one's rating if he is not a resident of the province.

The foregoing paragraphs have followed the general rule of classifying purchasing policies according to whether the subsidizations implicit in the policies manifest themselves from the demand or from the supply side of the transactions. The following analysis of these different kinds of policies will first be carried out under the assumption that one can look at a government in isolation; afterwards it will be extended to the case when many governments exist, as in a federal state. Only after this latter analysis is performed will I consider the implications of paying these subsidies through higher taxes than would otherwise prevail, or in the form of lower alternative expenditures. For the time being, I will assume that the government has at its disposal the resources required to pay the subsidies.

Consider first the policy of override prices—that is, the policy of paying a higher than necessary price for a product. In this case, a given entrepreneur gets a subsidy which is equal to the difference between the price he receives and the lowest price at which the product could have been bought by the government, a magnitude which crucially depends on the elasticity of the demand curve. The subsidy is larger when a rise in prices results in a relatively small reduction in the quantity demanded. One of the consequences of the subsidy is that the gross revenue of the chosen entrepreneur is larger than it would otherwise be, and as a result the rewards to some or all of the factors of production (land, labour, and capital) will be higher than they would be in the absence of the subsidy.

It has generally been observed that in situations of this kind the rewards to all the factors of production will increase. The increase will be greater for some inputs than for others, but it will not be negative for any. Consequently, if override prices are based on regional priorities (in the sense that the selected entrepreneur is chosen because of his residence or region), then the labour of that region will receive a higher income, and the property values of that region will be raised. It follows that the relative economic position of that region vis-à-vis other regions inside as well as outside the government's jurisdiction will have been improved. It can be improved in another respect whenever there is unemployment in the region where the selected entrepreneur lives. In that case, the increase in gross revenue resulting from the subsidy will probably reduce unemployment as well as increase the income of employed labour and raise land and property values.

In the case of changes in contract specifications after the contract has been awarded, we have seen above how to measure the size of this subsidy; again the subsidy will lead to an increase in the gross revenue of the entrepreneur who was awarded the contract, and this will be distributed to the factors of production in the fashion described in relation to override prices.

Finally, in the case of prequalification imposed on potential suppliers, the subsidy originates from the fact that supply is smaller than it otherwise would be, so that, in fact, the price paid by the government is higher. The effects of the subsidy are exactly as described above. For this general category of subsidies, one must consider the case of content specification separately. This arises whenever it is required that "local" inputs be used if an entrepreneur wishes to sell to the government. Two cases must be distinguished: one which arises when a very definite content requirement is specified, as when an entrepreneur must incur a given fraction of his costs on "local" inputs; the second case is when the content requirement is not precisely specified, but it is required that some local inputs be used. In both instances, content specification shifts the cost curve upwards and changes the slope of the curve, at least for that fraction of total cost that must be spent on the more expensive "local" inputs. Since the government pays for the purchase and, therefore, for the extra cost due to content specification, those factors which are used in the production process receive a subsidy which is equal to the difference between the price they receive for their services and what they could get in the absence of content requirements.

We must now consider what happens when the government is not pursuing its purchasing policy in isolation but instead is part of a system of interdependent jurisdictions. We must also take into account the fact that to pay the subsidies, the government must tax the population.

To analyze this problem, we must distinguish between two cases: one which arises when factors of production are mobile between jurisdictions, and another when such mobility does not exist. If a government implements purchasing policies and if the factors of production in its jurisdiction are mobile, the tax required to pay for the implied subsidies will, given the removal costs and the preference of individuals for the jurisdiction, tend to push the factors of production out of the jurisdiction. If the degree of mobility of factors (labour and capital) resulting from changes in taxes is called the tax elasticity of factor movements, then, assuming that the value of this elasticity is low, it will be easier for the government of a given jurisdiction to tax a fraction of its population and to pay the proceeds in subsidies to another. Measured against its effects on the reward of the factors employed in the subsidized firm, industry, or region, a purchasing policy will therefore be more efficient if the tax elasticity of factor movements is low. If it is high, purchasing policies will be less efficient—against the background just described—because the government will be unable to raise money to pay for the subsidy without losing some labour and capital employed in the taxed sections of the economy. As a consequence, one should expect governments in jurisdictions where factors of production are relatively immobile to adopt and implement purchasing policies more than other governments. There is an additional dimension to this problem, resulting from the fact that the subsidies are effectively preventing suppliers of other jurisdictions from selling to the government implementing purchasing policies. Such policies in fact invite retaliation. We should consequently expect those jurisdictions which stand to lose a great deal from the purchasing policies of a government in another jurisdiction to adopt purchasing policies themselves or to adopt policies which have similar effects.

As a last point, one would like to be able to answer the question of whether or not purchasing policies adopted by governments increase or reduce the available output and the welfare of the population of the region. The answer depends on whether or not we assume that the government can replace purchasing policies by other subsidization policies. If we assume that the government must use purchasing policies, we can show that, by starting with an economy in which all the markets are in full equilibrium, the subsidies extended through purchasing policies will interfere with the efficient working of the system and will produce a lower level of output. On the other hand, if we start with a situation of disequilibrium in some markets—disequilibria which may appear because of the existence of monopoly elements, taxes,. subsidies, external economies or diseconomies, and other things—then it is not possible to say whether the implementation of purchasing policies would improve or worsen the general welfare and whether such implementation would increase or reduce output. To arrive at an answer, one would require empirical knowledge of the technology used and of the structure of industry as well as of the structure of wants.

Suppose now that the government is free to choose between purchasing policies on the one hand and a mix of other policies on the other to attain its goal, should it implement purchasing policies or should it choose another combination of policies? The answer to this question is very heavily dependent on what the goals of the government are and, consequently, also on the hypothesis one chooses as the proper framework to analyze and understand the process of government; in other words, the answer is dependent on one's theory of government. . . .

34   Defence Expenditures, Priorities and Controls*

Canadian Manufacturers' Association

Defence Expenditures, Priorities and Controls

While international tensions may ease, the foreseeable future does not offer justification for relaxation in defence preparedness. The maintenance of our armed forces on a substantial basis will, we feel, be necessary for many years to come. The fact that Canada has had a well-equipped defence force over the prolonged period of international tension which we have experienced, has, we believe, acted as a deterrent to aggression.

Our feeling is that should a war situation arise, the old concept of a force in being, the purpose of which is to hold an enemy at bay until the manpower and industrial resources of the country can be mobilized, may not be realizable. It is possible that a critical situation may arise within a short period following the outbreak of hostilities, and it may be that our standing force will be not only the first but the only line of defence under such circumstances. For this reason we believe that our armed forces must be maintained on a basis which reflects the best procurable in arms and equipment, restricted as to supply only by the limits of our financial resources. The maintenance and expansion of Canada's defence production potential is therefore of paramount importance and defence purchasing policies should be consistently aimed at the greatest possible degree of self-sufficiency. Defence stores in all categories should be standardized wherever practical on Canadian-produced items in order to avoid the risk of an interruption in supply from outside sources should an emergency arise.

It is realized, of course, that it is not possible at all times to keep our defence forces supplied with equipment which represents the very latest devised, due to the continuous development of new weapons and equipment resulting from research and trial and due also to ever-changing ideas on the tactical uses to which such material may be put. We believe that the policy of our Defence Departments should, however, aim as closely as possible to the achievement of this ideal.

In keeping with the policy of self-sufficiency and to sustain and encourage Canadian industry, our Defence Departments should, we submit, expand their efforts to keep abreast of future developments in the material field by placing in the hands of private industry, for research and engineering, defence development projects of a long-range nature. Such long-range

---

*From: Canadian Manufacturers' Association, *Representations to the Royal Commission on Canada's Economic Prospects,* Toronto, December 1955, (pamphlet), p. 11 (reprinted by permission).

projects should not, we suggest, be confined only to the engineering and production facilities under the control of the Department of National Defence, but opportunity should also be given to private industry to develop them. In this way, industry which has shown its ability to meet and solve the challenge of involved technical problems in its own sphere of operations, would be brought into closer partnership with the Defence Departments and the Defence Research Board, a partnership which undoubtedly would be developed to a marked degree in the event of an emergency.

If, because of defence emergency or other supply difficulties it becomes necessary to reimpose a system of government priorities and controls, this should be carried out, as in the past, with full consultation with the industries affected.

35 Defence Procurement Policies*

Gideon Rosenbluth

. . . Canadian military procurement policy has been characterized by protectionism, by barter-type arrangements with other countries, by noncompetitive arrangements at home, and by strong efforts to increase the dependence of Canadian defence industry on the United States market. All these devices have served the objective of protecting and promoting Canadian defence industry. This objective both coexists and conflicts with that of obtaining defence requirements at the lowest cost, a goal which has received increasing emphasis in recent years.

Why are Canadian governments pursuing a policy of protecting and promoting defence industry, at the cost of the taxpayer and with the result of increasing Canadian economic dependence on the United States military market? It is hard to find a coherent rationale in official statements. This is not, in itself, surprising or alarming, since most government policies are shaped by a variety of considerations and are subject to conflicting pressures. Let us review briefly the main lines of argument that are apparent in official and unofficial discussions of procurement policy.

The traditional argument for the promotion of defence industry is that it is necessary for reasons of defence. Adam Smith, the father of economic science and high priest of free trade and free competition, wrote in 1776:

*From: Gideon Rosenbluth, *The Canadian Economy and Disarmament*, Toronto, Macmillan Co. of Canada Ltd., 1967) , pp. 40-48 (reprinted by permission of author and publisher) .

The defence of Great Britain . . . depends very much upon the number of its sailors and shipping. The act of navigation, therefore, very properly endeavours to give the sailors and shipping of Great Britain the monopoly of the trade of their own country. . . . As defence . . . is much more important than opulence, the act of navigation is, perhaps, the wisest of all the commercial regulations of England.

And again:

If any particular manufacture was necessary, indeed, for the defence of the society, it might not always be prudent to depend upon our neighbours for the supply; and if such manufacture could not otherwise be supported at home, it might not be unreasonable that all the other branches of industry should be taxed in order to support it. The bounties upon the exportation of British-made sailcloth, and British-made gun-powder, may, perhaps, both be vindicated upon this principle.[1]

Note, however, the frequent use of 'if', 'perhaps', and 'may' in these statements.

Thus the traditional ground for protection and subsidies to defence industry is the desire not to 'depend upon our neighbours' for defence requirements. While defence considerations are still cited as major grounds for these policies in Canada, the policy of not depending on our neighbours has, however, been abandoned. Complete independence of others in respect to the defence of Canada has, in fact, never existed. With entry into NATO, NORAD, and the Production and Development Sharing Programs, Canada has increasingly moved into a position described in official statements as 'partnership' with the United States in defence,[2] a term that is only appropriate if it is recognized that, in view of the difference in economic size and power, Canada is a very junior partner indeed. Official policy has in fact extended the concept of partnership to other countries. Describing the post-Korean situation, the White Paper on Defence says: 'Canada's defence programs now . . . made sense only in relation to the total capabilities of the entire group of NATO nations. . . .'[3] Thus, official policy no longer treats defence as a purely national task. Under these circumstances it would be appropriate for Canada's defence industries to contribute what they can on a competitive basis to the collective defence requirements. There can be no justification on grounds of defence for policies that encourage uneconomic industrial activity, such as the Canadian Content Policy, the various subsidies connected with the Development Sharing Program, non-competitive contracts, shipbuilding subsidies, and the like.

---

[1]*The Wealth of Nations* (New York, Random House, Modern Library Ed. 1937), pp. 429, 431, 488-89.

[2]White Paper on Defence (Ottawa, Queen's Printer, 1964), p. 6.

[3]*Ibid.*, p. 9.

The traditional argument for not 'depending upon our neighbours' would come into its own again if Canada were to adopt a neutralist policy or to introduce a greater degree of independence into its foreign policy. A more neutral policy has been proposed by a number of well-informed observers. It would require the maintenance of an industrial defence base that could not be justified on purely economic grounds, in order to achieve some degree of independence from United States sources of supply. It would not, however, be necessary to rely on domestic sources for all military requirements.[4]

It seems evident that in the context of present policies, 'defence' provides weak grounds for uneconomic practices designed to promote defence industry. A second major argument that has often been used is simply that Canadian government expenditures should serve to provide business for Canadian firms and employment for Canadian labour, rather than to benefit business firms and labour abroad. This argument is often voiced by members of Parliament as if it were a self-evident truth. Responsible civil servants will say, privately, that it is not 'politically feasible' to spend large sums of government money without ensuring that there is a benefit in terms of Canadian employment. The official pronouncements of government leaders have been very cautious in tone. A policy of using defence expenditure for the specific purpose of creating employment has not been asserted, and has even been denied. Nevertheless the 'benefits' of defence expenditure in terms of volume of business and employment have frequently been stressed.

The attitude of many members of Parliament is well expressed in questions such as the following, which appeared in Hansard on April 30, 1965:

> Is it the intention of the Department of Defence to purchase non-military vehicles direct from the manufacturers, thus by-passing local and franchised car dealers? If this is the case, this will help neither business nor employment in the country.[5]

---

[4]For examples of the case for neutralism see James M. Minifie, *Peacemaker or Powder-Monkey* (Toronto, McClelland and Stewart, 1960) and K. McNaught, on foreign policy, in M. Oliver (ed.), *Social Purpose for Canada* (Toronto, University of Toronto Press, 1961), pp. 445-72. McNaught argues that a neutralist policy is compatible with substantial unilateral disarmament, a view not shared by Minifie or the present writer.

It is doubtful if the present structure of ownership and control of defence industry would be appropriate for a neutralist policy. In many cases production will be most efficient if there is only one supplier, but in this case a private owner may exploit his monopoly position. Moreover, leading defence contractors are subsidiaries of foreign firms, largely United States firms (see Table 6:1). In United States law and governmental practice, parent companies are held responsible for the policies of their Canadian subsidiaries. Hence, situations are likely to arise in which the Canadian subsidiary faces a conflict of loyalties.

[5]*Debates,* (Commons), (April 30, 1965), p. 779.

The official attitude is reflected in the last part of the statement on production sharing quoted earlier from the White Paper on Defence, as well as in the following:

> During World War II and the years following, Canada undertook the manufacture of a wide variety of defence equipment. This production served as a useful stimulant for Canadian industry and was beneficial in many ways to the economy as a whole.[6]

The view of defence procurement and military bases as a source of employment is, of course, particularly prevalent in localities and regions in which business conditions are chronically or temporarily depressed. . . . [D]efence expenditure in proportion to total economic activity is particularly high in the Maritime provinces, and this is the region in which unemployment, on a long-term basis, is much higher than in other parts of the country. This situation accounts in large measure for the strong political support for the former policy of allocating naval shipbuilding and repair contracts on a non-competitive basis, and for the opposition to the new policy of competitive bidding. On February 7, 1966, the leader of the New Democratic Party raised a question in the House of Commons regarding the contract for repair and refit of H.M.C.S. *Bonaventure*. He asked: 'In view of the very severe economic conditions in Saint John, has the minister given any consideration to the possibility of granting this contract to the Saint John Drydock Company on a cost-plus basis . . .?' The Minister of Defence Production replied:

> . . . I think this would represent a very significant departure from government policy which, under successive governments, has followed the sound practice in relation to procurement for the Department of National Defence of using our defence funds to the maximum possible extent in obtaining value in defence equipment. This is the principal reason for strict adherence to a system of competitive bidding. If special assistance to an area is required by reason of a high level of unemployment, surely, as the hon. gentleman knows, there are both standing and emergency government programs which may be made use of for this purpose.[7]

This reply contrasts with the Minister's testimony of 1963 . . . in which he stated that regional economic and labour conditions were taken into account in the allocation of shipbuilding contracts. The contrast illustrates the change of emphasis away from employment considerations and towards maximum economy in defence procurement. Nevertheless, the domestic preference in shipbuilding and repair contracts, the Canadian Content Policy, production sharing, and negotiated contracts still tend to direct expenditure into uneconomic channels, and the benefit to business and

---

[6]*Op. cit.,* p. 29.
[7]*Debates,* (Commons), (February 7, 1966), pp. 802-803.

employment in particular industries or regions is still a major line of reasoning by which these policies are defended.

The weakness of this line of reasoning is indicated by the first of the Minister's two statements quoted above. Policies to maintain full employment on a national scale, without requiring special protection of particular industries, are well established and thoroughly discussed in the literature of economics and political science. . . . Chronic unemployment in particular regions calls for policies of regional development and mobility. . . . The use of uneconomic policies in defence procurement as a substitute for such policies places an unnecessary burden on the economy.

A third line of reasoning that has been used in the defence of present procurement policies is that they tend to raise the economy's level of productivity or its rate of increase of productivity. At any rate, an array of rather vaguely worded official (and other) statements mean something like this, if they have any meaning. The White Paper on Defence says: 'Defence expenditure can make a contribution to the efficient development of manufacturing.'[8] The Defence Production Department paper, 'Defence Expenditure and its Influence on the Canadian Economy', discusses the subsidies given to Canadian firms for defence development work and comments:

> The benefits of this assistance are not limited to defence production. The resulting technological advances in the complex production operations of highly sophisticated weapons systems spread readily into other areas of Canadian production. The economy as a whole is made stronger and better able to make its way in world markets.[9]

The Minister of Defence Production, in one of his appearances before the House of Commons Committee on Defence, said: 'We cannot overlook the benefit to the Canadian economy of the performance in Canada of the research, development, and production associated with advanced defence technology.'[10] The same belief was expressed by the Glassco Commission, (the Royal Commission on Government Organization), which stated in its report: 'Defence research, development and production now constitute collectively one of the major stimuli to technological progress, and thereby to the competitive strength and growth potential of a nation's industrial economy.'[11] It has also been asserted that the Defence Development and Production Sharing Programs raise the level of technological knowledge in the country by providing access to United States military technology, which

---

[8]*Op. cit.*, p. 29.

[9]House of Commons, *Special Studies Prepared for the Special Committee on Defence* (Ottawa, Queen's Printer, 1965) , p. 102.

[10]*Minutes*, (Commons) , Special Committee on Defence, July 30, 1963, p. 268.

[11]*Report of the Royal Commission on Government Organization* (Ottawa, Queen's Printer, 1962) , Vol. II, p. 119.

is presumed to represent the most advanced level of technological knowledge.

This line of reasoning is often linked with another defence of uneconomic procurement policies. These policies, it is said, benefit Canada's balance of international payments; that is to say, they make it easier to maintain a given value of the Canadian dollar without undue pressure on our reserves of foreign exchange. Such pressure arises from the operation of the defence program because of the policy (since the Avro Arrow cancellation) of purchasing major weapons systems abroad. It is counteracted by the Production and Development Sharing Programs and reduced by the protectionist policies followed in shipbuilding and repair contracts and more generally by the Canadian Content Policy. Moreover, the argument runs, it is reduced by the technological improvements in industry flowing from participation in defence research and production.

The Glassco Commission, while strongly endorsing the view that there were technological and balance-of-payments benefits to be reaped from defence production, was mildly critical of the absence of the study and planning on which the realization of such a potential would depend: 'The procurement effort must be guided by an adequate appreciation of the present and future potentials of the economy in the field of research, development, and technology which can, by proper stimulation and support, underpin the country's economic strength and potential economic growth.' However:

> There is less evidence of serious studies of the Canadian economy upon which confident judgments could be made about the significance of particular segments in relation to future strength and growth. Equally, little evidence has been found that this need is met elsewhere in the government. The degree of success this far attained has been dependent, to an uncomfortable degree, on the common sense and *ad hoc* judgements of practical men. . . .[12]

The justification of present procurement policies on the grounds of technological benefit to the economy is open to serious criticism. It is of course quite possible that scientific and technological knowledge and experience gained through defence work may be usefully employed in other economic fields. . . . [H]owever, United States and British studies indicate that such benefits are not to be expected as a matter of course and are, in fact, decreasing in frequency. Moreover, if the assumption of such benefits is used as a justification for subsidizing defence development and production which would otherwise be uneconomic, one must consider the alternative uses of the resources employed in this manner. As the United States President's Committee on the Economic Impact of Defence and Disarmament has put it:

---

[12]*Ibid.*

There are, to be sure, tangible and occasionally significant incidental benefits which flow from the defense program to the
civilian sector (peaceful uses of military technology, training of
personnel, and the 'spin-off' of new science-based enterprises).
However, there can be little doubt that the Nation could have
obtained the same benefits at substantially lower costs and with
more certainty if comparable research and training resources had
been devoted directly to civilian purposes.[13]

As the Glassco Commission has pointed out, procurement policies have
not been guided by any systematic attempt to ascertain what the economic
sectors or activities are in which these assumed benefits might be located.
Finally, it should be emphasized that the leading example of uneconomic
procurement policies is the shipbuilding industry—and no one would claim
that the Canadian shipbuilding industry is technologically advanced. On
the contrary, its high costs are largely due to technological backwardness
compared with the Japanese and German industries.

The promotion of defence production in order to improve the balance
of payments is also open to criticism. It is true that the stationing of troops
abroad under the NATO agreement and the purchases of major weapons
systems abroad are a significant drain on foreign exchange reserves, and
thus constitute grounds for the active promotion of exports. They do not,
however, provide a special reason for promoting the export of defence
goods. Exports of any kind are sources of foreign exchange, and thus are
equally useful for offsetting the drains arising from the defence program.
Government policy-makers· often appear to be preoccupied with the
balance of foreign payments in particular economic sectors, such as defence,
or the tourist trade, or automobiles, but there is no economic justification
for this preoccupation. A sensible policy of export promotion would concern
itself with those lines in which the prospects for stable growth are most
promising. Most defence exports are probably not in this category. Their
market is highly volatile since it is affected by rapid technological obsolescence, sudden shifts in military strategy, and political considerations.

It appears from our discussion that there are no sound economic grounds
for any deviation, in defence procurement, from the policy of seeking the
best value for money. A neutralist policy, or a move in that direction, might
call for special measures to protect an industrial defence base. But under
the present policy of integrating Canada's military effort with those of her
allies and not seeking significant independence in external affairs, the
subsidies and non-competitive features in defence procurement are inappropriate.

Procurement policies have important implications for the problem of
disarmament. The lower the proportion of business that is dependent on

---

[13]*Report of the Committee on the Economic Impact of Defense and Disarmament*
(Washington, U.S. Gov't. Printing Office, 1965), p. 8.

defence, the easier are the economic adjustments required by disarmament. Thus, under present defence and external policies, strict adherence to the principle of value for money in defence would not only make economic and military sense, but would prepare the ground for an easier transition in the event of disarmament. The defence production that would remain under such a policy would be performed by economically competitive firms. They would have strong incentives to diversify their activities and develop civilian markets, since they would not be able to exert political pressure for uneconomic government contracts. The shipbuilding industry, which at present is maintained by protective federal contract work and heavy federal subsidies for the rest of its business, would be 'phased' out or forced into radical technological change. The scale of output of the aircraft industry would be greatly reduced.

The government would cease to urge and subsidize firms to enter the United States defence market and the volume of business and employment exposed to the hazards of that market would be greatly reduced. Disarmament is one of these hazards.

Considered strictly from the point of view of the economic impact of disarmament, a policy of neutralism, which requires a domestic industrial defence base, would create greater problems of transition to a disarmed state. It may, however, offer better prospects for the achievement of a peaceful and disarmed world. This is a problem with which the present study cannot deal.

36   Research and Development in Canada *

H. E. English

The importance of research and development activity by Canadian firms is not easy to assess. . . . [F]ew Canadian firms would qualify by size as being able to support sizable industrial research and development expenditures. Only 14 per cent of all such expenditure in the United States is carried on by firms with less than 1,000 employees (and as noted already 86 per cent is done in companies with over 5,000). There are only a little over one hundred manufacturing establishments in Canada with more than 1,000 employees and more than half of these have less than 1,500. While . . . the

---

*From: H. E. English, "Industrial Organization and Technical Progress", in T. N. Brewis (ed.), *Growth and the Canadian Economy* (Toronto, Carleton Library, McClelland and Stewart, 1968), pp. 127-37, (reprinted by permission of author and publisher).

lesser importance of the defence industries partly explains the more modest scale of industrial R&D in Canada, it is clear that the size of firm must be of great importance. Nevertheless, it is interesting that the smaller firms engaged in research and development often spend slightly more as a percentage of sales.

A National Industrial Conference Board study in Canada[1] revealed that 68 companies out of 176 surveyed have research and development activities, but that only 19 employ more than 30 scientists each. It is apparent that Canadian activity in this area is more limited than that in the United States, United Kingdom, Japan, and, perhaps more significantly, than that in Sweden, Switzerland and the Netherlands, all of which are smaller countries than Canada.

The Minister of Industry has made the following comparison:

Compare if you will, Canada's performance with that of industrial nations and you will find that our 1961 national research ratio of 0.85% gross national product is relatively austere compared with the ratio of 1.7% for Sweden and France, 1.4% for the Netherlands and Switzerland and 1.3% for West Germany and Japan. At the same time, the corresponding American figure has risen to 2.8% while the United Kingdom ratio is 2.4%, due in part to their higher defence expenditure. Even if the latter are deducted, the balance of their civil research and development effort is in the neighbourhood of 1.5% of the gross national products for both countries.[2]

But these figures require careful interpretation. Economic growth has not been very closely correlated with R&D expenditures. The high ratios for the United States and the United Kingdom have not prevented them from being laggers in growth during much of the decade 1955-65, and Canada, in spite of its performance on R&D, has at times shown a rapid rate of growth. But even if we acknowledge that R&D might improve upon this performance, it should be remembered that many industries require very limited expenditures for this purpose, and only a share of such activity must be carried on near the point of production. Most research concerns product rather than process, and it is usually only at the development stage that the work must be carried on near the plant. In any firm which has more than one plant, there is little apparent need for R&D activities to be carried on at more than one producing any product.

For several reasons, Canadian plants can benefit more than those in most other countries from the technical know-how of a neighbour. This is not only, or even primarily, because of foreign ownership of much Canadian industry. The Canadian resource pattern so closely resembles that of the

---

[1]National Industrial Conference Board, *Scientific Research in Canadian Industry* (Montreal: September, 1963).

[2]"Secondary Industry and the Place of Canadian Economy in a Changing World," address by Hon. C. M. Drury to the Marketing Association of Canada (Montreal, October 16, 1964) (mimeo.), p. 5.

United States that the appropriate production techniques are likely to be similar on both sides of the border. Social characteristics are also so similar that consumer tastes differ little. Even Canadian-owned companies such as Dominion Engineering (before it was taken over by General Electric) and British-owned companies such as John Inglis have depended heavily upon American technology acquired through licensing arrangements. Perhaps one of the main problems associated with such dependency is that Canadian subsidiaries sometimes pay much less than a proportionate share of the costs of the technology they use; and the latter is (in any case) often not divisible in any meaningful sense.

In endeavouring to assess the quantity of resources which should be allocated to research and development in Canada, one cannot apply an aggregative standard. General incentives to expand research and development activities which at least match those of other countries can probably be defended; although they may beg the ultimate question about the rationale of inducements for reallocation on the time scale, they can find some support in the empirical measures of the return on past research endeavours.

But surely for a country such as Canada the hope for a distinctive and effective contribution is affected much more by circumstances which govern the opportunity for large enough and efficient enough production of particular products. A distinctive Canadian character can be given to products, but corporate research and engineering departments required to build in such distinctive characteristics can do so only if there is an opportunity to market substantial quantities of the products in question, in competition with well-established foreign products developed under similar expectations. The chief limitations upon any Canadian manufacturer attempting to achieve this objective have already been described. Foreign tariffs prevent Canadian producers from breaking into world markets; and Canadian tariffs, by making possible the division of the Canadian market, hamper the efforts of Canadian firms to exploit the various economies of scale, including those elements of research and development which require large fixed outlays. It is not difficult to understand why firms producing small quantities of a wide range of product lines will rely upon designs provided at low cost by parent firms, or through licensing arrangements. It is the circumstances that maintain such structural conditions that must bear the responsibility for the consequent restraint on development of distinctive techniques and products.

There is ample evidence that those firms which are not prevented by institutional factors (oligopoly relations and protective tariffs) from achieving the economies of scale required for this sector have been able to keep up with the latest techniques and in many cases have made a distinctive contribution to these techniques. In some industries, for example steel, petroleum and some chemicals, the Canadian domestic market is ample to support large-scale production operations and some research and development activity, directed primarily to adapting known techniques to Canadian production opportunities, and developing products based on particular Canadian resources and needs. In other cases, for example in most electronic office equipment and farm machinery, trade barriers do not prevent leading firms from achieving a rational international division of labour in their operations.

In still other instances, for example in the electronics sector, special research and production opportunities have been associated with defence and space programmes, and have relied in most instances on export activity. It is not surprising that in a country such as Canada, as for Sweden and the Netherlands, the factor most likely to make economically feasible greater R&D activities is the prospect of large specialized exports of the end-products of technical progress. This would appear to be true whether or not the bulk of the research is done in Canada.

Reasons for Encouragement to Canadian Research and Development

Even though commercial policy changes may be of most strategic import-ance, there are some arguments for direct incentives to Canadian R&D activities. The Minister of Industry has cited three of these:

. . . it must be appreciated that there are . . . certain inherent disadvantages in relying too heavily upon imported technology. . . . Any industry which is dependent upon licensed or imitated designs will always lag behind the state-of-the-art by at least one generation and is at an obvious disadvantage in the export market, quite apart from the problem of competing directly with the licensor. Nor is it clear that the needs of our domestic market are always best served by this practice, at least to the extent that the Canadian environment differs from other countries . . . perhaps the most unfortunate consequence of all is the lack of opportunity afforded to our best graduates in science and engineering to practice their skills in Canada and thus contribute to the progress of their native land.[3]

What I have already said casts some doubt on these arguments. The final statement is not borne out by the experience of those industries (already cited) which have had the chance to use existing techniques in efficient ways to capture positions in world or domestic markets. While it is true that licence arrangements usually do preclude export by the licensee to the domestic market of the licensor (and perhaps to certain of his export markets), the same restraints will not normally apply to parent-subsidiary relationships. In cases where American subsidiaries have not exported to the United States, it would be wrong to assume that this is always the result of a formal policy, or even where it is, that this policy could not change if commercial policy changes created the opportunity and the necessity of closer integration of Canadian with American operations and more special-

---

[3]*Ibid.*, pp. 6-7.

ized production and export. Under such circumstances, there is no apparent reason why the Canadian producer needs to (or should be able to) lag behind the American, unless the Canadian production facilities can be profitably used in the production of "old-fashioned" products, as is sometimes the case. The reason why there may be such a lag in present circumstances is that while the Canadian market for a new product is growing, it does not pay to commence production as early here as it would in the United States, where a large market is available immediately a product is proven effective and economical. This obstacle is removed as soon as access to foreign markets is assured.

Thus the main reasons for encouraging research and development activity in Canada would appear to be to reduce dependence on technical licensing agreements (but not parent-subsidiary relationships), and to subsidize Canadian scientists and engineers. However, the latter raises questions which go beyond economic criteria, and direct promotion of R&D may not be required for either purpose, except perhaps as transition measures, if commercial policy changes can be used to enlarge the market available to subsidiary and Canadian-owned plants.

Specific Proposals for Promoting Research and Development

Among the specific policy proposals for directly stimulating invention and innovation are:

        (a) patents

        (b) tax incentives or subsidies

        (c) cooperative research

The patent is the oldest of the devices used to promote technical progress. Since it gives the user a monopoly, the patent must be defended on the grounds that the new technique or product would not have come into being and into use without the monopoly and the related social cost in the form of higher prices and restricted output during this period.

A distinction must be made in this connection between individual and corporate research. It is doubtful whether the patent system is essential to the research programme of the corporation. Large companies in partially competitive (oligopolistic) industries have money to spend on it and typically these companies vie with one another for product improvement, using what might otherwise be short-term profits for this purpose. The research competition is primarily a requirement for maintenance of position among established firms especially since the results of research are often pooled.

There is good reason to expect that the product or process improvements would take place anyhow since the emulative motives are independent of patent privileges, and the firms have the financial reserves to maintain research establishments.

The varied structure of industry probably means that the patent system encourages the assignment of relatively more resources to investment in those industries which are less competitive in structure, since these have the financial means themselves to take advantage of the opportunity involved or to buy up the new ideas of individuals or prospective competitors. In those industries in which individual producers do not have finances for research because of relative small scale, highly competitive operations, e.g., primary industries such as agriculture and fishing, the patent has not provided a sufficient incentive and government sponsored research organizations have been established. Thus the patent system in the modern institutional setting would appear to be unnecessary for some and insufficient for others. Is there a sufficiently large third group for whom it provides just the right sort of incentive?

One of the curious anachronisms of the patent system is the duration of the monopoly granted. Although technical progress is such that the life of many new processes or products is seldom more than a few years, patent monopolies have characteristically extended over much longer periods, for example seventeen years.

In relative terms the Canadian patent system seems to have very little effect in promoting Canadian research, since about 95 per cent of all patents taken out in Canada are held by foreigners.[4] One of the few reasons for the preservation of the patent system under such circumstances would appear to be the need to match incentives to research in other countries under conditions of international competition. However, other forms of incentive might still be preferred as more efficient.

The *tax incentive or subsidy approach* has recently become more popular. For the past several years, firms have been able to deduct from taxable income 150 per cent of any increase in their research and development expenditures (both capital and operating) over the 1961 base year. The scheme was welcomed, although there were suggestions that the base year should be an average of several years, and some firms which have long been involved in research felt that the incentive discriminated against them. In a survey conducted by the National Industrial Conference Board,[5] companies were asked if the tax incentives had encouraged them to establish or enlarge their R&D facilities. While firms typically indicated increases of between 10 per cent and 30 per cent, many firms indicated that their increases were due to plans already made, and more than half of the firms interviewed indicated that they had not as yet increased R&D spending as a result of the incentive. For the largest companies the incentive appears to have been incidental. For the smallest companies in the group, the incentive did not cause them to establish such facilities for the first time. A middle group of companies with modest R&D programmes seems to have been most

[4]T. N. Brewis, *et al., Canadian Economic Policy* (Toronto: Macmillan, 1961), pp. 88-93.
[5]National Industrial Conference Board, *op. cit.,* pp. 5-13.

influenced by the incentive, though even here it has been a marginal consideration. Equally or more important has been the supply of scientific personnel and the ability of firms to plan ahead, counting on the continuance of the incentives over sufficient time that returns on such investment can reasonably be anticipated.[6]

Finally, it should be noted that all incentive schemes of this sort can be relatively easily matched by other governments, and it is therefore important that any country which uses them should be confident it can benefit as much or more than other countries from the shift of resources into this particular form of investment.

The promotion of *cooperative research agencies* would seem to be a means of improving the efficiency and reducing the risk of research in industries in which the firms are small relative to the size of research projects required. Cooperative research is widely used in the United Kingdom and other European countries. In the United Kingdom there are 53 of these agencies, which spent £9 million in 1963.

Among the advantages of cooperative research cited by John Convey in his study of British experience[7] is the availability of R&D benefits to all firms, large and small; better planning of programmes and use of manpower; development of "scientific awareness" in the companies.

In assessing the qualities of the British associations Mr. Convey stresses such things as the quality of the research direction, the support of the particular industry for the agency serving it, the size of the Association and the planning of its programme. These are indications of administrative efficiency and perhaps broadly of the appropriateness of specific programmes. They do not relate to the productivity of the agencies, and indeed the familiar comparative figures for growth of G.N.P. per capita, which Mr. Convey lists, show that Britain has had a much poorer growth record than other countries, few of which also use cooperative research as much as the United Kingdom. Clearly other considerations are of paramount importance.

Pooled efforts by industry are only likely to have desirable economic

---

[6]In 1965 the Canadian government announced its intention to replace the tax incentive with "grants of defined amounts to be taken in cash or applied as credits against the tax liability of the business concerned." All with R & D expenditure above $50,000 a year would have to get "prior agreement from the Minister of Industry that the research and development proposed, if successful, would be likely to benefit Canada." The Economic Council's Advisory Committee on Industrial Research and Technology issued a Report supporting the earlier tax incentive scheme, primarily on the grounds of scepticism concerning the ability of the government to assess in advance the benefit to be derived from a prospective research grant. The government, for its part, seemed to be striving for greater equity and efficiency in its support of research and development. See *A General Incentive Programme to Encourage Research and Development in Canadian Industry*, Report to the Economic Council of Canada by the Advisory Committee on Industrial Research and Technology (Ottawa: Queen's Printer, December, 1965).

[7]John Convey, *A Study of Cooperative Research in the United Kingdom and Its Application to Canadian Conditions*, Department of Mines & Technical Surveys (Ottawa: October, 1963).

consequences if there are strong incentives for cooperation and for the application of the benefits of cooperation. To some extent there are conflicting motives in cooperative research. All firms are assured of access to the same technological advances, but none can expect to benefit relative to his rivals in applying the results. This would tend to breed conservatism, particularly where the market being exploited is shared only among the firms supporting the cooperative association. To the extent that such firms still compete among themselves, it is likely to be because the larger firms, which are better able to support research activities on their own, are tempted to break away from an arrangement which is of greater benefit to the smaller firms. It seems probable that cooperative research will be most likely to work effectively if the industry in question is thereby equipping itself for more effective exploitation of international markets, and thus has a common interest in both invention and innovation.

Conclusions

In the National Industrial Conference Board study on *Scientific Research in Canadian Industry* (cited earlier), the 176 firms were asked: "Have you lost domestic or foreign markets to competitors for technological reasons?" The Board summarized its results as follows: "Firms that report losses of domestic or foreign markets to competitors for technological reasons are a minority." Among the reasons cited for competitive problems in the international market, two seem most relevant to the foregoing argument. A former producer of switch gear apparatus stated: "A careful assessment of the domestic market for these products indicated to us that it could not support the development work entailed with the present large number of competing firms." A chemical manufacturer stated: "We are at a disadvantage when a foreign competitor can ship a product to Canada at a low tariff, while we face an unsurmountable tariff wall against us in shipping from Canada." These statements are borne out by my discussions on these questions with Canadian manufacturers, and support the main lines of the argument in this paper.

The main barrier to efficiency in manufacturing in Canada is the inability to rationalize production so as to take full advantage of the economies of scale in production and to spread the cost of development of distinctive Canadian products. Foreign tariffs provide a barrier to the expansion of exports and Canadian tariffs perpetuate the subdivision of the market and diversification of individual plants and firms. Methods for promoting Canadian manufacturers through government incentives or cooperative industry efforts are unlikely to be effective unless they are combined with changes in commercial policy. A scheme for allowing 150 per cent of the increase in a firm's R&D expenditures may give it a subsidy equal to a fraction of one per cent of its sales, but compared to the handicap imposed on Canadian productive efficiency through the structure of industry supported by the Canadian tariff (and the barrier to exports imposed by many foreign tariffs) these incentives are of modest significance.

However, in circumstances in which obsolete Canadian and foreign tariffs (restricting the rationalization and development of manufacturing in Canada) are being dismantled, various schemes for fiscal incentives and industry cooperation might well come into their own as means of aiding the transition to a stronger international competitive position.

37 Patents*

Canadian Manufacturers' Association

Industrial property is probably the least understood form of property known to the law. A patent grant does not confer upon an inventor a monopoly in the exercise of his invention. It merely confers upon him the right to exclude others, for a specified period of time, from using the fruit of his mind. All unpleasant connotations of the word "monopoly" are singularly inappropriate in the case of the protection of the property of inventors and authors. The origin of this type of property is production. It is based on the theory that every man is entitled to the fruits of his mind.

The word "monopoly" has become the victim of its history. The highly political expressions of some members of the parliaments of Elizabeth I, of the Stuarts, and of the Interregnum, if read by the uninformed mind and without the use of the critical faculty, would easily lead to the view that all monopolies granted during those periods were improper and resulted in grievances. It has long been the fashion, even in some text books on the law of patents, to refer to "the grievous weight of monopolies in the hands of courtiers and favourites of the Sovereign." A careful examination will show that, save for abuses associated with the manner of enforcement of some few illegal monopolies, the monopoly policy of the Tudor and Stuart sovereigns was directed toward the stimulation of trade and the self-sufficiency of the realm. This is perhaps best exemplified by a short quotation from S. R. Gardiner, recognized as the authoritative historian of the period. He states that these grants were "by no means the mere make-shift contrivances for extracting money from the purses of the subjects which it has now for two centuries and a half been the fashion to represent

---

*From: "Submission to the Royal Commission on Patents, Copyrights, Trade Marks, and Industrial Designs", (mimeographed), Toronto, (October 15, 1954), pp. 1-3 (reprinted by permission).

them" (1867) (41 Archaeologia at 226). In his "History of England", Vol. 4, page 6, Gardiner states that: "A careful examination of these grants will convince us that they were not open to the charges which are habitually brought against them."

The patent of invention ought not to be confused with the type of monopoly grant that the common law always regarded as improper. From the time of the first true patent of invention granted by Henry VI in 1449, the grant of an exclusive right to an inventor has always been recognized as being beneficial to the public.

The effectiveness of the patent policy of the Tudor and Stuart sovereigns was demonstrated by the attraction it offered to considerable numbers of skilled craftsmen who migrated to England bringing their new skills and improvements with them. As a direct outcome of the patent system in the reign of Elizabeth, the realm, for the first time in history, became self-sufficient in ordnance and armament and independent of Spain from which country it had theretofore purchased these commodities. Indeed, it may be confidently asserted that save for the patent of invention the Industrial Revolution of the late eighteenth century would not have taken its rise in England.

It should be remembered that the patent of invention was preserved as valid when the Statute of Monopolies of 1623 declared the illegality and abolition of monopolies generally. The law embodied in this exception has been accepted as the foundation of the patent statutes of all civilized countries of the democratic world.

It is believed by some that patents are objectionable because they confer exclusive privileges and are hence tinged with the reprehensible nature of the word "monopoly". To such people any right exclusively enjoyed should be abolished as being contrary to public interest. They fail, however, to perceive that ownership connotes exclusivity and that ownership of any property, real or personal, is purely monopolistic in character. Opposition to the system of patent grant in return for the donation to the public of a meritorious invention disregards entirely the practical benefit flowing to the public from a continued emphasis upon research and development by inventors and by corporations employing them. Patents are the spur that the law adds to the genius of invention.

It should never be forgotten that the grant of a patent is not a one-sided transaction but is based firmly upon the doctrine of valuable consideration. The protection of the state to the inventor in the exclusive enjoyment of his own property for a term of rather short duration must be based upon the consideration given by the inventor. This consideration is the disclosure to the public of the details of his invention in the fullest possible manner, so that, at the end of the patent term, the public will be able to exercise the invention in as full and beneficial a manner as the inventor himself. Without the reciprocal consideration of the patent grant an inventor would be a fool to make such a disclosure but would rather, in his own interest, maintain his invention in secrecy, which might accord to him an exclusivity many times longer than that accorded by patent, with consequent detriment to public interest. Such a practice the law would be powerless to prevent and would be the inevitable result of attempting to confine the patent grant within anything less than its already very restricted extent.

38   Federal Assistance to Manufacturing *

Dominion Bureau of Statistics

The federal Department of Industry was established in July 1963 to promote the growth, efficiency and improvement of manufacturing industries in Canada. The Department assists Canadian industries to adapt to technological changes and variations in domestic and export markets; it aids potentially sound industries to overcome problems of growth and development and promotes industrial research and design activity.

Program for the Advancement of Industrial Technology

In 1965 the Department of Industry initiated a Program for the Advancement of Industrial Technology (PAIT) to stimulate industrial growth by the application of science and technology to the development of new or improved products and processes. The basic aim of the Program is to help industry up-grade its technology and expand its innovation activity by underwriting specific development projects that involve a significant advance in technology and which, if successful, offer good prospects for commercial exploitation. PAIT is essentially a form of "development insurance" with the Government sharing the financial risk of the development with the sponsoring company.

PAIT assistance is available to individual Canadian companies or groups of Canadian companies for developmental projects to be carried out and exploited in Canada. Companies are expected to have the capabilities and facilities to undertake the development work and also to provide for the manufacture and sale of the resulting products in both domestic and export markets. This Program is designed to increase the technical competitiveness of Canadian industry and is also intended to help create an industrial environment attractive to Canada's best-qualified scientific, technical and managerial personnel.

Since the inception of the PAIT program, 109 Government-assisted

---

*From: *Canada Year Book, 1968*, Ottawa, Queen's Printer, (1968) pp. 718-22 (reprinted by permission).

development projects, representing a total effort of approximately $35,000,000, have been undertaken by Canadian firms.

Industrial Research and Development Incentives Act

The Department of Industry is responsible for administering the program of the Industrial Research and Development Incentives Act (IRDIA), enacted in March 1967. The Act provides for cash grants in place of the former tax allowance for research and development. Grants or equivalent tax credits are available for 25 p.c. of capital expenditures for scientific research and development in Canada, and for the increase in current expenditures in Canada for scientific research and development over the average of such expenditures in the preceding five years.

To qualify for a grant, expenditures must be for scientific research and development which, if successful, is likely to lead to or facilitate an extension of the business of the corporation. Accordingly, corporations must usually undertake to exploit the results of the research and development in Canada. Also, corporations must normally be free to export products resulting from the research and development to all countries in the world.

Automotive Program

The Canada-United States Agreement on Automotive Products, signed by Prime Minister Pearson and President Johnson on Jan. 16, 1965, provides for the removal of tariffs and other impediments to trade between the two countries in motor vehicles and original equipment parts. The basic objective of the plan is to provide access to expanded markets for Canadian motor vehicle and component producers. By increased production and specialization, they will be in a position to expand trade and employment and to improve the productivity and efficiency of the industry. In order to enable Canadian vehicle and parts producers to achieve these objectives, a number of important features were incorporated into the program. The most important of these was the undertaking of Canadian motor vehicle manufacturers to expand very considerably Canadian production by the end of the 1968 calendar year.

As a result of the new program, Canada is producing an increasingly larger share of the total North American output of vehicles and components. Canadian exports of vehicles and parts and employment in this industry have increased substantially since the implementation of the program and new investment in additional plants and expansions to existing facilities has been extensive.

Machinery Program

A Machinery Program was introduced by the Department of Industry in 1967 with two main objectives—to encourage efficiency by permitting Canadian industry to acquire capital equipment at the lowest possible cost, and to facilitate the development of more specialized lines of production by the

Canadian machinery industry. Under this Program, a new tariff item (42700-1) will replace 18 existing items. Rates on these items have ranged up to 22½ p.c., depending on whether a machine was of a "class or kind" made in Canada. This class or kind distinction will disappear, replaced by a common rate of 2½ p.c. British Preference, 15 p.c. Most-Favoured-Nation. At the same time, the new tariff rate will apply to any products under the item which Canadian machinery manufacturers can produce as soon as they are able to do so. (Former tariff provisions excluded Canadian-made machines from protective rates until such machines accounted for 10 p.c. of domestic consumption in their class.) This provision will especially encourage the production of custom-designed machinery in Canada.

The Program will provide for remission of duty where this is in the public interest and the machinery imported is not available from production in Canada. A Machinery and Equipment Advisory Board will advise the Minister of Industry concerning eligibility of machinery for remission of duty in accordance with the Program criteria, with final authority for granting remission lying with the Governor in Council. A Review Board will be established to deal with appeals on the Board's findings. Machinery producers may also apply for remission of duty on production parts included in Tariff Item 42700-1 which they must import. This provision should stimulate Canadian machinery manufacturers to specialize their production and enable them to compete more effectively.

Building Equipment, Accessories and Materials Program (BEAM)

In 1967, the Department of Industry introduced the BEAM Program to assist in achieving greater productivity and efficiency in the manufacture and use of building equipment, accessories and materials. The Program has five main objectives: to establish a comprehensive construction information system; to promote the adoption of modular dimensional co-ordination of building components; to encourage the industrialization of the building process; to promote the adoption of uniform building regulations and standards; and to establish a Design Awards Program. To assist the Department in defining the objectives and in developing and implementing the Program, three Industry Advisory Committees have been established on Modular Co-ordination, Construction Information Systems and Industrialized Building Techniques and Systems. These committees meet on a regular basis and include architects, engineers and representatives of trade unions and the manufacturing and building industries.

A study has been undertaken to determine the precise needs and priorities for construction information in Canada, to identify the ways in which a comprehensive and flexible information system could be developed and to enable government and industry to assess the feasibility of establishing such a system. The Industry Advisory Committee on Construction Information Systems is also considering the development of system designs and methods of coding and indexing information.

With the assistance of the Industry Advisory Committee on Modular Co-ordination, the Department has developed a program to encourage the increased use of dimensional standardization of building components. A series of six conferences was held at major Canadian centres during October and November of 1967 to acquaint policy-makers within the industry with the technological and economic advantages of modular dimensioning. Clinics were planned to instruct architects, engineers, draftsmen and building supervisors on modular principles in building. A Directory of Canadian Modular Building Materials is being prepared for publication by the Department.

To obtain a first-hand knowledge of industrialized building techniques, the Department sponsored three industrial missions to European countries to study building systems based on prefabricated concrete, masonry and steel components. A national conference, "A Systems Approach to Construction", is planned, to inform all sectors of the industry on the development of industrialized building techniques; it will be followed by a series of seminars and lectures with leading authorities participating. Because industrialized building would be greatly facilitated by the adoption of uniform building regulations, the development of performance standards, and the establishment of a means of assessing new building materials, systems and techniques, an in-depth study is being organized to point the way toward such developments.

The BEAM Design Awards Program being established will recognize design excellence of building equipment, accessories and materials which incorporate modular co-ordination, prefabrication, pre-assembly and standard component design. Submissions will be accepted in five categories—structural systems, exterior cladding, interior finishing systems and mechanical and electrical equipment.

Industrial Design

The National Design Council and the Department of Industry sponsored many activities in 1967 and provided an advisory service to assist designers to meet the challenges offered by Expo 67 and centennial year projects. Under the Canada-Design '67 Program, initiated in 1965 to encourage the manufacture of well-designed products for use in connection with centennial projects, catalogues of well-designed products were distributed to architects, contractors, buyers, retailers and business men in Canada and abroad and, to further promote these products, displays were shown across the country. More than 380 new product designs were accepted and promoted to prospective manufacturers and over 70 products were adopted and produced for centennial year.

Through the National Design Council and the Department of Industry, a very successful international congress and seminar on industrial design was held at Ottawa and Montreal in September 1967, attracting over 625 representatives from 32 countries.

Two Design-Canada awards projects, which are intended to recognize design achievements of Canadian manufacturers by offering awards and promotional benefits, were completed in 1967. The Structural Steel Awards Program attracted 62 entries—four designs of buildings or bridges received Awards of Excellence and seven entries were given Design of Merit recognition. The Concrete Awards Program, from 152 entries, recognized three designs for Awards of Excellence and 14 as Designs of Merit. In 1967, a Design-Canada Centre was completed at Place Bonaventure in Montreal which, with the Toronto Centre, serves as a focal point for the promotion and display of products and design.

The Design-Canada service includes a reference service of books, periodicals and technical papers on design subjects; a record of professional designers and design services; a speakers' service; an audio-visual service with films, slides and other material for distribution, lending or sale; and a product index, which is an illustrated record of all products accepted for design promotion by committees appointed by the National Design Council. An advisory service is available on request to designers, manufacturers, business men, educators and the general public; an advisory service is also available to government agencies responsible for office installations on the premise that good design can improve the operational efficiency of the working environment with considerable cost reductions.

Design-Canada scholarships and grants encourage advanced training and research in the field of industrial design and support the promotion of industrial design in Canada.

Area Development Program

The area development program fosters economic development in designated areas characterized by high chronic unemployment, slow employment growth and serious problems of under-employment as measured by low non-farm family income. Development grants of up to one third of the capital cost of new machinery and equipment and new buildings are available to assist new and expanding manufacturing and processing industries in the designated areas. In addition, special accelerated depreciation allowances are available for tax purposes on new machinery, equipment and new buildings, or on significant extensions of old ones.

The program embraces large regions of the country, in all provinces, with 92 Canada Manpower Centre areas and contiguous counties and census divisions being designated. The program covers areas comprising approximately 17 p.c. of the labour force. By the end of 1967, more than 1,200 firms had indicated intention to establish new or expanded facilities in designated areas and to invest more than $1,800,000,000. It is estimated that over 50,000 new jobs will be provided directly by these new or expanded facilities and that a similar number of additional jobs associated with supply and service industries will be provided.

Defence Product-Development Assistance

This program provides funds for Department activity to sustain techno-logical capability in Canadian industry by sharing the cost of selected defence development projects, the amount authorized for the year ended Mar. 31, 1968, being $25,000,000. In some cases, project costs are shared with the United States and other allied governments. Typical of projects sup-ported under the program to meet present or anticipated requirements of allied governments are: Helicopter Logistic Devices at Okanagan Helicop-ters (Vancouver); Air Transportable Maintenance Shop at ATCO (Calgary); Black Brant Family of Rockets at Bristol Aerospace (Winnipeg); Tilt Wing Aircraft at Canadair (Montreal); High Frequency Sounding Equipment at EMI Cossor (Halifax); Xenon Light Sources at Atlantic Films (St. John's, Nfld.); the Twin Otter Aircraft Turbinization Project at de Havilland (Toronto); the OT-4 Stationary Gas Turbine Engine at Orenda (Toronto); and Parachute Developments at Irvin Airchute (Fort Erie).

Adjustment Assistance (for Firms in the Automotive Parts Industries)

The Automotive Program offers increased opportunities to Canadian auto-motive parts manufacturers for expanded production, rationalization of output and reduced costs. In order to take advantage of these opportunities, Canadian parts makers must engage in substantial re-equipment and plant expansion programs. The Adjustment Assistance Program has been estab-lished to make term loans available to automotive parts manufacturers for the financing of the acquisition, construction, installation and moderniza-tion of facilities or machinery and for use as working capital.

A program of tariff remissions on imported machinery and equipment was also introduced in order to further assist the automotive parts producers to expand and modernize productive facilities. The tariff remissions cover machinery and equipment used in the production of original equipment automotive parts, accessories and tooling when such machinery and equip-ment are not available from Canadian manufacturers in time to meet production schedules.

Adjustment Assistance (General)

In late 1967, the Government put forward a program of adjustment assist-ance related to the Kennedy Round. Objectives of the program are, first, to enable Canadian industries to benefit as much as possible from the widening markets and the increased scope for specialization and longer production runs and, secondly, to assist firms adversely affected by Kennedy Round agreements to adapt to more competitive conditions. Some firms will be forced to reorganize and re-equip to meet new challenges and others may wish to extend their opportunities. Under this program, the Government proposes to offer insurance on the major share of risk of loss for industrial adjustment assistance loans made by private lenders. Where obvious injury can be proved, direct loans may be made available. Technical assistance may also be offered to manufacturers preparing adjustment proposals in order to improve production, managerial skills, marketing and financial operations.

To be eligible for insured loans, firms must establish injury resulting from Kennedy Round tariff reductions or show that their export opportunities are significantly decreased. A plan for re-structuring operations on a more competitive basis must be presented. An Adjustment Assistance Board will examine the feasibility of such plans. Finally, firms must demonstrate that suitable financing is not available from other sources on reasonable terms. Where a firm has incurred serious threat or injury due to the tariff changes, and where suitable private financing is not available, the Government may offer direct loans on the condition that a firm co-operate fully with the Board in seeking a workable solution to its difficulties. When necessary, firms may be assisted to find competent technical and professional advice from the private sector. The Government may contribute a maximum of 50 p.c. of the cost of such consulting services.

Shipbuilding Construction Assistance

During 1967, the Federal Government continued its program of encouraging a self-sustaining and efficient shipbuilding industry. The program included examination of financial measures in support of shipbuilding and the application of general assistance plans administered by the Department of Industry. Legislation introduced in 1967 included transfer of responsibility for shipbuilding matters from the Canadian Maritime Commission to the Department of Industry.

The industry continued to respond to the policy of national competition for government shipbuilding requirements. Similarly, the industry made active use of the subsidy program for commercial vessels which provides a subsidy rate of 25 p.c. for vessels other than fishing trawlers for the period 1966-69, after which time it will be reduced by 2 p.c. each year until a rate of 17 p.c. is reached in 1972. The subsidy rate of 50 p.c. for fishing tfawlers was reduced to 35 p.c.

With the support of other programs such as the Defence Development Sharing Program, the Department has encouraged the development of production of marine components and exports in this area have been increased.

Technical Missions

Technical missions concerning magnesium manufacturing, structural steel, and powder metallurgy technology were recently organized to visit industrial establishments in the United States and Europe. The purpose of these missions is to enable Canadian business men to examine and assess the latest technological developments taking place outside Canada in their particular industries. The information gained is prepared in report form and circulated to Canadian industry.

SUGGESTIONS FOR FURTHER READING

Allen, W. R., *International Trade Theory*: *Hume to Ohlin*, New York, Random House Inc., 1965.

Corden, W. M., *Recent Developments in the Theory of International Trade*, Princeton, N. J., Princeton University Press, 1965.

Dales, J. H., "Some Historical and Theoretical Comment on Canada's National Policies," *Queen's Quarterly*, Vol. 71 (Autumn, 1964).

Dales, J. H., *The Protective Tariff in Canada's Development*, Toronto, University of Toronto Press, 1966.

Danhof, C. H., *Government Contracting and Technological Change*, Washington, D. C., Brookings Institution, 1968.

Dominion Bureau of Statistics, "Manufacturing and the Changing Industrial Structure of the Canadian Economy, 1946-1965," special article in *Canada Year Book* (1967), pp. 665-678, Ottawa, Queen's Printer, 1967.

Eastman, H. C., "The Canadian Tariff and the Efficiency of the Canadian Economy," *American Economic Review*, Vol. 54 (May, 1964).

Eastman, H. C. and Stykolt, S., *The Tariff and Competition in Canada*, Toronto, Macmillan Co. of Canada Ltd., 1967.

Economic Council of Canada, "Science, Technology and the Economy," chapter 3 of *The Challenge of Growth and Change*, the Fifth Annual Review, Ottawa, Queen's Printer (1968), pp. 29-61.

Fullerton, D. H. and H. A. Hampson, *Canadian Secondary Manufacturing Industry*, a study prepared for the Royal Commission on Canada's Economic Prospects, Ottawa, Queen's Printer, 1957.

Hamilton, W. H. (with Thurman Arnold and I. M. MacKeigan), *Patent Monopolies, A Matter of Concern to Consumers*, Regina Leader Post and Saskatoon Star-Phoenix, 1955 (Reprinted in Skeoch, *Restrictrive Trade Practices in Canada.*)

Johnson, H. G., *The Canadian Quandary* (Toronto, McGraw-Hill Co. of Canada Ltd., 1963), especially chapters 8 and 9 on "External Economic Policy."

McIlroy, J. R., "The Case for Tariffs," *Dun's Review and Modern Industry*, July, 1962.

National Industrial Conference Board, *Problems and Policies in Canadian Manufacturing, A Symposium*, Montreal, 1964.

Royal Commission on Patents, Copyright and Industrial Designs, *Report on Patents of Invention*, Ottawa, Queen's Printer, 1960.

Slater, D. W., *World Trade and Economic Growth*: *Trends and Prospects with Application to Canada*, Toronto, University of Toronto Press (for the Private Planning Association of Canada), 1968.

Wilson, A. H., *Science, Technology and Innovation*, Economic Council of Canada, Special Study, Ottawa, Queen's Printer, 1969.

Young, J. H., *Canadian Commercial Policy*, a study prepared for the Royal Commission on Canada's Economic Prospects, Ottawa, Queen's Printer, 1958.

PART SEVEN

Policies Affecting the
Resource-Based Industries

INTRODUCTION

The preceding part examined a number of policies by which governments in Canada have sought to increase the amount of the country's productive resources allocated to the manufacturing industries. All these measures to some extent entail substituting human judgment in the form of administered controls for the impersonal competitive controls of the "ideal" market-economy. A person unfamiliar with the country might imagine that this promotion of manufacturing was part of a deliberate plan to focus our national energies on building up this kind of industry relative to agriculture and other resource-based industries—that is, to promote the "industrialization" of the country. Certainly the tariff policy and other measures to favor Canadian manufacturers have been seen by farmers, lumbermen, miners, and other resource-exporting groups to be harmful to their particular interests.

Yet there appears to be no such plan. As will be seen from the selections in this part, the primary industries too have been protected and subsidized by Canadian governments. In seeking the reasons for this one may not want to go any further than to note that farmers and other land-based producers also have votes, and some of them are well organized for the purpose of exerting political pressure. Are there reasons to believe that competitive market controls would not work well as regulators of these industries? Must government intervene to protect primary producers from exploitation by uncompetitive oligopolistic suppliers of credit, machinery, and other inputs

254

required by farmers and other resource-based businessmen? These are some of the questions with which the readings in this part are concerned.

It will be noted that many of the problems of the resource-based industries arise from the fact that they are inherently highly competitive in the economist's sense of the term. Many producers contribute to the total output of these industries, with the result that individually they find it difficult to influence the market price of their output. Such producers feel they are at the mercy of erratic market forces over which they have little control. They are unlikely to find much solace in the economist's assurance that this is exactly how things should be in a free-market economy, especially when they see that the bankers who lend them money, and the manufacturers who sell them machinery and consumer goods, are not only conspicuously able to exert an influence on the prices of *their* products, but are enabled to keep their prices high by virtue of tariff protection from foreign competitors.

Consequently we find, as noted in *Reading 39* that the declared purposes of agricultural policy in Canada are to establish a "stable agricultural industry" in the interests of the national economy, and to provide farmers with a "fair share of the national income". The spectrum of policies applied to these ends is surveyed in this same selection. Note the implication that agriculture, like manufacturing, is an essential national industry and that it would not be adequately sustained if exposed to unregulated market forces. Yet Canadian agriculture operates under conditions quite different from those surrounding our manufacturing industry. Most Canadian agriculture is relatively efficient and would seem to possess certain natural advantages that should enable it to compete effectively in world markets. Unlike manufacturing it can hardly be thought of as a struggling infant industry trying to break into world markets. As its spokesmen would be quick to point out, however, these world markets are not freely competitive, being dominated as they are by state purchasing agencies and by foreign selling agencies acting on behalf of farmers who are much more heavily and conspicuously subsidized than their Canadian counterparts.

Must we, in the light of this, tax ourselves for the doubtful privilege of maintaining an agricultural industry of a given size? To Adam Smith and his followers who sought to refute such "mercantilistic" positions, the answer was, emphatically, No. It is perhaps a measure of the political relevance of classical market theory today that most Canadians would accept the mercantilist's point of view and answer Yes, going on to cite national independence, strategic considerations, and the maintenance of employment as justifications for manipulating our agricultural as well as our manufacturing activities.

The same arguments, presumably, must apply to our other natural resource-based industries as well. Of these the mining and forest industries are the most important in terms of value of output and, perhaps, in terms of the subjective importance attached to them as sources of employment and national strength. The fisheries and fur trapping industries are of mainly regional importance as sources of employment and income, and because of this, aid to them is more likely to be regarded as a matter of regional than national importance. (It may be that the maintenance of regional income and employment levels is itself a matter of national policy in Canada, but such regional measures will be considered separately in the next part.)

An important difference separating agriculture from the mineral and forest industries is that the latter are based on resources that in Canada are usually publicly rather than privately owned. Because of this, private firms exploiting mineral and forest resources are being entrusted with the utilization of a national resource in a legal as well as an economic sense. This gives governments the ability not only to regulate these industries effectively but to directly influence the prices of their output by charging more or less for the right to exploit the publicly owned resources involved. *Readings 41* through *45* outline some of the main policies toward the mineral and some other resource industries and analyze, often critically, the economic effects of these policies. In the last selection Professor Anthony Scott analyzes the difficult question of how the public authorities could go about determining how they should act to bring about the preferred utilization of our natural resources.

39   Farm Assistance Programs*

Dominion Bureau of Statistics

Basic to the concept of Canada's national agricultural policy is the premise that a stable agriculture is in the interests of the national economy and that farmers as a group are entitled to a fair share of the national income. In pursuit of these objectives, the Department of Agriculture has carried on, over a long period, a program designed to aid agriculture through the application of scientific research and the encouragement of improved methods of production and marketing. Over the years, as conditions have warranted, programs have been initiated to deal with special situations such as the Prairie Farm Rehabilitation Act to deal with the results of the drought in the 1930s; the Prairie Farm Assistance Act to mitigate the effects of crop failure; Feed Grain Assistance Regulations to assist in the movement

---

*From: *Canada Year Book 1968,* Ottawa, Queen's Printer (1968) , pp. 418-87, (reprinted by permission) .

of western feed grains to Eastern Canada and British Columbia; and the Maritime Marshland Rehabilitation Act to save valuable soil in the Maritime Provinces.

Although much has been accomplished and is still being accomplished by these measures, changes in the past two decades have dictated a new approach to some problems. Large-scale mechanization was the sequel to the reduction of manpower available to farmers; the number of farms declined but the size of farms increased; marketing and income problems took different forms. Legislation enacted to meet these situations include price support (Agricultural Stabilization Act), production and markets stabilization (Canadian Dairy Commission Act), crop insurance (Crop Insurance Act), resource development (Agricultural and Rural Development Act), feed grain assistance (Livestock Feed Assistance Act) and credit facilities (Farm Improvement Loans Act, Prairie Grain Advance Payments Act, Farm Credit Act and Farm Machinery Syndicates Credit Act). These measures, with the exception of the Agricultural and Rural Development Act, are described individually below.

Agricultural Stabilization Act

The Agricultural Stabilization Act (SC 1958, c. 22, proclaimed Mar. 3, 1958) established the Agricultural Stabilization Board and repealed the Agricultural Prices Support Act, 1944. The Board is empowered to stabilize the prices of agricultural products in order to assist the agricultural industry in realizing fair returns for labour and investment, and to maintain a fair relationship between prices received by farmers and the costs of goods and services that they buy.

The Act provides that, for each production year, the Board must support, at not less than 80 p.c. of the previous ten-year average market or base price, the prices of nine commodities (cattle, hogs and sheep; butter, cheese and eggs; and wheat, oats and barley produced outside the prairie areas as defined in the Canadian Wheat Board Act). Other commodities may be supported at such percentage of the base price as may be approved by the Governor in Council. Since the Act came into force, the following farm products, other than the nine named commodities, have been supported at one time or another: honey, potatoes, soybeans, sunflower seeds, sugar beets, tobacco, turkeys, apples, peaches, sour cherries, apricots, raspberries, asparagus, tomatoes, milk for manufacturing and skim milk powder. The Board may stabilize the price of any product by an offer-to-purchase, by a deficiency payment, or by making such payment for the benefit of producers as may be authorized.

In stabilizing prices of certain commodities by means of deficiency payments, the price stabilization program has been assisting the agricultural industry to make production adjustments from a position of excessive supply to one of more normal relationship between supply and demand. The institution of limited deficiency payments by the Board assists in the adjustment of production in a relatively short time. During the period of adjustment, the Board guarantees a minimum average return to producers for a limited quantity of product.

The cost of stabilization programs under the Act averages $58,500,000 a year. The Board has available a revolving fund of $250,000,000. Losses incurred are made up by Parliamentary appropriations and any surplus is paid back to the Consolidated Revenue Fund. An Advisory Committee named by the Minister of Agriculture and composed of farmers or representatives of farm organizations assists the Board in its operations.

Canadian Dairy Commission Act

The Canadian Dairy Commission was established by the Canadian Dairy Commission Act, 1966, and became operative on Apr. 1, 1967. The affairs of the Commission are directed by three Commissioners, and its objects are "to provide efficient producers of milk and cream with the opportunity of obtaining a fair return for their labour and investment and to provide consumers of dairy products with a continuous and adequate supply of dairy products of high quality".

To perform its functions, the Commission is authorized to stabilize prices of major dairy products through offers to purchase at fixed prices, thus establishing stable prices in the interests of both producers and consumers. The Commission may borrow from the Minister of Finance the funds required for such purchases to a maximum of $100,000,000, which must be repaid.

The Commission administers the payment of funds provided to it by the Government for subsidies to producers of milk and cream used in the production of dairy products. These payments supplement returns to producers from the market and permit market prices to be kept at reasonable levels. The total quantity of milk and cream on which subsidy is paid is restricted to the volume required to serve the Canadian domestic market. Each producer is given a quota for the amount for which he is eligible for subsidy. The Commission, indirectly, pools returns to producers from products sold on the domestic and export markets through an export equalization fund. Money for this is deducted from the subsidy and payments are made to equalize export prices with domestic prices for any surplus products that must be exported.

The Commission also has authority, under regulation by the Governor in Council, to exercise control of the interprovincial and export movement of dairy products, and to perform other functions related to its responsibilities.

Crop Insurance Act

To assist in making the benefits of insurance protection on crops available in all provinces, the Crop Insurance Act was passed in 1959. This Act does not set up any specific insurance scheme but rather permits the Federal

Government to assist the provinces to do so by making direct contributions toward the cost of providing crop insurance. The initiative for establishing schemes to meet their own regional requirements rests with the provinces. Schemes may be organized on the basis of specific crops or areas within the provinces and agreements between the provinces and the Federal Government set out the terms of insurance coverage.

Under the Act and amendments of 1964 and 1966, the Federal Government will pay 50 p.c. of the administrative costs incurred by a province and 25 p.c. of the amount of premiums required to make the scheme actuarially sound. In addition, the Federal Government may make loans to any province equal to 75 p.c. of the amount by which indemnities required to be paid under policies of insurance exceed the aggregate of the premium receipts for that year, the reserve for the payment of indemnities, and $200,000. As an alternative to such loans, the Federal Government may re-insure a major portion of the provincial risk in a program operated under the Crop Insurance Act. Farmers insured under the Act are not eligible for payments under the Prairie Farm Assistance Act, nor are they required to pay the 1 p.c. levy on grain sales as provided for under that Act.

In 1967, 33,042 farmers purchased $90,419,146 worth of insurance coverage for their crops, compared with 24,500 farmers and $52,000,000 worth of coverage in 1966. The increase was largely a result of the 1966 amendments to the Crop Insurance Act which broadened its scope by: (a) raising the limit of coverage from 60 p.c. of the average crop yield to 80 p.c.; (b) increasing the Government's contribution to the individual farmer's premium from 20 p.c. to 25 p.c.; (c) extending coverage to fruit trees or perennial plants, and to summerfallow that had been prepared but could not be seeded because of agricultural hazards; and (d) calculation of the average yield from the records of an individual farm where feasible, instead of from the area records.

Farm Improvement Loans Act

The Farm Improvement Loans Act (RSC 1952, c. 110), administered by the Department of Finance, is designed to provide credit by way of loans made by the chartered banks to assist in almost every conceivable purchase or project for the improvement or development of a farm and includes the purchase of agricultural implements, the purchase of livestock, the purchase and installation of agricultural equipment or a farm electrical system, the erection or construction of fencing or works for drainage on a farm, and the construction, repair or alteration of farm buildings including the family dwelling. Credit is provided on security related to the purchase or project and on terms suited to the individual borrower.

The legislation, originally operative for three years (1945-48), has been continuous by way of extensions usually for three-year periods. The latest extension was for the period July 1, 1965 to June 30, 1968. The maximum term of a loan and the interest rate remain at ten years and 5 p.c. simple interest, respectively. The borrower is required to provide from 10 p.c. to 33⅓ p.c. of the cost of his purchase or project, depending on the loan category to which it belongs. The Federal Government guarantees each bank against loss sustained by it up to an amount equal to 10 p.c. of loans granted by it in a lending period.This guarantee does not apply to any loan made after the aggregate of all loans made by all banks in a given period reaches an amount fixed by statute. The current maximum stands at $700,000,000. By Dec. 31, 1966, 3,147 claims amounting to $2,342,613 had been paid under the guarantee since the inception of the Act, representing a net loss ratio of less than one-tenth of one per cent after recoveries have been taken into account. The maximum loan or amount which may be outstanding to a borrower at any one time stands at $15,000.

Prairie Grain Advance Payments Act

This Act, which came into force on Nov. 25, 1957, provides for interest-free advance payments to producers for threshed grain (wheat, oats and barley) in storage other than in an elevator under a unit quota. Advance payments of 50 cents per bu. of wheat, 20 cents per bu. of oats and 35 cents per bu. of barley are made, subject to certain restrictions as to quota and acreage. Maximum advance payment per application is $3,000. Repayment is effected by deducting 50 p.c. of the initial payment for all grain delivered subsequent to the loan, other than for grain delivered under a unit quota. The amounts deducted are paid to the Board until the producer has discharged his advance.

Farm Credit Act

The Farm Credit Act (SC 1959, c. 43, proclaimed on Oct. 5, 1959) established the Farm Credit Corporation as successor to the Canadian Farm Loan Board established in 1929. The Corporation, which is a Crown agency, reports to Parliament through the Minister of Agriculture.

The Act provides two types of long-term mortgage loans for farmers. Under Part II of the Act the Corporation may lend up to 75 p.c. of the appraised value of the farm land and buildings taken as security, or $40,000, whichever is the lesser. Under Part III the Corporation may lend 75 p.c. of the appraised value of the farm land and buildings and of the livestock and equipment taken as security, or $55,000, whichever is the lesser. To qualify for a loan under Part III a farmer must be under 45 years of age and have had at least five years of farming experience. Part III loans are further secured by mandatory insurance on the life of the borrower, and his farming operations are subject to supervision by the Corporation until the loan is reduced to 75 p.c. of the appraised value of the farm land and buildings. Similar life insurance and supervision are available on an optional basis to borrowers under Part II.

The interest rate on the first $20,000 borrowed under Part II or the first $27,500 under Part III is set by statute at 5 p.c. On that part of the loan which exceeds these amounts the interest rate is set by the Corporation with the approval of the Governor in Council. This rate can vary according to the interest rate on money borrowed by the Corporation, the operating costs of the Corporation and the allowance made for reserves against capital losses. The interest rate on the amount of loan under Part II exceeding $20,000 and the amount under Part III exceeding $27,500 is, at present, 6¾ p.c. All loans are repayable on an amortized basis within a period not exceeding 30 years.

The Corporation has 127 field offices administered by 224 credit advisers who are responsible for informing local farmers about the services available, for pre-loan counselling on credit use, farm planning and farm management, for accepting applications and for making farm appraisals.

In addition to the amounts repaid by borrowers, funds for lending to farmers may be borrowed by the Corporation from the Minister of Finance. The aggregate amount of such borrowings outstanding at any time may not exceed 25 times the capital of the Corporation. This capital was raised by amendment to the Act in 1966 from $24,000,000 to $40,000,000. There were 58,258 loans to the amount of $770,554,169 outstanding as of Mar. 31, 1967.

Farm Machinery Syndicates Credit Act

The Farm Machinery Syndicates Credit Act (SC 1964-65, c. 29, proclaimed Dec. 11, 1964) provides the Farm Credit Corporation with authority to make loans to qualified groups of farmers (referred to as syndicates) to purchase farm machinery to be used co-operatively and primarily on the syndicate members' farms. Under this Act, the Corporation may lend a syndicate up to 80 p.c. of the cost of the machinery to be purchased but loans outstanding to any syndicate may not exceed $15,000 per member or $100,000. Funds for this purpose are advanced to the Corporation by the Minister of Finance.

To qualify for a loan a syndicate must have three or more members, all of whom are farming and the majority of whom have farming as their principal occupation. Loans are repayable over a term not exceeding seven years. Security is provided by a promissory note signed by each syndicate member and such other security as may be required.

The interest rate, set by the Corporation with the approval of the Governor in Council, is based on the cost of funds to the Corporation, the expenses in servicing loans and an allowance for a reasonable reserve against losses; at present it is 6½ p.c. There is an initial service charge of 1 p.c. on the amount of each loan. The Corporation's field staff provide assistance to groups of farmers in making their local arrangements with respect to sharing in the use of the machinery and repayment of the loan. Up to Mar. 31, 1967, the Corporation had approved 262 loans totalling $1,988,025.

Prairie Farm Assistance Act

The Prairie Farm Assistance Act, passed in 1939, provides for direct money payments by the Federal Government on an acreage-and-yield basis to farmers in areas of low crop yield in the Prairie Provinces and in the Peace River area of British Columbia. Its purpose is to assist in dealing with a relief problem which the provinces and municipalities cannot do alone and to enable the farmers to put in a crop the following year. Payments for the 1966-67 crop year, as at July 31, 1967, totalled $3,116,437; payments made under the Act since 1939 amounted to $361,054,822.

Payments are made from the Prairie Farm Emergency Fund to which farmers contribute 1 p.c. of the value of all sales of wheat, oats, barley, rye, flaxseed and rapeseed. The additional funds required are provided from the federal treasury. The total collected through the 1 p.c. levy in the 1966-67 crop year, as at July 31, 1967, was $11,674,082; the amount collected since 1939 was $185,902,984.

Farmers operating land in the spring wheat area, and not covered by a federal-provincial crop insurance scheme, are eligible for awards. Crop failure and natural causes preventing seeding and summerfallowing are taken into account in making awards. These may not exceed $800 in respect of any one farmer's total cultivated acreage.

Feed Grain Assistance

The activities of the Feed Grain Administration of the Department of Forestry and Rural Development include the administration of a program respecting freight and storage assistance on Western Canada feed grains used for feeding livestock in Eastern Canada and British Columbia. Under the Feed Grain Assistance Regulations of the Appropriations Act, the original policy was initiated in October 1941 to enable eastern Canadian feeders of livestock and poultry to obtain western-grown feed grains at reduced cost so that livestock and poultry production could be maintained at a high level. This program was amended over the years with the introduction of a storage assistance program, freight assistance to truck movements of grains and feeds and a zone system of payment. Orders in Council passed in 1966-67 amended zone rates to more equitably equalize transport costs to all zones.

On Nov. 17, 1966, Royal Assent was given to the Livestock Feed Assistance Act authorizing the establishment of a Crown corporation known as the Canadian Livestock Feed Board, the function of which is to carry out the administration of the freight and storage assistance programs, to administer the broader objects of the Act of ensuring an availability of feed grain stocks and storage to meet the needs of livestock feeders, and to ensure reasonable stability and a fair equalization in feed grain prices in Eastern Canada and British Columbia.

During the year ended Mar. 31, 1967, $20,263,373 was spent on the freight assistance program, aiding in the transport of 2,607,510 tons of feed grains and grain products into Eastern Canada and British Columbia, and $570,714 was spent on the payment of storage charges on western feed grains in store in elevators and vessels in Eastern Canada.

40 Controls Affecting the Marketing of Farm Products*

Dominion Bureau of Statistics

Subsection 1. — Control of the Grain Trade

The agencies exercising control of the grain trade in Canada include the Board of Grain Commissioners for Canada which, since 1912, has administered the provisions of the Canada Grain Act, and the Canadian Wheat Board which operates under the Canadian Wheat Board Act, 1935.

The Board of Grain Commissioners for Canada

The Board of Grain Commissioners was established in 1912 under the authority of the Canada Grain Act, 1912 (RSC 1952, cc. 25 and 308 and amendments). It is a quasi-judicial and administrative body of three—a chief commissioner and two commissioners—reporting to the Minister of Agriculture.

The Canada Grain Act has been called the Magna Charta of the Canadian grain trade or, more particularly, of the Canadian farmer, and the Board's chief duties are to ensure that the rights conferred on the different parties by the provisions of the Act are properly protected. Transportation of grain is restricted except from or to licensed elevators, and restriction is placed on the use of established grade names. The Act does not provide for any control or supervision of grain exchanges and the Board of Grain Commissioners has no power or duties in the matter of grain prices.

The Board manages and operates, under semi-public terminal licences, the Canadian Government elevators situated at Moose Jaw and Saskatoon, Sask., Lethbridge, Edmonton and Calgary, Alta., and Prince Rupert, B.C. The Executive Offices of the Board and other principal offices are situated at Winnipeg, Man., but branch offices are maintained at numerous points from Montreal in the east to Victoria in the west. Total personnel is approximately 1,100, including Canadian Government Elevators staff.

On a fee basis, the Board provides official inspection, grading and weighing of grain, and registration of warehouse receipts. All operators of elevators in Western Canada and of elevators in Eastern Canada that handle western-grown grain for export, as well as all parties operating as grain commission merchants, track buyers of grain, or as grain dealers, are required to be licensed by the Board annually and to file security by bond or otherwise as a guarantee for the performance of all obligations imposed upon them by the Canada Grain Act or by the regulations of the Board.

---

*From: *Canada Year Book 1968*, Ottawa, Queen's Printer (1968), pp. 918-23, (reprinted by permission).

To protect the rights of the different parties, the Board has jurisdiction to inquire into and is empowered to give direction regarding any matter relating to the grading or weighing of grain; deductions made from grain for dockage; shortages on delivery of grain into or out of elevators; unfair or discriminatory operation of any elevator; refusal or neglect of any person to comply with any provision of the Canada Grain Act; and any other matter arising out of the performance of the duties of the Board.

In the Prairie Provinces the Board maintains four assistant commissioners—one in Alberta, two in Saskatchewan and one in Manitoba. These assistant commissioners investigate complaints of producers and inspect periodically the country elevators in their respective provinces; all elevators with their equipment and stocks of grain are subject at any time to inspection by officials of the Board.

The Board sets up, annually, Committees on Grain Standards and also appoints Grain Appeal Tribunals to give final decisions in cases where appeals are made against the grading of grain by the Board's inspection officials. To assist in maintaining the uniform quality of the top grades of Red Spring wheat handled through terminal elevators, the Canada Grain Act provides that wheat of these grades shall be stored with grain of like grade only.

The Grain Research Laboratory, located at Winnipeg, is the main centre of research on the chemistry of Canadian grains. It is well staffed and equipped to provide the service required to help maintain and expand domestic and foreign markets for all types of grain. The Laboratory collects and tests samples of various crops to obtain information on the current quality of all grains shipped during the crop year. Fundamental research is also undertaken; the program is directed toward better understanding of what constitutes quality in cereal grains and toward improvement in the methods of assessing quality.

In addition to its duties under the Canada Grain Act, certain other duties are performed by the Board. Under the provisions of the Inland Water Freight Rates Act (RSC 1952, c. 153), the Board maintains records of rates for the carriage of grain from Fort William or Port Arthur, Ont., by lake or river navigation and is empowered to prescribe maximum rates for such carriage. Under the provisions of the Prairie Farm Assistance Act (RSC 1952, c. 213 as amended), the Board collects from licensees under the Canada Grain Act 1 p.c. of the purchase price of wheat, oats, barley, rye, flax and rapeseed purchased by such licensees.

The Canadian Wheat Board

The Canadian Wheat Board was established under the Canadian Wheat Board Act of 1935 for the purpose of "the marketing in an orderly manner, in interprovincial and export trade, of grain grown in Canada" and now operates under RSC 1952, c. 44 as amended. The Board accomplishes its objective through regulation and agreement. It owns no grain handling facilities but, by entering into agreements with the owners of these facilities, it attempts to bring about an orderly flow of grain through each of the steps involved in merchandising the grain from the producer to the domestic or overseas buyer.

In the selling of wheat, the Board utilizes the services of shippers and exporters. In its sales operations, the Board endeavours to meet the wishes of overseas buyers and, on occasion, enters into direct contracts. When an exporter completes an export sale, in his capacity as an agent of the Board, he is responsible for the transaction; he completes the transaction with the buyer and settles with the Board for the purchase of the wheat from the Board.

When the commercial storage facilities are inadequate to handle all the grain produced, it is necessary for the Board to regulate the flow of grain from the producer to these forward positions. The first step is accomplished by the use of producer's delivery permits issued annually by The Canadian Wheat Board. Every delivery of grain made to country elevators by a producer is entered in his permit book. By regulating the amount of grain delivered by the producer to the country elevator by the use of a quota system and, by apportioning shipping orders to country elevators according to the needs created by sales commitments, the Wheat Board regulates the amount of grain coming into the marketing channel.

The next step is the handling of the grain by the country elevator. The maximum charges for the handling and storing of the grain are set by the Board of Grain Commissioners, but the actual charges are subject to negotiation between the elevator companies and the Wheat Board.

The third step in the marketing process—transporting the grain from the country elevators to large terminal elevators in Eastern Canada, Churchill or on the West Coast—is carried out by the railways. The Wheat Board determines the kinds and grades of grain that are required at the different terminal destinations to meet its sales commitments and informs the elevator companies and the railways of these needs. The maximum tariffs are set by an agreement between the railways and the Government of Canada.

The fourth major step—storing and handling of the grain at terminal elevators—is done in privately or co-operatively owned elevators. Maximum charges are established for this service by the Board of Grain Commissioners.

In the case of oats and barley, the Board's operations are less extensive than those relating to wheat. These two grains are sold in store positions at the terminal elevators at Fort William-Port Arthur and Vancouver. Oats and barley are marketed either on a straight cash basis at prices quoted daily by the Board or on the basis of exchange of futures concluded through the facilities of the Winnipeg Grain Exchange. The Board controls the movement of coarse grains to the Lakehead. The private trade is responsible for the movement of oats and barley from Lakehead or Vancouver positions.

The producer receives payment for his wheat, oats and barley in two or three stages. An initial payment price is established early in the crop year by Order in Council. The initial payment price less the cost of handling grain at the local elevator and the transportation costs to the Lakehead or Vancouver is the initial price received by the producer. This price is a guaranteed floor price in that if the Wheat Board, in selling the grain, does not realize this price and the necessary marketing costs, the deficit is borne by the Federal Treasury. However, with very few exceptions, the Wheat Board has operated without financial aid from the Federal Treasury.

After the end of the crop year, but prior to the final payment being made, if the Wheat Board can confidently foresee a surplus accumulating and if authorized by Order in Council, an interim payment is made to producers. This interim payment is the same amount per bushel to all producers of the same grade of grain. When the Board has sold all the grain or otherwise disposed of it in accordance with the Canadian Wheat Board Act, the Board, if authorized by Order in Council, makes a final payment to producers.

Under the Prairie Grain Advance Payments Act, administered by the Board, producers may receive, through their elevator agents, cash advances on farm-stored grain in accordance with a prescribed formula. The purpose of this legislation is to make cash available to producers pending delivery of their grain under delivery quotas established by the Board. Cash advances are interest-free as far as producers are concerned.

Western Canadian producers receive the price for their grain that the Wheat Board receives, less its operating costs including carrying charge, and the general level of prices received by the Board is determined by competitive conditions in world markets. The only subsidy received by the farmer in the Canadian wheat marketing system is the part-payment of storage costs for wheat made by the Government of Canada. Under provisions of the Temporary Wheat Reserves Act, the Minister of Finance, out of the Consolidated Revenue Fund, pays to the Wheat Board the storage costs on wheat in storage at the end of the crop year in excess of 178,000,000 bu.

Subsection 2. — Controls Over Farm Products Other Than Grain

The Government of Canada and provincial governments have, through legislation and in other ways, given marketing aids such as those related to research, education, information, inspection, grading and many other service measures of this type, designed to assist in making adjustments in marketing within agriculture and between agriculture and the remainder of the economy. Closely related is regulatory action designed to protect the consumer.

Producers have been concerned about another type of market control, namely that which will give either their organizations or a government agency influence over the price received. In a highly specialized commercial agriculture such as Canada now has, the producer is dependent on the price of his product for his livelihood. Canadian farmers have long attempted to obtain some measure of market control through voluntary organizations, mainly marketing co-operatives. All provinces have made provision for the incorporation of such co-operatives and most, if not all, have provided other assistance to them. In the federal field, the Agricultural Products Co-operative Marketing Act encourages marketing under a co-operative plan.

Other legislation provides for legal control over the marketing of agricultural products, either by a producers' board or a government agency. Legislation of this type includes that pertaining to milk control boards, to producer marketing boards and to industry marketing commissions.

* * *

Product Controls

The federal and provincial departments of agriculture cooperate in establishing and enforcing grades of quality standards for various foods. Some control over size and type of containers used for distribution of agricultural products is exercised by the Canada Department of Agriculture and the Department of Trade and Commerce enforces regulations pertaining to weights and measures. . . .

Controls related to health and sanitation in food handling are developed and enforced at all three levels of government—municipal, provincial and federal. Examples of provincial and municipal action include laws pertaining to the pasteurization of milk, inspection of slaughterhouses and sanitary standards in restaurants. At the federal level, inspection by the Health of Animals Branch of the Department of Agriculture of all meat carcasses that enter into interprovincial trade is required. The Food and Drug Directorate of the Department of National Health and Welfare has wide control over the composition of foods sold and over misleading advertising of foods and drugs.

Marketing Controls

The Agricultural Products Co-operative Marketing Act.—In the late 1930s, the Federal Government decided to assist orderly marketing by encouraging the establishment of pools which would give to the producer the maximum sales return for his product, less a maximum margin for handling expenses agreed upon in advance. Thus, the Agricultural Products Co-operative Marketing Act and the Wheat Co-operative Marketing Act were passed in 1939. The latter was used in one year only but the Agricultural Products Co-operative Marketing Act, which covers the marketing of all agricultural products except wheat, has continuously served agricultural producers since 1939.

The purpose of this Act is to aid farmers in pooling the returns from sale of their products by guaranteeing initial payments and thus assisting in the orderly marketing of the product. The Government may undertake to guarantee a certain minimum initial payment to the producer at the time of delivery of the product, including a margin for handling; sales returns are made to the producer on a co-operative plan. The guaranteed initial payment may be up to a maximum of 80 p.c. of the average price paid to producers for the previous three years, the exact percentage to be recommended by the Minister of Agriculture who enters into an agreement with the selling agency for the product. In 1967 the only agreement made was with respect to apples for processing.

Milk Control Legislation.—Most of the provinces enacted milk control legislation before 1940. Many of them finance these milk-control agencies out of public funds, others finance through the collection of licence fees and assessments from those engaged in the fluid milk industry, and some combine the two methods. Most milk-control agencies have authority to carry out some system of licensing which provides for the revocation of such licences if those engaged in the fluid milk business do not conform with the orders of the milk control board.

In all provinces with such boards, the milk control board sets the minimum price which distributors in specified markets may pay producers for Class I milk, that is, milk actually sold for fluid consumption. In Ontario and British Columbia, formulas are taken as a guide in the setting of minimum prices. Most provinces also set either minimum or fixed wholesale and retail prices for fluid milk. The wholesale and retail prices are fixed in Prince Edward Island, Nova Scotia and Saskatchewan; minimum prices are established in New Brunswick, Quebec and Alberta. However, maximum but not minimum prices are set in Manitoba and no control is exercised over milk prices at the wholesale and retail levels in Ontario and British Columbia; in these three provinces some degree of price competition between store and home delivery sales has developed.

The powers given to or requirements made by milk control boards include: (1) authority to inquire into all matters pertaining to the fluid milk industry, to define market areas, to arbitrate disputes, to examine the books and records of those engaged in the industry, to issue and revoke licences, and to establish a price for milk, and (2) authority to require a bond from distributors, periodic reports from distributors, payments to be made to producers by a certain date each month, distributors to give statements to suppliers, distributors to give notice before ceasing to accept milk from any producer, producers to give notice before ceasing to deliver milk to any distributor, and the prohibition of distributors requiring capital investment from producers.

At the national level, a *Canadian Dairy Commission* was established and started operating on Apr. 1, 1967. This is a new departure in the area of agricultural marketing; it is the first time with any farm product that a national agency and privincial agencies have authority to deal with the same industry in their respective areas of jurisdiction. The Canadian Dairy

Commission complements provincial function by regulating the marketing and pricing of milk and milk products that move in interprovincial or international trade. Briefly, the function of the Commission is to provide efficient producers of milk and cream with the opportunity of obtaining a fair return for their labour and investment and to provide consumers with a continuous and adequate supply of dairy products of high quality. The Commission administers the funds provided by the Federal Government for stabilization purposes. . . .

Producer Marketing Boards.—During the 1930s strong support developed for legislation whereby agricultural producers could exercise legal authority under certain conditions to control the marketing of their produce. The Natural Products Marketing Act of 1934 attempted to provide this power at the federal level but proved *ultra vires.* The Natural Products Marketing (British Columbia) Act 1936 was *intra vires* of provincial government powers and provided the model from which marketing board legislation has evolved in all ten provinces.

While marketing board legislation has been revised from time to time on the basis of experience and there are variations in detail from province to province, the same basic powers are given to producers in all provinces. These powers include authority for a duly constituted producer board to control the marketing of 100 p.c. of a specified commodity produced in a designated area. A producers' board, in at least some provinces may set production quotas for each farmer. One producers' board may control the marketing of several related commodities and the designated area may be either the whole or part of a province. A producer vote is usually required to establish a producer marketing board whose powers are delegated either by a provincial marketing board, which has certain supervisory authority, or by the Lieutenant-Governor in Council.

The powers of a producers' board provided by provincial legislation are necessarily limited to intraprovincial trade. Under the Agricultural Products Marketing Act, the Federal Government may delegate to a marketing board with respect to interprovincial and export trade similar powers to those obtained with respect to intraprovincial trade under provincial authority. This Act also gives the Governor in Council the right to authorize a provincial marketing board to impose and collect levies from persons engaged in the production and marketing of commodities controlled by it for the purposes of the board, the creation of reserves and equalization of returns.

In 1966 there were 107 such marketing boards, including the Canadian Wheat Board (previously excluded from the total), organized in Canada, 62 of which were in the Province of Quebec and 20 in Ontario; each of the other provinces with the expection of Newfoundland had one or more boards. It is estimated that about 42 p.c. of the 1966 farm cash income was received from sales made under the control of provincial marketing board plans, including the following commodities: hogs, certain dairy products, poultry, wool, tobacco, wheat, soybeans, sugar beets, potatoes, other vegetables, fruits, seed corn, white beans, honey, maple products and pulpwood. As at Oct. 31, 1966, 41 of these provincial boards had received an extension of powers for purposes of interprovincial and export trade from the Federal Government. Five boards had received authority with regard to seven commodities to collect levies in excess of administrative expenses.

41   The Tax System and the Allocation of Resources*

Royal Commission on Taxation

The Incentives to the Oil and Mining Industries Provided by the Depletion Allowances and the Three-year Exemption for New Mines.

The incentives to the two resource industries can be presumed to have increased investment in these industries relative to what it otherwise would have been. Because both industries are highly specific geographically, there is a presumption that the income tax system shifted factors of production to the regions where the basic resources were located.

The effects of these and similar features of the tax system on the output of the economy depends essentially upon the answers to four questions:

1. Did the tax system change the allocation of resources to the industry relative to a neutral tax system?

2. If so, in what direction and to what extent?

3. Would the market have efficiently allocated resources among industries and regions had the tax system been reasonably neutral?

4. If not, did the tax system compensate for the market imperfection or compound the imperfection?

If the market would have worked well in the absence of the special tax provision for an industry, and if that provision had an effect on the allocation of resources, the tax provision must have brought about a misallocation of resources. If the market would not have worked well, and if the provision had an effect that compounded rather than compensated for the imperfection, the provision must have brought about a misallocation of resources. Only if the tax provision had no effect, or had an effect that compensated

---

*From: *Report*, Ottawa, Queen's Printer, Vol. II (1966), pp. 132-35, (reprinted by permission).

for a market imperfection, can the provision be given a clean bill of health from an efficiency point of view. It may, of course, still be unacceptable from an equity point of view. On the other hand, changes that have undesirable economic effects may still be justified if the improvement in equity was thought to be overriding.

To be more specific, if all product and capital markets worked perfectly, and if there were no other interferences with the allocation of the market, the Canadian tax treatment of oil, mining and service industries would distort the allocation of resources. This would come about because the tax treatment would induce more resources to flow to these industries relative to other industries. The value of the additional output in the favoured industries would be less than the value of the forgone output in other industries.

Unfortunately there is no method of determining in a completely objective, and hence incontrovertible, way how well product and factor markets work or the precise impact of particular features of the tax system on the allocation of resources. Even if we knew the marginal value productivities of each resource, that is, the value of the output produced by the last additional unit of the resource used in each industry (and we do not), these data would be difficult to interpret because of the possible imperfections in the market. For example, if those in command of some industries are able to control output and prices to some extent, the marginal value productivities of resources used in such industries is likely to be high relative to other industries that do not have the same degree of market control. But tax incentives are unlikely to increase the flow of resources into these industries, and thus bring the marginal value productivities of labour and capital in these industries into line with those in other industries. The tax incentives will only raise the profits of the firms in the industry or the return to those who supply the factors of production.

. . . [W]ith respect to the oil and mining industries . . . the available evidence suggests to us that the market may, to a limited extent, discriminate against investment in the resource industries because of the risks involved in some aspects of those activities. Some tax incentives therefore seem justified; but we have concluded that the present incentives are too liberal in relation to the imperfection they are intended to offset and extremely inefficient. They bonus investments that would have taken place in the absence of the tax concessions. We are of the opinion that they induce too much investment in this sector relative to other sectors. Furthermore, the present incentives do nothing to meet the greatest risk of all, loss of the original capital put into a risky venture. We intend to meet this problem, to the extent that a tax system can legitimately do so, through our proposed treatment of losses. We shall therefore recommend that depletion allowances and the three-year exemption for new mines should be removed. However, we will also discuss a number of means of providing more efficient incentives to these industries where this is warranted.

42   The Proper Tax Treatment of Mines and of Oil and Gas Income *

Canadian Manufacturers' Association

The Association takes the position that the existing three-year exemption for new mines and the depletion allowances for income from mining and oil and gas production should be retained. It does not believe that the Commission has proven its case for withdrawal of the three-year exemption for new mines and of depletion allowances on income from mining and oil and gas production. It is noted that its conclusions are based in part on assumptions of doubtful validity, on arguable points of economic theory, and on premises which seem to be at variance with the facts and informed industry opinion. Some vital areas of the problem seem to have been explored inadequately or not at all. Generally, the Association regards the prospective gains from implementation of the Commission's mining and petroleum proposals, viz. equity and neutrality of the tax base and some increase in income tax revenues, as too unsubstantial to offset the risk of inhibiting the growth of these major industries, of decreasing our export potential and of discouraging foreign investment.

The following are the Association's specific observations:

(i)   There is no proof in the Commission's Report that encouragement of these industries has produced or will produce a misallocation of Canada's resources of labour and capital. Indeed there is the very strong presumption that exploitation of natural resources, for which there is an ever growing world market at stable prices, is well suited to the structure of Canada's economy. This view seems to be strengthened by the knowledge that these industries are not labour-intensive and that the bulk of the capital required has come from foreign sources, probably ear-marked for use in this type of endeavour wherever in the world physical, political and taxation conditions are most favourable.

(ii)   There is no reason to suppose, as the Commission does, that foreign investors are indifferent to after-tax rates of return and general tax climate stability, and, at the same time, there is no way of predicting how great will be the withdrawal and diversion from Canada of foreign capital in response to any particular degree of unfavourable change in the tax rules.

---

*From: Submission of the Canadian Manufacturers' Association to the Minister of Finance on the Recommendations of the Royal Commission on Taxation", (mimeographed) , September (1967) , pp. 79-85, (reprinted by permission) .

(iii) The Association cannot accept the Commission's view that Canada should import natural resource products if they are made cheaper than its own by other countries' more favourable tax treatment of their producers. On the contrary, we continue to believe in the principle that Canada's prosperity and favourable balance of payments depend upon encouragement of those activities for which Canada has the greatest relative aptitude. The discovery and efficient exploitation of natural resources deserve much consideration in this regard as demonstrated by the contributions of the mining and petroleum industries to the current prosperity of the country.

(iv) Absolute neutrality of government fiscal policy in allocating resources is nowhere considered desirable, as evidenced by the use of tariffs in most countries to promote their manufacturing industry.

(v) The Commission appears to base the major part of its case with regard to petroleum on the imminent competitiveness of Athabasca tar sands oil, believing that the extraction processes are now perfected and that these can be applied to exploit the whole of those vast reserves. From this viewpoint, the Commission expresses relative indifference to the need for new discoveries of conventional oil. The Association submits these views are not in accord with the facts and expert industry opinion: the economic success of the first large-scale enterprise in this field seems far from assured at this point, even under the present tax law. The industry is continuing to spend as much as ever of its after-tax funds on conventional exploration and substantial new pools of oil are currently being discovered, the exploitation of which is presumably cheaper than Athabasca extraction.

(vi) The Commission has not established a clear position with regard to the future of natural gas as a Canadian energy source and major export item, a matter which is not related to the Athabasca tar sands development. It appears that the existence of plentiful reserves enables the industry to bargain for long-term contracts and attract the necessary capital for the building of plants and pipelines for processing and transport.

(vii) The Association does not believe it is clearly established that the income stream representing liquidation of discovered ore deposits and oil and gas pools should be taxed on the same basis as other income. As a group, these enterprises appear to have not yet recovered capital invested, and this reflects the inherent uncertainty of discoveries, the extraordinarily unpredictable timing of outlays and revenues and the degree of abortive outlay by many of them. We are also made aware of the fact that substantial appropriations of interests in discovered pools are made by the provinces, which could be considered a form of taxation. These factors suggest that the

Commission has not sufficiently considered the special nature of the income of these industries in implementing its basic theories of equity and neutrality.

(viii) The Commission has not adequately considered the implications of retroactivity in its mining and petroleum proposals, at least not to the extent that it has in other segments of its Report. Realization of discoveries made before the date of new legislation, including realization of a reasonable after-tax return on investment by those who have purchased interests therein after discovery, would be unjustifiably penalized by the abrupt and substantial change in the taxation basis. Perhaps the chief source of concern is the general loss of confidence this might engender in the stability of Canada's tax climate.

(ix) There appear to be several forms of special levies imposed on the mining and petroleum industries by the provinces—Quebec's education tax and the provincial mining taxes, royalty payments and appropriations of interests in discovered oil and gas reserves—the significance of which the Commission does not seem to have fully assessed in its thesis of equity and neutrality in taxation. The Commission, for example, estimated that the depletion allowance reduced petroleum industry federal taxes otherwise payable in 1964 by about $19 million. It did not emphasize the fact that the same industry provided some $300 million towards the revenues of the provincial governments in the same year. Moreover, it is not clear how much revenue might be lost to the provinces through implementation of the recommendations, for example in lower prices bid for provincial rights to proven oil and gas properties.

(x) The fact that most of the present allowances are shared by large and successful mining and oil companies would not seem to demonstrate their wastefulness and inefficiency as incentives. Rewards which go to the efficient may well be preferable to a uniform system of subsidy outlays by government, which merely require certain activities to be undertaken and are not conditional upon efficient use thereof or the production of future taxable income. As a basis for maintaining stimulation and competitiveness of whole major industries, a general subsidy procedure might be impossible to administer effectively, producing unwarranted windfalls in some cases and failing, perhaps on a judgment basis, to reach its objective in others.

In addition to its conclusion that the present depletion allowance and the three-year exemption for new mines should be retained, the Association is also of the opinion that the provisions of Section 83A of the Income Tax Act should be revised to permit all corporations to deduct the expenses of drilling and exploring for minerals, petroleum or natural gas from any source of corporate income.

43   Government Aid to the Mineral Industry*

Dominion Bureau of Statistics

Federal Government Aid

Federal assistance to the mining industry takes the form of the provision of detailed geological, topographical, geodetic, geographical and marine data which are of basic importance to the discovery and development of the mineral resources of Canada; the provision, through laboratory and pilot-plant research, of technical information concerning the processing of ores, industrial minerals and fuels on a commercial scale; financial and technical assistance to the gold-mining industry under the Emergency Gold Mining Assistance Act, and certain tax incentives.

The Department of Energy, Mines and Resources

The federal Department of Energy, Mines and Resources came into being on Oct. 1, 1966. It embraces all of the functions of the former Department of Mines and Technical Surveys, and new functions pertaining to water and energy resources. Apart from its administrative establishments, the Department is made up of four Groups—Mines and Geosciences, Mineral Development, Water, and Energy Development—each headed by an assistant deputy minister and each aiding the Canadian mineral industry in some way.

   The Mines and Geosciences Group.—This Group contains four branches —the Mines Branch, the Geological Survey of Canada, the Observatories Branch and the Surveys and Mapping Branch.

   The *Mines Branch* is a large laboratory and pilot-plant complex carrying out applied and basic research to discover new and better methods of ensuring mine safety, extracting and refining ores and other minerals, and using metals and minerals in industry and defence. Gratifying results have been achieved in the extraction of metals from ores and in the refining of low-grade crude oil, in the automation of grinding circuits and cyanide leaching processes in gold mills and in the leaching of ground or crushed uranium ores by bacteria. In pyrometallurgy—the extraction of metals by heat— applied research is concentrated principally on the combination of shaft and electric furnaces for smelting iron ore. In petroleum refining, research concerns hydrogenation, catalytic cracking, and catalyst development. This work is highly significant because of the opening-up of unconventional sources such as the Athabasca tar sands and the so-called Colorado oil shales, whose economic importance has been recognized by the Mines Branch for many years. A close tie-in with producers is maintained in mineral proces-

---

*From: *Canada Year Book 1968*, Ottawa, Queen's Printer (1968), pp. 609-17 (reprinted by permission).

sing in which the emphasis is on the concentration of metallic ores and on the processing and improvement of industrial minerals. In the field of mineral sciences, the physical, chemical, crystallographic and magnetic studies being undertaken on sulphide minerals are of fundamental interest. In physical metallurgy, experiments on new alloy combinations continue to yield valuable practical benefits for Canadian industry.

The Mines Branch, on the advice of experts from industry and the universities, also awards an annual series of research grants in mining sciences to Canadian universities. In 1966, the total amount to be distributed annually was raised from $50,000 to $100,000.

The *Geological Survey of Canada* carries out geological investigations in Canada and compiles and publishes information in the form of reports, maps and other graphic representations. The scope of its activities extends into many aspects of the geological sciences, including geochemistry, geophysics, geomorphology, mineralogy, palæontology, petrology, surficial and bedrock geology, and petroleum geology. The Survey's objectives are to systematically study, describe and explain the geology of Canada in order to find out more about the nation's potential mineral resources, and to provide this information to those engaged in discovering, exploring and developing these resources; to increase fundamental knowledge on the origin of rocks and minerals and to develop new theories, methods and instruments; and to help in the scientific training of young Canadians in these fields. Each year, the Geological Survey sends about 100 parties into many parts of Canada. They conduct broad regional investigations in the Canadian Shield, the Appalachian and the Cordilleran geosynclinal belts, the sedimentary basins of the mainland and the Arctic Archipelago, and unconsolidated sediments. As the first systematic reconnaissance of Canada is approaching completion, the country's major geological features are reasonably well known and attention is now given to more fundamental aspects of Canadian geology. An example is the recently concluded agreement with the Province of Quebec for a jointly financed aeromagnetic survey on both sides of the lower St. Lawrence River. The agreement is part of a 12-year $18,000,000 federal-provincial program of aeromagnetic surveys.

The headquarters of the Geological Survey are at Ottawa but it has several regional offices and a recently opened Institute of Sedimentary and Petroleum Geology in Calgary, which will serve the special needs of the western provinces. The Survey each year awards a large number of grants in support of geological research in Canadian universities, at present totalling $150,000.

A great deal of geophysical work of interest to prospectors is being carried on by several divisions of the *Observatories Branch*. Its airborne geomagnetic surveys, which have ranged all over Canada and across the Atlantic to Scandinavia, have become famous. There is also a network of nine permanent geomagnetic observatories, and temporary observatories are placed at many widely distributed sites each summer. The Branch also operates 23 first-order seismic stations and many temporary stations. Gravity research, yet another means of studying the composition of the earth's crust, is also being intensively pursued by field parties in all parts of Canada, including the Arctic and the bottoms of the Gulf of St. Lawrence and Hudson Bay.

No mineral development is possible without accurate, large-scale topographical maps, and progress in this field by the *Surveys and Mapping Branch* continues to be gratifying.

The Mineral Development Group.—This Group conducts broad economic and mineral-commodity studies and gathers comprehensive domestic and world data on all minerals, including energy minerals, for the use of government and private industry. It also licenses and leases mineral exploration in offshore areas south of the 60th parallel and in Hudson Bay, administers the Emergency Gold Mining Assistance Act and the Explosives Act, and co-ordinates the Department's foreign-aid work.

Current activities in these fields include regional studies of the mineral economy of the Atlantic Provinces, including the Cape Breton coal situation; assessment of mineral projects in various parts of Canada for which federal support has been requested; and the safeguarding of Canadian mineral interests through participation in international agencies such as the United Nations Lead-Zinc Study Group, the United Nations Steel Committee, the Organization for Economic Co-operation and Development, the General Agreement on Tariffs and Trade, and the International Tin Council. In collaboration with the External Aid Office, the Group is setting up training courses for mineral scientists, technologists and economists brought to Canada under the various aid programs, chiefly the Colombo Plan, and is advising on mineral projects undertaken by Canada as an aid to developing countries. The Group publishes an extensive series of reports and other material, and maintains the Mineral Occurence Index, which is a listing of about 10,000 mineral showings and deposits in Canada that may be consulted by anyone interested. Also of considerable value to the mining industry are the federal-provincial roads programs. . . .

The Water Group.—The Water Group advises on federal water policies, undertakes joint programs with provinces for water conservation and development, co-ordinates the work of federal agencies in water-resource management and water pollution, carries out broad hydrometric and hydrographic surveys, and conducts oceanographic and limnological research. Of interest to the mining industry is the study of pollution problems in mining areas, such as current projects in northeastern New Brunswick and on the headwaters of the Saskatchewan River system.

The Energy Development Group.—This Group examines Canada's total energy situation and requirements, and recommends policies and projects concerning Canada's energy resources. Among the administrative agencies that report to the Minister of Energy, Mines and Resources, four are concerned with some aspect of energy development. These are the National Energy Board, the Dominion Coal Board, Atomic Energy of Canada Ltd., and Eldorado Mining and Refining Ltd. The Assistant Deputy Minister for Energy Development serves as adviser on over-all plans and policies relating to energy.

The Dominion Coal Board

The Board was established by the Dominion Coal Board Act (RSC 1952, c.86) which was proclaimed on Oct. 21, 1947. By this Act the Board was constituted a department of government to advise on all matters relating to the production, importation, distribution and use of coal in Canada. The Board is also charged with the responsibility of administering, in accordance with regulations of the Governor in Council, any coal subventions or subsidies voted by Parliament.

The Board is empowered to undertake research and investigations with respect to:—

(1) the systems and methods of mining coal;

(2) the problems and techniques of marketing and distributing coal;

(3) the physical and chemical characteristics of coal produced in Canada with a view to developing new uses therefor;

(4) the position of coal in relation to other forms of fuel or energy available for use in Canada;

(5) the cost of production and distribution of coal and the accounting methods adopted or used by persons dealing in coal;

(6) the co-ordination of the activities of government departments relating to coal; and

(7) such other matters as the Minister may request or as the Board may deem necessary for carrying out any of the provisions or purposes of the Act.

In addition, the Dominion Coal Board Act provides authority in the event of a national fuel emergency to ensure that adequate supplies of fuel are made available to meet Canadian requirements.

The Act authorizes a Board membership of seven, including the chairman. The latter is the Chief Executive Officer, has the status of a deputy minister, spends full time on the Board's business, receives a salary and is in charge of a public service staff. The other members, men of long experience and expert knowledge of aspects and regions of the Canadian coal industry, receive *per diem* payments and travelling expenses while attending Board meetings or while otherwise officially engaged on Board business.

In general, the Board and its staff constitute a central agency through which representations on coal matters are made to the Government from any sector of the industry or the public. Conducting a continuous study of developments and problems within the industry, exchanging information with provincial authorities concerned with coal and with national authorities and agencies in other countries and maintaining the most complete files of Canadian coal information in existence, the Board makes recommendations to the Government and reports to Parliament through the Minister of Energy, Mines and Resources.

Since its inception, the Board has worked toward the co-ordination of the activities relating to coal of various government departments and other agencies. Its own responsibilities in research on the mining and utilization of coal have been carried out mainly by the Fuels Research Centre, Mines Branch, Department of Energy, Mines and Resources, although on occasion, the Board has recommended or commissioned specialized types of research to be conducted outside the government service. As a contribution to the co-ordination of coal research and to the dissemination to the industry of technical information resulting from research, the Board initiated the now annual Dominion-Provincial Conferences on Coal. The Dominion Bureau of Statistics collects much of the statistical information required by the Board.

Government purchases of fuel, which constitute an important outlet for coal, claim a part of the time of the Board's staff in an advisory capacity. Advice on fuel matters is also continuously available to all government departments and agencies. A senior official of the Coal Board is chairman of the Interdepartmental Fuel Committee, which advises on the supply, purchase and utilization of fuel for the Department of National Defence, and of the Dominion Fuel Committee, which is organized along similar lines as an advisory body to other government departments.

The subvention assistance on the movement of Canadian coals, which the Board administers, is authorized by votes of money by Parliament; payments are in accordance with Regulations established by Order in Council. This assistance, which has been provided in varying degrees for the past 30 years, was designed to further the marketing of Canadian coals by equalizing as far as possible the laid-down costs of Canadian coals with imported coals. During the year ended Mar. 31, 1967, a total of 6,420,513 tons of coal was shipped under subvention and $37,698,975 was paid in assistance.

As agent to the Minister of Energy, Mines and Resources, the Board administers loans under the Coal Production Assistance Act (RSC 1952, c. 173, as amended by SC 1958, c. 36; SC 1959, c. 39; SC 1960-61, c. 20; and SC 1962-63, c. 13). The Board also administers payments under the Canadian Coal Equity Act (RSC 1952, c. 34), which provides a subsidy on Canadian coal used in the manufacture of coke for metallurgical purposes. In the year ended Mar. 31, 1967, payments under this Act totalling $82,260 were made on 166,182 tons of coal.

Emergency Gold Mining Assistance Act

Under this Act, which came into force in 1948 (RSC 1952, c. 95), financial assistance is provided to marginal gold mines to counteract the effects of increasing costs of production and a fixed price for gold. By enabling gold mines to extend their productive life, the subventions help communities dependent on gold mining to adjust gradually to diminishing support.

In 1963 an amendment extended the provisions of the Act to Dec. 31, 1967 and also introduced a restriction which affects lode gold mines coming into production after June 30, 1965; such mines are eligible for assistance only if the mine provides direct economic support to an existing community, that is, if the majority of the persons employed at the mine reside in one or more of the established communities that are specified in a schedule to the Act. The restriction does not apply to lode mines in production before July 1, 1965 nor to placer gold mines. A second amendment passed Nov. 28, 1967, extended the application of the Act to Dec. 31, 1970, without changing the method of computing the amount of assistance payable.

The amount of assistance payable to an operator is determined by a formula and is based on the average cost of production per ounce and the number of ounces produced; it ranges from zero to $10.27 per ounce produced. Gold mines having a cost of production of $26.50 or less per ounce receive no assistance and those having a cost of production of $45.00 or more per ounce receive the maximum rate of $10.27 per ounce.

Under the current formula, the assistance payable to the operator of a gold mine is computed by adding 25 p.c. to the product of two factors, "rate of assistance" and the number of "assistance ounces". The number of assistance ounces is two thirds of the total ounces produced and sold to the Royal Canadian Mint by a mine in a calendar year. The rate-of-assistance factor is two thirds of the amount by which the average cost of production exceeds $26.50. The rate-of-assistance factor is limited to a maximum of $12.33 which is reached when the average cost of production rises to $45 per ounce of gold produced. The average cost of production is determined by dividing the total allowable costs by the total number of ounces produced in the form of bullion from the mine in a calendar year. Only those ounces of gold that have been sold to the Royal Canadian Mint are eligible for inclusion in the assistance-ounces factor. The cost of production includes mining, milling, smelting, refining, transportation and administration costs. Allowances are made for depreciation, pre-production costs and expenditures on exploration and development on the mine property in accordance with the Regulations.

The amounts paid to operators of gold mines to Mar. 31, 1967 for the years 1948-66, inclusive, totalled $231,024,273 on a production of 53,380,055 oz.t. of gold produced and sold in accordance with the requirements of the Act. The assistance payable for gold produced and sold under the Act in the calendar year 1966 is estimated to be $15,600,000.

The Act is administered by the Department of Energy, Mines and Resources with the aid of the Office of the Comptroller of the Treasury in accounting matters.

Provincial Government Aid

Newfoundland

The Newfoundland Government, through the Mines Branch of the Department of Mines, Agriculture and Resources, provides several valuable services to those interested or involved in exploration and mining, including: the conduct of a continuing program of mineral assessment designed to encourage development of the mineral resources of the province; the inspection of exploration work carried out on concession areas and the examination of mining operations; the administration of beaches (control of removal of sand and gravel as a conservation measure) and the collection of data relevant to the control of sand removal; the identification of mineral rock specimens submitted by the public and the examination of corresponding occurrences where such is warranted; the dispensing of technical advice, in so far as possible, to those who seek such service (i.e., in hydrological problems and on the availability of quarryable peat moss to be removed by permit); co-operation with the Geological Survey of Canada and other Federal Government agencies; and the preparation and publication of data useful for educational and general informational purposes, including the preparation of mineral and rock sample sets. Geological reports, geophysical maps and compilations of general data pertaining to specific areas are procurable at nominal cost and other information from unclassified files is made available to interested parties. Prospector's or miner's permits are issued by the Mines Branch and mining claims are recorded.

Nova Scotia

Under the provisions of the Mines Act (RSNS 1954, c. 179), the Government of Nova Scotia may assist a mining company or operator in the sinking of shafts, slopes, deeps and winzes and the driving of adits, tunnels, crosscuts, raises and levels. This assistance may take the form of work performed under contract, the payment of bills for materials and labour, or the guarantee of bank loans. Any such work must be approved by the Department of Mines. Mining machinery and equipment to be used in searching for or testing and mining minerals may be made available through the Government. Such equipment is under the direct supervision of the Chief Mining Engineer.

The Government of Nova Scotia is also empowered to make any regulations considered necessary for increasing the output of coal. Such regulations cover the appropriation, on payment, of unworked coal lands, the operation of coal mines, and loans or guarantees for loans. Close co-operation is maintained with the Federal Government in carrying out federal regulations made to secure increased production and economical distribution of coal from the mines of the province.

New Brunswick

The Mines Division of the Department of Natural Resources has three Branches. The *Mineral Resources Branch* administers the disposition of Crown mineral rights including the issuing of prospecting licences, recording of mining claims, issuing of mining licences and leases and other matters pertaining thereto. Detailed and index claim maps are prepared for distribution. The Branch is responsible for general and detailed geological mapping and investigations. Maps and reports are prepared for distribution, mineral and rock specimens are examined for prospectors and preliminary examinations of mineral prospects are made when requested and circumstances warrant. The *Mines Branch* administers the safety regulations governing operations under the Mining Act. All mines are regularly inspected, laboratory facilities are maintained and certain equipment used in mines must be approved. The Branch is responsible also for the collection of mining taxes and royalties and the preparation of statistics on mineral production. The *Water Branch* administers the Water Act, is responsible for the use and allocation of all surface, ground and shore waters and for pollution control measures and implements policy matters as determined by the New Brunswick Water Authority. A Regional Office, staffed by geologists and inspectors, is maintained at Bathurst, serving as a recording office for northeastern New Brunswick. Claim maps and topographical, geological and aeromagnetic maps are available for perusal and distribution.

Quebec

Through its Mineral Resources Branch, the Department of Natural Resources implements the Mining Act (SQ 1965, c. 34). The Branch has four Divisions—Geology, Mining, Laboratories and Pilot Plant.

The *Geological Surveys Division* is concerned with geological exploration, mineral deposits, mapping and hydrogeology. It conducts studies on the geological composition of Quebec territory for the development of mineral resources; following yearly expeditions, detailed reports of the findings and geological maps of different regions are made available for the use of interested persons. A unique system of index plans affords prospectors a precise, quick and valuable technical documentation. The Division also conducts surveys on underground water and supervises drilling and boring by private companies exploring for hydrocarbons.

The *Mining Division* is concerned with civil engineering and mining exploration and inspection. It issues prospecting and development permits, grants mining lands for working purposes, and collects fees for mining rights. It is responsible for the inspection of mines, quarries and processing plants to ensure that operations are consistent with regulations and to ensure the safety of mine workers. A trained rescue crew of about 375 members operates as three main groups and nine secondary groups. In addition, all workers in active underground mines are trained in rescue operations. The Department undertakes the construction and maintenance of mining roads as authorized under the Mining Act; it has constructed and paid the full cost of certain highways leading to new mining districts. In addition, to avoid the establishment of slums in the vicinity of mining enterprises, the Department regulates the use of the land and authorizes the building of well-organized residential areas.

Laboratories, operated for the use of prospectors, geologists, engineers and mine operators, include equipment for mineralogy, petrography, the dressing of ore, wet and dry assays, spectrography or X-ray photography. Mineral determinations are made free of charge but the assaying of ore content is subject to a fee; free coupons are issued by the Department to be used by prospectors for payment of assays. The laboratories have patented 12 new processes for the extraction and treatment of minerals and, because of the development of such new metallurgical processes, certain minerals once deemed valueless are now of great commercial importance.

To provide for the future development of the mining industry, scholarships are granted to students wishing to follow a career in geology, mining and metallurgical engineering, as well as to students in hydrology or other relevant fields of science (hydro-electricity, hydraulics or meteorology). The Department, in co-operation with universities in Quebec and Montreal, gives yearly courses in prospecting and lectures are given by departmental geologists and engineers at various points in the province.

Ontario

The Ontario Department of Mines renders a multiplicity of services of direct assistance to the mining industry within the province. The *Mining Lands Branch* of the Department handles all matters dealing with the recording of mining claims, assessment work, etc., and the preparation of title to mining lands. As a service to the mining public, individual township maps are prepared and kept up to date showing lands open for staking and recorded and patented claims therein. District Mining Recorders maintain offices at strategic locations throughout the province. The *Geological Branch* carries on a continuing program of geological mapping and investigation and prepares, for the use of the public, detailed reports and maps of the areas studied. A program is under way, in co-operation with the Geological Survey of Canada, through which the whole province is to be flown and mapped in a series of airborne magnetometer surveys. In many active areas of the province, resident geologists gather and make available to the public information concerning geological conditions, exploration and development within their respective districts. A geologist specializing in industrial minerals investigates methods of treatment and recovery of such minerals and compiles data on the uses, specifications and markets for such products. During the winter months, courses of instruction for prospectors are held in various centres throughout the province.

The work done by the *Laboratory Branch* includes wet analyses and assays of metal and rock constituents on a custom fee basis, as well as mineralogical analyses and physical testing. The same service is given free of charge to holders of valid assay coupons issued for the performance of assessment work on mining claims. The *Temiskaming Testing Laboratories,* situated at Cobalt, operate a bulk sampling plant mainly to assist the producers of the area in marketing their silver-cobalt ores; they also perform fire assays and chemical analyses. The *Inspection Branch* administers the operating rules of the Mining Act which call for the regular examination of all operating mines, quarries and sand and gravel pits and certain metallurgical works with a view to ensuring proper conditions of health and safety to the men employed. District offices to serve the local areas are maintained in the major mining centres of the province. Mine rescue stations in the principal mining sections are operated under the supervision of the Branch and all hoisting ropes in use at mines are periodically tested by a Branch-operated cable-testing laboratory.

Since 1951 the Department has been engaged in a road-building program to give access to mineralized areas and open them for full development. In 1955 this became an interdepartmental project with other interested departments participating through an interdepartmental committee of Ministers which decides on priorities and locations. Actual construction is carried out by the Department of Highways. Under the federal-provincial Roads to Resources Program inaugurated in Ontario in 1959, the provincial government shared equally in the cost of constructing roads to otherwise inaccessible areas. . . . The agreement expired on Mar. 31, 1967.

The *Public Relations Branch* of the Department carries out a regular publicity and information program and maintains a library of films on mining subjects which are available for free loans to the public. Each year, displays pertaining to mining are prepared and presented at the Canadian National Exhibition and elsewhere in the province.

Manitoba

The Mines Branch of the Manitoba Department of Mines and Natural Resources offers five main services of assistance to the mining industry: maintenance, by the Mining Recorder's offices at Winnipeg and The Pas, of all records essential to the granting and retention of titles to every mineral location in Manitoba; compilation, by the geological staff of the Branch, of historical and current information pertinent to mineral occurrences of interest and expansion of this information by a continuing program of geological mapping; enforcement of mine safety regulations and, by collaboration with industry, introduction of new practices such as those concerned with mine ventilation and the training of mine rescue crews which contribute to the health and welfare of mine workers; and maintenance of a chemical and assay laboratory to assist the prospector and the professional man in the classification of rocks and minerals and the evaluation of mineral occurrences. Manitoba also aids the mining industry by assisting in the construction of access roads to mining districts.

To encourage the exploration for minerals in Manitoba, the Mineral Exploration Assistance Act was passed in April 1966. This Act provides for the payment of grants to individuals to assist in defraying the cost of exploration within designated areas. If assisted exploration results in the discovery of a deposit, the grant is repayable from the profits of the mine; a grant for exploration that proves unsuccessful is not repayable.

Saskatchewan

Assistance to the mining industry in Saskatchewan is administered by the Department of Mineral Resources. The *Mineral Lands Branch* of the Department is responsible for administering the Precambrian Assistance Program. This Program, designed to stimulate development and utilization of the mineralized areas of northern Saskatchewan, offers to industry a 50 p.c. rebate of approved exploration expenditures on a specified area or property to a maximum of $50,000 a year for each individual or company and a maximum of $150,000 on any one area or property. This Branch is also responsible for making disposition of all Crown minerals and maintains records respecting areas let out by lease, permit or claim. Recording offices, located at Regina, La Ronge, Uranium City and Creighton, assist the public in determining the lands available and accept applications.

Officers of the *Engineering Branch,* under the authority of the Mines Regulation Act, make regular examinations of all mines to ensure proper conditions for the health and safety of the men employed. Safety education, particularly in the form of first aid and mine rescue instruction, is also a part of the work of this Branch. All Branch officers are stationed at the Regina headquarters.

The Precambrian Geology Division of the *Geological Sciences Branch* conducts geological surveys in the shield areas of the province and publishes maps and reports for the information and guidance of the industry. Resident geologists are maintained at Uranium City and La Ronge and at the latter centre a laboratory provides for the storage and examination of core and samples. The Division processes exploration data and assessment work to be made available for inspection by the industry.

Alberta

Alberta Government assistance to the mining industry is diversified in character. The Mines Division of the Department of Mines and Minerals regulates coal mines and quarries and maintains standards of safety by inspection and certification of workers. The Workmen's Compensation Board also maintains safety standards and pays the cost of training mine rescue crews. The oil and gas industries are served in a similar way by the Oil and Gas Conservation Board. Its regulatory measures, however, are also concerned with preventing the waste of oil and gas resources and with giving each owner of oil and gas rights the opportunity of obtaining a fair share of production. This Board compiles periodic reports and annual records which are of invaluable assistance in oil development in Alberta. The mining industry is also served by the Research Council of Alberta which has made geological surveys of most of the province and has carried forward projects concerned with the uses and development of minerals. The Council has studied the occurrence, uses and analyses of Alberta coals and their particular chemical and physical properties, the use of coals in the generation of power, and the upgrading and cleaning of coal, and has also studied briquetting, blending, abrasion loss, shatter and crushing strength, asphalt binders and dust-proofing of coal. Studies have been made of glass sands, salt, fertilizers, cement manufacture and brick and tile manufacture. . . .

The province from time to time has had commissions examine various aspects of the mining industry when it has considered that their findings would be of assistance in developing such industries. The province, together with the Canadian Association of Oil Well Drilling Contractors and the Western Canada Petroleum Association, maintains a detailed supervisory and safety training program concerned with the drilling of oil and gas wells. Of assistance also to mining companies and oil companies are the special deductions provided for in the Alberta Income Tax Act. These follow the parallel provisions in the federal Income Tax Act.

British Columbia

The Department of Mines and Petroleum Resources of British Columbia provides the following services: detailed geological mapping as a supplement to the work of the Geological Survey of Canada; free assaying and analytical work for prospectors registered with the Department; assistance to the prospector in the field by departmental engineers and geologists; grub-stakes, limited to a maximum of $700, for prospectors; assistance in the construction of mining roads and trails; and inspection of mines to ensure safe operating conditions.

44 Public Management and Mismanagement of Natural Resources in Canada*

P. H. Pearse

A lack of economic logic in government policies toward natural resource exploitation and management is observable throughout the western world.

*From: P. H. Pearse "Public Management and Mismanagement of Natural Resources in Canada", Queen's Quarterly, Vol. LXXIII, (Spring, 1960), No. 1, pp. 86-99 (reprinted by permission of author and publisher).

Canada is no exception. But misdirected policies are particularly costly in Canada because of our exceptional economic dependence on our natural resources and the pervasive influence of government on their use and development. This paper consists of a brief critique of natural resource policies in Canada.

Canadian governments have followed a policy of retaining public title to natural resources to a greater extent than is common in other advanced western countries. Land for agriculture has, of course, been sold or given away since the earliest times. But during the last hundred years or so governments have been less and less inclined to alienate forests, sub-surface mineral and petroleum resources, water, and fish and game resources. In some cases this policy is the result of technical difficulties in dividing up and selling common-property resources such as marine fisheries and some water resources. But more often public retention of title to natural resources has been a deliberate policy surprisingly consistent in view of the traditions Canada has inherited and pursued with increasing rigour throughout the history of Canadian settlement and economic development. As a result we now find throughout the most recently settled parts of the country, and particularly in the West, title to most natural resources remains firmly in the hands of government.

It is not the purpose of this paper to examine the desirability of a policy of maintaining Crown ownership of natural resources. There are undoubtedly different arguments for non-alienation of different resources, and often the reasons are rather unclear. But it is reasonable to assume that where governments choose to remain the landlord, their objective is to manage the resources in such a way that the nation or province will derive a maximum benefit from these assets. Yet even a very cursory examination reveals that present policies cannot possibly maximize the benefit to be derived from natural resources. They lead, on the contrary, to a startling amount of economic waste, and create problems of rural poverty and retarded technology.

Natural resources policies must be judged in at least two ways. The first is the way in which particular resources are managed by particular government agencies for particular purposes (e.g. the way in which a forest service administers Crown forests for wood production). The second is the way in which conflicts between different demands on the same natural resource base are dealt with (e.g. the way in which conflicts between recreation and industrial exploitation are reconciled).

*　　　*　　　*

An evaluation of policies toward specific kinds of natural resources in Canada is complicated by the existence of as many as eleven separate policies which inevitably differ. Yet within those jurisdictions where a given resource occurs and is exploited, there is a good deal of uniformity in the general characteristics and effects of government policies. Thus, recognizing that exceptions are called for here and there, it is possible to refer briefly to common features of government policy toward certain natural resources in Canada and draw general conclusions about the implications of these policies for the contribution of resources to Canadian welfare.

Agriculture

Agricultural land might justifiably be excluded from the category of "natural" resources. But agriculture places extensive demands on our natural resource base, and policies relating to agriculture have important implications for other uses of resources.

From the earliest days, governments in Canada have encouraged agricultural activity. Special privileges were given to farmers to attract population and push back the frontiers of settlement. Today, the special need for this particular kind of economic activity—farming—no longer exists, in the sense that it has any special virtue over other kinds of production. Yet the policies of encouraging agriculture persist and indeed they have been intensified. Governments still act as if agriculture warrants support at almost any cost, and in their faltering pursuit of this objective, aggravate rather than alleviate agricultural problems.[1]

As a result, we find across Canada large areas of marginal or sub-marginal farming; poor, uneconomic farms occupy much of the rural landscape. Sub-marginal farming is the source of many of our problems of rural poverty which are attracting increasing attention through A.R.D.A. and other programmes; and rural depressed areas, through their direct sociological consequences as well as their associated misuse of rural resources, place a heavy burden on our economy.

It is abundantly clear that we have too many people in Canada trying to eke a living from too many uneconomic farms. This problem is in part a result of the changed technology of agricultural production which has substantially increased the optimum size of the production unit, leaving many small farms relatively uneconomic. But it is due in large measure to our public policies which, instead of facilitating the evolution of our agricultural sector, have aggravated the situation. We have deliberately encouraged and continue to encourage people to become farmers. Farmers get special fiscal concessions (particularly under property and income taxation), special land purchasing rights, special credit facilities, technical and marketing assistance, certain direct subsidies on production, and a host of privileges and priorities which are not available to other users of natural resources. In provincial legislation pertaining to forests, water, game and most other natural resources, special rights and privileges are specifically provided to farmers. In addition, farmers commonly receive concessions under legislation dealing with taxation, trespass, motor vehicles and so on, and agricultural demands usually get preference when conflicts with other resource uses arise.

---

[1]See Lucy I. Morgan, "Price Supports and Farm Surpluses: The Canadian Experience", *The Bank of Nova Scotia Monthly Review* (December 1960).

Through a wide variety of special rights and privileges to agriculture we continue to provide special incentives for people to become, or remain *bona fide* farmers when the problem is one of too many farmers and too many poor farms. Some farmers themselves are beginning to suspect that the long-run effects of present programmes of aid to farming are not in the interest of the agricultural industry,[2] and experts are searching for methods of reforming the policies that have obviously been failing to solve our agricultural problems.[3] The reasons for these policies are complicated, but they obviously have much to do with the political difficulty of discouraging farming in the face of our traditions about the virtues of living on the land and the contribution of our early pioneer settlers.

These comments do not apply, of course, to the efficient farming and ranching activity which produce most of our marketed agricultural output. There are many areas in Canada where agriculture is highly efficient, and can compete successfully for the land and the other resources used. The pernicious effect of agricultural policies is on the large number of small marginal farms across the country, where the largest proportion of our agricultural population is found. By encouraging uneconomic farming we not only prejudice the development of agriculture itself and aggravate the problem of rural poverty, but we place a heavy long-run burden on the economy and hence on the welfare of Canadians generally.

Commercial fisheries

The marine fisheries provide a classic example of an economically "sick" industry. Recently, a number of highly competent studies have shown conclusively that the economic value of most of our commercial marine fisheries is zero or negative, because the cost of harvesting and processing the fish is equal to or greater than the value of the product. These costs are as high as they are because the government steadfastly refuses to control access to the resource by selling or otherwise rationing fishing licences, with the result that there are far too many fishing units for efficient exploitation of the fisheries.[4] The industry is immensely over-capitalized in boats and gear, which, like the large and mostly unnecessary labour force, is employed for only a small fraction of the year.

With uncontrolled entry, new fishermen continue to enter the industry as long as a profit can be earned, which means until total costs rise to the value of output. Having thus allowed the potential value of the fishery to be dissipated through excessive entry into the industry, the government must then face the problem of excessive fishing pressure on the resource base.

2See, for example, *Time* (September 3, 1965), pp. 22-26.

3See W. J. Anderson, "The Basic of Economic Policy for Canadian Agriculture," *Canadian Journal of Agricultural Economics,* Vol. XI, no. 2 (1964), pp. 19-28.

4See, for example, H. Scott Gordon, "The Economic Theory of a Common-Property Resource: The Fishery," *Journal of Political Economy,* Vol. No. 62 (April 1954), pp. 124-42.

Since every individual fisherman has an incentive to harvest as many fish as possible, with no incentive to manage the fishery, the government attempts to prevent depletion of the resource through controls on fishing time, gear, and fishing methods. Thus inefficient fishing is made compulsory through legislation.

In order to maximize the benefit of our marine resources, the object must be to harvest the yield of fish with minimum inputs of labour and capital in the form of boats and gear, allowing these resources to be as fully and efficiently employed as technical circumstances will allow. Policies aimed at accomplishing this have repeatedly been suggested.[5] A system of licence regulation (which, incidentally, is advocated by many fishermen themselves) is an obvious first step toward building a healthy and prosperous industry, and has been widely accepted by most interested parties. Yet the federal government continues to aggravate the depressed state of the industry through subsidies to boat-building and to fishermen at the expense of consumers, taxpayers, and potentially efficient fishermen.

Forests

Forests provide the base for Canada's largest industry, and a large proportion of Canada's forests remain under public ownership. Government policies relating to forest management consistently include two related objectives —to grow forests in such a way as to produce the maximum volume of wood, and to regulate exploitation on management units in such a way as to yield equal annual harvests in perpetuity.

These principles are a carry-over from classical European forest practice and are still advocated in most of our textbooks on forest management. Yet neither principles can possibly maximize the value of our forest resources. Growing timber to an age that will maximize volume is very different from growing it over the period that will maximize the value it generates. And a fixed allowable harvest year after year not only ignores the certainty of changing economies of production and the cost of tying up capital, but it also reduces the gains to be derived by altering rates or production as markets and costs fluctuate. Maximum sustained yield is accepted as the essence of "good foresty," but it involves the pursuit of biological and administrative neatness instead of social and economic efficiency.

The forestry industry has, on the whole, been prosperous in recent years, and private profits and public revenues reflect a considerable net economic benefit from exploitation of this resource. But because of the exceptional importance of this resource to the Canadian economy, policies that impose economic inefficiency in its exploitation are particulary costly, and the economic waste resulting from public forest policies in many parts of Canada is alarming.

5Among others, James Crutchfield, "An Economic Evaluation of Alternative Methods of Fishery Regulation," *Journal of Law and Economics* (October 1961).

Petroleum

Except for a few early alienations (and the questionable stature of off-shore discoveries) most underground oil resources in Canada remain provincial property regardless of the tenure over surface rights. As a result, the extraction of oil and gas, hitherto concentrated in Alberta, has been regulated by provincial agencies. The policies these agencies have adopted up to the present make little economic sense, and have resulted in such high and unnecessary costs that the value of this lucrative resource has been substantially reduced.

An oil pool in its entirety is the obvious management unit: a single plan of co-ordinated drilling and pumping is required to exploit the pool most efficiently. If several operators compete for the oil in a pool, the "common property" problem (as in the case of the fishery), arises with all its associated tendencies for economic waste.

In Alberta, where Canada's oil exploitation has been concentrated (policies differ considerably in other provinces), the provincial government deliberately sets about to fragment the ownership of pools by selling leases, checker-board fashion, over blocks of land with rights to extract the oil beneath. The predictable result is competition between operators on a common pool for the oil underground. Each operator has an incentive to pump oil as fast as he can before his neighbours get it and to extract as much as possible of the oil under his neighbours' leases (by, for example, drilling additional wells along the boundary of his lease).[6]

This competitve drilling has two important economic results. First, by exploiting pools too quickly, and with too many wells, the natural pressures within pools are dissipated and the amount of oil that can be recovered is reduced, and/or the costs of extracting it are increased. Second, the industry becomes vastly over-capitalized, as a result of the incentive to drill an excess of expensive wells.

Having created these tendencies for physical and economic waste, Alberta's Oil and Gas Conservation Board tries to mitigate the situation through the so-called pro-rationing system. Concentrating its attention too much on the technical problem of regulating extraction so as to prevent physical waste, each well is allocated a quota, made up in part by an allowance based on its cost of drilling so that the more costly (i.e. the economically less efficient) wells get a preferred share. This provides an incentive to drill even more wells, since the only way a company can increase its allowed extraction is to own more wells. So, finally, minimum spacing limits are prescribed; but these too are based on technical considerations and are acknow-

---

[6]For a thorough discussion of these effects, see M. A. Adelman, "Efficiency of Resource Use in Crude Petroleum," *The Southern Economic Journal,* Vol. XXXI, (October 1964), p. 103.

ledged to be inadequate in most cases, and always ill-suited to individual circumstances.[7]

The basic problem, and this complex of hopelessly inadequate regulations, arises from the public policy of fragmenting the rights to oil underground and hence creating an incentive for competitive extraction from a common pool. The result is an industry with far too many expensive wells—totally unnecessary wells—frequently badly located and spaced, and all operating at a fraction of their capacity. Since the cost of drilling oil wells is very high, and most costs in extraction are fixed costs, this situation leads to costs in oil extraction several times higher than technically necessary. No firm can use its technical and economic expertise to extract its oil in the most efficient manner. The alternatives to this policy, which would avoid the incentives to extract inefficiently, are to retain public title to oil until it is extracted, to allocate to private companies whole pools or sufficiently large areas of pools so that operators will not interfere with each other's operations, or to require "unitization" (co-ordination) of the operations of the several firms involved before well drilling begins, so that drilling and extraction might proceed in an orderly and efficient way. Examples of each of these alternatives can be found in foreign countries. Yet, instead of seriously considering any of these alternatives, Alberta has seen fit to continue to add more and more detailed regulations on operators, in a vain attempt to legislate efficiency in a situation where it has systematically provided incentives to be inefficient.

Water

Public retention of title to water increases from east to west in Canada, and in British Columbia the ownership of essentially all fresh water is vested in the Crown. Provincial water laws are based on an archaic mixture of riparian rights and arbitary priorities over water use. It is difficult to discover any clear objectives to water policies in Canada—certainly none that systematically attempt to allocate water to its most valuable use.

The inadequacies of water policies have not been obvious in the past because water has been a cheap resource, and sufficiently plentiful that serious conflicts for its use have not arisen. But this is unlikely to be the case much longer.

*   *   *

More could be said about the failure of governments to provide for the efficient use of resources of other kinds—for recreation, mineral exploitation, wildlife, parks, etc.,—but enough has already been said to demonstrate that public policies relating to specific resources tend to be remarkably wasteful.

---

[7]See G. David Querin, "Economic Issues in the Regulation of Oil and Gas," (mimeographed paper presented at the annual meeting of the Canadian Political Science Association, Hamilton, June 8, 1962).

Different kinds of problems are involved at the second level of management —that of resolving conflicts when competition develops between users for the same government-managed resource base.

After allocating land and water resources for particular kinds of exploitation, they are typically classified according to use, and jurisdiction falls to the several government departments—of forests, parks, agriculture, water, and so on. These departments typically see their responsibility as one of managing the resources under their surveillance for the production of the products of some particular specified use—for timber in the case of forest land, for aesthetic qualities in the case of parks, for farm production in the case of agricultural lands, and so on. This is understandable, but it has serious implications where resources can best serve more than one purpose and where changing economic and other conditions change the value of the resources under alternative uses.

Resources will be allocated to their highest use or combination of uses only if there is some clearing-house in which competing demands can be systematically weighed against each other. When a concession to some secondary use of a resource (say, to recreation on timberland) would generate benefits to society that exceed the loss to the primary use, then the concession must be made if the highest total benefit from the resource is to be realized. Yet typically a forest service concentrates its interest on forest production on forest land giving reluctant lip service to the palliative "multiple-use," but usually drawing a hard line at any concessions to recreation, aesthetics, etc., that have the effect of interfering with forest production. Departments of agriculture jealously watch over farmers and farm lands, and resent any intrusion that would increase the benefits of farm and rangelands that accrue to others at the expense of farm production. Recreation authorities concentrate their attention to parks and other areas allocated for recreation purposes, and often see their main role as one of excluding other resource users. All agencies resist changes that might reduce the areas under their jurisdiction. In short, there tends to be little co-ordination between agencies and very rarely any concessions in favour of a secondary interest.

It is obviously impossible to achieve a rational pattern of resource use when resources are administered through such an unsystematic and uncoordinated set of institutions. The best allocation of resources can be determined only by weighing alternative uses against each other in an unbiased way. It is unrealistic to assume that whenever agriculture or some other activity is given priority this will be the most valuable use of the resource to the nation. There is no effective machinery in any province in Canada for dealing in an organized way with conflicting demands on resources. As a result, we can never be certain that resources are put to their best purpose, or purposes, and as pressures on our resource base increase through time this will become an increasingly wasteful and costly situation.

*   *   *

The objective so far has been to make two general points. The first is that public management policies directed toward particular resource uses generally lack a clear objective, tend to be technologically oriented, and are, from an economic point of view, alarmingly expensive and wasteful. Where objectives are discernable, they tend to be in the interests of the resource itself rather than in the interests of the public that owns them (e.g. policies aimed at producing the greatest volume of timber, the most fish, the purest scenery in parks, etc.) .

The second point is that we have so fragmented administrative responsibilities for resource responsibilities in Canada that efficient over-all management is precluded. Management of resources is allocated to particular government departments with specific interests, and which are rarely prepared to concede much to alternative users. Recent administrative innovations such as the Council of Resource Ministers and A.R.D.A. are unlikely to alleviate this problem significantly. It will require a major change within government departments to permit adequate weighing of alternative demands, and to create a disposition among field administrators to consider resource uses outside the interest of the particular department or agency in which they are employed. Despite the increasing need for a broader perspective, present arrangements, by and large, encourage a narrow-minded single-use outlook among administrators.

It is remarkable that public policies should remain so wasteful and inappropriate in the natural resource field; and it is especially disturbing in a nation which depends so heavily on its natural resource base. That these policies should persist in a society as scientifically and politically sophisticated as this is doubly frustrating. Competent authorities have demonstrated repeatedly the waste and inconsistencies in our policies toward fisheries, agriculture, recreation, and so on. Yet the situation does not improve. There seems to be at least two main reasons why this is so: the political difficulty of gradually altering situations which involve established people 'close to the land', and the conflicting guidance of experts.

Now every biologist, forester, geologist and fishery expert is quick to admit that there is a good deal he has yet to learn about the nature of his resource. But it is very difficult to find cases where the obstacle to improvements in management are inadequacies in technical knowledge. It is a characteristic of the resource industries that management policies and practice are so far out of date in relation to our technical competence that the problems associated with present management no longer interest the experts. In the federal fisheries building in Vancouver technical experts on one floor work out more efficient methods and equipment for catching fish, and on another floor legislation is drafted to make more efficient gear illegal. The efficient management and exploitation of oil and game resources especially, and other resources to a lesser extent, is similarly frustrated by the framework of public legislation and regulation within which the managers must work. Economic efficiency begins at the secondary stages of manufacturing, processing and refining the resources, where entrepreneurs are relatively free from public control.

The bottleneck to better management is not inadequate technical knowledge; it is the political will required to put technical knowledge to work. Natural resource policies possess a high degree of political sensitivity. A great deal of irrational emotion about the exploitation of natural resources exists in the public generally. Besides this, substantial and relatively immobile sections of the electorate—fishermen, farmers, small loggers, and sport hunters and fishermen—work within the present policies and change would upset them in one way or another, at least in the short run. Changing resource policies seems to offer the politican much greater opportunities for loss than for gain in terms of public support. No wonder, then, that governments have been reluctant to adopt even widely-advocated changes in policy.

The professionals involved provide the other main reason for the lack of improvement; their training leads them to concentrate their attention on their specific resource itself rather than on its role in the total socio-economic complex. Foresters define "good forestry" as growing and harvesting the maximum volume of wood, which makes no sense unless they admit they are interested only in wood for its own sake. They spurn the economic argument that maximizing wood production cannot maximize the value of the resource. They refuse to question the economic virtue of extracting every branch and twig from the forest. Outdoorsmen fight to maintain the purity and remoteness of vast wilderness areas at the expense of making them accessible and enjoyable for a greater number of people. Geologists advocate the fullest possible extraction of oil without respect to its economic cost. The main interest of fisheries biologists tends to lie in the size and health of the fish population rather than the fishing industry, and hence they advocate regulations in the interests of the fish. The same is true for wildlife managers. As a general rule, the way professional people see and carry out their jobs implies that maximizing the output of resources will serve society's interests best—regardless of the costs or of more desirable alternatives.

The magic word to public approbation is "conservation," and all groups cloak their recommendations under the same winning guise. In fact, "conservation" describes policies ranging from "full use" (foresters and geologists), to rehabilitation (agriculturists), to complete preservation (aesthetes). The term is a virtuous one but it no longer has any useful meaning for management purposes. Insofar as government policy is influenced by professional resource experts within and without the civil service, and these specialists fail to formulate their recommendations in the light of their full economic implications, government policies will rarely encourage efficient use of resources.

Economists should be able to evaluate the economic efficiency of alternative policies and offer guidance in the formulation of policies that will maximize the benefits to be gained from resources net of the costs of exploitation and management. But training in the resource professions rarely includes a study of basic economic principles. Moreover, economists have only recently begun to address themselves specifically to natural resource development, and they are only now beginning to attack the problem of non-marketed benefits (such as recreation and aesthetic values, and the indirect effect of one activity on another), which are often of critical importance in natural resource management. As a result, economists' lamentations over the waste and costliness of present policies and their suggestions for reform remain voices in the wilderness.

*　　　*　　　*

The first requirement for efficient natural resource use is clear objectives. Present policies lack this, or where objectives are discernable they seem to be directed toward either the "welfare" of the resource itself or the maintenance of the *status quo* rather than toward the contribution of resources to the welfare of Canadians. Suppose, for example, the objective "to manage all resources in such a way as to yield the highest benefit to Canadians" were adopted. This is a simple objective, and perhaps even obviously acceptable, but most of our present policies are thoroughly incompatible with it. We know that public policies relating to almost every natural resource can be shown to have the effect of reducing their value—whether financial or intangible—to Canadians.

Alternative uses and combinations of uses of resources must be considered and evaluated in a way which does not involve arbitrary priorities among users. This is unlikely to be achieved as long as land and water are rigidly classified by use and placed under the jurisdiction of departments and agencies with single-minded interests.

There are strong and (in the opinion of this writer) valid arguments against unrestricted *laissez-faire* in the ownership and development of natural resources. But in a system where governments maintain public ownership of resources yet depend in large measure on the market for exploitation and development, governments bear a heavy responsibility in making the market work in the best interests of society.[8] The performance of governments in managing the vast public resources in Canada does not strengthen the case for increased government involvement in economic affairs. Both federal and provincial governments have a record of resource management which does not augur well for a Canadian economy with an expanded public sector.

---

[8]For an interesting discussion of this point, see Anthony Scott, "Resourcefulness and Responsibility," *The Canadian Journal of Economics and Political Science,* Vol. XXIV, No. 2, (May 1958), pp. 203-15.

45   The Social Policy of Intervention*

Anthony Scott

"It does not of course follow that wherever laissez faire falls short government interference is expedient." Sidgwick

It would be unreasonable to demand that the state make economic policy decisions on the grounds of efficiency alone, especially when "efficiency" is used in the sense of thrifty production of saleable goods. For the legislature is free of the limitations of market valuations and may make policies independently of prices and costs, heeding only its own—or its servants'—appraisals of the losses and gains resulting from its decisions. Such losses and gains may well transcend the estimates of the market pricing process and reflect some notion of social benefits and social costs. Another way of expressing this is to say that the state may adopt burdens and confer benefits upon any individual or group. In our problem this means that the legislature can exercise its own judgment rather than confine itself to projects justified by market estimates of costs, values and the collective rate of time preference.

This view of the supremacy of the legislature in economic matters obviously applies to the Western variants of the representative system of government. It must be qualified by the necessity for the legislature to receive periodic support from the electorate; obviously it cannot pursue indefinitely a policy which conflicts with the attitudes and threatens the incomes of the populace.

In addition to these democratic restrictions on its freedom of action, the legislature is in the final analysis constrained by the same limitations as those which govern the conduct of individuals and businesses; the scarcity of resources and the need to make economic decisions which are compatible with the tastes of consumers and the techniques of production. Nor can the economic planning of any body, including the legislature, start *ab initio,* but must take as given the past allocation of resources to various uses and the past decisions to hoard or exhaust the services of wasting assets. The legislature is therefore confronted with an economy already pressing heavily on its inheritance of energy, materials, education, and techniques, and using to the full its flow of labour-power within the life-span of the people.

Any contemplated change will raise difficulties: for every step which is believed to be on the whole beneficial will impose hardship or loss on some social group. In carrying out any policy, therefore, the administration should move in short stages, pausing before each to estimate the magnitude of ex-

*From: Anthony Scott, *Natural Resources: The Economics of Conservation* (Toronto, University of Toronto Press, 1955) , pp. 99-102 (reprinted by permission of author and publisher) .

tra social losses which may be inflicted, and getting assurance that they are more than offset by the expected extra social gains. That this procedure is not impossible is shown by the contemporary process of settling annually the budget. Here the government may be conceived of as weighing benefits of expenditure against costs of raising revenue; not in money terms so much as in terms of social satisfactions.

Indeed, in a model economy where all values could be expressed in a single medium (for example, in a world-state with a single currency and an acceptable distribution of income and wealth) the legislature would become in economic matters simply a maximizing unit. Its job would be to estimate in money terms the benefits and the costs of every conceivable action and of every conceivable combination of actions, its object to allocate resources so that the absolute maximum of welfare or profit (by assumption commensurable) was obtained. In such a state, marginal conditions would be found to hold at the maximum, so that the marginal social benefit of every dollar's worth of input was equal to one dollar. The allocation of resources would be such that there could be no improvement—every projected reallocation of resources would inflict losses on deprived users in excess of the gains of new users.

The legislature of the real world cannot hope to approach such perfection in the allocation of resources. All that it can do is undertake the reallocations which will bring about significant improvements, leaving small marginal changes to be made in a better world. But it is the assumption of this study that the legislature can and should make policies which tend toward the same absolute maximum that could be achieved in the simpler model economy.

Other authors are less hopeful that the legislature can make such detailed cost-benefit studies as are implied by the process described above. They believe that large public conservation projects can only be properly planned if they are actually based on some knowledge of the preference systems of the public. How much are individuals willing to pay (in taxes) for a collective irrigation project of a certain size? How much more will each offer to pay for one on a greater scale? Bowen and Ciriacy-Wantrup believe that the legislature can, by survey and questionnaire, get reasonable, indicative answers to such questions. This is not the place to comment on their proposals, except to suggest that, whatever may be found by the rather elaborate survey and statistical techniques necessary, the legislature will still need to carry out the fundamental maximizing process suggested above. A survey can not establish an allocation of resources; at the best it can only determine a demand curve.

Let us assume that the legislature has determined to attempt to approach the social optimum, using the step-by-step system sketched above, and perhaps also using surveys and statistics to establish the intensity of needs and benefits. With this background, we can see in perspective the meaning of "the benefits of conservation" discussed in this part.

Imagine now that all the social benefits we have described elsewhere were to be become private benefits. This might happen if the scale of management were so enlarged that each resource became "specific." Then all the consequences of investment and depletion would be enjoyed entirely by each resource's owner. All "social economies" would be services which the owner could sell to the public, the current flow of which he could renew if it were a renewable resource, or diminish if he felt that approaching shortages would make it worth his while to save his deposits for the lean years ahead. At the same time all those who knew of or who owned the means of providing substitutes for an exhaustible resource would prepare to augment its flow with their own products, and would bid up the prices of the relevant inputs. All stocks of the resource and of the materials for its substitutes would increase in value as those who foresaw the approaching shortage attempted to profit by anticipating the eventual increase in current demand. "Conservation" would then be an individual problem. As long as the prevailing social philosophy was that the individual should attain his desires efficiently, the state would find the laissez-faire economy a satisfactory mechanism for maximizing satisfaction.

This analysis suggests that the first task of the state in actual circumstances would be to change the ownership of property so that each resource became specific. . . . In general [this] . . . involves the reallocation of land so that the user costs or the present values appertaining to conservation became coextensive with the owner's property rights. Thus, the state would need only to make social values into private values, and every necessary action with respect to allocation among uses and allocation among periods would be taken by the hidden hand of the economy.

But this model world is far too simple to tell us much about the actions our legislatures should initiate. For even the satisfactory reallocation of property is impossible to any legislature now functioning. Since the economic effects of the methods of using natural resources may be widespread, nation-wide, or even world-wide, there is no institution by which a single owner can be given jurisdiction over them. This unappropriable characteristic of the gains from such resources as deepsea fisheries is shared by many municipal resources which it is impracticable to appropriate for technical or social reasons. Forest and watershed resources give so many services to so many classes of consumers in so many places that there is no single way that all can express in a market their valuation of these services. Consequently the owner can only respond to that smaller class of users who actually buy services from him. Here then is the first place in which public authority with its larger scale may intervene to provide all the services of natural resources and to pay for them by the collection of social contributions. In the case of international resources, this task becomes complicated, as we shall see, and it is necessary to make treaty or even supranational arrangements for allocating the resource.

A related difficulty is far less directly remediable. This occurs when the social loss due to depletion is not registered by a fall in market values, because the loss occurs only in a local, political sense. Thus any country whose resources are becoming depleted may in the extreme case be in danger of national extinction, through the emigration of those who seek higher rewards for their services. In many cases this will be experienced as a genuine loss. Yet unless the government or the state finds some method of raising the value (and the expectation of future value) of the resource, the individual will not direct his demand in such a way as to make conservation of the resource privately profitable.

The same non-market loss will occur when there is unemployment of resources. No matter how large the scale of the private enterprise, it is unlikely that ownership of a resource can be made so comprehensive that the entrepreneur will manage the deposit or investment over time in such a way as to keep high home employment. In these cases, then, the legislature must intervene in allocation, for merely enlarging the scale of the enterprise will not be sufficient.

There are further shortcomings in the allocation of natural resources, even when the scale is adequate to allow the owner to sell the services of his resources to all its users. In the first place, the owner's knowledge may be inadequate to the appreciation of present and future profits of appropriate management. Further, he may lack the technical knowledge to enable him to manage the resource in the way that would satisfy all the market demands for its services over time. It is probable that as the scale of the resource increased, knowledge would become more accessible to the owner or manager, but this is not certain. Once again, the state might find it necessary to step in, perhaps merely to induce the owner by "liaison" to act in his own interest.

Once the state has intervened, it may find it necessary to intervene again This is because the furtherance of one social aim, such as financing communal purchase of services of certain resources, may involve measures such as tax collection which themselves inhibit the best use of resources over time. Consequently the state must step in to offset its own previous incentive. An example mentioned above of this conflict of state policies is seen in the conflicting desires to achieve the best allocation of the services of natural resources over time, and at the same time to keep the other resources of society fully employed. Another example is the incompatability of the encouragement of private resource conservation (or stock-piling) against wartime shortages and anti-inflationary price control in wartime. A more significant example is the fact that the large-scale ownership of resources, urged above in order to overcome the difficulty of diverging private and social benefits, may provide unacceptable instances of large-scale monopolistic control of large sectors of the economy. These are of course two sides of the same coin, but it is not unusual for society to want the best of both worlds. Therefore, it may be impossible so to enlarge the scale of exploitation and replacement as to substitute private revenues for social economies.

If this is true, then the scope for state intervention broadens to authorizing monopolistic exploitation on the one hand and controlling it on the other, or to achieving some at least of the effects of large-scale management by the adoption of piece-meal incentives and prohibitions.

This conflict of state policies explains the mass of legislation creating systems of subsidies and tax adjustments, "liaison" with small producers, controls, licences, and socialization which can be observed everywhere natural resources are the subject of state concern. Rejecting on grounds irrelevant to this inquiry the massive change in ownership which if permitted would in many cases exempt legislatures from further concern over conservation of natural resources, governments have been forced to improvise methods not in conflict with social policies which—let it be confessed—they feel to be more important.

There is one further characteristic wherein business may fail to achieve the socially desirable degree of conservation: its undoubted inability to recognize a different rate of time preference from that prevailing in the market. . . . [The] declaration of a "social rate of interest" leaves everything to be desired as a foundation for social policy. Nevertheless, if a nationalistic or introverted social policy leads to the adoption of such a concept, in spite of its threats of inflation, and of unharmonious individual decisions about investment and consumption, the economist *qua* economist can only counsel that, in order that this régime may prevail, the state must intervene continually in all sectors of the economy; no simple reform of ownership or taxation will suffice to establish and stabilize the sought-for degree of conservation.

It follows from what has been said in this chapter that the state usually cannot replace the exploitation of natural resources with steps of universal force which will by themselves completely change the degree of conservation of the economy. Because of the conflict of conservation policy with other social aims—or, to put it another way, because of the necessity of fitting conservation policy into already existing social and economic systems—the state will find it politic to enact many small measures of encouragement, assistance, and control which will lead private owners to act in the appropriate manner.

Only in emergency, or in pursuance of a variety of acceptable objectives, will outright collective management of resources on the one hand or the granting of large-scale private management rights on the other find place in the legislative agenda. . . .

SUGGESTIONS FOR FURTHER READING

Anderson, W. J., "The Basis of Economic Policy for Canadian Agriculture," *Canadian Journal of Agricultural Economics,* Vol. 11 (1963).

Boulding, K. E., "Economic Analysis in Agricultural Policy," *Canadian Journal of Economics and Political Science,* August, 1947.

Britnell, G. E. and V. C. Fowke, *Canadian Agriculture in War and Peace 1935-50,* Stanford, Stanford University Press, 1962.

Burton, I., "Investment Choices in Public Resource Development," in A. Rotstein (ed.), *The Prospect of Change,* Toronto, McGraw-Hill Co. of Canada Ltd., 1965.

Campbell, D. R., "Farm Marketing and Price Support Programmes," Institute of Public Administration of Canada, Eleventh Annual Conference, Proceedings, Toronto, 1959.

Campbell, D. R., "The Economics of Production Control: The Example of Tobacco," *Canadian Journal of Economics,* Vol. 2 (February, 1969).

Canadian Council of Resource Ministers, *An Inventory of Joint Programmes and Agreements Affecting Canada's Renewable Resources,* Ottawa, Queen's Printer, 1964.

Ciriacy-Wantrup, S. V., *Resource Conservation,* Berkeley, University of California Press, 1952.

Davidson, C. B., "The Canadian Wheat Board and its role in Grain Marketing," special article in Dominion Bureau of Statistics, *Canada Year Book* (1960), pp. 625-630.

Dominion Bureau of Statistics, "Canada's Commercial Fishery Resources and their Conservation," *Canada Year Book* (1960), pp. 625-630.

Drummond, W. M., and W. Mackenzie, *Progress and Prospects of Canadian Agriculture,* a study prepared for the Royal Commission on Canada's Economic Prospects, Ottawa, Queen's Printer, 1957.

Economic Council of Canada, "Productivity in Agriculture," chapter 5 in *The Challenge of Growth and Change,* the Fifth Annual Report (Ottawa, Queen's Printer, 1968).

Fowke, V. C., *Canadian Agricultural Policy,* Toronto, University of Toronto Press, 1947.

Fowke, V. C., *The National Policy and the Wheat Economy,* Toronto, University of Toronto Press, 1957.

Goundry, G., "Comments on Conservation," *The Canadian Banker,* Vol. 66, (Summer, 1959).

Innis, H. A., "The Historical Development of the Dairy Industry in Caanda," in M. Q. Innis, *Essays in Canadian Economic History,* Toronto, University of Toronto Press, 1962.

Martin, C. B., "Dominion Lands Policy," in W. A. McIntosh and W. L. G. Joerg, (eds.), *Canadian Frontiers of Settlement,* Vol. 2 (Toronto, Macmillan Co. of Canada Ltd., 1938).

Morgan, L. I., "Price Supports and Farm Surpluses: The Canadian Experience," Bank of Nova Scotia, *Monthly Review,* December, 1960 (reprinted in M. H. Watkins and D. F. Forster, *Economics Canada,* Toronto, McGraw-Hill Co. of Canada Ltd., 1963).

Resources for Tomorrow Conference, *Papers and Proceedings* (Ottawa, Queen's Printer, 1961-62), 4 Vols.

Scott, A., "The Development of the Extractive Industries," *Canadian Journal of Economics and Political Science,* Vol. 28 (February, 1962).

PART EIGHT

Area Development Policies

INTRODUCTION

The preceding part was concerned with policies whereby the government, for various reasons, seeks to influence the allocation of resources among different industries rather than rely on unregulated markets to perform this essential economic function. In an unregulated free-market economy resources would be allocated to those employments offering the prospect of the highest returns to the owners of these resources. Thus, if labor could be more productively employed in manufacturing than in farming, the owners of labor services would, presumably, leave agriculture for the higher returns obtainable in manufacturing. But if this shift was thought undesirable for some reason, policies to subsidize incomes in agriculture might serve to check such an adjustment. If the country wants to have a manufacturing industry of some particular size and this is not the size that a purely market allocation of economic resources would achieve, policies to subsidize manufacturing through tariffs and other devices might serve to achieve such a goal.

In a large, geographically diverse country, all these policies will have a differential impact on different parts of the country. Governments in the past have not been unmindful of the incidental regional implications of such policies for their electoral appeal in different parts of the country. Consequently we have probably always had some form of implicit regional economic policy in Canada. Federal governments, for example, have had to balance the promotion of manufacturing, agriculture, and the fisheries in order to satisfy electors on the Prairies, in central Canada, and on the coasts. But is there also an economic case to be made for deliberately interfering with the spatial allocation of economic resources within the economy?

This question has been brought to the fore in recent years by the proliferation of various kinds of explicit regional development programs. Again, this is not a new kind of government participation in economic life because many historical precedents for deliberate regional development schemes can be found, especially in Canada. As noted in Part 5, for example, Federal policies toward rail transportation in the nineteenth century were greatly influenced by the importance attached to encouraging the agricultural settlement of the interior. Provincial and municipal governments have for even longer engaged in practices designed to attract particular industries to their jurisdictions. Only recently, however, has an attempt been made to analyze the effects of some rational plan for coordinating them into a consistent set of policies.

It should be noted that many of the issues raised concerning these area development programs are closely connected with the government interventions in labor markets described in the next part. One, and probably the most important political and economic reason for governments to become involved in promoting the development of a particular geographical area is to improve the living of those residing in the area. But this could be done by encouraging migration to areas where better livings could be earned. Given its natural resource endowment, employment and income can be raised by transfering capital and enterprise into any area. Alternatively, labor could be encouraged to move out. Thus, policies affecting the allocation of capital and business enterprise among regions may be interchangeable with policies to influence the uses to which labor resources are put.

How one could proceed to assess the economic merits of such alternatives is explored by Professor Breton in *Reading 49*. Helen Buckley and Eva Tihanyi assess the impact of a specific program that they carried out under the provisions of the Agricultural Rehabilitation and Development Act, in the light of such economic-political criteria. The use of taxes and subsidies, and of provincial "development funds" for promoting the development of particular areas by means of altering the flows of capital among regions and industries are the subject of *Readings 47* and *48* drawn from the reports of the Carter Royal Commission and from the Porter Royal Commission respectively.

The use of measures to affect the flow of the other mobile economic factor of production, labor, as an alternative to such policies of influencing capital allocations will be taken up in the selections of the next part where we consider a number of labor market policies.

46 The Economic Impact of the Agricultural Rehabilitation and Development Act*

Helen Buckley

Eva Tihanyi

Apart from the possibility of some form of direct payment to residents, governments have two basic ways of promoting the growth of per capita income in an area. The first alternative is to assist "development projects"; in the present context these may be defined as investments in physical capital with the intention of raising output locally. The second alternative, which we would prefer to label the promotion of "labour force adjustment", covers measures that encourage movement out of the area. The potential gain from the second approach is, of course, the greatest if those who move can go to regions with labour-absorptive capacity and if they possess the specific skills there in demand. In the long run, departures from the area of origin will tend to improve the local balance between labour and available physical capital (including natural resources) in favour of the latter, making possible the attainment of higher productivity for the remaining labour force.

Under the conditions prevailing in most parts of Canada, it is likely that a low-income rural area must rely heavily on downward adjustments in the size of its labour supply before significant increases in local productivity and income levels per person can be hoped for. The recognition of this necessity has been very slow to come and is still far from being generally accepted. Out-migration continues to be regarded as a hindrance to improving local standards, partly because so little has been done by senior governments to alleviate some of its truly damaging side effects, and partly because population growth has all too frequently been misused as a measure of political success.

The ARDA programme is strongly influenced by local preferences which, in many provinces, continue to run strongly in favour of the resource programmes, and against bolder policy experiments bearing the seeds of controversy or threatening vested interests. Viewed from a purely provincial standpoint, there are benefits to be had in resource investments, and these cannot but be enhanced when the federal government pays a large part of the cost. The resource approach is also attractive to communities which are hard-pressed to maintain services in the face of low incomes, declining tax

---

*Helen Buckley and Eva Tihanyi, *Canadian Policies for Rural Adjustment: A Study of the Economic Impact of ARDA, PFRA, and MMRA,* Economic Council of Canada, Special Study No. 7 (Ottawa, Queen's Printer, 1967), pp. 17-26 (reprinted by permission).

revenues, and the loss of young persons to the city. Provincial governments are not unmindful of such problems, nor do they fail to see that the problem of financing services becomes more difficult, not less, if reduction in the rural labour force is encouraged. There exists, therefore, not only 'a strong demand for development at the local level but also a similar interest at the provincial level in measures intended to impart greater strength to rural communities.

Throughout the early years ARDA's activities were chiefly aimed at satisfying local desires for development, though action was generally on a limited scale. Even projects referred to in ARDA terminology as land-use "adjustment" tended to be land development schemes promoting some form of intensification. The alternate land-use projects (which accounted for a large proportion of expenditures) seldom aimed at removing underemployed labour from marginal and submarginal lands, although some of the western community pasture developments sought this as a secondary objective. More commonly, however, ARDA funds were used to acquire lands for blueberry production, recreation, reforestation or similar projects, the benefits from which are frequently exaggerated. The justification for many such projects was to salvage lands abandoned as agriculture retreated from marginal areas. There exists a very common—but erroneous—zeal for "economy" which cannot tolerate the waste of land but easily overlooks the waste of labour on the tidy parcels of the small farmer.

What seems a misplaced concentration of effort through the early ARDA years is not entirely to be explained as mistaken diagnosis. An important part of the original ARDA message could be interpreted as saying: "we don't know the solution, but we will underwrite research and implement pilot projects in the hope of finding solutions".

The search for solutions went on during these formative years of ARDA. In fact, few programmes in Canada have ever devoted such energies to social and economic research as did ARDA (e.g., the BAEQ programme in Quebec) and federal funds played an essential role in making this research possible. It was an important side benefit that the issues were kept alive and much debated; this tended to bring about a more favourable atmosphere for change.

While ARDA was not entirely innocent in prolonging many of the popular myths that surround the benefits from resource development, it is a major accomplishment of the programme that it also helped to soften public attitudes towards genuine adjustments in the rural economy. Today, in many parts of Canada, the transfer of labour from agriculture and other rural occupations is more widely accepted as a solution worthy of governmental support. This made it possible to launch major new programmes in New Brunswick and Manitoba shortly after the observation period of the present study ended. The new approaches will be discussed at the end of this summary.

ARDA cannot remain immune from the pressures to provide "development" of a locally tangible nature even if programme planners themselves realize the stronger need for "adjustment". This pressure can easily lead to situations in which economic principles are compromised and projects are accepted for ARDA financing even when they are economically unsatisfactory. Two additional circumstances work in this direction.

First, the regular ARDA programme is still too closely linked to the concept of land development and even in rural development areas allows only a limited choice of alternatives. With authorities under pressure to utilize the allotted funds but having a small range of choices, the result can easily be the selection of a project of dubious merit.

Second, it should be recognized that the combination of resource development with the social objective of poverty reduction can reduce efficiency in the promotion of either goal. In many circumstances, income improvement is urgent; but in a society which is not committed to a general policy of minimum income maintenance and which attaches a stigma to "being on welfare", inefficient projects become acceptable solutions for help. From the hundreds of projects listed in the ARDA Catalogue, it would not be difficult to pick out many in which the taxpayer pays one dollar so that a farmer somewhere in a fringe area can make (say) fifty cents. One wonders how much consolation it provides that he will have to work for it and thus avoid the alleged humiliation of direct income maintenance.

The 1:1 benefit-cost ratio . . . as a minimum criterion of efficiency is not intended as a guide by which the work of those implementing the ARDA programme in practice should be evaluated. In many circumstances, strict adherence to at least a 1:1 ratio would lead to inaction—a course understandably unattractive to a dedicated public servant. If he selects, say, the least inefficient alternative possible under ARDA to alleviate a poverty situation, is his action less desirable than leaving a pressing social problem unattended?

Only if the executors of public policies are free to choose among all feasible approaches to attain a certain objective can they be expected to give consistent preference to the one that economic criteria recommends. Under too much pressure to provide "development" and with too much constraint on the types of development to consider, they are—despite the best intentions—hardly in a position to assure at least a 1:1 benefit-cost ratio in programme implementation.

This frustrating predicament may help to explain the gap between intended and actual adherence to economic principles. According to the current federal-provincial ARDA agreement, for example, development projects approved under certain sections, and all development projects with a total cost of above $100,000, must be subjected to benefit-cost analysis. The importance of good economics has been frequently emphasized in public statements by leading ARDA representatives. Yet, in everyday ARDA operations, statements of benefits in the most rudimentary terms are apparently acceptable as a basis for evaluating the merits of a project sponsored from ARDA funds. ARDA has sponsored a number of feasibility studies; yet we could not find evidence that systematic research was directed towards *ex post* evaluation of implemented projects.

The valuable tool of benefit-cost analysis has played a very limited role in PFRA and MMRA operations, and perhaps in government investments generally, until quite recently. The shortcomings stated above are by no means peculiar to ARDA; on the contrary, ARDA at least made some beginning in working out the methods of more rigorously applied benefit-cost principles. However, as annually submitted provincial policies rather than single development projects become the subject of federal-provincial cost-sharing negotiations, there is some danger that this modest beginning will not be followed by full commitment. A drainage assistance policy, grants for clearing or for the construction of ponds, woodlot management services and similar ARDA-sponsored activities are not considered suitable for benefit quantification; yet federal cost-sharing is automatically expected if any province has established a precedent with a similar programme. Frequently our inquiries revealed a resentment against a federal role in benefit-cost evaluation; some provinces would have preferred to treat it as an internal matter at the discretion of the departments in question.

The reorientation in the ARDA programme referred to earlier occurred gradually over the years and culminated in the adoption of certain new programmes. We attempted to analyze these programmes on the basis of the plans as approved, but had no occasion to follow up on the first experiences of implementation.

The farm consolidation and rehabilitation section of the regular ARDA Agreement provided the operative framework for a major new farm programme launched in Ontario and expected to be followed elsewhere in Eastern Canada, mainly as an element of comprehensive regional programmes. It is hoped that increased scale on the consolidated farms and the additional assistance in credit and management will create units that can provide incomes of a satisfactory level. Departing farmers (whose lands ARDA will purchase for cash) will be able to retire or retrain for other employment.

That ARDA has turned its attention to basic deficiencies in farm structure and organization appears to be a step forward, but there is no assurance that essential changes will result. With the right emphasis, the programme will become primarily a means of labour transfer from agriculture. With the wrong emphasis the programme could become a means to arrest, with further subsidies, the land-abandonment process taking place spontaneously in areas of high-cost marginal farming.

An outstanding milestone in ARDA's history to date was the launching of the first major comprehensive regional programmes late in the summer of 1966. The idea of programme concentration in selected areas, to be based on co-ordinated research and planning, was always an element of the ARDA programme. Although the most intensive regional research took place in the Gaspé Region of Quebec, the first province to commit itself to long-range regional programmes was neighbouring New Brunswick. . . .

If the first plans reveal the essentials of others to follow, then Canada will finally see, in a number of regions, a co-ordinated application of highly desirable "adjustment" policies combined with prudently designed "development". This is a very important breakthrough.

These first plans approximate what is described in these final paragraphs as an optimum set of rural policies.

An optimum set of rural policies in Canada today must have a vigorous educational and manpower programme as its backbone; the up-grading and mobilizing of the rural labour force is the most important adjustment process for governments to pursue. Provisions for land-use and farm adjustment could play an important complementary role to a good manpower programme but, without the latter, these provisions will fail to result in substantial income improvement. It appears that the new comprehensive programmes are based on the correct diagnosis that inefficient use of land is the reflection, not the cause, of rural poverty, and that the latter will yield only to measures which improve the quality and utilization of rural labour resources.

The backbone, however, is not the whole skeleton. Manpower policies alone cannot bear the burden of solving the problem of rural poverty in all situations. The removal of excess labour from rural areas and from low-income regions generally will tend to increase earnings for the remaining labour force, but this positive tendency might be countered by the unfavourable repercussions consequent to population decline or stagnation. Areas of continuous out-migration are familiar with such undesirable phenomena as the deterioration of commercial and public services, the concentration of the aged, and other shifts in population structure. The resistance to government-sponsored out-migration is, at least partly, motivated by the real hardships migration imposes on the areas of origin. A firm government commitment to effective manpower policies should be coupled with a firm commitment to share the financial burdens of maintaining a high level of social services, so that the unfavourable effects of out-migration will not be allowed to dissipate the gains from the adjustment process.

It is very much in the interest of society at large that a high standard of social services be maintained in all rural areas even though sparse population makes those services more expensive than elsewhere. This is particularly important with respect to education: if rural depopulation results in substandard educational services, the long-run losses to society are likely to be enormous. A similar argument could be made for maintaining a high level of health services, community facilities and housing. The ARDA-provided public subsidies so ineffectively spent for soil and water developments and rural enterprises of dubious merit would command much higher returns if ways were found to channel them into social infrastructure improvements within or adjacent to depressed rural communities. The apparent recognition of this is perhaps the strongest feature of the special area programmes that resulted from ARDA planning.

Realistic rural policies should give recognition to the fact that many poor people have not the ability to make a successful adjustment in a new and unfamiliar environment. Age and poor health are among the more important reasons and both are likely to be prevalent in low-income rural areas. For some groups at least it would be highly desirable to adopt a policy of direct income maintenance. The guaranteed minimum income for farm operators 55 years of age and over who sell their land to ARDA was first adopted in the Ontario consolidation programme. It appears to be a step in the right direction, although it might be suggested that its applicability is too restricted and the proposed income level too low.

Very few of the elements of "optimum" policies described above could be accommodated under the regular ARDA programme; the new comprehensive plans are financed in large measure from other federal and provincial sources. Plainly, the provisions of the federal-provincial ARDA Agreements in effect to 1970 do not fill the most important gaps in policies for rural Canada. The funds made available for rural development cannot be used for the kinds of development which promise the largest returns to society and best serve the long-run interests of rural residents: education, health and other community services. Instead, the funds are channeled into agricultural land and water investments, which have a strong tendency to become hardship payments to primary producers for the lack of commercially justifiable opportunities to expand. By the same token, ARDA funds cannot be used for a comprehensive manpower mobility programme; even the new Agreement's Rehabilitation section could at best serve as a supplement. So it is that land-use adjustment is promoted instead of adjustments in the rural labour force.

Through the promotion of rural conservation, some ARDA projects are likely to contribute to incomes in a more distant future. While this factor should appropriately raise the value of the benefits considered as relevant, the writers have not encountered evidence of any major conservation inputs being attributable to ARDA, nor do they consider it desirable that the programme concentrate future efforts in that direction. This is suggested for two reasons. First, there is no evidence that present agricultural practices in Canada endanger the future value of rural resources in a significant way;[1] to the extent that natural resources *are* in danger, Canadians would be well advised to search for other culprits—a task well beyond ARDA jurisdiction. Second, it appears that regular ARDA funds are too small to serve the dual objectives of resource conservation and socio-economic adjustments; the combination of these objectives as the responsibility of one agency may perpetuate the misconception that the two are solvable by the same means.

---

[1] For this opinion, see H. Van Vliet, Address to the Saskatchewan Resources Conference, (Saskatoon, 1964).

The future will undoubtedly see a concentration of efforts in "special" areas such as Northeastern New Brunswick and Interlake in Manitoba. This is logical enough in view of the concentration of poverty and the limitation on funds available. There could be a danger, however, that the association between rural poverty and regional poverty will become over-emphasized as the mainstream of ARDA action shifts into the poor, agri-culturally marginal areas, while the rural low-income problem dispersed throughout the rest of Canada is left to "traditional" agricultural policies and to the land resource development projects of the regular ARDA programme.

It is not altogether certain how deeply the reorientation in rural policies apparent in the new comprehensive plans will affect the regular ARDA programme; there are few, if any, signs that a shift away from the physical resource orientation will generally characterize ARDA action of future years. Many provinces appear willing to settle for a continuation of the pattern established by the action projects of the early ARDA years, and the new approaches, even though they appear to have general applicability, could easily remain special experiments isolated from the mainstream of Canadian rural policies.

47 The Use of Taxes and Subsidies for Area Development*

Royal Commission on Taxation

. . . [T]he government introduced in 1965 the *Area Development Incentives Act*. Under this Act the Minister of Industry is empowered to make sub-sidies to firms establishing new facilities or expanding existing facilities in designated areas. The subsidies are established by a formula based on the approved capital cost of the facility. A subsidy under this Act is not taxable to the firm.

We commend this change from tax concessions to subsidies. We believe that investment credits (subsidies) are at least as efficient as accelerated depreciation and, per dollar of revenue forgone, more efficient than the three-year exemption of income for new businesses. The fact that the costs of the subsidy can be readily determined is also a desirable feature, for it encourages the comparison of costs and benefits. Because the present tax incentives allow a business to postpone the deduction of any capital cost

---

*From: *Report*, Ottawa, Queen's Printer, Vol. II (1966), pp. 135-37 (reprinted by per-mission).

allowances until after the three-year exempt period has expired, they provide a much larger concession than is immediately apparent. It is not possible to say how great the resulting tax concession may be. We do not think this feature of the present measure is desirable.

We do not feel that we can take a position on the probable effectiveness of the area development incentives. We believe, as we have already said, that there may be grounds for subsidizing the movement of capital to depressed areas. We are doubtful whether subsidies that do not take into account the specific needs of specific areas will lead to an efficient allocation of capital among the areas; but we are aware of the other efforts that are being made to provide funds for depressed areas through provincial and federal regional development bodies. To the extent that the latter can help to develop both the infrastructure of these depressed areas, through better education, roads and cheaper power, and geographic focal points for development that can help to realize economies of scale, the unselective character of the area development incentives may be compensated for to some extent. We are also aware that highly selective subsidies involve a risk of serious error, unless those who allocate the funds are extremely knowledgeable. The state of knowledge about regional development is still so fragmentary that heavy reliance on government planning for industrial development within regions is perhaps premature. Selective subsidies to industry also have the disadvantage, at least to many people, that they require a high degree of government intervention in business decision making. We strongly recommend that a full-scale research programme on the problems of regional economic development be undertaken with all speed. The problem is of great importance and complexity. Every effort should be made at an early date to assess the effectiveness of the new programmes.

Although we cannot be certain how effective the area development incentives will prove to be, we are reasonably certain that they will be more efficient than the present tax incentives. Because the former will be more useful, and because our recommendation for accelerated capital cost allowances for new business, regardless of location, should assist in meeting the financing problems of such businesses, there seems no reason to keep the depressed area tax incentives; we believe they would be redundant. It is our recommendation that they be removed from the Act, but, of course, not in such a manner as to remove the incentive to those businesses now availing themselves of the provisions.

48   Provincial Development Funds*

Royal Commission on Banking and Finance

The provincial development funds and similar facilities have been set up to assist local businesses unable to obtain funds from other sources, including the federal Industrial Development Bank. Some—as in New Brunswick, Newfoundland and Saskatchewan—may either lend directly or guarantee the repayment of funds to other lenders; in contrast, the Ontario Development Agency confines itself to guarantees, while still other provincial agencies make only direct loans. Their rates of interest are usually relatively low, indeed lower than the I.D.B. lending rate which is itself below those of competing private institutions. The term of loans is frequently limited by legislation to 10 years, but in at least one case may be for as long as 20 years.[1] The provinces' main aim is to assist small businesses, but some are prepared to guarantee quite substantial bond issues.

The General Investment Corporation recently established in Quebec jointly by the provincial government and private interests is intended to promote the expansion of manufacturing and other industrial development in the province. It stands prepared to provide equity funds or lend to applicants depending on the circumstances, being particularly interested in assisting medium sized businesses which are expected to grow rapidly. Its first three transactions averaged about $700,000. Thus the Corporation's objectives differ substantially from those of the direct provincial agencies in other parts of the country, although it may well provide assistance to smaller enterprises as it develops.

Some of these agencies also go beyond lending or guarantee activities, the Alberta Provincial Marketing Board for example having a subsidiary which buys materials for small businesses, often at advantageous prices, and holds them until needed. By requiring only a partial cash deposit, this agency relieves smaller companies of part of the cost of carrying inventory. Moreover, the Alberta Treasury Branches also invest a substantial share of the funds collected in their deposit accounts in loans. In 1961, $23 million of the $38 million of Treasury Branch loans were to small businesses, and a further $7 million were to farmers' and feeders' associations. This was by a considerable margin the largest amount lent to businesses by any provincial agency. The government of Manitoba provides management advice as well as financial assistance to small enterprises through its Development Fund. Considerable emphasis is laid on attempts to foster balanced economic development in the province as a whole and on regional economic problems within the province. About two-thirds of the Development Fund's lending

---

*From: *Report,* Ottawa, Queen's Printer (1964), pp. 226-27, (reprinted by permission).

has been in small centres and rural areas where the government has also promoted Community Development Corporations to pool local resources for industrial investment.[2] In Nova Scotia, Industrial Estates Limited was set up in 1957 to promote secondary manufacturing and reduce the need for equity funds by building plants for lease and financing purchases of equipment. The new Ontario agency, in common with some others, is prepared to assist companies with technical and other advice. Thus the provinces provide help for small businesses in many ways, although the outstanding amount of advances or guarantees is not very large, probably not in excess of $50 million, and their policies have become more selective as the I.D.B. has broadened its activities.

49 Area Development Policies*

Albert Breton

As the title . . . seeks to make clear, the policies described in it are all designed for the promotion of specified areas. All these policies, in one way or another, involve the subsidization of actual or potential residents of a given area. One fundamental economic question is this: Do these subsidies improve or worsen the allocation of resources in terms of maximizing the per capita income of the population under the government's jurisdiction? Put in less abstract terms, would the same amount of resources devoted to the retraining and relocation of labour in the areas which are deemed to have substandard levels of well-being increase the economic welfare of these people by more or less than subsidies to help them on the spot?

The answer must rely on a number of important facts which are not always in the investigators' hands: facts dealing with the mobility of labour and capital in the absence of all subsidies and, just as important, facts related to the principles which determine government behaviour. The traditional recommendation of economists, based on the assumption of a disinterested government bent on maximizing the common good, has been that whenever externalities exist, the proper policy is one of taxes and subsidies to close the gap between the marginal social and the marginal private benefits and costs. It is often difficult to reconcile the actual pattern of taxation with that which would prevail if this tradition were followed.

One of the difficulties in making such a reconciliation, however, comes

*From: Albert Breton, *Discriminatory Government Policies in Federal Countries,* Canadian Trade Committee, Private Planning Association of Canada, pp. 47-49 (Montreal, 1967) (reprinted by permission of author and publisher).

from efforts of governments to hide their own actions, either by trying to give the impression that subsidies are not in fact being paid, as with the GIC[1] and the CDC[2] or simply by refusing to make the amount of the subsidies known, even to Parliament, as with the IEL[3]. However, one must be careful in interpreting this type of behaviour. Provincial governments may be careful to hide some of their actions, in the same way that oligopolists are also careful not to reveal certain of their actions to rivals. If this is the case, it becomes difficult to interpret government behaviour as that of an omniscient calculator weighing private and social magnitudes and devising the proper taxes and subsidies to equalize them. It also poses the problem of the efficiency of area development policies in a different and more meaningful context.

Two questions must be asked. First, can and do the area development policies increase the total flow of savings that all the provinces have at their disposal, either by inducing economic units to reduce their current expenditures and their current consumption or by inducing "foreign" savings to flow into the country? The second question is, in a way, more basic. Can a given province increase the flow of savings at its disposal when all or many of the other provinces are also using area development policies for the same purpose? It is not easy to answer the first question nor even to say anything rigorous about it. Indeed, since the subsidies have to be paid out of taxes, the effect of the higher rate of return (due to the subsidies) on the flow of savings must also take into account the effect of taxation on that flow. Furthermore, changes in the rate of return and in the rate of taxation induce, first, substitution among goods and services and, secondly, changes in the level of real income, operating in opposite directions and strictly dependent on the preferences of individuals. It is not possible, therefore, to decide on whether the amount of savings supplied by all the provinces will increase or not.

The answer to the second question, whether one province can increase its share in the over-all flow of savings when other provinces are also trying to do this, depends on the reply to another question: Can a province, by paying subsidies, eliminate or reduce the importance of other factors which are responsible for the small flow of savings in the first place? For example, savings may not flow into a given province in an amount which is large enough to satisfy the objectives of the government because the level of income of the population is too low. This in turn may depend on a low level of education, initiative, health, and mobility. Since the profitability of investment also depends to a large extent on these factors, the amount of subsidy required to attract one dollar of extra savings may have to be very large indeed. Because of this the "poorer" provinces may be the ones least capable

---

[1]General Investment Corporation of Quebec (eds.).
[2]Canada Development Corporation (eds.).
[3]Industrial Estates Limited of Nova Scotia (eds.).

of increasing the flow of savings to themselves. Only intervention by a higher-level government, such as the federal government, may be able to break the deadlock. However, the capacity of the federal government to pay subsidies is limited by its capacity to levy taxes. Since the use of the proceeds of these revenues cannot by definition produce as high a rate of growth as they would have in their initial use, it follows that a redistribution of savings will reduce the over-all rate of growth. To return to our initial query, it would appear that in a world of interdependence, the efficiency of area development policies can be nil in the degree that resources are used to attract capital and wasted when capital is not attracted; or this efficiency can be negative for some provinces in the sense that the total flow of capital accruing to these provinces is smaller than it would have been if none of the provinces had implemented these policies. In that case also, some resources are wasted from an over-all point of view.

Does this mean that the policies are useless? Again, as always, the answer depends on the criterion adopted. In the foregoing paragraph, the discussion was implicitly based on the ethical norm that the object of policy is the maximization of per capita measured income. However, if the criterion is the positive norm that the government is striving to maximize its probability of re-election and the strength of its political organization, it may well be that the redistribution of income which is implied by area development policies makes the policies very efficient.

SUGGESTIONS FOR FURTHER READING

Brewis, T. N., "Area Economic Development: Pursuit of a Policy," *Business Quarterly,* Vol. 29 (Summer, 1964).

Brewis, T. N., "Regional Development," in T. N. Brewis (and others) *Canadian Economic Policy* (revised edition), (Toronto, Macmillan Co. of Canada Ltd., 1965), chapter 13.

Brewis, T. N., "Regional Development: The Need for a Federal Policy," *Business Quarterly,* Vol. 27 (Fall, 1962).

Economic Council of Canada, "Regional Aspects of Federal Economic Policies," chapter 7 in *The Challenge of Growth and Change,* the Fifth Annual Review (Ottawa, Queen's Printer, 1968).

Howland, R. D., *Some Regional Aspects of Canada's Economic Development,* a study prepared for the Royal Commission on Canada's Economic Prospects, Ottawa, Queen's Printer, 1957.

Slater, D. W., "Trends in Industrial Locations in Canada," *Resources for Tomorrow,* Vol. 1 (Ottawa, Queen's Printer, 1961), pp. 409-416.

Whalen, H., "Public Policy and Regional Development: The Experience of The Atlantic Provinces," in A. Rotstein (ed.), *The Prospect of Change,* Toronto, McGraw-Hill Co. of Canada Ltd., 1965.

PART NINE

Labour Policies

INTRODUCTION

In an "ideal" free-market economy the incomes of individuals would be determined by the prices established in markets for the productive services they were able to supply to producers, and by the quantities of these services available to them. Those who owned and sold the services of large amounts of highly-priced property in the form of land or capital would receive large incomes, as would those who could supply large amounts of highly-priced labor services. Others, who owned no property and had for sale labor services that would command only a low price in the market would obtain relatively low incomes.

The function of labor markets in such a system would be to establish wage rates at which the quantity of labor offered for sale would just equal the quantity that employers would be willing and able to employ at such rates. It would not be the functions of such markets to provide a "living wage" or a "just wage," or any particular level of income to wage earners. Consequently, in the nineteenth century economists sought, with the approval of employers, to explain that wages would find their own levels in a free-market system and that attempts to tamper with these levels would create serious problems of long-term labor supply and living conditions.

Dissatisfaction with such an approach led workers to organize unions for the purpose of trying to influence wage rates and working conditions. Governments eventually came to encourage these efforts by guaranteeing, subject to certain limitations, the right of workers to organize unions and to engage in collective bargaining.

In addition to this body of labor law regulating the relations between employers and their workers, governments have also sought to influence the

318

wages of labor and conditions of work more directly by establishing minimum wages and minimum standards of safety and health protection, and by prohibiting discrimination and other practices restricting the individual's right to work.

In Canada, all this has been greatly complicated by the division of responsibility for such measures among the provinces and the Federal government. Businesses under Federal jurisdiction, such as banking and railroads, are subject to Federal labor laws—others to the laws of the particular province in which they operate.

The general principles underlying this type of policy are set out in *Reading 50.* It will be noted that although the policies designed to regulate the processes of bargaining between employees and their employers indirectly affect the competitiveness of labor markets by enabling workers to combine and to demand recognition, only a fraction, perhaps one-third of all Canadian workers are members of unions. The other policies referred to, those that set minimum wages and labor standards, represent both a more direct and a more pervasive form of government intervention in labor markets in that they apply to all workers whether unionized or not. Even so, it would be easy to exaggerate the effect of the latter policies, as the minimum standards and wages set have probably not often led to the establishment of higher wage rates or better working conditions than might have prevailed in their absence. The minima have probably been more market-determined than market-determining in these respects.

Since World War II the general drift toward some rationalization of economic policies through planning has shown up in the labor field in the form of "labor market policy". As described in *Reading 51,* this represents a much more concerted attempt by government to influence the behavior of labor markets than do the more traditional policies referred to above. The purpose of labor market policy, as explained by the Economic Council of Canada, is to effect a matching of the supply and demand of labor "in specific localities and occupations" in such a way as to maximize the productivity of the available labor resources of the country. This seems explicitly to suggest that the market mechanism itself cannot achieve such an optimum use of our labor resources.

The selections will also indicate in their description of these programs how closely related labor market policy is to area development policies as mentioned in the introduction to the preceding part. Note here how important it is that policies in such closely related fields be coordinated with one another. This is a good illustration of how the case for more and more comprehensive *planning* of public policies is built up once a conscious effort is made to rationalize government intervention in a system of interrelated markets.

With all this discussion of how labor markets may be made to work more efficiently as devices for allocating "labor resources" among alternative employments, it would be easy to forget that we are also talking about how the standards of living most of us enjoy, or suffer, are determined, the point with which this introductory note began. To the extent that labor markets (despite the existence of unions), minimum wage laws, and the attempts by government to raise the productivity and earning power of particular groups of workers all fail to provide some workers with an "adequate" level of income—however that may be defined—private and public "welfare" payments will be required to sustain some members of the community. Such social welfare policies fall outside the scope of this collection in that they have not customarily been practiced in this country by governments acting on markets or through controls over private business. It is true, as we have seen, that governments in Canada do establish minimum wages, but these have not been set at levels that guarantee that any employed person could support a family at more than a bare subsistence level. It is also true that our labor codes provide workers with some protection against capricious dismissal or refusal to employ on the part of private businessmen. And compulsory education laws, worker training, and upgrading programs do contribute something toward making us all employable. But to date, guaranteed employability, guaranteed employment, and guaranteed incomes have not been explicit objectives of public policy in Canada. The possibility of working in this direction is tentatively explored by the Economic Council of Canada in *Reading 53*.

50 Labour Markets *

Task Force on Labour Relations

The Role of the Labour Market[1]

The labour market is only one of a series of interdependent markets which in the aggregate make possible the operation of a mixed enterprise economy. The labour market serves as a mechanism in which buyers and sellers of labour can accommodate their common and competing interests. The result of this interaction is a hierarchy of wages and salaries that allocate the available labour force in a manner consistent with a similar operation of all other factor and product markets.

The imperfections in the labour market, such as inadequate knowledge in the hands of employers and workers, have been partially overcome by public

---

*From: *Canadian Industrial Relations*, Ottawa, Queen's Printer (1968), pp. 32-37 (reprinted by permission).

[1]For an account of the history of the labour market, see H. C. Pentland, "The Development of a Capitalistic Labour Market in Canada", *Canadian Journal of Economics and Political Science*, November 1959, pp. 450-61.

and private counselling and placement agencies, including the Canada Manpower Service. Although many deficiencies remain in the labour market in spite of these efforts, over time it serves to distribute labour and income in a fashion that no other mechanism could easily match. The continuing reconciliation of the interacting forces of supply and demand which is produced by the labour market leads to a relative distribution of workers and their incomes between different areas, industries, employers and occupations which is not readily undone.

Employers often have a range of discretion within which they may operate in setting wages and other terms and conditions of employment, because of imperfections in the labour market and the time required by the forces of supply and demand to take effect. Employers must reconcile their own internal wage and salary structures with external market forces, but they can reduce the need to accommodate the two by building in benefits which tend to tie workers to their employment. This strategy has limitations.

Personnel administration is the name traditionally given to the process by which management formulates and implements its manpower and human resource policies. Some small enterprises have no personnel department; they simply accept what the market dictates or the union negotiates. Others have a carefully worked out personnel policy without having a specialized personnel officer. Many large corporations have complex personnel departments that handle everything from preliminary interviewing of job applicants and career counselling of regular employees through manpower planning and fringe benefit administration to salary adjustments and merit rating plans.

Where all or part of the work force is organized, a special industrial relations unit is usually created to assist in negotiations and to handle continuing relations with unions. How this activity fits into the complete personnel function varies from case to case. It can present difficult administrative problems where the employer wishes to maintain common personnel practices throughout his enterprise but deals with a union or unions only in part of it.

Collective Bargaining

Where workers are dissatisfied with what the market or their employer suggests is an adequate return for their services, they often seek to form common cause to improve their situation. Through unionization they compel those employing their services to give them a voice in the determination of their terms and conditions of work. Collective bargaining is the process by which groups of organized workers and those desiring their services seek to resolve their differences through reason, the threat of economic conflict or actual conflict. As a result of collective bargaining, more and more issues are subject to joint determination and management's unilateral decision-making power is being reduced accordingly.

The collective bargaining process has adapted itself to an increasing range of normative and procedural issues. Normatively, negotiations now cover everything from wages, hours and working conditions to elaborate fringe benefit and income and job security plans. Procedurally, collective bargaining has led to the introduction of grievance and many other procedures, including job posting and advance notice for layoffs.

An obvious feature of the collective bargaining system is its limited coverage of the labour force. The scope of the process varies with the manner in which the labour force is delineated and with the ways in which collective bargaining and trade unionism are defined.

The term "labour force" can be interpreted in a variety of ways.[2] At its broadest—the "total labour force"—it may be described as the number of persons willing and able to work. More meaningful for our purpose is the "total non-agricultural paid work force" which is the total labour force less agricultural, self-employed and unpaid workers. Narrower still, reference may be made to the labour force of a region, locality, industry or plant. Other possibilities include labour force breakdowns by occupation, skill or sex. Finally, there are frequent references to the distinction between blue and white collar workers, a distinction not always easily drawn.

The extent of collective bargaining is not the same as that of trade unionism, although they tend to cover the same groups of workers. In practice collective bargaining is more all-embracing than trade unionism. First, there are many collective agreements which apply to non-union as well as union members. Under the prevailing concept of exclusive bargaining rights, this coverage is mandatory within designated bargaining units. Second, the *Collective Agreement Decrees Act*[3] in Quebec provides for decrees under which certain terms and conditions in a collective agreement may be made applicable to all establishments in a given jurisdiction, including the unorganized. Less stringent legislation of a similar kind exists in several other jurisdictions. Less formally, the results of collective bargaining also affect many other workers whose employers seek to emulate union standards.

As indicated earlier, the term trade union also poses some difficulty. Conventionally it is limited to organizations of workers acting collectively to protect and improve their conditions of employment. In that sense it embraces virtually all groups, including most of the non-affiliated public employee associations at the federal and provincial levels, and many associations of professional workers, such as teachers and nurses,[4] who have traditionally refrained from referring to themselves as unions though they may operate in a similar manner. Their contribution to the proportion of the

---

[2]For example, "The civilian labour force is composed of that portion of the civilian noninstitutional population 14 years of age and over who, during the reference weeks, were employed or unemployed." See Dominion Bureau of Statistics, *The Labour Force*, (Ottawa, Queen's Printer, monthly).

[3]R.S.Q., 1964, c. 143.

[4]See Shirley B. Goldenberg, *op. cit.* and J. Douglas Muir, *op. cit.*

labour force already covered by collective bargaining can only be estimated because data on the extent of their participation in that process is limited.

At least two other groups add to the total. The first covers dependent contractors as described above; the second embraces independent practitioners in professions where they join together to agree on a fee schedule or the equivalent. Their adherence to the schedule may vary; yet there is an affinity between a doctor agreeing with his colleagues on what their services are worth and a local union of electricians negotiating their hourly rate. It is hard to justify the view that one group is participating in collective bargaining while the other is not. Again, however, one runs into data limitations when attempting to ascertain how much independent practitioners would add to the proportion of the labour force covered by collective bargaining.

Even if all these groups were totalled, it is unlikely that they would surpass 45 or 50 per cent of the non-agricultural work force. There will doubtless always remain large numbers of workers not covered by collective bargaining. This is the situation in virtually all countries where there is a free labour movement. In the exceptional case of Sweden, a high proportion of the labour force is covered by collective bargaining. In most other countries, however, the proportion is much closer to that prevailing in Canada.

Labour Standards Legislation[5]

Labour standards have been designed for a number of purposes and have performed with varying degrees of effectiveness. They range from general minimum wage programs to special protective measures aimed at hazardous employment practices in particular occupations. We limit our attention for the most part to wage and hour standards, since these are the areas where such programs are most prone to impinge on the results of collective bargaining. . . .

Wage and hour standards are usually designed to serve one or more of three basic purposes. First, they may be designed as part of an anti-poverty program to ensure workers a minimum standard of living without being exploited by having to work unduly long hours. This was probably the main purpose of most early wages and hours legislation. This purpose was later combined with that of eliminating "unfair" competition if only to garner employer support for the legislation. Lately a new and more sophisticated purpose has been added. The pressure of higher standards can be used to improve productivity and the rate of growth by forcing marginal employers to use their labour forces more efficiently or go out of business. In the latter event, the result could be unemployment in the absence of com-

---

[5]See Gérard Hébert, S. J., "Labour Standards Legislation", H. Carl Goldenberg and John H. G. Crispo (eds.), *Construction Labour Relations*, (Ottawa, Canadian Construction Association 1968), pp. 230-303; and Mamhood A. Zaidi, *A Study of the Effects of the $1.25 Minimum Wage Under the Canada Labour (Standards) Code, Impact of Minimum Wage and Industrial Standards Legislation*, Task Force Study.

plementary fiscal, monetary and manpower programs to facilitate the movement of displaced labour into other more productive undertakings.

The mixture of objectives which underlies standards programs in Canada is reflected in the variety of approaches within and between the different jurisdictions. Most jurisdictions now have a variable or general minimum wage program that is presumably intended to provide a basic minimum standard of living. But none of the general minimum wage standards and few of the variable ones meet the minimum family budget needs suggested by recognized social welfare agencies. Failing this objective, a more modest purpose of such legislation might be described as the prevention of severe exploitation. If an acceptable minimum standard were the goal, there would be something akin to an escalator clause built into the program to keep the minimum increasing at least in line with the cost of living. Yet no such feature is present in any of the general minimum wage legislation, whether comprehensive or variable in its application.

An objective beyond the maintenance of a bare minimum standard is inherent in the industrial standards programs of most provinces and the collective agreement decree system in Quebec. In both systems the purpose clearly includes the protection of employers paying something approaching union rates. Under the industrial standards programs in the provinces, rates are publicly set for an industry upon the request of and after consultation with employers and unions affected, and are then enforced with varying degrees of rigour by government inspectors. In addition, under the decree system in Quebec the role of the private parties is greater in determining the standards and in policing the system. Under each decree there is established a parity committee, composed of the interested parties, which can levy a payroll tax against both workers and employers to provide a fund with which to employ auditors and inspectors to enforce the rates and other conditions specified in the decree. As a result, under the Montreal construction decree system alone there are more auditors and inspectors in the field than there are employed for the entire standards program in most of the other provinces. The parity system leads to comparatively higher standards that are relatively better enforced than in most other jurisdictions. It also has a number of desirable indirect effects, especially in the construction industry where subcommittees of the parity committees are doing effective work in everything from apprenticeship and safety to the settlement of jurisdictional disputes.

The Results of the System[6]

The results of the Canadian industrial relations system take various forms, depending on the processes of interaction from which they flow. Primary attention in this Report is devoted to the operation of the collective bargain-

[6]See S. Jamieson, *Toil and Trouble: Labour Unrest and Industrial Conflict in Canada, 1900-1966,* Task Force Study; and John Vanderkamp, *The Time Pattern of Industrial Conflict in Canada, 1901-1966,* Task Force Study.

ing process and to the outcome in the form of terms and conditions of employment, obtained with or without a work stoppage, and in the form of such stoppages themselves. Rarely does a strike or lockout end in an unresolvable impasse.

Unions may be looked upon as power centres concerned with advancing the welfare of their members. The basic objective of unions in industry is improved working conditions of those they represent. The principal method is collective bargaining with employers. Union power in the extreme is manifested through the concerted withdrawal of labour from the employer—the strike. Management's equivalent is its capacity to withstand a strike and to lock out its employees. But the power of both sides, and especially the union, is felt in the bargaining process even without a work stoppage. The fact that a strike or a lockout is a possibility induces unions and management to try to reach agreement. The cost of settlement is set against the calculated cost of a work stoppage. . . . As expensive as they may seem, [work stoppages] play an indispensable part in the present collective bargaining process. The threat of a stoppage or an actual stoppage may be needed to induce the parties to narrow and eventually resolve their differences.

Whatever may be the verdict of those who judge the behaviour of the parties, and particularly unions, the logic of their behaviour is clear. On the union side, the power to negotiate effectively derives from the power to inflict economic damage on the employer and those who are allied with him. Few unions strike frequently, many strike infrequently, and some rarely. Yet the right to do so, and the possession of the organization and support to do so, are of prime importance in the bargaining relationship.

Terms and conditions of employment produced by collective agreements are of interest from many points of view. Their costs are of concern because of their potential impact on inflation and on the reconciliation of various national economic goals. . . .

The Internal Interdependence of the System

There is a flow of influences throughout the Canadian industrial relations system . . . starting, basically, with a host of environmental features which play upon the parties of interest and their various processes of interaction. The results feed back into the system at many points, so as to lead to further accommodation. Adjustments at any one point lead to additional adjustments elsewhere; there is constant change. Any tampering with the system must be based on an appreciation of the implications of such adjustments, not merely at the point of impact but everywhere in the system.

51 Labour Market Policy*

Economic Council of Canada

High employment can be sustained without rising prices and a deterioration of the nation's balance of payments only if there is efficient use of manpower resources. This concept has become widely recognized throughout the western world in recent years. It is for this reason that increasing attention has been focused on the development of labour market policies by European countries, and more recently by the United States. No country can achieve maximum efficient utilization of manpower resources without effective labour market policy.

Both the theory and practice of labour market policy are, generally speaking, a post-war development. Labour market policy is concerned with facilitating fuller and more efficient use of manpower. It has acquired increasing importance in many countries with the growing realization that it is crucial to the attainment of national economic goals.

The term "active and positive labour market policy" has recently come into circulation. This concept of labour market policy, which has been developed in practice to its highest degree in many European countries, implies that it must have the status of an important national economic policy *integrated* with general fiscal and monetary policy. Its objectives, like those of the latter, are the same: to promote not only full employment, important as this is, but other national economic goals as well. Labour market policies can contribute to these objectives to the extent that they can influence efficient use of manpower resources. They are a necessary and vital complement to fiscal and monetary policy.

The central purpose of this section is to examine Canada's present labour market policy and to consider what improvements are required in this area to help promote our broad economic objectives.

Object of Labour Market Policy

The object of labour market policy, as we conceive it, is to bring about the matching of the supply and the demand for labour in specific localities and occupations in a way that manpower resources can be most productively utilized. It has as its purpose both the achievement of high employment and the utilization of the labour force at its maximum productive potential. Workers who are employed at less than their productive potential, whether it is because of problems associated with lack of occupational, industrial or geographical mobility, earn less than they are potentially capable of earning. They contribute less to national productivity than they are potentially

---

*From: *First Annual Review: Economic Goals for Canada to 1970,* Ottawa, Queen's Printer, (1964) , pp. 170-73, (reprinted by permission) .

capable of contributing. There is thus an important loss of goods and services to the country as a whole. The national economic loss from inefficient use of manpower resources can be just as great as the economic loss arising from unemployment. Equally important, when there is a mismatching of the supply of and the demand for labour in an economy operating at a high level of demand, inflationary pressures inevitably arise.

The removal of obstacles to desirable labour mobility is a chief function of labour market policy. For example, effective labour mobility is indispensable to minimizing the duration of unemployment when workers are displaced from their jobs. Shortening the duration period of unemployment can contribute significantly to economic growth and stability by increasing the supply of labour needed to match demand. Inadequate labour mobility, by impeding the flow of labour at a time of high demand, results in shortages and bottlenecks which produce upward pressures on production costs.

In an economy affected by change, some industries will be contracting while others are expanding. As so often happens in the case of contracting industries, they may seriously affect over-all employment in the geographical area in which they are located. Consequently, a declining industry and a depressed locality often go hand in hand. Under these circumstances, a breakdown in labour mobility may not only prolong problems of the locality, but may also result in expanding industries elsewhere being deprived of needed manpower. There is thus a two-fold adverse effect on the national economy: the growth of the national product is retarded by unused manpower resources bottled up in a depressed industry or locality; and, at the same time, inflationary pressures may be created as a result of labour shortages in expanding industries or localities. Rigidities of this nature act as a deterrent to growth and handicap a country's competitive ability and its balance of payments position. Furthermore, since idle manpower must also be supported, this imposes an additional cost on the nation as a whole.

There are three major kinds of labour mobility: occupational, industrial and geographical. An unemployed worker may face the need to undergo one, or two, or all three. In some cases, a worker may become displaced because his skill has become obsolete, and cannot be transferred elsewhere. To be re-absorbed into the labour market, he will have to acquire a new skill. This means re-training. In other cases, a displaced worker may be the victim of a declining industry. To become re-employed he will have to go to another industry. This may or may not require his learning a new skill, depending on whether or not his present skill is transferable. If he lives in a community where there are no alternatives, he will have no choice but to move to a new locality if he is to find employment.

The importance of labour mobility has increased in recent years, largely as a result of an acceleration in technological change and a more closely interdependent international economy. Occupational skills can be quickly wiped out through a new technical process. Whole industries can be sent into decline, either from technological advancements, from increasing import competition, or from changes in consumer demand. The day is probably gone when a new entrant into the labour force could reasonably expect to make one skill last throughout his working life, or, perhaps, to stay permanently in the same occupation, industry or locality.

With labour mobility having such critical importance to the viability of the economy, it cannot be dismissed as the sole responsibility of the individual. Nor can any local community be expected to assume the entire financial burden of providing training and re-training of its displaced workers when such workers, after training or re-training, may have to move elsewhere for re-employment. The dimensions of the problems associated with mobility are such that they can be dealt with adequately only with the assistance of appropriate public policy. An integrated programme to facilitate all forms of mobility is necessary if economic inflexibilities are not to thwart the achievement of national economic goals.

There is little point in re-training a worker for a job that exists outside of his locality if he lacks the financial resources to move himself and his family. Likewise, there is no point in a worker moving to a new area if he is uninformed about the labour market in that area, or is technically unequipped to take advantage of existing job opportunities once he gets there. Effective mobility cannot be promoted in this piecemeal fashion. It can only be promoted by the development of an integrated programme of labour market services. Nor can effective labour mobility be promoted if functions and responsibilities under labour market policy are dispersed among various agencies, whose activities are not properly co-ordinated.

52   The Problem of Low Incomes*

Economic Council of Canada

Sources of Income

The principal source of income for most families, including low-income families, is earnings in the form of wages, salaries and income from self-employment. Any factors that adversely affect the market value of labour services, or which prevent the services from being offered, may result in income falling below poverty lines. Among the more notable factors of this kind are lack of job skills (often associated with low levels of formal education), old age, disablement, ill health, and participation in low-paying occupations. The necessity of caring for young children may also

*From: *Fifth Annual Review: The Challenge of Growth and Change*, Ottawa, Queen's Printer (1968), pp. 114-16, 133-35 (reprinted by permission).

prevent labour services from being offered. A small percentage of families are able to offset deficient labour income with returns from wealth holdings. But most must rely on some form of government transfer payment, such as pensions, unemployment insurance, or family allowances; hence the higher degree of reliance on such payments among low-income families, who, as a group, received 27 per cent of their income from this source in 1961, compared with a figure of 8 per cent for all families.

Where a low-income family is for one reason or another incapable of offering labour services, and is therefore largely dependent on government payments, the policy problem of how to aid that family is in one sense relatively simple: the major issue is the size of the income to be provided. But where there are earnings, but on an insufficient scale, or where there is an unexploited potential for earnings, the policy choices are less simple. Other things being equal, it is far better to help people to help themselves —to put them in a position to upgrade their earnings permanently through such measures as training and manpower mobility programs, and to exploit unused earnings potential (provided this does not involve a sacrifice of future to present earnings, as in the case of the youth who drops out of high school to augment family income). But self-help takes time, and meanwhile income support in the form of government payments may be needed. It seems a fair generalization that in the past Canadian social policy has tended to emphasize various forms of income maintenance, and has only recently moved strongly into the more difficult area of promoting self-help among low-income people.

Low Income Occupations

Where the head of a family is in the labour force, his chances of having a low income are very much greater in certain occupations than in others. This statement is a well-worn commonplace, but the extent of the differences revealed in Table 1 is nevertheless striking. The incidence of low incomes in 1961 was more than twice the over-all average in four occupational groups: farm workers; loggers and related workers; fishermen, trappers and hunters; and labourers.

Once again, it is necessary to draw a careful distinction between incidence and total numbers, and to note that the four occupations named accounted for only 22 per cent of all the low-income family heads in the Table. Nevertheless, it is worth remarking that the four occupations tend to be characterized by much seasonality and other irregularity of employment and earnings. This cross-checks with other information suggesting that, across the whole occupational spectrum, insufficiency of wage and salary earnings is often associated with intermittent and part-time work.

The Spectrum of Existing Policies

A Canadian attack on poverty does not of course start from scratch. Canada already has in operation, or on the statute books scheduled for implementa-

Table 1

Occupational Distribution of Male Nonfarm Family Heads, 1961

	(1) Number of Nonfarm Family Heads		(2)	(3) Incidence of Low Income
	Total (000)		Low Income (000)	(2) as a percentage of (1)
Managerial*	419		42	10
Professional and technical	256		12	5
Clerical	200		21	11
Sales	182		24	13
Service and recreation	246		50	20
Transport and communications	256		61	24
Farm workers**	34		19	56
Loggers and related workers	35		20	57
Fishermen, trappers, hunters	20		14	70
Miners, quarrymen, related workers	44		8	18
Craftsmen, production process and related workers	991		183	19
Labourers	149		60	40
Not stated	39		10	26
Total of male nonfarm family heads in current labour force	2,871		524	18

*Includes self-employed, as do other occupational classifications.
**Includes farm *workers* not living on farms.
SOURCE: Based on data from Dominion Bureau of Statistics.

tion within the relatively near future, an impressive inventory of social legislation. There are important Canadian policies in all four of the major categories of anti-poverty programs mentioned in our brief survey of the U.S. war on poverty: manpower programs, individual improvement programs, community betterment programs, and income maintenance programs. In some areas, particularly income maintenance, the coverage of Canadian programs is superior to that of their U.S. counterparts.

It should be noted also that the comprehensiveness of this inventory has been significantly improved in recent years. Under the Canada Assistance Plan, for example, provinces may at their option combine four previously separated federal-provincial assistance programs (for the aged, the blind, the disabled, and the unemployed) into a single program. Assistance is based on a more comprehensive and flexible assessment of recipients' budgetary needs, and federal cost-sharing is extended for the first time to aid to needy mothers and their dependent children. In general, the Plan sets out to close previous gaps in the social security system. Some of its features are rehabilitative and preventive in character, designed to help people by their own efforts to rise and remain above poverty.

A selection of other relatively recent additions to the stock of social legislation and social policies would include the monthly guaranteed income supplement to certain Old Age Security pensions, major developments in manpower policy by both federal and provincial governments, and new training and other manpower initiatives sponsored by municipal governments and voluntary agencies.

But while the inventory is impressive, the means immediately available for assessing its impact on Canadians are not. Apart from a few illustrious exceptions, remarkably little has been done by way of systematic evaluation of these policies in operation, either separately or in combination.

One of the great uncertainties is the extent to which the existing structure of policies in fact constitutes an attack on poverty—the extent, that is, to which its benefits flow to those most in need. This uncertainty comes very much to the fore when proposals are made for major new anti-poverty measures such as the negative income tax or other income guarantees.[1] We do not wish to pass judgment one way or another on such proposals at the present time; we confine ourselves to noting that their adoption has been advocated by a number of distinguished figures, and to recommending that the possibility of their usefulness for Canada be subjected to serious and thorough study. But such a study must embrace, among other things, an examination of the costs and anti-poverty effects of a considerable range of existing policies which income guarantees would to some extent replace and to some extent supplement. Only in this way will it be possible to form a proper judgment as to whether some type of broader income guarantee might usefully be added to the Canadian armoury of weapons against poverty.

It will be clear that we have not ourselves been able to conduct at this stage a thorough and searching examination of the existing structure of Canadian social policies. Some very limited and preliminary enquiry has suggested, however, that both the coverage and efficacy of many parts of

---

[1]Various forms of guaranteed minimum income have been proposed by different writers. The simplest form would be a minimum income grant paid by the government to all, regardless of means; if it were subject to income tax, part of it would be recouped in this fashion. Other forms of guarantee have been proposed that would operate more directly through the existing tax system. Under one form of "negative income tax", an official minimum income level would be established; all family heads and nonfamily individuals would be required to complete income tax returns; and where actual income fell below the official minimum, a "negative tax payment" by the government would make up the difference. Under another form, the payment would consist of "unused" income tax exemptions by those with incomes too low to be subject to tax. Many negative income tax proposals incorporate graduated incentives for recipients to seek work. The Guaranteed Income Supplement now payable to certain old age security pensioners is a type of negative income tax.

the structure leave much to be desired. Objectives are not always clearly defined, or have not been redefined in the light of changing circumstances. It is difficult, for example, to discover an authoritative statement of the fundamental objectives of the Family Allowances program in the circumstances of 1968. This is not to say that Family Allowances and other long-established programs are not continuing to serve some highly useful purposes but these purposes should surely be re-examined in the light of the many important economic and social changes that have occurred over the last generation.

In some areas of policy, there appears to be an undue bias towards the mere alleviation rather than the eradication and prevention of poverty. Lack of co-ordination, not only between but within levels of government, is often apparent. In some places there is overlapping; in others, gaps. Objectives of policies and success in achieving objectives are rarely subjected to regular review. Often the data that would be required to do this are lacking. There is fairly strong evidence in some areas of high administrative overheads and inefficiencies.

The above must of course be regarded as a very limited and tentative assessment. Its main significance is that it appears enough to indicate the desirability of a much more thoroughgoing appraisal.

SUGGESTIONS FOR FURTHER READING

Forsey, E., "History of the Labour Movement in Canada," special article in Dominion Bureau of Statistics, *Canada Year Book* (Ottawa, Queen's Printer, 1967), pp. 773-781.

Hamilton, D., *A Primer on the Economics of Poverty*, New York, Random House Inc., 1968.

Kovacs, A. E., (ed.), *Readings in Canadian Labour Economics*, Toronto, McGraw-Hill Co. of Canada Ltd., 1961.

Meltz, N. M. and A. Kruger, (eds.), *The Canadian Labour Market*, Toronto, University of Toronto Centre for Industrial Relations, 1968.

Schlesinger, B., (ed.), *Poverty in Canada and the United States: Overview and Annotated Bibliography*, Toronto, University of Toronto Press, 1966.

Woods, H. and S. Ostry, *Labour Policy and Labour Economics in Canada*, Toronto, Macmillan Co. of Canada Ltd., 1962.

PART TEN

Consumer Protection Policies

INTRODUCTION

The satisfaction of consumer wants is widely held to be the ultimate purpose of all economic activity. Consequently all policies that affect the use made of our available resources will have some effect on the consumer's welfare. Indeed, as we saw in Section One, it may be argued that the economic case for preferring a free-market, private-enterprise system of economic organization is that this system will prove superior to the known alternatives as a device for ensuring that our resources of all kinds will be used to produce the things consumers most want, in the desired relative quantities, and with optimum efficiency. And, as we saw in earlier selections in Section Two, the principal guarantee of such performance is the force of competition. It is competition that, in the theoretical argument for this system, ensures that the interests of consumers, not producers, will be served. It is competition that is supposed to ensure the "sovereignty" of the consumer. To the extent that competition is not present in the real world markets, the various government policies described in parts 4 and 5 are introduced. At the same time, as we have also seen, some policies are used to over-ride the forces of competition in order to promote goals other than economic efficiency, although many unintentionally have the same effect.

How very difficult it is to reconcile regulation and other forms of non-market decision-making with the objective of preserving the logic of a market-controlled system will by now have become apparent.

When markets are imperfect and cannot perform "satisfactorily," or when we believe that we can or should improve upon the market's performance, we substitute policies of regulation and public decision-making for them. But is it possible to assess fully the ultimate effect of these policies on consumer welfare? Just as there are no operative measures that we can use to assess the economic costs of monopoly to society, there are no measures that we can use to assess the social costs or benefits of public policies which, for better or worse, influence the efficiency with which we use our resources. Indeed, economists cannot often agree, even at a theoretical level, on the direction, let alone the magnitude, of many of these effects. Perhaps this helps to explain the ambiguity of some of our public policies toward markets. Even more disturbing is the fact that in the real world, when we do think that we know what the economic effects of a policy will be, we may find that they are perverse. And this brings us to the subject of this concluding part in Section Three.

If, because of imperfections in markets, consumers' interests are demonstrably harmed, it would seem that policies to correct this should be implemented. If consumers, for example, are led by false advertising or by other deceptive selling practices to spend their income on things they do not want, the satisfaction they derive from their income is not maximized. Therefore, some regulation of selling practices would seem to be warranted. To take another example, if the quality of a product being sold can only be appraised by experts, ordinary consumers are likely to be deceived. Consider medical care. Only medical doctors know enough about medicine to assess the quality of the work done by physicians on their patients. And probably only an ophthalmologist can evaluate the performance of another ophthalmologist. The ordinary consumer is unable to make such assessments. Short of trying to make medical experts of us all, the appropriate public policy would seem to be to regulate the practice of medicine in such a way that sub-standard or dangerous medical care would simply not be available to the consumer. In other instances, an even more severe kind of regulation is imposed. That is, when the community decides that a good or service is entirely harmful its production and sale may be made illegal to prevent its reaching the consumer.

Thus, there seem to be strong common-sense reasons to have specific policies to protect the interests of consumers. A wide range of these policies currently in effect in Canada will be found described in *Reading 53*. But despite the apparent strength of the arguments for policies like these, it is impossible to assess their ultimate economic benefits and cost to consumers. One reason for this is that many of them, like the policies considered in Part 6, have the effect of lessening competition and creating monopoly situations. Often licensing, for example, discussed in *Reading 54*, seems deliberately to eliminate competition, as in the case of municipal taxi-cab licensing. And sometimes, as in the case of the professions, regulation confers upon professional bodies the power to set the prices consumers have to pay for their services. Paradoxically, in the case of the prohibited occupations and products, the inevitable black markets that arise tend to take on a monopolistic structure organized by professional criminals, as will be seen from *Reading 55*.

What general conclusions the reader will draw from the outline of government policies of intervention in the functioning of a supposedly free-market economy provided in sections Two and Three must be left open. The general impression created by any such catalogue, however selected, must be one of confusion and some inconsistency. Clearly-defined policy positions are conspicuously absent. As we have seen, there is not even a clear commitment to "competition" as the preferred means of regulating economic life in our society, all supposedly authoritative statements to the contrary notwithstanding. Perhaps it is just this ambiguity of policy that has made so much public regulation politically acceptable in what is so often called a "free market" economy. For this, and possibly other reasons, it may not be desirable or necessary to try to "rationalize" this immense body of specific policies to make it part of an integrated, ordered system. Or is there a trend toward such a rationalization of policy within some kind of "planning" framework? This is one of the questions that will be considered in Section Four.

53 Present Federal Government Activities in the Consumer Field*

Economic Council of Canada

The purpose of this Chapter is to outline briefly the present extent of the major federal government policies and programmes which are most directly concerned with consumer affairs. The main objective of these measures, which are fairly considerable in number, is to set out certain basic requirements which consumers can normally expect to be observed when they shop for and use goods and services.

Before proceeding to examine these matters, it is necessary to emphasize one point in particular. All of these federal government activities have evolved in the light of the division of legislative responsibilities under the Canadian constitution. In some cases, such as weights and measures, the British North America Act has assigned specific responsibility to the federal Parliament. In other cases the activities arise from the more general federal responsibility for criminal law. A leading example here is the Food and Drugs Act. Still others have developed under federal responsibilities for

---

*From: *Interim Report,* Consumer Affairs and The Department of the Registrar General, July 1967, Ottawa, Queen's Printer (1967), pp. 10-18 (reprinted by permission).

regulating trade and commerce of an interprovincial or international character. Typically, these activities must take account of provincial legislation affecting intraprovincial trade in the same product areas. In addition, there is an important area of concurrent jurisdiction, the field of agriculture, in which both federal and provincial legislatures may make laws of major significance to consumers.

There are also many areas of concern to consumers which come entirely within the constitutional responsibilities of the individual provinces, especially those which are closely related to property and civil rights. These include the nature of contractual relationships between buyers and sellers, the regulation of many forms of commerce conducted on a purely local or provincial basis, and the incorporation of companies with provincial objects. Finally, the provinces have delegated to municipalities responsibility for a variety of laws affecting consumer interests.

Thus under the Canadian constitution no single level of government has jurisdiction over all the matters in which consumers are interested. Each level of government undertakes a number of activities affecting consumers, and the degree of protection afforded any individual Canadian can and does vary significantly from one location to another within the country. It is clear that a satisfactory over-all approach to this important area of public policy can only be fully developed through effective co-ordination and co-operation among the federal, provincial and municipal authorities concerned. We will return to this vital matter again later in this report. In this Chapter, we are concerned essentially with those activities over which the federal government exercises jurisdiction under the present distribution of responsibilities.

There are, however, some important areas of interest to consumers where the federal government has responsibilities but which do not fall within the scope of this Chapter. For example, we do not attempt to deal with such matters as policies affecting over-all levels of economic activity, matters relating to combines, the regulation of rates in transportation and communications. Rather, the policies and programmes which concern us here are those whose principal objective is to influence the framework for normal day-to-day relationships between business and consumers. These various functions and responsibilities are based on a wide range of legislation. They have developed over several decades and are scattered almost haphazardly through a large number of government departments and agencies. In many cases they have emerged as the result of the preoccupations and efforts of these departments. The present distribution of policies and programmes thus inevitably reflects the lack of a co-ordinated approach to consumer affairs in the past. The functions of certain departments overlap to a significant extent, and some programmes may attempt to fulfil several purposes, not all of which are directly related to consumer interests as such.

In the circumstances, it is not surprising that there are no simple and clear-cut categories into which all these programmes and policies will fall.

Nevertheless, taking the consumer's point of view, it appears that they attempt to serve one or more of the following objectives:

(a) protection against fraud and deception;

(b) protection against hazards to health and safety;

(c) promoting the development of suitable quality standards and grades;

(d) providing information of assistance to consumers.

For families to whom every penny counts, these measures are obviously of very immediate concern. Indeed, the efficiency with which they are carried out will have a direct bearing on consumer confidence in the operations of our market economy.

The existing distribution of a number of federal government activities affecting consumers is illustrated in Chart 1. . . . What follows in this Chapter is of necessity a highly condensed summary of this activity.

Protection Against Fraud and Deception

One key piece of federal legislation is the group of general criminal code provisions against fraud, deception and misleading sales techniques. For the most part, enforcement of these laws has been left to provincial governments, but a number of federal agencies do have responsibilities for enforcement activities based on criminal law. For example, there are prohibitions against fraud and deception in the food and drug legislation administered by the Department of National Health and Welfare. The Combines Investigation Act contains a section directed against misleading price advertising. The Royal Canadian Mounted Police is actively concerned with the suppression of counterfeit money, and the Post Office engages in a number of activities to prevent the use of the mail for criminal purposes.

In addition, under the constitution, the Standards Branch of the Department of Trade and Commerce has a particular responsibility for ensuring the accuracy of weights and measures used in commerce. The Broadcasting Act provides that the Board of Broadcast Governors may make regulations respecting the character of advertising on radio and television. Under federal responsibilities for trade and commerce, the Departments of Agriculture and Fisheries also attempt to prevent the use of deceptive descriptions of the quality of a variety of food products. Similar provisions exist in regard to the sale of certain other specified commodities and services. However, no single federal agency is regularly concerned with assessing and ensuring the over-all adequacy of enforcement activities to prevent fraud and deception. There seem to be some areas in which enforcement is virtually non-existent.

Protection of Health and Safety

A number of measures have been adopted to protect the health and safety of consumers. This is a major concern of inspection and regulatory activities

Chart 1

Existing Distribution of

Federal Government Activities

Affecting Consumers

PROTECTION AGAINST FRAUD AND DECEPTION

Justice   Finance
Combines Investigation Branch   Insurance
Food and Drug Directorate   Registrar General
Agriculture   Board of Broadcast Governors
Fisheries   Trade and Commerce
Post Office   (Standards Branch)
CMHC

PROTECTION OF HEALTH AND SAFETY

Food and Drug Directorate   CMHC
Agriculture   Atomic Energy Control Board
Fisheries   Transport

ESTABLISHING PRODUCT STANDARDS AND
GRADES

Food and Drug Directorate   Trade and Commerce
Agriculture   (Standards Branch)
Fisheries   CMHC
Industry   NRC

PROVIDING CONSUMER INFORMATION

Agriculture   CMHC
Food and Drug Directorate   Board of Broadcast Governors
Fisheries   Dominion Bureau of Statistics
Finance   Trade and Commerce
Insurance   (Standards Branch)

carried on by the Food and Drug Directorate and the Departments of Agriculture and Fisheries. The Department of Transport and its various agencies have responsibilities relating to the safety of air, rail and marine transportation services. Some activities, such as the sale of narcotics and prescription drugs, are regulated in great detail. In other areas, enforcement is focused on setting minimum safety standards which have to be observed. This is a very complex field in which a high degree of technical competence is essential for effective administration. At the same time, although considerable effort has been made to achieve close working relationships among agencies with overlapping responsibilities, divided jurisdiction can and does create difficulties in administration. For example, there seem to be significant gaps in the retail inspection of meats. In addition, there are some areas, such as automobile safety, in which no federal department has had clear responsibility for investigating whether there is need to revise existing policies.

Establishing Product Standards and Grades

Several departments have been concerned with promoting the development and use of widely accepted standards and grades to indicate product quality and safety. Apart from the few instances where standards have been imposed as the necessary part of regulatory activities, most have been developed with the active co-operation of representatives of the producers concerned. Occasionally they have involved active consultations with consumers and users as well. The most important agencies in this field have been the Food and Drug Directorate, the Departments of Agriculture and Fisheries, and the Standards Branch of the Department of Trade and Commerce through its activities under the National Trade Mark and True Labelling Act. There are also the important provisions of the National Building Code developed by the National Research Council in co-operation with the Central Mortgage and Housing Corporation and other interested bodies, as well as the incidental consumer benefits derived through the operations of the Canadian Government Specifications Board in setting standards applicable to purchases by the federal government for its own use. These programmes supplement many private activities of a similar nature, such as those of the Canadian Standards Association.

The use of standards and grades is not applicable in every area of interest to consumers. But there are a number of areas where standards and grades can and do act to provide buyers with an objective source of useful information and guidance. They also serve as a means by which responsible members of an industry may move to prevent the sale of products of an unacceptable or dangerous quality.

In the future the development of standards work in Canada will also be influenced to an increasing extent by the trend towards the wider use of standards and grades in many areas of international trade in which this country has a vital interest. We understand that the Government is currently giving intensive study to its policies and programmes in the field of standards and grades. One of the possibilities which has been mentioned is the establishment of a new widely representative body at the national level to develop a more co-ordinated approach to standards work on a voluntary basis. We would commend such a development. Standards work should not be left to government alone; there should be active participation by both producer and user groups if the future development of standards is to be fully effective and able to meet changing needs over time.

Providing Consumer Information

Many government departments have policies and programmes designed to provide information of assistance to consumers. In part this is done through labeling requirements which stipulate the information that must be shown on packages or containers. Moreover, the consumer service branches operated by a number of agencies, including particularly the Food and Drug Directorate and to a more limited extent the Departments of Agriculture and Fisheries, provide information helpful to consumers. In addition, some financial support has been provided for the work of the Consumers' Association of Canada. Recently the Department of National Health and Welfare has begun to provide support for studies and experimental programmes in the field of credit counselling services for low-income families. Requirements also exist for business firms to make public certain information regarding their operations. However, the present consumer information services are not conducted on a co-ordinated basis, and there does not seem to be an over-all policy in this area. Also, some agencies such as the Dominion Bureau of Statistics provide information intended mainly for other purposes which is also of great potential value to consumers, but frequently more could be done to put it into a form which meets consumer needs.

Protection in Financial Transactions

The consumer is also afforded some protection in his financial dealings, including borrowing, saving, insuring and investing, with institutions coming within federal jurisdiction. Among other purposes, legislation in this area serves to provide for inspection and regulation to ensure minimum standards of performance, for measures to prevent fraudulent activities by unscrupulous operators, and to encourage the dissemination of reliable information to assist the public to make informed decisions regarding their financial transactions.

* * *

Our survey of these current activities has left us with two main impressions. The first is that many of these programmes have arisen as *ad hoc* reactions to periodic crises or pressures in particular problem areas. Consumer protection programmes are generally carried on in departments whose primary concern is with other matters, and in some cases they have not always been given adequate attention. In certain instances, lack of staff appears to have hampered enforcement. We have been very much impressed, for example, by the rapid expansion in the staff of the Food and Drug Directorate which occurred *after* the thalidomide incident. Although their scope is very wide, the existing responsibilities are widely diffused and are not the result of a coherent over-all plan. There has in fact been no single part of government which has had specific responsibility for the essential task of providing a continuing review and assessment of the total package of policies and programmes relating to consumer affairs.

Our second impression is that there has been no effective means for ensuring efficient co-ordination of the administration of these programmes. Those who bear responsibility for their administration seem to be engaged in an uneven battle against the problems of duplication and gap-closing. In the present maze, there is a great risk of making an unwarranted, but understandable, assumption that "somebody else" is taking responsibility for a specific matter. At the same time, a number of different departments may be drawn more or less independently into closely related activities which would seem more suited to administration on a co-ordinated basis.

Two specific examples illustrate the present lack of co-ordination:

(a) Not only are existing responsibilities scattered widely among different departments and agencies, but published information about them is generally sparse. Indeed, it frequently requires a very considerable research effort even to find the precise location of existing responsibilities. As a consequence, both consumers and businessmen are frequently puzzled about where they should go with complaints and requests for information and guidance. When their inquiries are misdirected, replies may be inadequate or at least needlessly delayed. There is a pressing need to improve the channels of communication between the government and the public regarding programmes in this area.

(b) A number of policies require retail inspection services for effective administration. For some time, at least three agencies have been concerned with making periodic visits to retail food stores for the purposes of their own programmes: the Food and Drug Directorate, the Standards Branch of the Department of Trade and Commerce, and the Department of Agriculture. The latter department in particular has a very extensive programme involving regular inspection of agricultural products in stores in large urban centres which account for roughly 65 per cent of total retail food sales. Recently, the Department of Fisheries initiated a retail inspection service in Montreal and is considering extending it to other cities. The present organization of retail inspection services raises the distinct possibility of unnecessary duplication, and it would appear that these services could be carried on more efficiently by co-ordinating them within a single inspection service. Where feasible, individual inspectors could be trained to perform a larger number of functions during the course of their visits to retail establishments.

The present organization of federal government programmes and responsibilities inevitably gives rise to considerable confusion and frustration for consumers, businessmen and government officials alike. It also raises the possibility of serious gaps developing in essential programmes. It is a tribute to the dedication of the government officials concerned that they have made these programmes operate as effectively as they have. Certainly there have been few complaints regarding the competence of the public servants involved—rather the complaints have concerned the organizational labyrinth in which these public servants must work. Clearly changes are necessary to improve the co-ordination and efficiency of administration of the laws which are now on the books, if the public is to be assured that this legislation is adequately fulfilling the objectives for which it is intended. There is also a need for continuing research to detect and deal with emerging problems before they reach crisis proportions.

54   Licensing Powers*

Royal Commission Inquiry into Civil Rights

The Personal and Public Interests Involved

As a general principle that which is not prohibited is, in the eyes of the law, permitted. There is a personal and public interest that the law should not unnecessarily fetter the individual's basic right to engage in any lawful means of earning a livelihood that he sees fit and to develop whatever talents he may have to this end. This principle bears on both the basic legislative decision to license and on the standards which should be imposed to implement the licensing power.

It is not our function to consider competing economic values or principles. However, the interest of the individual and the public interest may suffer if licensing requirements are unnecessarily imposed or unreasonable standards are required in their implementation. Generally, there is still a basic truth expressed in the judgment of Harrison, C. J. in *Regina v. Johnston*:

> "The great law governing the conduct of man in serving his fellowmen is the law of competition. The less that law is interfered with the better for the general interest of society."[1]

---

*From: *Report No. 1*, Toronto, Queen's Printer, Vol. III, (1968), pp. 1096-1114 (reprinted by permission).
[1] (1876), 38 U.C.Q.B. 549-552.

This philosophy has received legislative recognition in the Municipal Act, which provides, subject to certain expressed exceptions, that ". . . a council shall not confer on any person the exclusive right of exercising within the municipality any trade or calling or business . . . unless authorized or required by this or any other Act so to do. . . ."[2]

The power to suspend or revoke a licence is more far-reaching than the power to license. It involves not only the right of the individual to engage in the activity of his choice, but it may affect a substantial investment in time and money in the building up of the licensed business, together with goodwill attached to it. When proceedings are commenced to revoke, or to some lesser extent, to suspend a licence, all this must be taken into account. It should likewise be considered in the framing of standards to be met for the procedure to be followed before a revocation or suspension order is made.

LEGISLATIVE DEFINITION OF THE PURPOSES OF LICENSING

In the statutes of Ontario there is a wide variation in the legislative definitions of the purposes of licensing schemes.

The British North America Act[3] confers legislative power on the provinces with respect to "shop, saloon, tavern, auctioneer, and other licences in order to the raising of a revenue for provincial, local, or municipal purposes." The raising of revenue is only one of the many purposes of imposing licensing requirements. Licences are often required for the purpose of: facilitating the collection of revenue,[4] enforcing minimum standards of competence;[5] protecting the public health;[6] ensuring a minimum level of competence in certain trades serving the public, e.g., electricians;[7] protecting natural resources;[8] regulating various aspects of the provincial economy, e.g., the schemes provided for by the Farm Products Marketing Act[9] and the Milk Act;[10] or a licence may be required for several combined purposes, e.g., collection of revenue, having a record of the names of persons enjoying a privilege, and public safety, e.g., the operation of motor vehicles on public highways.[11]

---

[2]R.S.O. 1960, c. 249, s. 248 (1).

[3]B.N.A. Act, s. 92, para. 9.

[4]Retail Sales Tax Act, Ont. 1960-61, c. 91.

[5]Highway Traffic Act, R.S.O. 1960, c. 172.

[6]Air Pollution Control Act, R.S.O. 1960, c. 12, superseded by the Air Pollution Control Act, 1967, Ont. 1967, c. 2, at the time of writing not proclaimed in force; Meat Inspection Act, Ont. 1962-63, c. 78.

[7]Municipal Act, R.S.O. 1960, c. 249, s. 401, para. 5.

[8]Game and Fish Act, Ont. 1961-62, c. 48, s. 38.

[9]R.S.O. 1960, c. 137.

[10]Ont. 1965, c. 72.

[11]Highway Traffic Act, R.S.O. 1960, c. 172, s. 13.

Definition of Standards

"A prime source of justified dissatisfaction with the type of federal administrative action which I will shortly specify is the failure to develop standards sufficiently definite that decisions will be fairly predictable and that the reasons for them will be understood; this failure can and must be remedied."[12]

It is essential for the guidance of licensing agencies that the government policy be reflected in the legislative definition of the standards required to enable a person to obtain and retain a licence. While in most areas a rigid and exhaustive code cannot be laid down for the administration of the licensing policy and it is necessary to leave to the licensing tribunal the power to exercise a well-informed discretion, the scope of the policy should be made clear in the defined standards. The licensing legislation of Ontario leans much too heavily in favour of unfettered discretion.

The case law on municipal licensing illustrates the deficiencies of the enabling sections of the Municipal Act and the deficiencies of licensing by-laws passed thereunder. Most of the enabling sections of the Act simply employ the formula that by-laws may be passed "for licensing, regulating and governing" the particular trades or businesses, etc., mentioned. The requirements to be satisfied to obtain a licence, or to retain a licence, appear either to be left to the body enacting the by-law—to be inserted in the by-law—or to be laid down in actual cases by the body administering it.

Standards in Municipal By-Laws

Some of the by-laws passed in Ontario providing for the licensing of taxicabs usefully illustrate how licensing powers may be implemented where no or insufficient standards are provided.

The taxicab by-law enacted by the Board of Commissioners of Police for the City of Ottawa[13] empowers the Board to revoke a licence "if the circumstances shall appear to it to warrant such action." It would be difficult to frame a more subjective legislative ground for revoking a licence. There is nothing in the enabling section of the Municipal Act[14] expressly authorizing such a basis for revocation, nor, on the other hand, is there anything in it which would tend to indicate that the test is beyond the powers of the Board.

The Windsor taxicab by-law enables the Board of Commissioners of Police to revoke a licence "upon such grounds as the Commission may deem

---

[12]Friendly, *The Federal Administrative Agencies: The Need for Better Definition of Standards,* 75 Harv. L. Rev. 863, 867 (1962).

[13]By-Law No. 184 of the Board of Commissioners of Police for the City of Ottawa, s. 31 (2).

[14]R.S.O. 1960, c. 249, s. 395, para. 1.

sufficient".[15] The same language is used in the Sault Ste. Marie by-law.[16] The Hamilton by-law contains no provisions respecting the grounds for which a licence may be revoked. Its revocation section commences: "Upon the Board's decision to suspend or revoke any licence which may be lawfully revoked. . . ."[17] This section implies that a power to revoke exists and that the grounds for revocation are at large.

The Fort William by-law[18] provides that a licence may "be refused, revoked, or cancelled by the Board in its discretion and it shall not be bound to give any reason for refusing, revoking, or cancelling any licence". While there is nothing in the enabling section of the Municipal Act[19] expressly authorizing this provision, it accords with section 247 (4) of the Act which contains similar language. A like provision is in the London taxicab by-law.[20]

The Port Arthur taxicab by-law frankly states that "any licence issued pursuant to the provisions of this by-law may be revoked or cancelled at any time by the Board without cause assigned".[21] The next sub-section of this by-law, by contrast, is objective in the extreme. Upon conviction for trivial offences carrying nothing more than a nominal fine, a taxicab operator shall—not may—lose his means of livelihood. It states:

"54. (2) Every licence issued to a person as driver of a taxicab shall be forthwith revoked upon the conviction of that person for any offence under the Criminal Code of Canada, the Liquor Control Act of Ontario or the Highway Traffic Act of Ontario, s. 111 (1) (a) or (b) ."

This is discrimination against taxicab operators and an unjustified encroachment on their civil rights. Mr. Gellhorn's observation on similar licensing laws in the United States is fully warranted: "In practical terms . . . a blanket proscription of this sort seems more vindictively punitive than it does selectively preventive."[22]

These examples demonstrate how far bodies exercising subordinate legislative power will depart from sound principles[23] when given the power to do so. The effective remedy does not lie in merely amending these arbitrary by-

---

[15]By-Law No. 91 of the Board of Commissioners of Police for the City of Windsor, s. 41 (b) .

[16]By-Law No. 18 of the Board of Commissioners of Police for the City of Sault Ste. Marie, s. 34 (b) .

[17]By-Law No. 4 of the Board of Commissioners of Police for the City of Hamilton, s. 13.

[18]By-Law No. 20 of the Board of Commissioners of Police for the City of Fort William, s. 13.

[19]R.S.O. 1960, c. 249, s. 395, para. 1.

[20]By-Law No. 58 of the Board of Commissioners of Police for the City of London, s. 6.

[21]By-Law No. 11 of the Board of Commissioners of Police of the City of Port Arthur, s. 54 (1) .

[22]Walter Gellhorn, *Individual Freedom and Governmental Restraints,* 128.

[23]See Chapter 23 *supra.*

laws but in amending the provisions of the Municipal Act which gives the licensing tribunals power to be arbitrary. Proper guide lines are required.

Limitation on the Number of Licences to be Issued

Licensing authorities are empowered under the Municipal Act[24] to pass by-laws in certain cases limiting the number of licences of a particular class that may be issued.[25]

The power to limit the number of licences that may be issued and to refuse a licence on the ground that the specified number has been granted, is a control over the relevant area of the economy with monopolistic attributes. Where the power to limit is conferred and exercised the licence takes on the characteristics of a franchise. The real purpose of limiting the number of licences to be issued should be to promote the welfare of the licensee in the public interest. This principle has received statutory acknowledgment in statutes other than the Municipal Act,[26] such as the Public Commercial Vehicles Act,[27] and the Farm Products Marketing Act.[28] The power to limit the number of licences issued is a far-reaching one and should only be conferred when accompanied by adequate safeguards for the rights of the individual. Under the Municipal Act the power is to be exercised by the passage of a "by-law". The limitation, or an objective formula for determining the limitation, should be expressed in the by-law.

The Metropolitan Licensing Commission of Metropolitan Toronto in its licensing by-law[29] used this formula: "There shall not be issued by the Commission a greater number of taxicab owner licences than the number set by resolution of the Commission." The number of taxicab owner licences in the Metropolitan Toronto area was provided for in a formula fixed by a resolution of the Metropolitan Licensing Commission at one licence per thousand population of Metropolitan Toronto. This did not

---

[24]*Ibid.*

[25]Pursuant to the Municipal Act, the number of licences may be limited for the carrying on of the business of a public garage or automobile service station where gasoline is stored or kept for sale (s. 379 (1), paras. 127, 128, 129); for the carrying on of the taxicab business (s. 395, para. 1); for the business of operating "victualling houses, ordinaries and houses where fruit, fish, oysters, clams or victuals are sold or to be eaten therein, and places for the lodging, reception, refreshment or entertainment of the public" (s. 399 (1), para. 5); and for the having in possession for hire or gain of any billiard, pool, or bagatelle table, including the limiting of the number of tables that may be licensed (s. 401, para. 1). And see s. 248 (2), which enables the council to limit the number of licences and the number of tables "to such number as the council may deem fit even if the number be limited to one".

[26]R.S.O. 1960, c. 249, s. 399 (1) para. 5.

[27]R.S.O. 1960, c. 319.

[28]R.S.O. 1960, c. 138, s. 18, as enacted by Ont. 1962-63, c. 45, s. II, as amended by Ont. 1965, c. 39, s. 5 (1) (2), and as further ameneded by Ont. 1966, c. 56, s. 2 (1) (2).

[29]By-Law No. 49, enacted on the 24th July, 1963, Schedule 8, para. 48.

comply with the Municipal Act,[30] which states: "By-laws may be passed . . . for limiting the number of cabs . . . used for hire." The principle or the formula for determining the number should have been fixed in a by-law.[31]

Quite apart from this interpretative point, subordinate or delegated legislative power of a monopolistic character, affecting the rights of the community as a whole, should not be exercised by a non-elected body. If the number of licences for taxicabs or restaurants or other facilities serving the public is to be limited in any community, the principle or the formula for fixing the number should be determined by legislation publicly debated and passed by the elected representatives of the people. This is an elementary safeguard for the rights of the individual. This principle is consistent with the general policy of section 247 (2) of the Municipal Act[32] which provides that it is the council and not a Board of Commissioners of Police, where such Board is the licensing body, which fixes the fee to be paid for a licence.

In making this recommendation we are not unmindful of the fact that before decisions of this nature can be made intelligently they must be based on accurate information and a substantial element of administrative expertise. If relevant information is required in order to determine the number of licences that should be issued for any trade or calling, an inquiry procedure could be provided, through which the information would be acquired, and the general public could have an opportunity to be heard. An analogous practice is followed under the Public Commercial Vehicles Act[33] in determining public necessity and convenience. Where it is intended to fix quotas for licences there should be no difficulty in holding a public hearing by a committee of the municipal council before a decision is made.

The Farm Products Marketing Act[34] provides another illustration of a delegation, and of a subdelegation, of legislative power to non-elected bodies, which when exercised produces monopolistic results. The Farm Products Marketing Board is empowered, *inter alia,* to make regulations providing for "the fixing and allotting to persons of tobacco acreages or other production quotas on such a basis as the Board deems proper".[35] This gives power to the Board to restrict a tobacco farm owner from growing tobacco on his own land beyond the stipulated acreage and to prohibit others from growing tobacco. The Act goes on to provide that the Farm

---

[30]R.S.O. 1960, c. 249, s. 395, para. 1.

[31]By-Law 49 has since been repealed and replaced by By-Law No. 68, requiring that the number of taxicab licences be fixed by by-law.

[32]R.S.O. 1960, c. 249.

[33]R.S.O. 1960, c. 319, s. 4, as amended by Ont. 1961-62, c. 114, s. 4.

[34]R.S.O. 1960, c. 138, s. 18, as enacted by Ont. 1962-63, c. 45, s. 11, as amended by Ont. 1965, c. 39, s. 5 (1) (2), and as further amended by Ont. 1966, c. 56, s. 2 (1) (2).

[35]*Ibid.,* s. 18 (2) (b) (ii).

Products Marketing Board may delegate this power to the local board. This has been done.[36]

The Ontario Flue-Cured Tobacco Growers' Marketing Board has passed (May 6, 1963) what are called "General Regulations" pursuant to this sub-delegation to implement the acreage allotment provisions of the Farm Products Marketing Act. The local board derives its legal power to limit a farmer in the use of his land from a regulation passed by the Farm Products Marketing Board—an appointed body. If such a power is needed in the public interest it is one of such consequence to the general public that it should only be exercised by the Legislature, or by the Lieutenant Governor in Council, a body directly accountable to the Legislature. Under the present law the cabinet is two levels away from the formulation and enforcement of a detailed policy of land use.

The Transfer of Licences Having a Monopoly Value

Where the law restricts the number of licences which may be issued to those engaging in a particular trade or occupation, difficult questions arise concerning the right of an owner to transfer his licence to another person. Three main interests are involved:

(1) The interest of the licence holder in selling his property for whatever it will fetch in the market place. The law of supply and demand will give the licence a market value quite apart from any goodwill attached to the business carried on by the licensee;

(2) The interest of the qualified and deserving person who wishes to engage in the trade or occupation in question to do so on a fair and equitable basis without having to "buy a licence" from another licence holder;

(3) The interest of the public in having the benefit of free competition.

Apart from licences issued for the purpose of collecting revenue and maintaining records, the only justification for a licensing scheme is the promotion of the public interest in good service, safety, health, and in some cases, the economic welfare of the licensees. Generally speaking, there can be no justification for a scheme of licensing that creates a franchise with a marketable value for the licensee. It may be that this is a necessary consequence in some cases, but the public interest demands that adequate safeguards be provided against public and private exploitation.

Special representations were made to this Commission concerning the licensing procedure adopted in Metropolitan Toronto with respect to taxi-cab licences. The Licensing Commission maintains a list of applicants who are eligible to receive a licence in their turn when new licences are issued by reason of an increase in the population of Metropolitan Toronto.[37] However, licensees are free, in effect, to transfer their licences to purchasers who may not be on the list, in accordance with the relevant by-law of the Com-

---

[36]O. Regs. 107/63, 108/63 and 125/63.

[37]By-Law No. 68 of the Metropolitan Licensing Commission, Schedule 8, s. 48A.

mission.[38] A cab owner "may sell his cab and its equipment to any person and upon such sale the owner's license issued in respect of such cab shall be terminated. . . . [T]he Commission may in its discretion issue a new licence to the purchaser of such taxi-cab vehicle and equipment subject to the following conditions:

. . . (i.) That the new applicant qualifies under all other provisions of this By-law, and is a resident of Metropolitan Toronto."[39] Six other conditions follow. Under this system, when the Commission issues a licence to the purchaser, as in practice it does, the vendor realizes a monopoly value of his licence on the sale of the vehicle and equipment.[40] While the licence fee payable to the Commission for a new licence is only $300, it was recently reported that a cab and licence were "sold", with the approval of the Commission for the sum of $14,500.[41] Whether this figure is correct or not, the monopoly value of taxicab licences in Metropolitan Toronto is very high and in the last analysis it is the members of the public who use taxicabs who bear this cost.

In the years prior to 1963, the Licensing Commission followed the policy of requiring cab owners intending to sell their vehicles as cabs, to sell to the next eligible person on a list kept by the Commission, at a price determined by the Commission—which price did not take into account the monopoly value of the licence. However, it was decided, in 1963, to depart from this practice. In the brief filed with us by the Metropolitan Licensing Commission, the reason for the change was explained in this way.

". . . [E]xperience indicated that there was widespread flouting and circumvention of these regulations, which tended to bring the whole by-law into disrepute and contempt. Most of the revocations of cab owners' licences arose from attempts by this Commission to enforce the by-law in regard to illegal sales. Finally, the Commission in 1963 decided to bring matters into the open by permitting the sale of a taxicab at whatever price the parties agreed to. Section 27 of Schedule 8 of the by-law now permits the making of an Agreement for the sale of a taxicab upon an all-cash basis. If the Agreement is approved by the Commission the existing licence is terminated and a new licence is issued.

In the two years since this change was made it has been noted that the monopoly value of a cab owner's licence has increased from $1,500.00 to $5,000.00 or more, which would appear to indicate that cab ownership is a desirable asset and presumably a profitable business under the present regulations.

Recognition of the right to deal in the monopoly value of a licence in addition to being more realistic has made it possible for

---

[38]*Ibid.*, Schedule 8, s. 27.
[39]*Ibid.*, Schedule 8, s. 27 (1) (2) (i).
[40]Brief of the Metropolitan Licensing Commission, 7-8.
[41]Toronto Star, June 15, 1967, p. 7.

the Licensing Commission to insist upon higher standards in the industry in dealing with the public, especially as regards the mechanical condition of taxicabs and the regulations have been tightened in regard to the age of taxicab vehicles, and some of the monopoly value of the licence has been channelled back to the Licensing Commission, representing the public, in the form of increased licence and licence renewal fees."[42]

On our request, the Chairman of the Licensing Commission elaborated on this submission in a letter to this Commission:

"The type of transactions [under the transfer system existing until the change in 1963] that were used to effect a transfer of the ownership without a sale were varied but generally took the form of rental agreements, partnership agreements and management agreements, none of which came before the Commission. These were the methods used to circumvent the Commission's regulations as referred to in the submission to the Royal Commission. The Commission attempted to regulate management agreements by requiring affidavits to be taken by the owner of the licence and by prescribing the form of contract to be used by the manager and licensee. It was found that notwithstanding the form of contract for management, licences were in essence being sold. This is best illustrated in the reported case *Re Szabo and Metropolitan Toronto Licensing Commission,* [1963] 2 O.R. 426."[43]

We recognize that in a large urban area such as the Municipality of Metropolitan Toronto, in a field such as the taxicab industry,[44] it may be difficult to police a licence-issuing and transfer policy, but we do not find the reasons given by the Commission convincing.

Any argument based upon cab ownership being a "desirable asset and presumably a profitable business under the present regulations", is neither sound nor logical. It should not be the purpose of a licensing system to enhance the profitability of the business of a licensee beyond what is necessary to give good service to the public and a reasonable return to the licensee from his labours. The latter interest is guaranteed by the limitation on the number of licences that may be issued, and not by the right to make a profit on the sale of licences under the present government-created monopoly. It is hard to see any relationship between the right to deal in the monopoly value of a licence and the ability of the Commission to insist on higher standards in the industry.

If there was difficulty in preventing trafficking in licences prior to 1963

42Brief of the Metropolitan Licensing Commission, 7-8.

43Letter, June 13, 1967.

44See the Report of the Advisory Committee on Taxicabs to the Board of Commissioners of Police of the City of Toronto, April 12, 1932, 30-32; and the Report of the Committee on Taxicabs to the Board of Commissioners of Police for the City of Toronto (1952), 13-16.

by reason of illicit transfers through "rental agreements, partnership agreements and management agreements", the real cause for the difficulty must have been that the fares were so high that, taken with the limitation on the number of licences issued, the licences had a very high marketable value.

Finally, the argument that "some of the monopoly value of the licence has been channelled back to the Licensing Commission, representing the public, in the form of increased licence and licence renewal fees" is untenable. If this were true it would be an indirect tax on the users of taxicabs for the benefit of the public at large, which is not the purpose of the licensing scheme. But the thesis is not sound. The purchaser from a licensee pays the monopoly value to the licensee and it is he, not the vendor, who pays the increased licence fee to the Commission. The purchaser of the licence must recoup for himself, out of fares collected from users of taxicabs, not only the purchase price of the licence but the "increased licence fee". This policy of the Licensing Commission of Metropolitan Toronto appears to be in direct violation of the intent of its general licensing by-law:[45]

"17. (1) No person shall enjoy a vested right in the continuance of a licence and upon the issue, renewal, transfer, cancellation or suspension thereof, the value of a license shall be the property of the Metropolitan Licensing Commission.

(2) No license shall be transferred except with the consent in writing of the Commission and the Commission shall not be bound to give such consent."

In practice, a cab owner may not transfer his licence; he may only sell his taxicab vehicle, equipment and the goodwill attached to the business. The licence is terminated and the Commission issues a new licence. It however treats "the value of a licence" as the property of the licence holder and not that of the Commission. The public interest demands that licensing laws should be written so as to make it clear that the monopoly value created by the limitation of numbers of licences cannot be turned to private advantage. A licensee should not be able to reap a benefit for himself by reason of the limitation of the number of licences. He has done nothing to create this wealth. It is the users of the taxicab, together with the limitation on licences that may be issued, that have created it.

If there is to be a limitation on the number of licences issued, the licensing tribunal should maintain a list of applicants for licences, available for public inspection. When the holder of a licence no longer wishes to use it, he should return it to the tribunal and a new licence should be issued to the person qualified and entitled to it whose application has been filed with the Commission for the longest period of time.

---

[45] By-Law No. 68 of the Metropolitan Licensing Commission, s. 17.

55 Black Markets and Competition*

T. C. Schelling

. . . A difference between black-market crimes and most others, like racketeering and robbery, is that they are "crimes" only because we have legislated against the commodity they provide. We single out certain goods and services as harmful or sinful; for reasons of history and tradition, and for other reasons, we forbid dope but not tobacco, gambling in casinos but not on the stockmarket, extra-marital sex but not gluttony, erotic stories but not mystery stories. We do all this for reasons different from those behind the laws against robbery and tax evasion.

It is policy that determines the black markets. Cigarettes and firearms are borderline cases. We can, as a matter of policy, make the sales of guns and cigarettes illegal. We can also, as a matter of policy, make contraceptives and abortion illegal. Times change, policies change, and what was banned yesterday can become legitimate today; what was freely available yesterday, can be banned tomorrow. Evidently there are changes under way in policy on birth control; there may be changes on abortion and homosexuality, and there may be legislation restricting the sale of firearms.

The pure black markets reflect some moral tastes, economic principles, paternalistic interests, and notions of personal freedom in a way that the rackets do not. And these tastes and principles change. We can revise our policy on birth control (and we are changing it) in a way that we could not change our policy on armed robbery. The usury laws may to some extent be a holdover from medieval economics; and some of the laws on prostitution, abortion, and contraception were products of the Victorian era and reflect the political power of various church groups. One cannot even deduce from the existence of abortion laws that a majority of the voters, even a majority of enlightened voters, oppose abortion; and the wise money would probably bet that the things that we shall be forbidding in fifty years will differ substantially from the things we forbid now.

What happens when a forbidden industry is subjected to legitimate competition? Legalized gambling is a good example. What has happened to Las Vegas is hardly reassuring. On the other hand, the legalization of liquor in the early 1930's swamped the criminal liquor industry with competition. Criminals are alleged to have moved into church bingo, but they have never got much of a hold on the stockmarket. Evidently criminals cannot always survive competition, evidently sometimes they can.

The question is important in the field of narcotics. We could easily put insulin and antibiotics into the hands of organized crime by forbidding their sale; we could do the same with a dentist's novocaine. (We could,

---

*From: "Economics and Criminal Enterprise", *The Public Interest*, No. 7 (Spring 1967), pp. 75-78 (reprinted by permission of author and publisher).

CONSUMER PROTECTION POLICIES 353

that is, if we could sufficiently enforce the prohibition. If we cannot enforce it, the black market would be too competitive for any organized monopoly to arise.) If narcotics were not illegal, there could be no black market and no monopoly profits; the interest in "pushing" it would not be much greater than the pharmaceutical interest in pills to reduce the symptoms of common colds. This argument cannot by itself settle the question of whether (and which) narcotics (or other evil commodities) ought to be banned, but it is an important consideration.

The greatest gambling enterprise in the United States has not been significantly touched by organized crime. That is the stock market. (There has been criminal activity in the stock market, but not monopoly by what we usually call "organized crime.") Nor has organized crime succeeded in controlling the foreign currency black markets around the world. The reason is that the market works too well. Federal control over the stock market, designed mainly to keep it honest and informative, and aimed at maximizing the competitiveness of the market and the information of the consumer, makes it a hard market to tamper with.

Ordinary gambling ought to be one of the hardest industries to monopolize. Almost anybody can compete, whether in taking bets or providing cards, dice, or racing information. "Wire services" could not stand the ordinary competition of radio and Western Union; bookmakers could hardly be intimidated if the police were not available to intimidate them. If ordinary brokerage firms were encouraged to take horse-racing accounts, and buy and sell bets by telephone for their customers, it is hard to see how racketeers could get any kind of grip on it. And when any restaurant, bar, country club or fraternity house can provide tables and sell fresh decks of cards, it is hard to see how gambling can be monopolized any more than the soft-drink or television business, or any other.

We can still think gambling is a sin, and try to eliminate it; but we should probably try not to use the argument that it would remain in the hands of criminals if we legalized it. Both reason and evidence seem to indicate the contrary.

The decisive question is whether the goal of somewhat reducing the consumption of narcotics, gambling, prostitution, abortion or anything else that is forced by law into the black market, is or is not outweighed by the costs to society of creating a criminal industry. The costs to society of creating these black markets are several.

First, it gives the criminal the same kind of protection that a tariff gives to a domestic monopoly. It guarantees the absence of competition from people who are unwilling to be criminal, and an advantage to those whose skill is in evading the law.

Second, it provides a special incentive to corrupt the police, because the police not only may be susceptible to being bought off but can even be used to eliminate competition.

Third, a large number of consumers who are probably not ordinary criminals—the conventioneers who visit prostitutes, the housewives who bet on horses, the women who seek abortions—are taught contempt, even enmity, for the law by being obliged to purchase particular commodities and services from criminals in an illegal transaction.

Fourth, dope addiction may so aggravate poverty for certain desperate people that they are induced to commit crimes, or can be urged to commit crimes, because the law arranges that the only (or main) source for what they desperately demand will be a criminal (high-priced) source.

Fifth, these big black markets may guarantee enough incentive and enough profit for organized crime so that large-scale criminal organization comes into being and maintains itself. It may be—this is an important question for research—that without these important black markets, crime would be substantially decentralized, lacking the kind of organization that makes it enterprising, safe, and able to corrupt public officials. In economic-development terms, these black markets may provide the central core (or "infra-structure") of underworld business.

A good economic history of prohibition in the 1920's has never been attempted, so far as I know. By all accounts, though, prohibition was a mistake. It merely turned the liquor industry over to organized crime. In the end we gave up, probably because not everybody agreed drinking was bad (or, if it was bad, that it was anybody's political business), but also because the attempt was an evident failure and a costly one in its social by-products. It may have propelled underworld business in the United States into what economic developers call the "take-off" into self-sustained growth.

SUGGESTIONS FOR FURTHER READING

Borrie, G. J. and A. L. Diamond, *The Consumer, Society and the Law*, revised edition, London, MacGibbon and Key Ltd., 1966.

Consumer Council, *Consumer Consultative Machinery in the Nationalised Industries*, a Consumer Council study, London, Her Majesty's Stationary Office, 1968.

Friedman, M., "Occupational Licensure," chapter 9 in *Capitalism and Freedom* (Chicago, University of Chicago Press, 1962), pp. 137-160.

Fulop, C., *Consumers in the Market: A Study in Choice, Competition, and Sovereignty*, London, Institute of Economic Affairs, 1967.

Lees, D. S., *The Economic Consequences of the Professions*, London, Institute of Economic Affairs Monograph No. 2, 1966.

McClellan, G. S., *The Consuming Public*, New York, H. W. Wilson Co., 1968.

Magoruson, W. G., *The Dark Side of the Market Place*, Englewood Cliffs, N.J., Prentice-Hall Inc., 1968.

Morrell, C. A., "Federal Food and Drug Legislation in Canada," special article, Dominion Bureau of Statistics, *Canada Year Book,* 1962, pp. 217-222.

Packer, H. L., "The Crime Tariff", *American Scholar,* Vol. 33 (Autumn, 1964).

SECTION

4

Toward a New
Political Economy

PART ELEVEN

Re-Thinking Old Assumptions

INTRODUCTION

The foregoing sections of this volume have included a wide range of readings outlining both the capitalist ideology and the shift in theory and practice toward collectivism in contemporary political economy, as well as analyses of particular policies implemented by the Canadian state to promote or limit the operation of free market forces. Thoughtful readers will probably have arrived at this point with more questions in mind than answers. That is only another way of repeating the truism that the modern world is bafflingly complex and that there are no simple answers to social questions.

But any student may fairly demand: what does it all mean? What should we conclude? Is the "private sector" now controlled too much or too little, badly or well, by public authorities?

Any editorial process of selection implies conclusions. The reader must accept, reject or modify those conclusions. Our judgment is that the role of the modern state in economic life has grown inexorably, is growing, and is likely to continue to grow, and that on balance this is desirable. But whether government intervention in the economy expands or shrinks, all non-communist nations will be confronted continuously by complex problems of public policy related to the private sector that must be settled, one way or another, by society's value judgments as informed by the analyses of social scientists. Therefore, the final selections in this book are intended, not to provide answers, but to indicate new ways to view reality and new formulations of essential questions.

In the light of contemporary realities in the mixed or collectivist economy, are the assumptions of orthodox economic theory still the most useful guides to the solution of present and future problems? Karl Polanyi mounts

359

a biting attack on traditional capitalist assumptions and "Our Obsolete Market Mentality" in *Reading 56*. Polanyi advances the unusual view that economic determinism holds true, but holds true only in a market society. He calls for a new view not only of our capitalist past but also of the nature of man and of society, a shift toward more "democratic collectivist" rather than orthodox liberal assumptions.

Counterpoised against the Polanyi challenge to market concepts is the salutary reminder of Yale's Professor Lindblom in *Reading 57* that, with or without private property and private decision-making, the tough criteria of market determinations may remain the most useful means of allocating scarce resources. Market concepts, he argues, still provide the most useful tools of analysis for any pattern of social organization, and "the market mechanism can be serviceable to planned and unplanned economies alike".

Lindblom is right, at least within limits; but what are those limits? Does orthodox economic theory bear sufficient relevance to contemporary reality, and what of politics and the role of the state? Another set of questions floods in. We must ask ourselves not only whether the "private sector" can continue to be regarded realistically as private, but whether that keystone of capitalism discussed in Part 1, private property, remains private any more. In an age of high concentrations of economic power, typified by giant multi-national corporations with highly fragmented common-stock ownership and an equally high degree of centralized managerial control, surely it is no longer reasonable to postulate the small individual entrepreneur as the basic unit of production. It is now naive to ask who "owns" the C.P.R. or General Motors. Increasingly, in the corporate economy, those who "own" do not control, and those who control do not "own". Probably J. K. Galbraith is right when he suggests that real economic power is passing from the owners of tangible private property to the "technostructure," the highly trained professional technocrats in engineering, law, accounting, economics, and other disciplines who control the corporate leviathans. In his book *The New Industrial State,* Galbraith observes that "Man will look back in amusement at the pretense that once caused people to refer to General Dynamics . . . and A.T. & T. as *private* business."

Having begun this book with the contention that private property is the foundation of capitalism, should we end it by stating that private property is being replaced by collectivized technology? Not quite. We have still to consider, though only briefly, the concepts of democracy and of what used to be called (before the fashion changed) political economy. The two concepts are inextricably inter-related.

The capitalist ideology and normative economic theory regard every producer and consumer in a free market as equal, but they are not. Thus the orthodox capitalist ideology usually ignores the fundamental ethical questions of the primary distribution of wealth, social elites, and power. As Professor Harold Lasswell of Yale University puts it, the problem of who gets what, when, and how is *the* problem of politics, yet this is a question that traditional economic theory tends to beg, ignore or assume away. Only a very few Canadian scholars have turned their minds to such problems.

One of those few is the distinguished political theorist C. B. Macpherson of the University of Toronto. From his avowedly Marxist perspective, Macpherson has argued repeatedly that both the negative liberal state and the capitalist market economy are expressions or reflections of the basic class organization of society—the power structure. In the Western world, he contends, the liberal state first emerged as a construction required by the market economy and naturally reflected the power structure built into it. The concept of democracy was added later. Hence we have confused the liberal state and democracy; they are not the same. But in the developing nations of the East, democracy arose as a modern political movement against the liberal state and the market economy which were associated with Imperialism. Thus, in the developing nations, says Macpherson, democracy means government by the mass of the people, a Rousseauian reflection of the General Will, whereas Western democracy has meant the election of governments chosen from elite groups within the ruling bourgeoisie, a Lockean construct of possessive individuals.

It becomes apparent that the most difficult question is posed by the relationship between economic liberalism and democracy. Although in the introduction to Part 1 we recognized the view that democracy and capitalism are two different things, this position may now appear to be a gross oversimplification.

And now that we have traced the erosion of the market economy by the pragmatic techniques of modern collectivism, we must also re-assess the adequacy and appropriateness of our concept of democracy. Unfortunately that would require a separate book; but many students will want to read at least Professor Macpherson's stimulating analysis of the subject in *The Real World of Democracy*.

The last question raised above hinges on the problem of power. Who gets wealth? Who rules? If orthodox political scientists have left the theory of democracy confused, and if the conventional wisdom of economic analysis cannot cope with the problem of power, perhaps neither economists nor political scientists have been asking the most important questions. Modern economic theory yields admirable answers to problems of resource allocation and price determination, but it is almost silent on problems of power. Is there no branch or school of economic or political philosophy that can help us?

There is at least one. Buried beneath the Hegelian obfuscation and obsolescent Ricardian value theory of Marxian dogma lies the penetrating social analysis of Karl Marx. One need not adopt C. B. Macpherson's position without reservation or become a Marxist to recognize that Marx possessed great insight and posed the crucial questions. The most effective recent plea for a reconsideration of the analytic tools of Marx is by the moderate, liberal economist of New York's New School of Social Sciences, Professor Robert Heilbroner in *Reading 58*. Heilbroner suggests that Marx got most of the answers wrong, but put the most important questions and put them correctly. As a way out of our present social and philosophical dilemmas, Heilbroner builds a compelling case for a merging of Marxian insights with neo-classical economic theory. Orthodox political theory might benefit from the same infusion.

The result could be a revivification in a more sophisticated form of the traditions of economics and political science, recombined into a more vital and useful discipline of political economy. As Heilbroner observes, economics is in danger of becoming excessively abstract and socially irrelevant. Similarly, a "science" of politics divorced from economic insights may be equally irrelevant. If recombined, the two disciplines could emerge as a mutually reinforcing partnership of increased social utility. By urging the creation of a new political economy, we are proposing not a marriage but a reconciliation.

In a Canadian context, the case for ending the artificial dichotomy between economics and political science as separate academic subjects is best put by Professor Melville H. Watkins. The Task Force on the Structure of Canadian Industry (the Watkins Report), from which we included a selection in Part 3, demonstrated the utility of reconciling the two disciplines. The essay included here as *Reading 59* casts further light on many of the problems raised in sections Two and Three of this volume, and puts them into a fresh perspective. Professor Watkins reminds us that the analytic model of the free market is by no means philosophically neutral. He sounds the call for a more sensitive political and social approach to economic questions, and underlines the need for a re-affirmation of non-market values by students of the social sciences. If a sharper challenge has been issued to Canadian scholars, we have not heard it.

56   Our Obsolete Market Mentality*
Civilization Must Find a New Thought Pattern

Karl Polanyi

The first century of the Machine Age is drawing to a close amid fear and trepidation. Its fabulous material success was due to the willing, indeed the enthusiastic, subordination of man to the needs of the machine.

Liberal capitalism was in effect man's initial response to the challenge

*From: *Commentary*, Vol. 3, No. 2 (February 1947), pp. 109-17 (reprinted by permission of the author's estate and publisher).

of the Industrial Revolution. In order to allow scope to the use of elaborate, powerful machinery, we transformed human economy into a self-adjusting system of markets, and cast our thoughts and values in the mold of this unique innovation.

Today, we begin to doubt the truth of some of these thoughts and the validity of some of these values. Outside the United States, liberal capitalism can hardly be said to exist any more. How to organize human life in a machine society is a question that confronts us anew. Behind the fading fabric of competitive capitalism there looms the portent of an industrial civilization, with its paralyzing division of labor, standardization of life, supremacy of mechanism over organism, and organization over spontaneity. Science itself is haunted by insanity. This is the abiding concern.

No mere reversion to the ideals of a past century can show us the way. We must brave the future, though this may involve us in an attempt to shift the place of industry in society so that the extraneous fact of the machine can be absorbed. The search for industrial democracy is not merely the search for a solution to the problems of capitalism, as most people imagine. It is a search for an answer to industry itself. Here lies the concrete problem of our civilization.

Such a new dispensation requires an inner freedom for which we are but ill equipped. We find ourselves stultified by the legacy of a market-economy which bequeathed us oversimplified views of the function and role of the economic system in society. If the crisis is to be overcome, we must recapture a more realistic vision of the human world and shape our common purpose in the light of that recognition.

Industrialism is a precariously grafted scion upon man's age-long existence. The outcome of the experiment is still hanging in the balance. But man is not a simple being and can die in more than one way. The question of individual freedom, so passionately raised in our generation, is only one aspect of this anxious problem. In truth, it forms part of a much wider and deeper need—the need for a new response to the total challenge of the machine.

The Fundamental Heresy

Our condition can be described in these terms:

Industrial civilization may yet undo man. But since the venture of a progressively artificial environment cannot, will not, and indeed, should not, be voluntarily discarded, the task of adapting life *in such a surrounding* to the requirements of human existence must be resolved if man is to continue on earth. No one can foretell whether such an adjustment is possible, or whether man must perish in the attempt. Hence the dark undertone of concern.

Meanwhile, the first phase of the Machine Age has run its course. It involved an organization of society that derived its name from its central institution, the market. This system is on the downgrade. Yet our practical philosophy was overwhelmingly shaped by this spectacular episode. Novel notions about man and society became current and gained the status of axioms. Here they are:

As regards *man,* we were made to accept the heresy that his motives can be described as "material" and "ideal," and that the incentives on which everyday life is organized spring from the "material" motives. Both utilitarian liberalism and popular Marxism favored such views.

As regards *society,* the kindred doctrine was propounded that its institutions were "determined" by the economic system. This opinion was even more popular with Marxists than with liberals.

Under a market-economy both assertions were, of course, true. *But only under such an economy.* In regard to the past, such a view was no more than an anachronism. In regard to the future, it was a mere prejudice. Yet under the influence of current schools of thought, reinforced by the authority of science and religion, politics and business, these strictly time-bound phenomena came to be regarded as timeless, as transcending the age of the market.

To overcome such doctrines, which constrict our minds and souls and greatly enhance the difficulty of the life-saving adjustment, may require no less than a reform of our consciousness.

The Market Trauma

The birth of laissez faire administered a shock to civilized man's views of himself, from the effects of which he never quite recovered. Only very gradually are we realizing what happened to us as recently as a century ago.

Liberal economy, this primary reaction of man to the machine, was a violent break with the conditions that preceded it. A chain-reaction was started—what before was merely isolated markets was transmuted into a self-regulating *system* of markets. And with the new economy, a new society sprang into being.

The crucial step was this: labor and land were made into commodities, that is, they were treated *as if* produced for sale. Of course, they were not actually commodities, since they were either not produced at all (as land) or, if so, not for sale (as labor).

Yet no more thoroughly effective fiction was ever devised. By buying and selling labor and land freely, the mechanism of the market was made to apply to them. There was now supply of labor, and demand for it; there was supply of land, and demand for it. Accordingly, there was a market price for the use of labor power, called wages, and a market price for the use of land, called rent. Labor and land were provided with markets of their own, similar to the commodities proper that were produced with their help.

The true scope of such a step can be gauged if we remember that labor is only another name for man, and land for nature. The commodity fiction handed over the fate of man and nature to the play of an automaton running in its own grooves and governed by its own laws.

Nothing similar had even been witnessed before. Under the mercantile regime, though it deliberately pressed for the creation of markets, the converse principle still operated. Labor and land were not entrusted to the market; they formed part of the organic structure of society. Where land was marketable, only the determination of price was, as a rule, left to the parties; where labor was subject to contract, wages themselves were usually assessed by public authority. Land stood under the custom of manor, monastery, and township, under common-law limitations concerning rights of real property; labor was regulated by laws against beggary and vagrancy, statutes of laborers and artificers, poor laws, guild and municipal ordinances. In effect, all societies known to anthropologists and historians restricted markets to commodities in the proper sense of the term.

Market-economy thus created a new type of society. The economic or productive system was here entrusted to a self-acting device. An institutional mechanism controlled human beings in their everyday activities as well as the resources of nature.

This instrument of material welfare was under the sole control of the incentives of hunger and gain—or, more precisely, fear of going without the necessities of life, and expectation of profit. So long as no propertyless person could satisfy his craving for food without first selling his labor in the market, and so long as no propertied person was prevented from buying in the cheapest market and selling in the dearest, the blind mill would turn out ever-increasing amounts of commodities for the benefit of the human race. Fear of starvation with the worker, lure of profit with the employer, would keep the vast establishment running.

In this way an "economic sphere" came into existence that was sharply delimited from other institutions in society. Since no human aggregation can survive without a functioning productive apparatus, its embodiment in a distinct and separate sphere had the effect of making the "rest" of society dependent upon that sphere. This autonomous zone, again, was regulated by a mechanism that controlled its functioning. As a result, the market mechanism became determinative for the life of the body social. No wonder that the emergent human aggregation was an "economic" society to a degree previously never even approximated. "Economic motives" reigned supreme in a world of their own, and the individual was made to act on them under pain of being trodden under foot by the juggernaut market.

Such a forced conversion to a utilitarian outlook fatefully warped Western man's understanding of himself.

Hunger and Gain Enthroned

This new world of "economic motives" was based on a fallacy. Intrinsically, hunger and gain are no more "economic" than love or hate, pride or prejudice. No human motive is *per se* economic. There is no such thing as a *sui generis* economic experience in the sense in which man may have a religious, aesthetic, or sexual experience. These latter give rise to motives that broadly aim at evoking similar experiences. In regard to material producton these terms lack self-evident meaning.

The economic factor, which underlies all social life, no more gives rise to definite incentives than the equally universal law of gravitation. Assuredly, if we do not eat, we must perish, as much as if we were crushed under the weight of a falling rock. But the pangs of hunger are not automatically translated into an incentive to produce. Production is not an individual, but a collective affair. If an individual is hungry, there is nothing definite for him to do. Made desperate, he might rob or steal, but such an action can hardly be called productive. With man, the political animal, everything is given not by natural, but by social circumstance. What made the 19th century think of hunger and gain as "economic" was simply the organization of production under a market economy.

Hunger and gain are here linked with production through the need of "earning an income." For under such a system, man, if he is to keep alive, is compelled to buy goods on the market with the help of an income derived from selling other goods on the market. The name of these incomes—wages, rent, interest—varies accordingly to what is offered for sale: use of labor power, of land, or of money; the income called profit—the remuneration of the entrepreneur—derives from the sale of goods that fetch a higher price than the goods that go into the production of them. Thus all incomes derive from sales, and all sales—directly or indirectly—contribute to production. The latter is, in effect, *incidental to the earning of an income.* So long as an individual is "earning an income," he is, automatically, contributing to production.

Obviously, the system works only so long as individuals have a reason to indulge in the activity of "earning an income." The motives of hunger and gain—separately and conjointly—provide them with such a reason. These two motives are thus geared to production and, accordingly, are termed "economic." The semblance is compelling that hunger and gain are *the* incentives on which any economic system must rest.

This assumption is baseless. Ranging over human societies, we find hunger and gain not appealed to as incentives to production, and where so appealed to, they are fused with other powerful motives.

Aristotle was right: man is not an economic, but a social being. He does not aim at safeguarding his individual interest in the acquisition of material possessions, but rather at ensuring social good-will, social status, social assets. He values possessions primarily as a means to that end. His incentives are of that "mixed" character which we associate with the endeavor to gain social approval—productive efforts are no more than incidental to this. *Man's economy is, as a rule, submerged in his social relations.* The change from this to a society which was, on the contrary, submerged in the economic system was an entirely novel development.

Facts

The evidence of facts, I feel, should at this point be adduced.

First, there are the discoveries of primitive economics. Two names are outstanding: Bronislaw Malinowski and Richard Thurnwald. They and some other research workers revolutionized our conceptions in this field and, by so doing, founded a new discipline. The myth of the individualistic savage had been exploded long ago. Neither the crude egotism, nor the apocryphal propensity to barter, truck, and exchange, nor even the tendency to cater to one's self was in evidence. But equally discredited was the legend of the communistic psychology of the savage, his supposed lack of appreciation for his own personal interests. (Roughly, it appeared that man was very much the same all through the ages. Taking his institutions not in isolation, but in their interrelation, he was mostly found to be behaving in a manner broadly comprehensible to us.) What appeared as "communism" was the fact that the productive or economic system was usually arranged in such a fashion as not to threaten any individual with starvation. His place at the camp fire, his share in the common resources, was secure to him, whatever part he happened to have played in hunt, pasture, tillage, or gardening.

Here are a few instances: Under the *kraal-land* system of the Kaffirs, "destitution is impossible: whosoever needs assistance receives it unquestioningly" (L. P. Mair, *An African People in the Twentieth Century,* 1934). No Kwakiutl "ever ran the least risk of going hungry" (E. M. Loeb, *The Distribution and Function of Money in Early Society,* 1936). "There is no starvation in societies living on the subsistence margin" (M. J. Herskovits, *The Economic Life of Primitive Peoples,* 1940). In effect, the individual is not in danger of starving unless the community as a whole is in a like predicament. It is this absence of the menace of individual destitution that makes primitive society, in a sense, more humane than 19th-century society, and at the same time *less "economic."*

The same applies to the stimulus of individual gain. Again, a few quotations: "The characteristic feature of primitive economics is the absence of any desire to make profits from production and exchange" (R. Thurnwald, *Economics in Primitive Communities,* 1932). "Gain, which is often the stimulus for work in more civilized communities, never acts as an impulse to work under the original native conditions" (B. Malinowski, *Argonauts of the Western Pacific,* 1930). If so-called economic motives were natural to man, we would have to judge all early and primitive societies as thoroughly unnatural.

Secondly, there is no difference between primitive and civilized society in this regard. Whether we turn to ancient city-state, despotic empire, feudalism, 13th-century urban life, 16th-century mercantile regime, or 18th-century regulationism—invariably the economic system is found to be merged in the social. Incentives spring from a large variety of sources, such as custom and tradition, public duty and private commitment, religious observance and political allegiance, judicial obligation and administrative regulation as established by prince, municipality, or guild. Rank and status, compulsion of law and threat of punishment, public praise and private reputation, insure that the individual contributes his share to production.

Fear of privation or love of profit need not be altogether absent. Markets occur in all kinds of societies, and the figure of the merchant is familiar to many types of civilization. But isolated markets do not link up into an economy. The motive of gain was specific to merchants, as was valor to the knight, piety to the priest, and pride to the craftsman. The notion of making the motive of gain universal never entered the heads of our ancestors. At no time prior to the second quarter of the 19th century were markets more than a subordinate feature in society.

Thirdly, there was the startling abruptness of the change. Predominance of markets emerged not as a matter of degree, but of kind. Markets through which otherwise self-sufficient householders get rid of their surplus neither direct production nor provide the producer with his income. This is only the case in a market-economy where *all* incomes derive from sales, and commodities are obtainable exclusively by purchase. A free market for labor was born in England only about a century ago. The ill-famed Poor Law Reform (1834) abolished the rough-and-ready provisions made for the paupers by patriarchal governments. The poorhouse was transformed from a refuge of the destitute into an abode of shame and mental torture to which even hunger and misery were preferable. Starvation or work was the alternative left to the poor. Thus was a competitive national market for labor created. Within a decade, the Bank Act (1844) established the principle of the gold standard; the making of money was removed from the hands of the government regardless of the effect upon the level of employment. Simultaneously, reform of land laws mobilized the land, and repeal of the Corn Laws (1846) created a world pool of grain, thereby making the unprotected Continental peasant-farmer subject to the whims of the market.

Thus were established the three tenets of economic liberalism, the principle on which market economy was organized: that labor should find its price on the market; that money should be supplied by a self-adjusting mechanism; that commodities should be free to flow from country to country irrespective of the consequences—in brief, a labor market, the gold standard, and free trade. A self-inflammatory process was induced, as a result of which the formerly harmless market pattern expanded into a sociological enormity.

Birth of a Delusion

These facts roughly outline the genealogy of an "economic" society. Under such conditions the human world must appear as determined by "economic" motives. It is easy to see why.

Single out whatever motive you please, and organize production in such a manner as to make that motive the individual's incentive to produce, and you will have induced a picture of man as altogether absorbed by that particular motive. Let that motive be religious, political, or aesthetic; let it be pride, prejudice, love, or envy; and man will appear as essentially religious, political, aesthetic, proud, prejudiced, engrossed in love or envy. Other motives, in contrast, will appear distant and shadowy since they cannot be relied upon to operate in the vital business of production. The particular motive selected will represent "real" man.

As a matter of fact, human beings will labor for a large variety of reasons as long as things are arranged accordingly. Monks traded for religious reasons, and monasteries became the largest trading establishments in Europe. The Kula trade of the Trobriand Islanders, one of the most intricate barter arrangements known to man, is mainly an aesthetic pursuit. Feudal economy was run on customary lines. With the Kwakiutl, the chief aim of industry seems to be to satisfy a point of honor. Under mercantile despotism, industry was often planned so as to serve power and glory. Accordingly, we tend to think of monks or villeins, western Melanesians, the Kwakiutl, or 17th-century statesmen, as ruled by religion, aesthetics, custom, honor, or politics, respectively.

Under capitalism, every individual has to earn an income. If he is a worker, he has to sell his labor at current prices; if he is an owner, he has to make as high a profit as he can, for his standing with his fellows will depend upon the level of his income. Hunger and gain—even if vicariously —make them plough and sow, spin and weave, mine coal, and pilot planes. Consequently, members of such a society will think of themselves as governed by these twin motives.

In actual fact, man was never as selfish as the theory demanded. Though the market mechanism brought his dependence upon material goods to the fore, "economic" motives never formed with him the sole incentive to work. In vain was he exhorted by economists and utilitarian moralists alike to discount in business all other motives than "material" ones. On closer investigation, he was still found to be acting on remarkably "mixed" motives, not excluding those of duty towards himself and others—and maybe, secretly, even enjoying work for its own sake.

However, we are not here concerned with actual, but with assumed motives, not with the psychology, but with the ideology of business. *Not on the former, but on the latter, are views of man's nature based.* For once society expects a definite behavior on the part of its members, and prevailing institutions become roughly capable of enforcing that behavior, opinions on human nature will tend to mirror the ideal whether it resembles actuality or not.

Accordingly, hunger and gain were defined as "economic" motives, and man was supposed to be acting on them in everyday life, while his other motives appeared more ethereal and removed from humdrum existence. Honor and pride, civic obligation and moral duty, even self-respect and common decency, were now deemed irrelevant to production, and were significantly summed up in the word "ideal." Hence man was believed to consist of two components, one more akin to hunger and gain, the other to honor and power. The one was "material," the other "ideal"; the one "economic," the other "non-economic"; the one "rational," the other "non-rational." The Utilitarians went so far as to identify the two sets of terms, thus endowing the "economic" side of man's character with the aura of rationality. He who would have refused to imagine that he was acting for gain alone was thus considered not only immoral, but also mad.

Economic Determinism

The market mechanism moreover created the delusion of economic determinism as a general law for all human society.

Under a market-economy, of course, this law holds good. Indeed, the working of the economic system here not only "influences" the rest of society, but determines it—as in a triangle the sides not merely influence, but determine, the angles.

Take the stratification of classes. Supply and demand in the labor market were *identical* with the classes of workers and employers, respectively. The social classes of capitalists, landowners, tenants, brokers, merchants, professionals, and so on, were delimited by the respective markets for land, money, and capital and their uses, or for various services. The income of these social classes was fixed by the market, their rank and position by their income.

This was a complete reversal of the secular practice. In Maine's famous phrase, "contractus" replaced "status"; or, as Tönnies preferred to put it, "society" superseded "community"; or, in terms of the present article, *instead of the economic system being embedded in social relationships, these relationships were now embedded in the economic system.*

While social classes were directly, other institutions were indirectly determined by the market mechanism. State and government, marriage and the rearing of children, the organization of science and education, of religion and the arts, the choice of profession, the forms of habitation, the shape of settlements, the very aesthetics of private life—everything had to comply with the utilitarian pattern, or at least not interfere with the working of the market mechanism. But since very few human activities can be carried on in the void, even a saint needing his pillar, the indirect effect of the market system came very near to determining the whole of society. It was almost impossible to avoid the erroneous conclusion that as "economic" man was "real" man, so the economic system was "really" society.

Sex and Hunger

Yet it would be truer to say that the basic human institutions abhor unmixed motives. Just as the provisioning of the individual and his family does not commonly rely on the motive of hunger, so the institution of the family is not based on the sexual motive.

Sex, like hunger, is one of the most powerful of incentives when released from the control of other incentives. That is probably why the family in all its variety of forms is never allowed to center on the sexual instinct, with its intermittences and vagaries, but on the combination of a number of effective motives that prevent sex from destroying an institution on which so much of man's happiness depends. Sex in itself will never produce anything better than a brothel, and even then it might have to draw on some incentives of the market mechanism. An economic system actually relying for its mainspring on hunger would be almost as perverse as a family system based on the bare urge of sex.

To attempt to apply economic determinism to all human societies is little short of fantastic. Nothing is more obvious to the student of social anthropology than the variety of institutions found to be compatible with practically identical instruments of production. Only since the market was permitted to grind the human fabric into the featureless uniformity of selenic erosion has man's institutional creativeness been in abeyance. No wonder that his social imagination shows signs of fatigue. It may come to a point where he will no longer be able to recover the elasticity, the imaginative wealth and power, of his savage endowment.

No protest of mine, I realize, will save me from being taken for an "idealist." For he who decries the importance of "material" motives must, it seems, be relying on the strength of "ideal" ones. Yet no worse misunderstanding is possible. Hunger and gain have nothing specifically "material" about them. Pride, honor, and power, on the other hand, are not necessarily "higher" motives than hunger and gain.

The dichotomy itself, we assert, is arbitrary. Let us once more adduce the analogy of sex. Assuredly, a significant distinction between "higher" and "lower" motives can here be drawn. Yet, whether hunger or sex, it is pernicious to *institutionalize* the separation of the "material" and "ideal" components of man's being. As regards sex, this truth, so vital to man's essential wholeness, has been recognized all along; it is at the basis of the institution of marriage. But in the equally strategic field of economy, it has been neglected. This latter field has been "separated out" of society as the realm of hunger and gain. Our animal dependence upon food has been bared and the naked fear of starvation permitted to run loose. Our humiliating enslavement to the "material," which all human culture is designed to mitigate, was deliberately made more rigorous. This is at the root of the "sickness of an acquisitive society" that Tawney warned of. And Robert Owen's genius was at its best when, a century before, he described the profit motive as "a principle entirely unfavorable to individual and public happiness."

The Reality of Society

I plead for the restoration of that unity of motives which should inform man in his everyday activity as a producer, for the reabsorption of the economic system in society, for the creative adaptation of our ways of life to an industrial environment.

On all these counts, laissez-faire philosophy, with its corollary of a marketing society, falls to the ground. It is responsible for the splitting up of man's vital unity into "real" man, bent on material values, and his "ideal" better self. It is paralyzing our social imagination by more or less unconsciously fostering the prejudice of "economic determinism".

It has done its service in that phase of industrial civilization which is behind us. At the price of impoverishing the individual, it enriched society. Today, we are faced with the vital task of restoring the fullness of life to the person, even though this may mean a technologically less efficient society. In different countries in different ways, classical liberalism is being discarded. On Right and Left and Middle, new avenues are being explored. British Social-Democrats, American New Dealers, and also European fascists and American anti-New Dealers of the various "managerialist" brands, reject the liberal utopia. Nor should the present political mood of rejection of everything Russian blind us to the achievement of the Russians in creative adjustment to some of the fundamental aspects of an industrial environment.

On general grounds, the Communist's expectation of the "withering away of the State" seems to me to combine elements of liberal utopianism with practical indifference to institutional freedoms. As regards the withering State, it is impossible to deny that industrial society is complex society, and no complex society can exist without organized power at the center. Yet, again, this fact is no excuse for the Communist's slurring over the question of concrete institutional freedoms.

It is on this level of realism that the problem of individual freedom should be met. No human society is possible in which power and compulsion are absent, nor is a world in which force has no function. Liberal philosophy gave a false direction to our ideals in seeming to promise the fulfillment of such intrinsically utopian expectations.

But under the market system, society as a whole remained invisible. Anybody could imagine himself free from responsibility for those acts of compulsion on the part of the state which he, personally, repudiated, or for unemployment and destitution from which he, personally, did not benefit. Personally, he remained unentangled in the evils of power and economic value. In good conscience, he could deny their reality in the name of his imaginary freedom.

Power and economic value are, indeed, a paradigm of social reality. Neither power nor economic value spring from human volition; non-cooperation is impossible in regard to them. The function of power is to insure that measure of conformity which is needed for the survival of the group: as David Hume showed, its ultimate source is opinion—and who could help holding opinions of some sort or other? Economic value, in any society, insures the usefulness of the goods produced; it is a seal set on the division of labor. Its source is human wants—and how could we be expected not to prefer one thing to another? Any opinion or desire, no matter what society we live in, will make us participants in the creation of power and the constituting of value. No freedom to do otherwise is conceivable. An ideal that would ban power and compulsion from society is intrinsically invalid. By ignoring this limitation on man's meaningful wishes, the marketing view of society reveals its essential immaturity.

The Problem of Freedom

The breakdown of market-economy imperils two kinds of freedom: some good, some bad.

That the freedom to exploit one's fellows, or the freedom to make inordinate gains without commensurable service to the community, the freedom to keep technological inventions from being used for the public benefit, or the freedom to profit from public calamities secretly engineered for private advantage, may disappear, together with the free market, is all to the good.

But the market-economy under which these freedoms thrived also produced freedoms that we prize highly. Freedom of conscience, freedom of speech, freedom of meeting, freedom of association, freedom to choose one's job—we cherish them for their own sake. Yet to a large extent they were by-products of the same economy that was also responsible for the evil freedoms.

The existence of a separate economic sphere in society created, as it were, a gap between politics and economics, betwen government and industry, that was in the nature of a no man's land. As division of sovereignty between pope and emperor left medieval princes in a condition of freedom sometimes bordering on anarchy, so division of sovereignty between government and industry in the 19th century allowed even the poor man to enjoy freedoms that partly compensated for his wretched status.

Current scepticism in regard to the future of freedom largely rests on this. There are those who argue, like Hayek, that since free institutions were a product of market-economy, they must give place to serfdom once that economy disappears. There are others, like Burnham, who assert the inevitability of some new form of serfdom called "managerialism."

Arguments like these merely prove to what extent economistic prejudice is still rampant. For such determinism, as we have seen, is only another name for the market-mechanism. It is hardly logical to argue the effects of its absence on the strength of an economic necessity which derives from its presence. And it is certainly contrary to Anglo-Saxon experience. Neither the freezing of labor nor selective service abrogated the essential freedoms of the American people, as anybody can witness who spent the crucial years 1940-1943 in these States. Great Britain during the war introduced an all-round planned economy and did away with that separation of government and industry from which 19th-century freedom sprang, yet never were public liberties more securely entrenched than at the height of the emergency. In truth, we will have just as much freedom as we will desire to create and to safeguard. There is no *one* determinant in human society. Institutional guarantees of personal freedom are compatible with any economic system. In market society alone did the economic mechanism lay down the law.

Man Vs. Industry

What appears to our generation as the problem of capitalism is, in reality, the far greater problem of an industrial civilization. The economic liberal is blind to this fact. In defending capitalism as an economic system, he ignores the challenge of the Machine Age. Yet the dangers that make the bravest quake today transcend economy. The idyllic concerns of trust-busting and Taylorization have been superseded by Hiroshima. Scientific barbarism is dogging our footsteps. The Germans were planning a contrivance to make the sun emanate death rays. We, in fact, produced a burst of death rays that blotted out the sun. Yet the Germans had an evil philosophy, and we had a humane philosophy. In this we should learn to see the symbol of our peril.

Among those in America who are aware of the dimensions of the problem, two tendencies are discernible: some believe in elites and aristocracies, in managerialism and the corporation. They feel that the whole of society should be more intimately adjusted to the economic system, which they would wish to maintain unchanged. This is the ideal of the Brave New World, where the individual is conditioned to support an order that has been designed for him by such as are wiser than he. Others, on the contrary, believe that in a truly democratic society, the problem of industry would resolve itself through the planned intervention of the producers and consumers themselves. Such conscious and responsible action is, indeed, one of the embodiments of freedom in a complex society. But, as the contents of this article suggest, such an endeavor cannot be successful unless it is disciplined by a total view of man and society very different from that which we inherited from market-economy.

57   The Rediscovery of the Market*

Charles E. Lindblom

What is the significance of the great debate, already several years old, on the appropriate role of profits in the planned economies of Communist Europe?

*From: *The Public Interest*, No. 4 (Summer, 1966), pp. 89-101 (reprinted by permission of author and publisher).

One interpretation of this sea change in Communist thinking is that Communism is turning capitalist. Since imitation is the sincerest form of flattery, many Americans are delighted to accept this interpretation. But the Communists do not see their reforms in this light; and Professor Liberman, whose name is foremost in the Soviet debate over the profit motive, has explicitly denied that Communist use of the profit motive is capitalistic. On his side of the argument there is some weighty evidence: namely, the existence of profit-oriented *socialist* enterprises all over the world—e.g., municipally-owned public utilities in the U.S., the nationalized industries of Britain and Western Europe, and the socialized enterprises of many developing nations (like Hindustan Machine Tools of India).

Indeed, the significance of the reforms has little to do with the antithesis capitalism-socialism. The new and growing use of profitability criteria in Communist enterprises can better be understood as a phase in *a worldwide rediscovery of the market mechanism.*

Now, capitalism and the market mechanism are not the same thing. Understandably, they are often confused with each other, because it was under capitalist auspices that the market mechanism first became, on a vast scale, the organizer of economic life. But the market mechanism is a device that can be employed for planned as well as unplanned economies, and for socialism and communism as well as capitalism. Today the market mechanism is a device both for the organization of the relatively unplanned sectors of the American economy and for such central planning as is practiced in the United States. In Britain and Scandinavia, it organizes both the private and the socialized sectors of the economy. In Yugoslavia it serves as an overall coordinator for an economy of publicly-owned enterprises. In many underdeveloped countries it is a powerful tool of development planning. It is this market mechanism rather than capitalism that the U.S.S.R. and its satellites are trying to employ—precisely to improve their planning.

Except for a convulsive attempt between 1918 and 1921, Soviet policy has never questioned the practical usefulness of money and prices. This does not mean, however, that the Soviet Union has heretofore made much use of the market mechanism. By the market mechanism, we mean the use of money and prices in a very particular way: prices and price movements are employed—instead of targets, quotas, and administrative instructions— to give signals to producers with respect to what and how much they should produce; and prices on labor and materials consumed are set to reflect the relative value of these inputs in alternative uses to which they might be put.

It is the possibility of using a pricing process to evaluate alternative possibilities and to cue producers accordingly—whether to suit the preferences of individual consumers in the market or the preferences of central planners, whether to administer the resources of an advanced economy or to guide the developmental choices of an underdeveloped economy—that has struck a new note in Communist economic policy, in the economic reorganization of Western Europe, and in the economic development of the nations still in early stages of growth. The significance of the development, of which Communist reforms are only a part, can be appreciated in the light of its own history.

Adam Smith and Laissez Faire

Most people who know anything at all about the market mechanism seem not to have advanced beyond Adam Smith's view of it. He saw it as *an alternative* to government control of economic life. He was concerned about inefficiency and other defects of mercantilism; and, to speak anachronistically, he thought he had found in the market mechanism a substitute for incompetent planners. His specific insights were profound. He saw the possibility that resources could be systematically allocated in response to human needs as a by-product of "selfish" individual decisions simply to buy or to sell. He saw that prices established by consumers in their trading with producers could establish a set of signals that could direct the productive processes of the whole economy. He saw that competitive bidding for inputs would establish a market value for them that would make possible a comparison of their productivities in alternative uses. He saw that a comparison of input prices and output prices, that is, of the money cost of production with money receipts, could control the flow of resources into each of their alternative possible uses. Finally, he saw that the market mechanism was for all these reasons an extraordinarily powerful device for decentralizing economic decisions. In all this, however, his vision was limited: the market mechanism was always a private enterprise market and always an alternative to planning.

Market Socialism

It was not until the development, over a century and a half later, of the theory of market socialism that any significant number of people perceived the possibilities of using the market mechanism in a completely socialized economy. Even today the idea of market socialism remains esoteric. In 1920, Ludwig von Mises published his now famous challenge to the socialists to indicate whether they had any system in mind for the actual administration of economic affairs in a socialist order. It was a challenge that many socialists brushed aside, believing that they could cross that bridge when they came to it. But a few socialists, conspicuous among them the late Oskar Lange, turned back to the 1908 work of the Italian economist Barone, to construct a model of a socialist economy that would practice a systematic and decentralized evaluation and allocation of its resources. They showed that prices could be manipulated by government in such a way as to reflect the values that consumers put on consumer goods and services, and also to reflect the values of inputs in alternative uses. Their discussion of the pricing process under socialism clarified the useful functions that prices can perform. If, for goods and services in short supply, prices are systematically raised by government pricing authorities, the high prices can be taken as signals for increased production, while being at the same time at least temporary deterrents to consumption. Similarly, if prices are systematically lowered for goods in overabundant supply, the low prices can be taken as signals by producers to curtail supply, and by consumers to increase consumption.

Lange's 1936 exposition of these possibilities made it clear that prices could be systematically regulated to perform the signalling and evaluating functions even in the absence of those competing private sellers whose rivalry sets prices in a private enterprise economy. Moreover, his exposition demonstrated that prices so set permit a systematic comparison of alternative patterns of allocation, a comparison that would not be possible without prices of this kind.

If the development of the theory of market socialism made it clear that the market mechanism could serve socialism as well as capitalism, it nevertheless did not much interest the socialists of Western Europe or the planners of Communist Europe. For the market socialist had developed a model of a socialist economy that left very little room for central planning. Their socialist market mechanism was designed, as was the market mechanism of classical economics, to serve the preferences of individual consumers rather than the priorities of central planners. As in a capitalist economy, in this kind of market socialism the consumer remained sovereign—at a time when most socialists, planners, and Communists were looking for ways to effect collective purposes and national goals, rather than individual preferences. Although socialist theory considered harnessing the market mechanism to centrally determined priorities, it did not construct a persuasive case as to how it could be done.

In the Communist countries, the possibilities of market socialism were underrated for still other reasons. Communist ideology was antagonistic to the very idea of the market, hence inevitably to market socialism. Academic and professional Soviet economics was also antagonistic to the orthodox tradition in economic theory out of which the theory of market socialism sprang. Finally, with respect to formal planning and resource allocation, the overwhelming concern of Soviet policy was "balance" rather than what economists call optimality. Optimality involves a careful evaluation of returns to production in alternative lines. To Soviet planners, however, the need for big allocations to steel, electric power production, and national defense seemed obvious. Speaking very roughly, all that remained to be done was to insure that allocations for the rest of the economy were roughly consistent with, or in balance with, the crudely calculated but obviously necessary allocations to these high priority sectors. And even this formal interest in balance was secondary to their interest in the crude growth of physical output.

The Market Mechanism for Centrally Determined Objectives

If the market mechanism was ever to be of any use for central planning, it had to be shown that prices could be set to reflect centrally determined values, and not merely individual consumer values. In the economics of the West, it has in fact long been clear that they can do so. For example, a subsidy to maritime shipping lines or to airmail carriers is a way of raising the price received by those who provide these transport services, thus signalling them to increase their production of the services. Similarly, a tax on liquor is a way of depressing the price received by manufacturers and distributors, hence a way of signalling them to restrict output. The result of these interventions—either subsidies or taxes—is to achieve a price that reflects both individual consumer preference *and* the preferences of governmental authorities.

A government can go even further—and in wartime often does. It can completely eliminate the effect on price of individual consumer demands so that producers respond to a price set entirely by government. This can be done either through the imposition of a legal price or by exclusive government purchase of commodities and services, after which government agencies either consume the purchased goods and services themselves or, in the case of consumer goods, redistribute them in some way to consumers.

Using the market mechanism in this way is an alternative to direct administrative control—to targets, quotas, physical allocations, specific instructions, etc. It is not always a good alternative, but it often is, since it is a way of manipulating incentives powerfully while leaving the actual decision—to produce or consume more or less—in the hands of the agency or enterprise whose price has been altered. Hence, a general virtue of the market mechanism as an instrument of central direction is that it permits extraordinary decentralization of detailed decision making.

To understand the possibility of subordinating the market mechanism to governmental rather than to individual choice, it is essential to distinguish between actions in which governments signal their production targets through prices, and actions in which they intervene in the market mechanism to alter the results without, however, actually using prices systematically as such a signalling device. To raise agricultural prices, for example, in order to stimulate agricultural production is a way of employing the market mechanism for the achievement of a centrally-determined goal of high agricultural production. On the other hand, to raise agricultural prices as part of a complex process of restricting farm output (as in the U.S.) is an entirely different kind of operation, in which direct administrative controls (such as acreage quotas) replace the market mechanism. Or again: depressing the price received by a manufacturer by imposing a tax on his output is a way of implementing a central decision to discourage consumption of the commodity, whereas the general imposition of legal maximum prices to control inflation has the effect of interfering with the market's ability to reflect either collective or individual choices and will ordinarily give rise to rationing, or to some other administrative device for the allocation of goods and services.

Perhaps it is the easy confusion of miscellaneous intervention in the pricing process (which the Communist economies have always practiced) with the skillful use of pricing to implement central planning of production that has contributed to Communist indifference to the latter. In any case, the Western demonstration that the market mechanism could be used to implement central priorities did not significantly affect Communist policy until certain other developments occurred. Even as late as 1950, the model of market socialism seems to be consigned to a limbo of interesting irrelevancies. Ideological barriers were still strong; so also was the obstacle of fundamental ignorance in Soviet economies about the pricing process.

Yugoslavia

The Yugoslav economy was the one sensational exception to Communist indifference to the market mechanism. Yugoslav Communism was indigenous, not imposed by the U.S.S.R. as in the satellites generally. Political relations with the Societ Union were such that in Yugoslavia independence in economic policy came to be valued rather than feared. Moreover, Yugoslav intellectuals and politicos had closer ties with their counterparts in the West than did any of the other Communist countries. Whatever the reasons, in 1952, recoiling from the inefficiencies of detailed administrative control over the economy, Yugoslavia brought into being a greatly decentralized market socialism. The change of direction, taken together with the rapid growth that ensued, excited much interest in the Communist world. The significance for Communism of the Yugoslav venture was greatly diminished on one score, however. For when the Yugoslavs abandoned detailed administrative control over the market mechanism they also went a long way toward consumer sovereignty as a replacement for the central direction of the economy. Hence, in the eyes of Communists elsewhere the Yugoslavs had largely abandoned central planning itself.

New Freedom for Economic Inquiry

New possibilities for economics were opened up by Stalin's death in 1953. Soviet economists, engineers, and administrators could finally look with some freedom at the lessons to be learned from foreign experience with the market mechanism. One especially noteworthy gain for economic analysis was the lifting of Stalin's capricious ban on mathematical economics (input-output analysis, and linear programming, etc.) .

Soviet mathematical economics, reaching back to work originating in the 1930's but not then pursued further, demonstrated independently of Western economics that pricing can be made useful to the planning of resource allocation even in the absence of any actual exchange between a buyer and seller. If we consider all the alternative combinations of end products that an economy can choose from, and all the alternative combinations of inputs that might be used to produce any given output, we see that there are vast possibilities of substitution—of one end product for another, and of one input for another. These possibilities of substitution can be represented by "substitution ratios"—and these substitution ratios can be expressed as a system of prices. (In the absence of any actual transaction in which a real price would be set, they are often called "shadow prices".) *Pricing turns out, therefore, to be implicit in the very logic of rational choice among alternative uses of resources.*

This discovery clearly removes certain traditional ideological objections to market pricing, for it makes clear that pricing is not a capitalist invention but a logical aid to rational calculation even in circumstances far removed from capitalist buying and selling. Whether in fact the discovery has yet achieved this consequence for Soviet thought is not certain, however; for Soviet mathematical economists have, on the whole, drawn the inference, not that the market mechanism might now be more openly examined, but that such pricing as might be achieved through the market mechanism can in principle now better be achieved through further mathematical analysis and electronic computation.

The "in principle" is crucial, since a prodigious amount of information needs to be gathered and processed in order to substitute computers for actual markets; and so far the accomplishment is beyond the capacity of economists, Soviet or Western. Nor can it be said with confidence that there is any way to gather and test the required information except by putting consumers or planners in the position of actual choice in a real market. Still, the exploration of the practical mathematics of resource allocation is far from its maturity.

The Rising Concern for Allocative Efficiency

In any case, the discovery of "shadow pricing" did not of itself overcome Communist disinclination to exploit the market mechanism. A final consideration was the growing complexity of the Soviet economy, with complexity outstripping admittedly growing Soviet competence in planning. The economy became more complex for at least two reasons: with the rising standard in living, the demand of consumers for varied and higher-quality consumer goods came to be more pressing; and with technological advance, alternative production possibilities became more numerous and complex. Soviet policy makers could no longer be satisfied with the simple mobilization of large quantities of capital, and the attendant mobilization of agricultural labor, for industry. As one student of the Soviet economy has written:

> "The Soviet economy again appears to be at a turning point. It is clear, as the debate shows, that it is becoming more and more difficult to plan *everything* centrally. The Soviet economy has grown not only in size, but in sophistication in concern for the consumer. As a result, campaigns and storming can no longer solve all the problems that arise. There are simply too many sectors which need attention. They can not all be manipulated from the center. It has

been estimated that, if the economy continues its present growth, by 1980 the planning force will have to be thirty-six times its present size."

It is especially noteworthy that the older Communist concern for "balance" is, in the face of this new complexity, no longer thought sufficient. It is increasingly difficult to find some clear superiority of one pattern for a few key industries over another alternative pattern. And that being so, Communist countries can no longer be satisfied with merely balancing the outputs and inputs of all other industries to satisfy a prior commitment to a few key programs. In short, consistency in an economic plan is no longer enough; optimality in a plan is now becoming a pressing objective. Hence, finally, the new interest in the market mechanism.

In their forthcoming study, *The Soviet Capital Stock 1928-1962*, Raymond P. Powell and Richard Moorsteen will document still another hypothesis to explain the new Soviet interest in improved resource allocation ("optimality"). The Soviet Union, they suggest, has been exhausting the possibilities for rapid growth through indefinitely larger and larger capital investment; it must now either find an alternative source of growth —i.e. a better allocation of resources—or resign itself to a lower growth rate.

Paradox of Planning

How far the Communist economics will go in employing the market mechanism of course remains to be seen. An ideological and traditional resistance to the market mechanism does not quickly evaporate and presumably will never wholly evaporate. Moreover, a market mechanism is not always and universally a serviceable instrument for economic organization. Even in an economy like that of the U.S., in which ideology is all on the side of the market mechanism, its use has to be constrained by the recognition of its limitations.

In the Communist case, there remains one conspicuous obstacle to extending the employment of the market mechanism, sometimes referred to as the "paradox of planning." The problem can be posed this way: if the planners intend to use prices to signal production goals for the economy, they cannot set appropriate prices for end products until they first decide what quantities of various end products they desire. But they cannot intelligently decide on appropriate quantities of end products unless they know their costs, i.e., the resources used up in their production. Now, in a market mechanism, these costs are represented by prices; and this is to say that they cannot determine desired quantities of end products until they know prices. But we have just said that they cannot determine prices until they know what quantities of end products they desire!

This problem does not arise when the price mechanism is used to implement any single collective choice, as in a Western economy, because a decision, say, to expand the production of maritime transport services can take as given the relevant prices already prevailing on the market. Planning an increase in the production of no more than a few commodities or services does not so alter price relationships and production patterns for the entire economy as to invalidate prevailing prices as guide lines for the planners. But to plan, through pricing, a production pattern *for an entire economy* promises readjustments of prices that will invalidate the very set of prices that the planners depend upon for making their plans.

It follows that the fullest use of a market mechanism as an instrument for central planning would require that central planners actually operate, not directly through a master plan in which all major lines of production for the economy are simultaneously established, but through a large number of (and a series of) specific choices for each of all outputs or industries to be planned. When a choice is made for any output or industry, the outputs and prices for other industries need to be regarded—for planning purposes—as unchanged. To make the fullest use of the market mechanism, central planners need to work out a strategy for goal-setting and pricing (against a background of the overall general plan) that proceeds through many specific *and sequential* price and production decisions.

Such a procedure, it may be the case, is already in embryo in the Communist economies—even though, for lack of understanding of its utility, it is more often hidden than openly displayed. Given the complexity of the task of comprehensive, synoptic national economic planning, and given also the inevitable limits on man's intellectual capacities, even where these capacities are extended by electronic computation, planning all over the world tends to break down into clusters and sequences of specific decisions. The mere construction of detailed five-year plans does not prove that anyone or any organization has achieved an integrated synopsis of the elements of the plan; instead these plans are typically a collection of targets and policies from many sources.

The Rediscovery of the Market in the West

Outside the Communist orbit, an appreciation of the usefulness of the market mechanism has been most conspicuously on the rise since World War II. With good reason, the market was under great attack in the depression of the '30's, the severity of disillusionment with its usefulness nowhere more vivid than in the American NRA, an attempt at partial displacement of the market in favor of private and public administrative controls. But in the late '30's, Keynesian economics began to hold out the promise of ending depressions by improving rather than eliminating the market mechanism; and Western governments, learning the lesson, have in recent years sustained higher levels of employment than used to be thought possible. Similarly, taxation and transfer payments, as well as provision of subsidized public goods like education, have attacked problems of inequality in income distribution—such problems can therefore no longer motivate proposals to disestablish the market mechanism. The result is that, in the West, the market mechanism is in better repute than ever before, as is indicated in the decline of socialist opposition to the market mechanism both on the continent and in Britain, where after World War II socialists deliberately subjected their newly nationalized enterprises to market controls rather than to the battery of administrative controls they had once contemplated. And the great event in Western European development in recent decades has been a substantial move toward unification, not through common government, flag, army, or language, but through the Common *Market*.

The Developing Nations

As a group, the underdeveloped nations of the world are lagging in their understanding of the usefulness of the market mechanism. Abstractly, they should be eager to exploit every possibility for economic advance; in fact, they stand in a kind of backwater.

One reason is that their leaders and intellectuals are often prisoners of a once exciting but now stifling orthodoxy. Some of them are prisoners of early Marxian doctrine on planning, the very orthodoxy from which European Communism is escaping. Others are prisoners of English socialism of the style and date of Harold Laski, or even of earlier versions of English socialism—in either case antagonistic to the market mechanism. But times change: although Nehru was a prisoner of both, his daughter may turn out to be a prisoner of neither.

Another reason is, oddly enough, the insistence of the United States, the World Bank, and other lenders that underdeveloped countries formulate national economic plans in order to qualify for aid. They mean by a plan a balanced and consistent set of investment outlays. The effect is to divert some of the best brains in these countries away from high priority questions of growth strategy to the construction of reconciled investment programs reminiscent of those the Communist countries are trying to leave behind as inadequate. In India, for example, the question of the size and internal consistency of the five-year plans overshadows in public discussion, and in the attention it receives from experts in Indian government, many more rewarding questions of growth strategy, including such questions as how the market mechanism might be employed to hold out incentives to farmers to raise food production or how it might ration scarce foreign exchange in such a way as to substantially raise the level of economic achievement.

To be sure, just how much the underdeveloped economies should count on the market mechanism is subject to much dispute. The point being made here is only that the underdeveloped countries themselves do not well understand the issues, and have often not tumbled to the fact that, for many of the specific developmental problems they face, they can employ the market mechanism in tandem with other methods of controlling and planning economic development.

The prospect that the underdeveloped countries may take a new view of the market mechanism as an instrument of development planning is, of course, greatly enlarged by what they now see developing in Communist

Europe. For even if they do not intend to follow the Communist path to development, the evidence that Western and Communist economies alike are finding the market mechanism useful is certain to impress them.

How they can best employ the market mechanism depends upon the particulars of their circumstances. But on a few counts a general usefulness of the market mechanism for these economies can be predicted. First, they all suffer desperately from a shortage of administrative skills and organization: they are not very competent in executing *any* kind of plan, economic or otherwise. Even the best of their civil services have developed procedures and traditions more suitable to keeping the peace than to stimulating economic development. Hence, on this score alone, they need the market mechanism more than do the advanced countries of the world.

Secondly, most of them have accumulated a mixed bag of administrative interventions in the market mechanism, such as price controls and exchange allocations, which have undercut the servicability of the market mechanism without putting any positive administrative program in its place. To impose, for example, maximum prices on food grains in order to hold down the price of food in towns and cities saps the farmer's incentive to produce more. It takes away the monetary incentive and puts nothing in its place— it destroys one mechanism of development without substituting another.

Thirdly, while the development of an economy through administrative techniques furiously engages the energies of a planning elite, participation in development through the market mechanism is open to everyone and, indeed, typically engages most of the adult population. Cueing, signalling, rewarding, and penalizing through the market mechanism are methods of drawing on the largest possible number of responses—and, in addition, a method of extricating a traditional peasantry from older institutions and habits of life that retard development.

Fourthly—and here is a consideration of enormous importance to most underdeveloped countries—they need the market mechanism because they cannot take the route to rapid development that the Soviet Union took from the 1920's to the '60's. Foreswearing in that period any hope for skillful allocation of their resources, the Soviets instead counted on achieving growth through restricted consumption and massive investment. Their strategy worked because the restriction of consumption was in fact possible. It was possible for two reasons: the standard of living was high enough to permit forced savings, and the Soviet government was willing and able to use compulsion. In many underdeveloped countries, neither of these conditions holds; in some, only one does. In many cases, the surplus over and above what is essential to consumption is much smaller than in the Soviet case, where development proceeded from an already advanced stage of early industrialization and food availability. And in ever more cases neither effective systems for tax administration nor other instruments of compulsion are sufficient to gather the savings that are hypothetically available. Hence, except to the extent that capital assistance from abroad can take the place of forced savings and investment, these underdeveloped countries cannot successfully imitate the older Soviet pattern. They need to understand, as even the Soviet Union in its new condition is coming to understand, the indispensibility of a judicious use of the market mechanism for efficient use of the limited resources they can command.

No Paradox for Planning

That the non-Communist underdeveloped nations can use the market mechanism to satisfy the individual needs of consumers is of course clear. But what of the usefulness of the market mechanism for implementing centrally-determined social priorities—to strengthen the industrial sector, for example, or to give a special push to agriculture, or to establish a steel-producing capacity? It follows from what was said above, about the paradox of planning, that it is just this kind of precise intervention for which the market mechanism is a demonstrably effective instrument of central planning. For this kind of *planning through selective intervention,* the paradox of planning does not arise; and no special techniques need to be devised to overcome it, as do need to be devised in the Communist countries of Europe. Hence, it turns out that the kind of "central planning" to which these underdeveloped economies are committed is the very kind for which the market mechanism is best suited.

Conclusion

That the market mechanism can be serviceable to planned and unplanned economies alike, to public and private enterprise alike, to collective and individual choice alike, is a discovery the significance of which may soon dwarf what we have seen of its consequences so far. To say this is not to take sides in the many disputes in many countries in which, for particular purposes at hand, the question has to be settled as to how far and under what circumstances market organization ought to be pushed. It is only to take note of the fact that, although these disputes will remain, and although different countries will choose different combinations of the market and other forms of organization of economic life, the market mechanism is now everywhere coming to be recognized as a fundamental method of economic organization which no nation can ignore and which every nation can well afford to examine freshly. Even China, bent on its own course, may come to be caught up in the movement toward the market. For lack of experience with, and personnel for, direct administration, China has perhaps gone less far in disestablishing the market under Communism than its ideological claims would suggest. If so, we may be witnessing a race in China between an old-fashioned Marxian determination to undermine the market as soon as administrative competence permits and a growing sophistication about the market's usefulness—with the result unpredictable, if momentous.

58 Putting Marx to Work

A Reappraisal of Marxian Economics*

By Robert L. Heilbroner

"Is society a branch of physics?" asked the Abbé Mably, a minor nineteenth-century pamphleteer and *philosophe*. The absurd question serves very well to introduce a discussion of what modern economics is about and whether Karl Marx still has something to contribute to economic thought. For, essentially, economics has always answered Yes to the Abbé's query. That is, it has always proceeded on the belief that there were enough regularities in the social process to enable a skilled observer to discover "laws" that described its movements, just as other laws described the motion of the planets in their orbits.

To be sure, economists have always recognized that there was a vast gulf between the unknowing planets and sentient human beings, and therefore they have never intended the laws to be as strict in the second case as in the first. Yet the gulf was not so wide as to destroy all similarity between the orderliness of the natural world and that of the social. For underneath the seeming disorder of the social universe, two processes could be discerned that imposed a degree of lawlike regularity on the events of economic society. One of these was the process of production itself—the actual technical sequences by which wheat became bread and grapes wine and iron ore steel. Although these sequences differed one from another, and although they changed over time with technological advance, nonetheless there seemed to be sufficient regularity, at least in the short run, so that we could talk of "laws" of production, such as diminishing returns or economies of scale or "coefficient of production" or "marginal elasticities of substitution" —all terms that describe the dependability of the productive element within the social universe.

The other order-bestowing element in the economic process concerned its human side, which is to say the behavior of workers and consumers and entrepreneurs. Clearly, this aspect of the underlying social orderliness could not be expected to demonstrate the same degree of invariance that is found in the physical world. Yet in the behavior of buyers and sellers there seemed to be a sufficient degree of repetitiveness so that we could talk of the "law" of supply and demand; and in the responses of consumers to changes in

*From: A Review Article by R. L. Heilbroner in *The New York Review of Books*, Volume XI, No. 10, 5 December, 1968, pp. 8-10 (reprinted by permission of author and publisher).

their incomes or of businessmen to changes in the interest rate other law-like patterns emerged.

Thus from the very beginning, economists have striven for a picture of society in which the interaction of laws of production and behavior—production and behavior *functions* is the modern term—would describe the major economic events of the social system much as if it were a branch of physics. Moreover, by reducing the complexity of the real world to the simplicity of a "model" dominated by these two great functions, economists, like physicists, have sought to predict the path of motion of their system.

How successful has been this audacious intellectual effort? On the face of it, the achievement has been astonishing. Models of the economy are now so complex that they require the facilities of a computer and the techniques of difference equations, matrix algebra, LaGrangian multipliers, and the like. Sophistication, elegance, rigor—the criteria by which mathematics has traditionally been judged—are now the standards of economic theorizing. Not least, the success of modern economics can be read in the flattery of imitation paid to it by its sister disciplines of sociology and political science which now seek to build models similar to those of the economist. Certainly, when the intellectual history of our times is finally written, the creation of the edifice of modern "neo-classical" economics will occupy a central chapter in it.

The only question is, what will that chapter say about the usefulness and relevance of this extraordinary enterprise? Here I suspect the appraisal of the future will not be uncritically admiring. The theory of economics, magnificent to behold, is considerably less impressive to use. It is true that it has given us a rough picture of how the market system works, both in allocating its resources and in determining the level of overall output. But beyond this conception, which can be taught with ease to a college freshman, the ramifications of economics have produced singularly little. A rococo branch called welfare theory, for example, has not, to my knowledge, yet resulted in a single substantive proposal that has added significantly to the welfare of mankind. The beautifully finished portion called price theory fails to explain the pricing operations of the great corporations. International trade theory does not adequately account for the most important single fact about international trade—to wit, the failure of an international division of labor to shed its benefits on poor countries and rich countries alike. The theory of economic development does not tell underdeveloped countries how to grow.

Even the central achievement of twentieth-century economics—the elucidation of the forces that determine prosperity and recession—fails when we seek to foretell the fortunes of the economy a few months hence. No doubt economists reading these words will deem them vastly exaggerated, which perhaps they are. Yet it is surely an opinion not wholly at variance with mine that must have moved Kenneth Arrow, a well-known economist, to sum up the collected papers of Paul Samuelson, the most brilliant theorist of our generation, with these words: "A careful examination of the papers both on theory and on policy yields only the most oblique suggestion that neoclassical price theory is descriptive of the real world. Of course, there is no denial, but Samuelson's attitude is clearly guarded and agnostic" (*Journal of Political Economy,* October, 1967).

Why is it that modern economic theory presents the spectacle of superb intellectual achievement without much social relevance? To my mind there are two reasons. One lies in the difficulties of reducing the real world—both in its technical and in its behavioral aspects—to reliable patterns with which we can then construct dependable models. It is one thing to ascribe an underlying "lawlike" character to the processes of production and to the responses of the economic actors, and quite another to reduce these activities to mathematical functions. In the case of production, for example, we encounter enormous difficulties in devising mathematical functions that will accurately account for the constantly changing nature of technology. And this difficulty is compounded by the even more intractable problem of finding functional representations of human behavior. No doubt, for instance, men tend to buy less when prices rise and to buy more when prices fall. Yet, on occasion, they will do just the opposite, as when they expect a price rise or price fall to *continue*—in which case their self-interest bids them to buy more in a hurry in the first case, and to hold off in the second.

Hence the inherent complexities of the production process and the vagaries of human behavior may well set limits to the predictive possibilities of economic theorizing, and these limits may account for much of the gap that exists between economic theory and economic reality. Yet, however much these difficulties explain the inaccuracy of economic theorizing, they do not account for its irrelevance. I have already mentioned the failure of price theory to explain the behavior of the large corporation and the gap between the theory and the reality of international trade. Now I must point out other areas of economic life over which modern economic theory passes in virtual silence. The distribution of wealth, for example, is a central economic fact about which it is mute. The effects on the distribution of income attributable to the process of growth is another, so that economics gives us no hint of the disturbances and frictions produced by long-run economic advance. The effect of a constantly improving technology on the level of employment is similarly ignored, so that today the theory of technological unemployment is in much the same shape as was the theory of mass unemployment in the days before Keynes. The nature of class interests in a capitalist system is not mentioned in any textbook, so that nothing in the nature of political or social constraints confines the free movement of the economic model.

In all of this, it will be noted, there is a common denominator. This is the systematic exclusion of matters that might connect the functional model with the pressures and resistances of the political world. This exclusion, which accounts for so much of the irrelevance of economics, is by no means accidental. Rather, it results from a fundamental failure of vision on the part of the modern model-builders, *who do not see that the social universe that they are attempting to reproduce in a set of equations is not and cannot be adequately described by functional relationships alone, but must also and simultaneously be described as a system of privilege.* In other words, if a model of economic reality is to be relevant, it must portray both the functional relationships peculiar to the provisioning process and those stemming from the clash of interests generated by this very functional process itself.

Is it possible to construct a system that is at one and the same time a portrayal of functional relationships and of privilege? There is one such system, Marxian economics—that vast *terra incognita* over which the average economics student flies while en route to the oral examination (where it may be mentioned as part of the History of Economic Doctrines) and at which he never again casts a glance. For what is unique about the Marxian system is that the categories, both of production and of behavior, into which it disaggregates the world are considerably different from those of the neoclassical system. On the production side, for example, Marxism lays great stress on the necessity for a "fit" between the output of the capital goods sector and that of the consumer goods sector, a relationship that is unnoticed in neoclassical economics where the aggregate output of *all* sectors is stressed rather than the relationship between them. Similarly, on the behavioral side, Marx approaches the problem of describing the great "human" functions by building up a picture of the actions of producers—that is, workers and capitalists—rather than by analyzing the activities of *buyers,* i.e., of consumers and investors. In different words, the Marxian analysis breaks down the total flow of economic activity into layers of costs, wages and profits rather than into the slices of consumption and investment characteristic of the Keynesian approach.

The result of the special categories of abstraction imposed by the Marxian view is to bring into the foreground a number of matters that fail to appear in neoclassical analysis, in particular the instability of the economy stemming from a failure of its productive components to interlock, and the changing division of the social product among the classes—profit receivers and wage earners—that compete for it. Now it should be said immediately that the manner in which classical Marxian analysis performs its task of constructing a model of society is very awkward and occasionally downright wrong. The "laws of motion" that it discerns within the capitalist system depend on rigid assumptions about the way in which technology permits labor to be combined with capital and loses sight of the central effect of productivity in changing the real shares of wage earners in the final product. Worse yet, as a means of explaining the price mechanism by which the system is coordinated, Marxian economics is hopelessly clumsy: if one examines the efforts of the more liberal Soviet or Czech economists to create a rational pricing system using Marxian concepts, and compares these efforts with the results obtained by nonMarxian price theory, the contrast is like that between a dull cleaver and a sharp scalpel.[1]

Why then bother with Marxian economics when, as virtually every economist will tell you, it is "wrong"? The reason is that, unlike neoclassical analysis, which is "right," the Marxian model has in surfeit the quality of social relevance that is so egregiously lacking in the other. The neoclassical model has rigor, but, alas, also mortis. The Marxian model has relevance, but, alas, also mistakes. The answer then, is clear. Marxian insights must be married to neoclassical techniques to produce an economic theory that is both elegant and consistent as a model and freighted with meaning as a theory of society. . . .

59   Economics and Mystification*

Melville H. Watkins

Economists have a hang-up about power. They have power, or appear to have it. But they use it to support the System—and the on-rushing status quo—and might not appear to be powerful if they didn't. Above all, they don't, as intellectuals, understand power. Economic theory, the kind of theory that economists use, just doesn't come to grips with it.

Now this essay is about mysteries and mystification. Why am I talking, then, about economics and power? Because it is the failure of economists to deal with power, analytically and theoretically, that constitutes the mystification. Complex theories and high-powered techniques are used to grapple with issues in a superficial way. By ignoring power the economist claims to be apolitical. In fact, he is trapped in a sense that only the innocent can be.

Let us repeat the tale more methodically. Economists have power, or appear to have it. No self-respecting government, corporation, or even university would think anymore that it could understand its present or probe

---

[1]Let me take a moment to call to the attention of interested readers an exceptionally useful group of books, all translations of works by Soviet or East European economists, published by the International Arts and Sciences Press, White Plains, N.Y. In particular I recommend *Toward a Theory of Planned Economy* by the Yugoslav Branco Horvat and *Plan and Market under Socialism* by the Czech Ota Sik. Both are technically demanding but enlightening efforts to combine the techniques and categories of Marxian and Western economics.

*From: *Journal of Canadian Studies*, Vol. IV, No. 1, (February, 1969), pp. 55-59, (reprinted by permission of author and publisher).

plan the University of Toronto, with the reasonable expectation that methods devised will have more general relevance. Whenever the Canadian government has an impossible assignment, like making sense out of the tax system or devising a policy toward foreign investment, it hires economists—and they are invariably ready and willing. Once dismissed as the dismal science, economics has been riding high ever since John Kennedy brought top American economists into the White House and, with a little help from the Cold War, made the American economy depression-proof. Canada soon followed suit with a modified less efficient version of the American system in the form of the Economic Council.

One measure of power is the capacity to disrupt. In the late 1950's, John Kenneth Galbraith made the New York stock market plunge billions when he told a Senate Committee that the existing situation had interesting parallels with the period prior to the Great Crash of 1929. Galbraith's views were suddenly shown to be on a par with Eisenhower's health. It is said that whenever the British economist Nicholas Kaldor visits an under-developed country to advise on the tax system, the completion of his work is followed by riots shortly thereafter. For my own part, after a recent speech to an audience of American businessmen, I was accused by a Canadian businessman who was present of having just cost Canada 100 million dollars. It was a sobering thought.

Lest you find this simply funny, consider the fact that the disastrous war in Vietnam was administered until recently by Robert McNamara with the help of some of America's brightest young economists.

But do economists really have power, or is it just an illusion? As an economist I would have to say, with regrets, mostly the latter. A distinction can be made between the expert as traditional intellectual who devotes himself to a critique of the way it is, and the expert as organic intellectual who devotes himself to working for the system—not only, or even primarily, by helping in his small way to solve its problems, which is largely legitimate and proper, but rather by rationalizing its operation; by developing theory which always ends up proving that this is really the best of all possible worlds; by endlessly debating minor differences in policy so that everyone forgets, partly through fatigue, that there may be major alternatives that no-one is even taking the bother to try to conceptualize.

In my prejudiced view, a classic example of all this is the Carter Commission. Faced with the appalling existence of poverty in Canada, and in spite of a clear commitment on the part of the Commission to improve the distribution of income, it managed to bog itself down in devising a perfect tax system to assure fairness to taxpayers and to allocate resources efficiently and largely lost sight of the need to use the tax system in some imaginative way—like the negative income tax—to redistribute income from the rich to the poor.

In the final analysis, however, the critical point is that the theory economists use has been emptied of the political. The economist has a trained incapacity to understand power; his innocence is not accidental. A modern day economist sees himself as concerned with allocating scarce means among competing ends. He sees economic theory as a set of techniques, or a technology, that gives the best solution to this fundamental problem. In the West, the answer invariably turns out to be the use of markets, and endless energy is devoted to discovering their minor imperfections and fighting false battles with businessmen and civil servants more openly committed to the free enterprise ideology. In the process, what is ignored is that *the market economy is not a neutral mechanism that can be allowed free reign in a society without the most profound political and social implications which then constrain the solutions which economists can put forward. The market economy creates the market society and thereby a set of institutions and values which are anything but neutral.*[1] Suddenly, important things like the distribution of wealth and of income become sacrosanct, for to challenge them would undermine the incentives requisite for the operation of the market economy—that is, it would undermine the power elite who have most to gain from the operation of the market economy. Economists become, without quite being aware of it, rationalizers of the status quo. Their theories deal with efficiency—and equity and humanity get neglected.

Jacques Ellul has written about the triumph of technique and its increasing autonomy from social and human considerations. As he makes clear, economics is a leading example of this disease. If economists say sensible and humane things, as they sometimes do, it is largely by accident, by a process of random truth. In politics, we talk of the radical right and the radical left. My colleague Abraham Rotstein has suggested that modern liberal economists belong to the radical center. As intellectuals and citizens, they are usually in the center of the mainstream, or at most slightly to the left. But as technocrats, using techniques increasingly developed out of the exigencies of economic theory or adapted from the natural sciences, they may build models and propose policies which are genuinely radical in the sense of the social disruption that would result from their serious application.

These are serious charges. They are also somewhat sweeping. Can they be sustained if one looks at particular issues? I think they can, and I propose to try two for size—poverty and foreign ownership.

The issue of poverty has already been touched on in passing. In the last decade, poverty has suddenly become visible in North America. The only economist who played any significant role in this discovery was John Kenneth Galbraith—and Galbraith, in spite of, perhaps even because of, his high standing among the lay public, is not well regarded by his professional colleagues. This oversight is not surprising for economists for at least the past century have not had anything important to say about the causes

---

[1]Emphasis added. (Eds.)

of poverty. Unwilling or unable to diagnose, prescription becomes haphazard. Economists talk about the poor as if they were dealing with dropouts who need a little help in shaping up. The possibility that industrialization, at least under capitalism, creates the poor in the very process of creating the affluent—or, worse still, that the affluent owe some considerable portion of their affluence to their ability to exploit others at home and abroad—is rarely perceived.

If you want to see how economists can mystify you on this matter, read Chapter 6 of the Fifth Annual Review of the Economic Council. It is a mixture of sentimentalism, paternalism, and technocracy—the latter in the guise of cost-benefit analysis. The Council's major recommendation is for further study, yet it gets headlines across Canada. Not only does it manage to substitute talk for action and assuage middleclass guilt, it mystifies us by implying that we could do something if we wanted—pending, of course, further study, careful weighing of priorities and so on. This masks the truth that liberal democratic societies like Canada appear unable, because of their power structure, to do anything serious about correcting poverty. One finally grasps the sickness of the joke that is being played upon us when the Council suggests that the cost-benefit techniques developed in the Pentagon to help the Americans lose the War in Vietnam be applied in the North American War on Poverty.

At the world level, matters are distinctly worse. The rich countries fight real wars to prevent the poor from adopting a social and political structure other than the capitalistic. The major policy advice we give is to stop breeding. The problem is people. If only there were fewer of them. Technology provides the answer and the pill will create economic growth. We show every willingness to subsidize the distribution of contraceptives but no willingness to stabilize the prices of the exports of the poor countries. The latter, unfortunately, would violate the market ideology.

Yet commodity price stabilization, albeit at the risk of increasing world prices, would genuinely help many poor countries and much more so than present and probable future levels of foreign aid. The economist's answer that equivalent transfers from rich to poor countries through foreign aid would be more helpful ignores the fact that the rich countries show no willingness to give openly such a level of aid. The rich and powerful of the world, like the rich and powerful within the nation, instinctively reject policies which would threaten their power and reduce their affluence. The economists get conned—which wouldn't matter all that much except that it helps the poor stay poor.

But I cannot do justice to the issue of world poverty, for my primary concern here is with Canadian issues. Let me move on to the contentious issue of foreign ownership of the Canadian economy—if for no other reason than that I have a vested professional interest in that topic.

As is well known, the extent of foreign ownership of our economy is the highest in the world and the investment comes overwhelmingly from the most powerful and nationalistic country in the world. Yet the prevailing view among Canadian economists is that it doesn't matter. As one of my colleagues says, it is a non-problem. He then has eight solutions—from abolishing the Canadian tariff to nationalizing any American controlled firm that refuses to sell to China. It all reminds one of the humourist Art Buchwald when he wrote of Americans: We have the answers. What are the questions?

Well, the questions in this case are there for the finding. Does it matter that most foreign direct investment, involving foreign control, results from the activities of a small number of giant multi-national corporations? Does it matter that the great majority of these corporations are American-owned and American-controlled?

In both cases, the answers have to be that it does matter. Furthermore, any economist who claims otherwise is displaying that irreverence toward power to which we have already alluded as being the essence of the process of mystification.

The fact that giant firms dominate foreign direct investment means that the economist's model of perfect competition, with consequent dispersion of power, is no longer relevant. Multi-national corporations are not small atomistic perfect competitors, but giant firms with monopoly power. They are not fully disciplined by the market, but rather have power and discretion. Now it is an accepted fact in liberal societies that even when such corporations are domestic, their private power should be countervailed by public power—though frequently this mostly takes the form of anti-combines or anti-trust policy involving more harrassment than anything else. When these firms are foreign-controlled, there is a second reason for exercising public policy, and something more than simply the anti-trust variety, for these firms are subject to foreign law and foreign policy and have the discretion to choose to obey these rather than Canadian law.

All of this is not simply a hypothetical possibility, as can be seen when we add the fact of these corporations being American-based to the fact of their being large. American-controlled firms in Canada are subject to American law on trade with Communist countries, American anti-trust law and American balance-of-payments controls on direct investment firms. The most recent dramatic example of this was provided by the Canadian dollar crisis on the foreign exchanges in January of last year, a crisis which resulted from American subsidiaries in Canada overresponding to President Johnson's New Year's Day message to send more dividends home, and a crisis which ended only when Mr. Sharp, then Minister of Finance, telephoned Mr. Fowler, the U.S. Secretary of the Treasury and asked him to tell the American firms to tell their Canadian subsidiaries to take it easy. Just for a moment, the power grid was lit up. Ottawa found it could communicate with Canadian incorporated firms only via Washington.

To recognize these facts is to realize that the economist's conventional prescription to apply American-style anti-trust policy in Canada and to lower the Canadian tariff is easier to say when the facts of power are ignored. Stiffer anti-combines policy in Canada, at least of the American variety, might inhibit the growth through merger of larger Canadian-owned firms able to challenge the dominance of present, and future, American-controlled giants. Just as historians can write of the British imperialism of free trade in the nineteenth century, we can speak of the American imperialism of anti-trust as well as of free trade, today. Unfortunately, economists have little to say about imperialism of any sort, and particularly varieties so subtle as we are talking about.

What about reduction of the Canadian tariff? A reasonable presumption is that it would increase the power exercised by American parents over their Canadian subsidiaries as a side-effect of rationalizing operations on a continental basis. A further presumption is that this would mean a lessened sensitivity to Canadian needs and aspirations and hence be a real political cost for Canadians. A policy that appears simply to make international markets function better, and to be apolitical, in fact carries the real possibility of subjecting the Canadian economy to even greater American control than is presently being experienced.

Enough by way of concrete examples. If I am right that Canadian economists are peculiarly innocent, why? Mostly because western economics is generally so, at least for the past century. But there is a further reason. Canadian economics in the last twenty years has been thoroughly Americanized, and more so than that of other countries. A tradition of Canadian economics with historical and political dimensions associated in particular with the work of the late Harold Innis has been all but obliterated. The doyen of Canadian economics today is Harry Johnson who, significantly, divides his time between London and Chicago as seats of the old and the new imperialism.

Now American economists today dominate the international profession, at least within the so-called free world. America is a liberal society and its economics is appropriately laissez-faire. Essentially, the United States, whose dominance in economics is very recent, took the neo-classical economics of Britain, including Keynes, and mathematized and computerized it. Technical sophistication has been achieved, though at the cost of emasculation. In the process, American economics has moved to the right within the neo-classical liberal mainstream. The intolerance toward Marxism, so much more marked in Cambridge, Massachusetts than in Cambridge, England, is a telling case in point.

As the neo-classical economics now filters into Canada via the United States—for our intelligensia has a branch plant mentality suitable to life in a branch plant economy—Canadian economics has similarly moved rightward. At the moment, the commitment of Canadian economists on issues like free trade stamp them as being even more laissez-faire than their American counterparts. Ultimately as Keynes insisted, it is ideas that matter and the subservience of Canadian economics to American economics to an extent more thorough than in the days of the British Empire, hardly bodes well for the Canadian future.

Except, of course, that an economics divorced from reality, as American economics seems increasingly to be, doesn't seem too viable in the long run —just as the American Empire doesn't look too viable. The War in Vietnam has made American power, and its soft underbelly, visible to many of us, even someone like myself who was trained in economics. Nothing destroys mystification like confrontation. At the rate the latter now occurs, the technocrat may be in for some more shake-ups. Economists may yet become humanists and economies communities.

SUGGESTIONS FOR FURTHER READING

Aron, Raymond, *The Industrial Society*, New York, Simon and Schuster, Inc., 1967.

Bell, Daniel, "Notes on the Post-Industrial Society," *The Public Interest*, No. 6 (Winter, 1967) and No. 7 (Spring, 1967).

Buchanan, J., and Tullack, G., *The Calculus of Consent*, Ann Arbor, University of Michigan Press, 1962.

Dahl, R. A. and Lindblom, C. E., *Politics, Economics, and Welfare*, New York, Harper & Row, 1953.

Downs, Anthony, *An Economic Theory of Democracy*, New York, Harper & Row, 1957.

Ellul, Jacques, *The Technological Society*, New York, Vintage Books, 1967.

Galbraith, J. K., *The New Industrial State*, Boston, Houghton Mifflin Co., 1967.

Ginzberg, Eli, Hiestand, Dale L., and Reubens, B. G., *The Pluralistic Economy*, New York & Toronto, McGraw-Hill Book Co., 1965.

Grant, George, *Technology and Empire*, Toronto, House of Anansi, 1969.

Gross, B. M., (ed.), *A Great Society?* New York, Basic Books, Inc., Publishers, 1968.

Harrington, Michael, *The Accidental Century*, Baltimore, Md., Penguin Books, Inc., 1966.

Heilbroner, Robert, *The Limits of American Capitalism*, New York, Harper & Row, 1967.

Kostelanetz, R., (ed.), *Beyond Left and Right*, New York, W. Morrow and Co., Inc., 1968.

Lloyd, T. O., and McLeod, J. T., *Agenda 1970: Proposals for a Creative Politics* (Toronto, University of Toronto Press, 1968), particularly chapters 3, 4 and 12.

Macpherson, C. B., *The Real World of Democracy*: The Massey Lectures, Fourth Series, Ottawa, Canadian Broadcasting Corporation, 1966, and Oxford, Clarendon Press, 1966.

Macpherson, C. B., "Post-Liberal Democracy," *Canadian Journal of Economics and Political Science,* Vol. XXX, No. 4 (November, 1964).

Moynihan, Daniel P., *Maximum Feasible Misunderstanding: Community Action in the War on Poverty,* New York, The Free Press, 1969.

Myrdal, Gunnar, *Challenge to Affluence,* New York, Pantheon Books, Inc., 1963.

Robinson, Joan, *Economic Philosophy* (London, Publishing Co. Ltd., 1964), chapter 6, "What are the Rules of the Game?"

Rotsein, A., *The Prospect of Change,* Toronto, McGraw-Hill Co. of Canada Ltd., 1965.

Servan-Schreiber, J.-J. *The American Challenge,* New York, Atheneum, 1968.

Contributors

Alexander Brady *Professor Emeritus, Department of Political Economy, University of Toronto.*

Albert Breton *Professor of Economics, London School of Economics and Political Science.*

Helen Buckley *Economist, Dominion Bureau of Statistics.*

E. H. Carr *Fellow of Trinity College, Cambridge.*

John Maurice Clark *Former Professor of Economics, Columbia Universitiy.*

T. C. Douglas *National Leader, New Democratic Party.*

H. E. English *Professor of Economics, Carleton University.*

Milton Friedman *Professor of Economics, University of Chicago.*

Scott Gordon *Professor of Economics, Indiana University.*

Friedrich A. von Hayek *Professor, University of Freiburg, West Germany.*

Robert L. Heilbroner *Professor of Economics, New School for Social Research.*

George Hogan *Former National Secretary, Progressive Conservative Party.*

A. B. Jackson *Vice-Chairman, Ontario Energy Board.*

J. C. H. Jones *Associate Professor Economics, University of Victoria.*

S. Judek *Professor of Economics, University of Ottawa.*

Maurice Lamontagne *Canadian Senate.*

Charles E. Lindblom *Professor of Economics and Political Scieince, Yale University.*

Lloyd D. Musolf *Professor of Political Science, University of California at Davis.*

P. H. Pearse *Associate Professor of Economics, University of British Columbia.*

Karl Polayni *Former Professor of Economic History, Columbia University.*

John Porter *Professor of Sociology, Carleton University.*

Eric Roll *Economist and a Director of the Bank of England.*

Gideon Rosenbluth *Professor of Economics, University of British Columbia.*

Eugene V. Rostow *Sterling Professor of Law, Yale University.*

T. C. Schelling *Professor of Economics, Harvard University.*

Anthony Scott *Professor of Economics, University of British Columbia.*

Andrew Shonfield *Chairman, Social Science Research Council, Great Britain.*

L. A. Skeoch *Professor of Economics, Queen's University.*

David W. Slater *Professor of Economics, Dean of the School of Graduate Studies, Queen's University.*

H. G. Thornburn *Professor and Head of the Department of Political Studies, Queen's University.*

Eva Tihanyi *Assistant Professor of Business Administration, University of Saskatchewan.*

Melville H. Watkins *Associate Professor of Economics, University of Toronto.*

G. W. Wilson *Professor of Economics, Indiana University.*

Paul Wonnacott *Professor of Economics, University of Maryland.*

Ronald Wonnacott *Professor of Economics, University of Western Ontario.*

Index